THE FLYER

The Flyer

British Culture and the Royal Air Force,
1939–1945

MARTIN FRANCIS

OXFORD
UNIVERSITY PRESS

OXFORD

UNIVERSITY PRESS

Great Clarendon Street, Oxford OX2 6DP

Oxford University Press is a department of the University of Oxford.
It furthers the University's objective of excellence in research, scholarship,
and education by publishing worldwide in

Oxford New York

Auckland Cape Town Dar es Salaam Hong Kong Karachi
Kuala Lumpur Madrid Melbourne Mexico City Nairobi
New Delhi Shanghai Taipei Toronto

With offices in

Argentina Austria Brazil Chile Czech Republic France Greece
Guatemala Hungary Italy Japan Poland Portugal Singapore
South Korea Switzerland Thailand Turkey Ukraine Vietnam

Oxford is a registered trade mark of Oxford University Press
in the UK and in certain other countries

Published in the United States
by Oxford University Press Inc., New York

British Library Cataloguing in Publication Data

Data available

Library of Congress Cataloging in Publication Data

Francis, Martin, 1964-
The Flyer: British culture and the Royal Air Force, 1939–1945 / Martin Francis.
p. cm.
Includes bibliographical references and index.
ISBN 978–0–19–927748–3
1. Great Britain. Royal Air Force—History—World War, 1939–1945. 2. World War, 1939–1945—Aerial
operations, British. 3. World War, 1939–1945—Great Britain. I. Title.
D786.F685 2008
940.54'4941—dc22   2008036751

Typeset by Laserwords Private Limited, Chennai, India
Printed in Great Britain
on acid-free paper by
Biddles Ltd, King's Lynn, Norfolk

ISBN 978–0–19–927748–3

1 3 5 7 9 10 8 6 4 2

Acknowledgments

I would like to begin by thanking my original commissioning editor at OUP, Ruth Parr, for her enthusiastic response to *The Flyer* in its formative days. I am also grateful to her successor, Rupert Cousens, and the rest of the team at OUP, especially Seth Cayley, for ensuring a speedy and professional path through the processes of editing and production. I should also like to thank the three anonymous reviewers for the Press, whose astute interventions did a great deal to sharpen and deepen my analysis during the writing of this book.

The following institutions and individuals granted permission to reproduce the images included in the book: the Imperial War Museum Department of Photographs, the Imperial War Museum Department of Art, the RAF Museum, Hendon, Granada International, London Features International, Marc Bryan-Brown (for the estate of Paul Tanquery), and Mrs. Norma Campbell-Vickers (estate of John Vickers). Conducting research for this book was made considerably easier by the good-humoured assistance of librarians and archivists at the Langsam Library, University of Cincinnati (especially the History bibliographer, Sally Moffitt), the British Library, the National Archives at Kew, the British Film Institute, the RAF Museum at Hendon and the Theatre Museum Archive at the Victoria and Albert Museum annex in Olympia. Special thanks are owed to the staff at the Imperial War Museum's Department of Documents, whose efficiency and comprehensive knowledge of their holdings is particularly valued by the US-based scholar trying to compress their archival research into a few, short, summer weeks.

This book originally took shape while I was a member of the Department of History at Royal Holloway, University of London. I would like to thank all of my former colleagues for their support, especially Tony Stockwell, whose decency and wise counsel I will always remember with affection and respect. In 2001 I was fortunate enough to spend sabbatical leave at the Center for European Studies at Harvard University, where I was able to benefit from the first-rate holdings on British history held in the stacks of the Widener Library. The majority of the research and writing of the book took place under the auspices of my current academic home, the History Department at the University of Cincinnati. Particular thanks go to Maura O'Connor, Hope Earls and my two Department Heads, Jim Murray and Man Bun Kwan. I owe a special debt to Jim, without whose efforts to secure me a one quarter leave in the spring of 2007, my manuscript might still remain unfinished. I am also grateful to the Charles Phelps Taft Research Center at the University of Cincinnati for awarding me a summer fellowship in 2004, and for generous assistance with the production costs for this book.

I count myself highly fortunate to have benefited from conversations with, and support and suggestions from, Deborah Cohen, Geoff Eley, Susan Grayzel, Nicoletta Gullace, Matthew Jones, Max Jones, Fred Leventhal, Peter Mandler, Laura Mayhall, Frank Mort, Sonya Rose, Penny Summerfield, Chris Waters, and Janet Watson. Moreover, I have been privileged that the ties of scholarship have so frequently been coupled with the rewards of lasting friendship. In London, both Alex Windscheffel and Michele Cohen provided a welcome blend of robust intelligence and heartfelt empathy. Becky Conekin offered moral support, a refreshing iconoclasm, and expert guidance on 1940s style and fashion. Amanda Vickery has been a staunch ally of both *The Flyer* and its author since the very beginning. I owe an inestimable debt to her, not merely for suggesting the book's title, but also—in surroundings as diverse as the commuter-packed carriages of the North London Line or the upstairs café in Harvey Nicks—for her infectious energy and sound advice. Stephen Brooke remains what he has been to me for over twenty years: an inspirational scholar, exemplary writer, and dearest friend. I thank him, and Amy Black and Theo, for their myriad acts of kindness.

In a book which emphasizes the centrality of domesticity to masculinity in the modern era, it seems particularly appropriate to acknowledge the contribution of my family to *The Flyer*. I would like to thank David and Gloria Reynolds for all that they have done for my family in recent years. I have also been extremely fortunate to be the recipient of the extraordinary generosity, hospitality and support offered by my in-laws, Henry Assael and Alyce Friedman Assael. My mother and father, Barbara and Brian Francis, selflessly encouraged me during the writing of this book, as they have done throughout my life, and I dedicate this book to them with love and gratitude beyond measure. Sadly, soon after I began *The Flyer*, my father was diagnosed with a cruel and merciless illness, and he did not live to see its completion. Not merely did he teach me, when I was eight years old, at an air display at RAF Coltishall, how to distinguish between a Spitfire and a Hurricane, but he was a true gentleman in every sense of the word, a model of uxoriousness, fatherhood and personal integrity. I miss him, but I take solace from the fact that this would have been a book he would have very much enjoyed.

Finally, I cannot even begin to find words to express my gratitude to my wife, Brenda Assael. As a fellow scholar, her almost forensic scrutiny of my manuscript helped sharpen my analysis, polish my prose, and save me from some of my more egregious flights of fancy. Her own research interests—in the histories of the body, emotions and popular culture—clearly informed and shaped many of the motifs of *The Flyer*. My debt to her is, of course, not merely an academic one. The ways in which she has enriched the texture and purpose of my life are truly infinite, and, in a spirit of happy expectation, I look forward to even greater adventures in the years to come. Devoting two chapters of *The Flyer* to the subjects of romance and marital companionship is a rather feeble acknowledgment of the extraordinary bliss that, through Brenda, I have come to enjoy in the domains of both love and marriage. Every day offers further testimony to the exceptional fortune that has settled upon me in the wake of her affirmative response to a somewhat nervous supplication, made on a Parisian summer evening, four years ago.

Contents

Abbreviations

ATS	Auxiliary Territorial Service
CO	Commanding Officer
DFC	Distinguished Flying Cross
DFM	Distinguished Flying Medal
DSO	Distinguished Service Order
FAA	Fleet Air Arm
LMF	Lack of Moral Fibre
RAF	Royal Air Force
RAFVR	Royal Air Force Volunteer Reserve
RCAF	Royal Canadian Air Force
USAAF	United States Army Air Force
WAAF	Women's Auxiliary Air Force
WRNS	Women's Royal Navy Service

List of Illustrations

Plate 1. Flyboy cosmopolitanism: (i) A. O. Weekes of Barbados and Flight Sergeant C. A. Joseph of Trinidad, two West Indian members of the Bombay Squadron (IWM Department of Photographs CH 11478)

Plate 2. Flyboy cosmopolitanism: (ii) Indian Air Force officers chatting with Lady Runganadehan and her daughter at a British Council reception, 1943 (IWM Department of Photographs CH 10521)

Plate 3. Love on the base: two WAAFs wave off a Hurricane pilot (IWM Department of Photographs Album 66)

Plate 4. A feminine presence: Bomber Command aircrew are debriefed by a WAAF intelligence officer at RAF Lakenheath (IWM Department of Photographs CH 12687)

Plate 5. The flyer married: Group Captain Al Deere and his new bride, Joan (RAF Museum)

Plate 6. Waiting wives: publicity photograph for Terence Rattigan's play *Flare Path*, Apollo Theatre, London, August 1942 (V&A Images/Victoria and Albert Museum, London); copyright John Vickers Archive/Norma Campbell

Plate 7. 'The heart being too strong for the physique': portrait of Wing Commander Peter Townsend by Cuthbert Orde, 1941 (RAF Museum); private copyright: refer to RAF Museum, London

Plate 8. The false flyer: John Mills as Flight Lieutenant George Perry in *Cottage to Let* (1941) (British Film Institute/London Features International)

Plate 9. The flyer as playwright: Terence Rattigan in RAF uniform, photographed by Paul Tanquery (V&A Images/Victoria and Albert Museum, London); copyright Marc Bryan-Brown Photography

Plate 10. 'A masterpiece of harmony and power': Spitfires at Sawbridgeworth, Hertfordshire, 1942 by Eric Ravilious (Imperial War Museum Department of Art LD 2125)

Plate 11. Homicidal Hun-hater or man of feeling? Wing Commander Guy Gibson reading in a poppy field near RAF Scampton, July 1943 (IWM Department of Photographs TR 1125)

Plate 12. The flyer-poet confronts the supernatural: David Niven as Flight Lieutenant Peter Carter in *A Matter of Life and Death* (1946) (British Film Institute/Granada International)

Introduction

In 1941 Lord David Cecil, commissioned to write an essay to accompany a collection of portraits of wartime flying personnel by the artist Sir William Rothenstein, went in search of the young men of the Royal Air Force. Finding the flyboys proved to be an easy assignment for the literary peer. Indeed, in the opening passage to his 'layman's glimpse' into the world of the wartime RAF, Cecil testified to the apparent ubiquity of the airman: 'All over the country, in lanes, in streets, saying goodbye at railway stations, leaning, glass in hand, over the bars of inns, we see the figures of the pilots, their faces for the most part so incongruously boyish above the misty blue of their uniform collars.'[1] Indeed, between 1939 and 1945 the war in the air was the war the British home front knew best. In the summer of 1940 Fighter Command fought the Battle of Britain in clear sight of the inhabitants of the villages of southern England and the London suburbs. In the remaining five years of the war British civilians went to bed to the sound of the thundering engines of hundreds of RAF bombers, setting out on their nightly missions to the continent. On the ground, RAF flying personnel were no less visible or familiar. From the hamlets of the South Downs and the market towns of East Anglia and Lincolnshire to the nightclubs of the West End, the fighter boys and bomber boys, with their glamorous slate-blue uniform with a set of silvery fabric wings sewn above the breast pocket, were a colourful counterpoint to the drab austerity of the home front. The British public was spellbound, not merely by the martial endeavours of the flyboys, but by their apparent good-natured charm and dashing style. Moreover, the flyer possessed an exotic quality that stemmed from waging war in what Cecil termed the 'remote life of the air', where they looked down on the terror and beauty of a cloudscape that resembled mountain ranges or vast frozen seas, or raised their eyes to the star-spangled blackness of outer space.[2] In an age before manned flight became a form of routine mass transportation, flyers enjoyed privileged access to a world of high adventure that was unknown and inconceivable to the overwhelming majority of the population. However, such rarefied associations were balanced by the flyer's celebrated modesty, the RAF's apparent informality, and the fact that aircrew were recruited from a range of social backgrounds. Given such star appeal, the flyer's decisive role in the British military effort between 1939 and 1945 was undoubtedly matched by an equally significant contribution to the propaganda war which accompanied it.

It is therefore surprising that there has, to date, been no sustained or scholarly study of the place of the flyer in British culture during the Second World War. This is despite the fact that the existing literature on the wartime RAF is immense, and continues to expand prodigiously, on an almost daily basis. There are minutely detailed accounts of individual campaigns (especially the Battle of Britain)[3] or even specific missions (the firestorm raids on Hamburg and Dresden recently receiving considerable attention).[4] Histories of individual squadrons are matched by biographies of, or recollections by, individual flyers, especially fighter pilots.[5] Those with a more technical bent will find countless appraisals of the design and capabilities of particular aircraft.[6] The overwhelming majority of books published on the wartime RAF are works of popular, rather than academic, history. Few of them engage with broader historiographical debates about the impact of the Second World War on British society or the extensive scholarship devoted to the relationship between warfare and gender roles. This is inevitable, given that their readership is usually composed of aeronautical enthusiasts and air-warfare aficionados. The few scholarly studies of the wartime RAF that have appeared are predominantly works of military history, focusing on strategic and operational issues, with only the occasional allusion to the social and cultural identities of flying personnel.[7] That said, a closer scrutiny of the literature dedicated to the wartime RAF suggests that there has been a subtle evolution in recent years, a shift which, while almost imperceptible, is definitely to be welcomed. An increasing recourse to oral history in popular histories of the air war has allowed us to get much closer to the sensibilities and experiences of individual flyers, especially those of bomber aircrew, whose wartime careers are now much less overshadowed than they were, even a decade ago, by their counterparts in Fighter Command.[8]

An important contribution to the literature on the wartime RAF, in this regard, has been Patrick Bishop's best-selling companion volumes, *Fighter Boys* and *Bomber Boys*.[9] Bishop's eloquent and evocative prose style, combined with a rich vein of interviews and unpublished testimony, genuinely succeeds in bringing the wartime flyboys to life. More successfully than any previous writer on the subject, he conveys the character, feelings, and motivations of those who flew. However, while he does consider flyer's friendships with fellow pilots, and their romantic entanglements with women, these are presented as brief intermissions in what are essentially established chronological narratives of, respectively, the Battle of Britain and the area-bombing offensive. He makes only a few fleeting references to how flying personnel were represented in popular culture or consciousness, and there is no attempt to relate the flyer to the wider cultural and social history of the Second World War. While *The Flyer* acknowledges its debt to this extensive corpus of writing (both popular and scholarly) on the wartime RAF, its concerns and content are much more closely aligned with the preoccupations of those engaged in the academic fields of cultural history and gender history. Despite being concerned with men in uniform, it is not intended as a contribution to military history as traditionally understood. Indeed, it repeatedly emphasizes commonalities between the RAF's apparently specialized military environment and the civilian world beyond. *The Flyer* is conceived as an exercise in cultural and social history, using the lives and representations of RAF flying personnel to illuminate much broader issues of gender, social class, national and racial identities, emotional life, and the creation of national myth in twentieth-century Britain. *The Flyer* is primarily intended as a contribution to the history of gender in modern Britain, especially the history of masculinity. In the decade-and-a-half since the appearance of Michael Roper and John Tosh's pioneering collection, *Manful Assertions: Masculinities in Britain Since 1800*, there has been a dramatic increase in the historical literature dedicated to evaluating how masculine identities evolved in late nineteenth- and twentieth-century Britain.[10] We now have scholarly studies of, to select just a handful of representative works, masculinity and the Victorian 'representative artisan', nineteenth-century male domesticity, aristocratic masculinity in the 1890s, masculinity and late Victorian street gangs, critiques of lower-middle-class manliness in the Edwardian era, male support for the women's-suffrage campaign, manliness in adolescent fiction, male pride among Coventry car-workers, imperial adventure narratives, masculinity and effeminacy in the late Victorian empire, masculinity and 'martial race theory', the late-imperial 'romance of manliness', masculinity, nationalism, and Irish team sports, West Indian men in 1950s Britain, men and sexuality, male fashion, masculinity, consumption and social space, the post-1945 'organization man', and male archetypes in post-war cinema.[11] This literature has been supplemented, and enriched, by studies undertaken in the history of male homosexuality in modern Britain.[12]

Historians of modern British masculinity were initially reluctant to tackle the subject of the two world wars. This relative lack of attention up to the mid-1990s stood in stark contrast to literary scholars, such as Sandra Gilbert, Elaine Showalter, Adrian Caesar, and Alfredo Bonadeo, who were already using poetry and other literary sources to link masculine degradation and suffering in combat to the attitudes of soldier-writers towards women and sexuality.[13] It is possible that some historians believed that essentialist arguments about men's innate capacity for violence rendered the study of male subjectivities during wartime superfluous. Alternatively, acknowledging men's participation in fighting and killing may have been embarrassing to those who had sought to use a gendered history of men to recover the more sensitive and reflective dimensions to men's lives. However, in the last decade this historical neglect has begun to be remedied. Joanna Bourke's pioneering *Dismembering the Male* appraised the impact of the First World War on men's bodies in Britain, but also considered the issue of male bonding in the services.[14] Nicoletta Gullace has provided a nuanced study of how the masculinity of fighting men in 1914–18 was related to that of various categories of non-combatants, while Deborah Cohen has investigated how, after 1918, limbless ex-combatants sought to maintain their masculine self-respect.[15]

However, the literature on war and masculinity in Britain during the Second World War remains less substantial than that which now exists on the 1914–18 conflict. Sonya Rose's study of 'temperate masculinity', in her *Which People's War? National Identity and Citizenship in Wartime Britain*, has therefore been a particularly welcome intervention. Rose contends that masculine heroism in 1939–45 deliberately rejected the old-style, elite, chivalric manliness of 1914, and instead emphasized the understated, self-deprecating, good-humoured courage of the 'little man'. Rose reveals how the templates of national identity and masculinity were fused in wartime Britain, the emotional restraint and 'common sense' of the British male matching the temperate tropes of Britishness.[16] However, Rose's study (as with the chapter dedicated to 'wartime masculinities and gender relations' in Penny Summerfield's *Reconstructing Women's Wartime Lives*)[17] focuses largely on non-combatants—civilian heroes or conscientious objectors—and we still lack a sustained analysis of how masculinity was understood and represented among servicemen. Joanna Bourke's follow-up to *Dismembering the Male, An Intimate History of Killing*, was only partly taken up with the years between 1939 and 1945, and (as its title implies) was exclusively interested in a single (albeit important) aspect of military experience.[18] There is, as yet, no equivalent for Britain of Christina Jarvis's insightful study of the cultural representation of male bodies in the United States during the Second World War.[19]

The Flyer, therefore, seeks to remedy a critical lacuna in the historiography of modern British masculinity. The complex identities and representations of RAF flying personnel during the Second World War reflect broader contradictions surrounding masculinity in a period characterized, conversely, by an intense focus on heterosexual desire and domestic attachments on the one hand, and a developed homosocial culture necessitated by military conscription on the other. John Tosh has, quite rightly, criticized some of the first generation of historians of modern British masculinity for focusing on all-male environments—the worlds of the public school, the ancient universities, the clergy, or aristocratic big-game hunters—from which women were largely excluded. He has stressed the need to write a gendered history of men which appreciates male domestic roles, as husbands and fathers.[20] While concerned with an apparently exclusively closed homosocial culture—the world of combat and the military—*The Flyer* fully endorses Tosh's insistence (reiterated by a leading historian of marriage in colonial-era America, Toby Ditz) that a gendered history of men must always register a female presence.[21] The RAF flyer constantly travelled back and forward across the frontier between the martial and domestic worlds, revelling in the all-male camaraderie of the mess while still being attracted to the responsibilities and pleasures of marriage and fatherhood. Even those flyers who were not married, found that their youth, their heroic deeds, and the allure of their grey-blue uniforms made it impossible for them to resist (even if they had wanted to) the attractions of female companionship and heterosexual romance. *The Flyer* is therefore a study of men in love, as well as at war. The fact that the militarization of men and the domestication of men were not incompatible has implications for the history of British masculinity which reach beyond both the specialized military culture of the wartime RAF and the chronological parameters of the Second World War.

A critical argument of *The Flyer* is that male and female experiences during the war were not polarized and antithetical, but were complementary and interrelated. It is conceived as a work of gender history in the broadest sense, and should therefore be read in conjunction with the extensive body of literature on women's roles in Britain during the Second World War which has been established by scholars such as Penny Summerfield, Gillian Swanson, Sonya Rose, Antonia Lant, and Lucy Noakes.[22] *The Flyer* should also contribute to a growing academic interest in gendering of airspace.[23] However, while *The Flyer*'s agenda is very much rooted in recent developments in gender history, it will also contribute to four other important fields of historical research.

First, it will help further understanding of the social history of Britain, during the Second World War and in the twentieth century as a whole. Traditionally, debates about how far British society became more egalitarian (in both subjective and objective terms) between 1939 and 1945 focused on the home front, following the lead of Angus Calder's classic *The People's War*, first published in 1969.[24] However, recently there has been more attention paid to the relationship between service life and social change in wartime. Jeremy Crang has shown how the egalitarian strictures of a so-called 'people's war' (and the fact that this was a conscript army) required army commanders to deploy the skills of persuasion and cooperation, not maintain a high-minded belief that troops were there to blindly obey orders. With Colonel Blimp dead and buried, the military was no longer a safe haven for those who wished to escape the democratic and populist impulses of the modern world.[25] *The Flyer* will include consideration of how these same issues of class and democracy were played out in the RAF. As the most junior of the three services, the RAF took pride in its lack of formality, and emphasized a technocratic and meritocratic vision of military life, appropriate to the supposed classlessness of the people's war. However, some flyers embodied old-style, public-school-derived notions of martial masculinity. In both Bomber and Fighter Commands, moreover, social distinctions between officers and NCOs, and between the aircrew and the ground crew who serviced their aircraft, remained deeply entrenched. In *The Flyer*, the attitudes and sensibilities of RAF pilots will always be located in a broader context of the social dynamics of mid-twentieth century Britain. The unique character of the service will be emphasized, but also how the flyer's masculinity owed much to notions of deportment, conduct, and sensibility derived from a middle-class culture which remained central to British life in this period.[26]

Second, *The Flyer* will be informed by recent discussions on citizenship and national identity in Britain during the Second World War. A critical motif in Sonya Rose's *Which People's War?* is who was included and who was excluded from wartime constructions of national belonging, an analysis which has been supplemented by the pivotal place accorded to the Second World War in recent general studies of national identity in England/Britain, and by specific case studies by Marika Sherwood (on West Indian workers and service personnel in wartime Britain) and Ian Spencer (on the contribution of the war to the formation of multiracial Britain).[27] The RAF is a particularly useful site on which to explore the relationship between war and national identity, since it was a genuinely multinational service. It contained volunteers from occupied nations such as France, Poland, and Czechoslovakia, and from neutral countries such as Ireland, the United States (before December 1941), and Argentina. Recruits from the white Dominions of Canada, Australia, New Zealand, and South Africa had to negotiate an RAF culture which appeared to them class-ridden and hidebound, and an acknowledgment of their frustrations provides another illustration of how claims for an essentially classless, youthful, and unpretentious masculinity were often projected by emerging Commonwealth nations as an indicator of their growing estrangement from the mother country. The RAF also recruited from among non-white subjects of the empire, some of whom became operational pilots, and their experience in facing the double challenge of combat and racial discrimination deserves particular attention, not least because it has been virtually erased from the dominant memory of the air war.

Third, given that this study is concerned as much with structures of feeling (relating to love, loss, fear, and aggression among pilots themselves and the romantic sensibilities of the public who idolized them), *The Flyer* engages with recent interest in the history of the emotions. Echoing Joanna Bourke's insistence that emotions be treated as more than a mere by-product in historical scholarship, it heeds the beating of hearts beneath the roar of the aero engines and the deafening explosion of the cannon shell.[28] It allies itself with those who have imaginatively employed a recognition of the importance of private emotions to provide fresh insight into established narratives of twentieth-century British history, for example, Frank Costigliola's discussion of how loneliness, isolation from families, and exhaustion may have impacted on the judgments of British diplomats in the early years of the Cold War, Michael Roper's study of 'emotional survival' among soldiers in the Great War, and Luisa Passerini's investigation of the convergence between proposals for European federation and discourses of romantic love, being discussed by scholars, novelists, and poets in the 1930s.[29] In common with these works, and in contrast to the dominant emphasis in much existing research into the history of the emotions, *The Flyer* goes beyond a focus on the public codes of conduct which register and regulate the expression (or repression) of private feelings of anger or shame.[30] It acknowledges the social norms which relate to the expression of emotions, but is no less interested in the subjective dimension, to how feelings registered in individual minds and actions. While it avoids a psychoanalytical methodology (those with a fear of Freud will undoubtedly be relieved to hear that there will be no attempt to put the flyer 'on the couch'), it comprehends emotion in relation to personal experience, and not merely as an aspect of cultural representation.[31]

Fourth, the last ten years have witnessed an explosion in studies concerned with the place of the Second World War in British popular memory, encompassing not merely patterns of official commemoration, but also museum exhibits, historic preservation, feature films, and television programmes. These studies focused on how the memory of the war was refashioned to accord with distinctly post-war shifts in British culture and politics: the end of empire, generational conflict during the 1960s, debates over Britain's role in a united Europe, and the Thatcherite project to reassert social discipline at home and national prestige abroad in the 1980s.[32] The RAF flyer certainly featured in many of these reconfigurations of the wartime experience. Anti-European Conservative Party election broadcasts in the 1980s contained archive footage of the Battle of Britain, while controversies over the moral and strategic efficacy of the strategic bombing campaign from the 1960s onwards dramatized a rejection by younger Britons of the uncritical and conservative narratives of the war subscribed to by their parents. *The Flyer* is inevitably entangled in these post-war mutations. Many of its sources, particularly the memoirs of RAF flying personnel, post-date the war, and we need to be aware that they may be addressing post-war matters, and not merely the wartime ones to which they are ostensibly dedicated. However, *The Flyer* is less interested in mapping, and accounting for, how the air war has been re-imagined in the last six decades than it is in explaining how the dominant cultural evaluation of the RAF flyer came to be developed during the war itself. As Lucy Noakes, in her *War and the British*, reminds us, participants in the war were already only too aware that they were living in momentous times, and themselves 'making history'.[33] As a result, key myths about the flyer were already in place long before 1945, and the pilots themselves were obliged to negotiate these stereotypes, often finding them simultaneously compelling and repellent. Indeed, flyers were often obsessed with the gulf between the mundane aspects of service life and the romantic expectations placed on the pilot by an adoring public. Others, however, either failed to escape from, or positively welcomed, the congenial association of the men in air-force blue with heroism and glamour. Either way, *The Flyer* would argue that both the dominant cultural representation of, and the subjectivity of, the RAF airman involved a complex dialogue between reality and imagination, or between combat and culture.

The RAF expanded dramatically during the war, with over a million men and women in the service by 1945. Of this figure, around 17 per cent were flying personnel, the vast majority serving as aircrew in Bomber Command.[34] It is these men who are the subject of this book, although their relations with ground-based personnel will be regularly touched upon. *The Flyer* is extensive in its coverage, but, inevitably, cannot profess to be comprehensive. There are relatively few references to Coastal Command, which was responsible (together with the Fleet Air Arm, which was part of the Royal Navy) for bringing air power to bear on the war at sea. The book's predominant focus is on that overwhelming proportion of flying personnel who were based in the United Kingdom, although several real-life and fictional flyers featured here were to fight in the skies over North Africa, Greece, Malta, and the Middle East. The RAF's war against Japan is largely absent, as are the missions conducted by the RAF from bases in liberated western Europe in 1944 and 1945. Clearly RAF men stationed in the Far East or the Levant were not able to enjoy the immediate access to family life and domesticity enjoyed by the home-based flyer. Their emotional ties to the civilian world were, of necessity, more indirect, relying on letters, cherished photographs, and other mementoes.[35] A similar condition obviously characterized overseas aircrew based in Britain, and those RAF flyers unfortunate enough to have become prisoners of war. However, to reiterate, these were a minority of flying personnel, the vast majority enjoying the peculiar privilege of dicing with death in the sky one moment, before sitting down to lunch with their wife and children, or chatting up the barmaid in the local pub, in the next.

The sources available for a study such as *The Flyer* are remarkably rich and diverse, but they also have to be handled with a certain degree of circumspection. For a start, they are being asked to provide insights into two different, although closely interlinked, issues: how RAF flyers were represented in British culture, and how flyers represented themselves and made sense of their lived experience. War writing requires vigilance from a researcher, who needs to separate fact from fiction, and be careful to distinguish between writing produced during wartime and works of subsequent reflection and reminiscence. Moreover, *The Flyer* often employs two different genres of war writing—first-person narratives and the fictionalized accounts of novelists, playwrights, and film-makers—in tandem. Since these two types of writing often shared similar content and sensibilities, *The Flyer* will always specify whether what is being placed before the reader is (or at least purports to be) fiction or real-life recollection.

Given the allure of the flyer, it is not surprising that there exists a range of published sources dating from the war years themselves which are dedicated to RAF flying personnel. Many laymen produced pen portraits of the service, while some flyers authored instant memoirs of the battles of France and Britain, and of the early years of the strategic bombing campaign. Features on flyers can be found in newspapers and magazines, while transcripts of radio broadcasts made by serving RAF personnel have also survived. Inevitably, these sources are distorted by the imperatives of censorship and propaganda, but this does not nullify their ability to tell us how the myth of the flyer was constituted and presented. Moreover, first-hand accounts produced by flyers during the war are often surprisingly candid on subjects that might be thought to have discomforted the publicity department of the Air Ministry, for example, references to the RAF's drinking culture or the consequences for German civilians of the violent destruction meted out by Bomber Command. Memoirs published after the war were free of the constraints of the censor's notorious red pencil, but they too are not entirely unproblematic. Memory can be selective and misleading, although RAF autobiographies have often drawn on official logbooks and operational diaries in a worthy aspiration to ensure accuracy.[36] No less significantly, flyer memoirs are often formulaic and tend to emphasize narrative at the expense of meaning, even if one or two of them (for example, the fighter-boy autobiographies of Geoffrey Wellum and Jim Bailey) are genuinely reflective and, in places, profound. A less justifiable criticism is that published recollections tend to emphasize the extraordinary and the outlandish, and obscure the more banal aspects of service life. While this is undoubtedly true at one level, the flyer's focus, in his memoirs, on the more emotionally charged aspects of wartime life was hardly impertinent or inadmissible, given the considerable significance of both love and death in the airman's lived experience and mental universe.

Some of the problems associated with post-war published memoirs can be tempered by using them in conjunction with the unpublished diaries and memoirs of flying personnel held in the archival collections of the Imperial War Museum and the Royal Air Force Museum. Once again, transparency is not guaranteed, since records presented to archives where they can be accessed by researchers may have been sanitized or compromised in some other form before they pass into the public domain. However, the archival collection of the Imperial War Museum in particular embraces a much broader spectrum of flyer testimony than that to be found in published sources, including as it does letters, diaries, scrapbooks, and manuscript memoirs composed by every type of flyer, from public-school pilot officers training to fly Spitfires to apprentices who became sergeant pilots in Lancasters. In addition, further insights into the world of the flyer are provided by the extensive testimonies of ground crew, non-operational aircrew, and WAAFs which the Imperial War Museum also holds. These essentially private records can be further supplemented by the institutional records of the Air Ministry held at the National Archive, which provide details about service life which were too mundane to receive wider publicity, and are particularly valuable for ascertaining official responses to issues relating to morale, social class, and relations between flying personnel and WAAFs.

The Flyer insists that fictional narratives, both literary and cinematic, play a critical role in shaping the dominant cultural construction of the wartime flyer. Unfortunately, such a statement risks immediate censure. For, while historians of twentieth-century Britain have become increasingly comfortable in recent decades with the use of feature film as a legitimate historical source, the notion that novels and plays can reconstruct or illuminate historical identities and sensibilities continues to be met by, at best, wary scepticism, and at worst, undisguised squeamishness. Historians rightly insist that one cannot assume that, just because a literary work possesses aesthetic merit, it is necessarily representative of wider experiences or reactions.[37] There is obviously some truth in this admonition. Literary and historical texts conform to the restrictions of the different genres in which they are conceived, which means they have to be subjected to rather different forms of analysis. However, the pioneering work of scholars such as Charles Bernheimer, Mary Poovey, and Alison Light has indicated the benefits to be gained from pursuing the suggestive connections between fiction and non-fiction.[38] As Janet Watson points out in her study of experience and memory in Britain during, and immediately after, the First World War, literary and historical texts are both 'constructions of experience that simultaneously respond to, and contribute to, social perceptions'.[39] For all their idiosyncrasies, novels and plays are an obvious means to recover the sensibilities and susceptibilities of a past age, and while they should be used with caution, it seems churlish for a historian to totally spurn the insights they provide, simply because authors of fiction might appear to be preoccupied with themes which they regard as universal and timeless, rather than those which are historically contingent.

It is true, as many historians have argued, that the canonical works of twentieth-century British literature would be an unreliable guide to the social and cultural history of the nation in the same period. For example, the restless experimentalism and violent disorientation found in the classic texts of literary modernism produced by T. S. Eliot, James Joyce, and Virginia Woolf in the inter-war years seem at odds with the relative stability and conservatism which characterized British society in this period. However, in the last decade literary scholars have moved away from these canonical authors and given increased attention to middlebrow writers, who either continued to write in older, more reassuring, traditions, or else embraced the modernist idiom in a manner that was more discreet and less dissonant than their illustrious contemporaries.[40] The great majority of the novels, short stories, and plays which feature in *The Flyer* certainly belong to this middlebrow category, although some of the authors discussed (notably Elizabeth Taylor and Terence Rattigan) have recently undergone major re-evaluation in regard to their literary reputations.[41] Most of the middlebrow literature dedicated to the wartime RAF has remained overlooked, not merely by historians but also by literary scholars, who, when they have considered the cultural significance of the RAF flyer at all, have focused almost exclusively on fighter-pilot-turned-author Richard Hillary.[42] Hillary appears regularly in *The Flyer*, but it will be evident that his perspective was not always widely shared in the service, and he was, in some respects, the least representative of those flyers who became celebrities during the war. Moreover, Hillary was certainly not unique in bringing first-hand experience to bear on the writing of air-war literature. H. E. Bates and John Pudney held commissions in the RAF, while, among others, Terence Rattigan, Roald Dahl, John Rhys, Arthur Gwynn-Browne, and Miles Tripp all served as flying personnel. Given that these writers both experienced life as operational aircrew and played a critical role in the creation of popular representations of the flyer among the broader public, it would surely be perverse to exclude them from consideration, merely because they articulated their subjectivities through the medium of a novel or stage-play, rather than through an official logbook or some other ostensibly more palpable type of historical record.

The Flyer is composed of eight core chapters. Chapter 1 opens with a discussion of the status of the RAF flyer in British culture at the beginning of the Second World War, before moving on to detail the main constituents of the allure which had attached itself to the flyboys by the winter of 1940–1, and which were to remain an enduring part of their appeal for the remainder of the war. It grants particular significance to the RAF's glamorous blue uniform and the particular magnetism of the fabric wings worn above the right upper jacket pocket, which indicated that the bearer was an operational pilot. Perhaps the most powerful testimony to the star appeal of the flyer was the close association between the air war and popular cinema. The arresting image of master bomber Guy Gibson relaxing by the swimming pool of legendary Hollywood director Howard Hawks is merely one example of the personal and creative relationships which were fostered between real-life RAF heroes and the world of the silver screen. It certainly provides a striking illustration of one of the major themes of this book: that the popular representation of the flyer was shaped by, and reflected the sensibilities of, a wider culture which lay beyond the airfield perimeter.

Chapter 2 considers how flyers bonded with each other, through shared rituals, leisure activities (especially a culture of heavy drinking), the RAF's peculiar verbal idiom, and a sense that they were all young men who had been thrown together into a world that was both exciting and terrifyingly macabre. However, this genuine comradeship was often simultaneously profound and perfunctory, and male bonding was regularly compromised by a number of divisions. There were distinctions between bomber boys and fighter boys or between different squadrons. Class divisions meant that relations between officers and NCOs could be fraught, and, despite its vaunted cosmopolitanism, national, ethnic, and racial differences among aircrew were all too evident.

The flyer in love is the subject of Chapter 3. While some flyers feared that romantic entanglements might compromise combat efficiency, many others found that falling in love offered an affirmation of life in the present and hope for the future. Romantic love and companionship appeared to be a reward for taking on the obligations of military service, and therefore the flyer's affairs of the heart, far from being esoteric, tell us a great deal about the intersections between masculinity, sexuality, and citizenship in modern Britain. What was especially unusual about the RAF was that the presence of female service personnel, in the form of the Women's Auxiliary Air Force (WAAF), allowed the possibility of heterosexual romantic attachments developing on the base itself. The romantic universe of the flyer ensured that the wartime RAF was never a closed all-male world, in which masculinity operated independently of a female presence. Moreover, as Chapter 4 reveals, many flyers were married. Despite belonging to a highly specialized service culture, the married flyer saw family life as a vital antidote to the dehumanizing consequences of military discipline and the violence of combat. The fact that the RAF was predominantly based on British soil (and that some RAF wives lived adjacent to the bases on which their husbands were stationed) meant that the flyer had a unique opportunity to maintain a presence in the domestic realm. That said, the fact that home remained the place where many of the flyer's deepest emotional needs were met, can be said to be true of British men as a whole in the 1940s, in spite of the competing pressures of duty to one's comrades and one's country.

The flyer's struggle with fear is considered in Chapter 5. It appraises how anxiety and stress were understood by medical experts, the RAF hierarchy, and by flyers themselves. It examines how aircrew coped with stress through various ameliorations and diversions, a common recourse to superstition, and a personal rationalization of the gruesome situation they found themselves in. These strategies provide important insights into the individual subjectivities of the men who flew. However, a discussion of fear and courage among flying personnel also requires reference to social norms, which allows this case study to illuminate how masculinity was more generally defined in Britain in the first half of the twentieth century.

Chapter 6 is dedicated to broken flyers (those disabled or disfigured in combat), flawed flyers (those with psychological problems), and false flyers (men who passed themselves off as airmen to facilitate their nefarious purposes, as spies or sexual predators). In contrast to the image of the carefree, debonair flyer which had so captivated the public, this chapter deals with darker imaginings of the men in blue, whether real or fictionalized. Here we get to meet the badly burnt airman William Simpson, who is spurned by his wife at first sight of his grotesquely misshapen face; the emotionally stunted ex-fighter pilot Freddie Page in Terence Rattigan's play The *Deep Blue Sea*; and Neville Heath, the sadistic serial killer who passed himself off as a dashing wartime group captain.

These discomforting visions of the flyer spoke to a broader ambivalence about the men of the RAF which is detailed in Chapter 7. The flyer could be presented as a gentle and chivalrous warrior, possessed of the sensibility of a poet. However, he might also be imagined as a brutal killer, an uncompromising agent of destruction. This binary was entwined with other contradictory understandings of the flyer, notably the discrepancy between flyboy philistinism and the presence in the wartime RAF of many artists and writers, or the contradiction between the association of flyers with a chivalric past and the fact that they fought through the medium of the most advanced technology yet seen in warfare. The RAF's participation in the controversial area bombing of Germany potentially made the contrast between the flyer as sensitive poet and flyer as savage psychopath even more acute. It certainly created an ambiguity which both contemporary observers, and the men of the RAF themselves, were more cognisant of than we might have supposed.

Chapter 8 is dedicated to the flyer's return to civilian life at the end of the war. It argues that, while most former flyers embraced the return to hearth and home, some found the transition problematic, and that the maladjusted flyer is a surprisingly common character in film and literature in the immediate post-war years. Consideration is also given here to flyers who entered public life after the war, not merely in Britain but, in the case of wartime fighter pilot turned white supremacist Ian Douglas Smith, in Britain's dwindling imperial possessions. The chapter concludes with a brief reflection on how dead comrades continued to cast a shadow over the post-war lives of those who had lived to see the end of hostilities.

The RAF's flying personnel were, for all the service's wartime expansion, an elite group. All operational pilots were either commissioned officers or NCOs. The wartime RAF also had some highly particular features, most notably its relatively lax discipline, rampant individualism, ostensible cosmopolitanism, regular access to women and families, and its proportionately high death rates. However, the story of the flyer is one that possesses a broader applicability, contributing as it does to the history of Britain during the Second World War, the history of British popular culture, and the histories of private life and the emotions. Representations of the flyer, and his own self-understanding, were certainly beset by ambivalence and instability. The flyer could be imagined as a classless meritocrat, a tribune of the people's war, or he could be envisaged as an anti-democratic superman, rendered omnipotent by his ability to literally ascend above the rest of humanity. He could be an emblem of scientific modernity or a reincarnation of the chivalric heroes of a medieval past. The airman might seek emotional solace in either the boisterous camaraderie of the mess or in the comforting arms of a WAAF lover. It was possible for him to be both a ruthless killer in the air, and a loving husband and father on the ground. The flyer could represent the breezy innocence of youth or the jaded cynicism of a manhood forged on the anvil of war. If he was unfortunate enough to be severely wounded, the airman might be lionized as a manly hero, or just as likely to find himself emasculated by responses of pity or revulsion. However, none of these ambiguities were exclusive to the wartime RAF. The flyer's world encompassed the egalitarian and the elitist, the cosmopolitan and the parochial, the homosocial and the domestic, the technical and the romantic. The fact that these oppositions may be found in other male worlds in twentieth-century Britain is obvious, but that, of course, only makes a study of the fighter boys and bomber boys of the Royal Air Force all the more significant and worthwhile.

1

The Allure of the Flyer

FROM HOOLIGAN TO HERO

In the early 1930s British military aviation was still in its relative infancy. The technology of air power remained rudimentary and unreliable. The majority of the RAF's air fleet was composed of open-cockpited biplanes, with wooden propellers, engines of no more than 650 horsepower, and top speeds which rarely reached beyond 200 m.p.h. Few aircraft possessed radio equipment, and navigation aids were embarrassingly primitive, most pilots getting back to base by a combination of a road atlas and following railway lines or rivers. Nevertheless, the flyers of the RAF were insistent that they represented the future of warfare. Military aviation throughout most of the First World War had been under the control of the army and navy, and it was only in March 1918 that an independent air force was created. When the war ended eight months later, the two senior services were eager to restore their authority over the fledgling Royal Air Force. The RAF's leaders and their political allies argued that air power could make a contribution to grand strategy in its own right, and protested that it should not be reduced to merely facilitating army and naval reconnaissance and conveyance. The advocates of an independent air force ultimately won the day, although it was a close-run thing, especially since the RAF was a tiny force in the early 1920s, a major victim of the financial retrenchment imposed in Britain after the ending of the First World War.

Despite (or possibly because of) the RAF's precarious status, the new service quickly developed a distinct culture and ethos. It had its own uniforms, insignia, and structure of ranks. It had opened a cadet school at Cranwell in Lincolnshire to train pilot officers and an apprentice school at Halston in Hertfordshire to prepare mechanics and technicians.[1] The RAF adopted a highly self-conscious aura of modernity. Flyers saw themselves as a completely new class of warriors, men whose bravery and skill would be tested by their ability to wage war using the most advanced technology available. RAF officers prided themselves on their lack of knowledge of horses, which were still central to the culture of the army. There were hunts at Cranwell, and at the base at Catterick in Yorkshire, but in general it was unwise for a flyer to admit he knew one end of a horse from the other. Those who did profess equestrian expertise or interest were likely to be labelled 'upstage' and shunned by their fellow officers.[2]

Repudiation of the horse was not merely intended to throw into sharper relief the RAF's association with the more advanced forms of warfare. Stabling and maintaining a horse were also expensive, and indicated that the mess life of the army remained confined to those possessed of a private income. The RAF, by contrast, appeared substantially less socially exclusive than the two other services. The RAF presented itself as essentially meritocratic, open to all those who were able to master the technological competence necessary to fly an aircraft in combat. Character, rather than social background, was emphasized as the criteria for recruitment into the service. The problem was that most senior RAF commanders identified good character in terms of the qualities exemplified by the private schools and elite universities they themselves had attended. As a consequence, pilot selection proved to be heavily dependent on possession of the right accent or the familiar stripes of an old school tie. The RAF's auxiliary squadrons were notorious for their social exclusivity, the force's 'weekend flyers' including grandees such as the son of the Duke of Westminster. Nevertheless, the possibilities of rising up through the ranks in the RAF were certainly greater than in the army or navy. Ten of the top-placed mechanics trained at Halston were eligible for scholarships at Cranwell, and many pilots were often unaware that some of their fellow officers were ex-apprentices. There was also a whole class of 'sergeant pilot' NCOs, selected men from the ranks who received air-crew training for five years, before returning to their previous duties. In 1936 the Royal Air Force Volunteer Reserve (RAFVR) was created, which opened up the service to lower-middle-class grammar-school boys looking for an alternative to dreary clerking jobs in the City. All recruits to the RAFVR shared the same initial instruction, and commissions were only awarded later, on the basis of performance in training.[3] Not merely did the RAF appear less class-ridden than its rivals, but the air force was characterized by an apparently relaxed attitude towards discipline, uniform, and deportment, which stood in marked contrast to the standards maintained by the army and navy. Pilots adopted an extremely lackadaisical attitude towards drilling or saluting, and even senior officers seemed oblivious to decorum or protocol. On one occasion, Air Commodore Richard Atcherley was discovered by a startled warrant officer playing with a squadron leader on a set of swings in a children's playground on the perimeter of his airfield.[4] The pre-war RAF appeared to possess a carefree culture which was more reminiscent of a private flying club than of a focused fighting service. Bomber aircrew received only limited training in navigation, while fighter pilots learnt even less about aerial gunnery.[5] In the last summer before the outbreak of war, fighter pilot Tony Bartley still had sufficient opportunity to learn to play golf, sail *Pimms No.4*, a yacht he had bought with four fellow flyers, go into Edinburgh every Saturday night to drink 'safaris', carry out a stunt in which he flew a decidedly cumbersome Oxford trainer under the Forth railway bridge, and fall in love with the provost of Edinburgh's daughter.[6]

The navy and army were appalled by the apparent indiscipline and youthful impudence of the RAF. In return, flyers could not resist provoking what they regarded as the more staid cultures of the two senior services. Peter Townsend, who joined the service in 1933, was contemptuous of 'the sea-dogs and the Colonel Blimps', delighting in the prospect that Britain would one day have to look for its protection to the pilots of the RAF, 'whom the old guard tended to despise as the rag-tail and bobtail of the country's youth'.[7] At the beginning of the war, Richard Hillary and his fellow fighter pilots—the 'long-haired boys'—took malicious pleasure in appearing 'slightly scruffy' while dining in upmarket London restaurants, thereby causing the 'beautifully turned out, pink-and-white cheeked young men' of the crack infantry regiments to 'feel uncomfortably related to chorus boys'.[8]

How did the wider British public view the flyers of the RAF in the 1930s? The answer is not a straightforward one, for popular attitudes ranged from enchantment to repulsion, and there was a definite ambivalence which the later heroic status of the RAF should not be allowed to obscure. The need for the RAF to ensure its independence during the inter-war years had led to an extensive campaign to publicize the service and to make the public more 'air-minded'. One way of furthering this end was the Hendon Air Pageant, which was held every summer between 1920 and 1937. This annual display included air races, mock battles, aerobatics, and a parade of types of aircraft which had just come into service, performed in front of crowds which reached over 150,000 by the early 1930s, supplemented by extensive coverage on BBC radio and in the illustrated press.[9] Enthusiasm for the flyers of the RAF was also disseminated indirectly, through biographies of the air aces of the Great War, such as 'Mick' Mannock and Albert Ball.[10] Adolescent and adult fiction also celebrated the flyer. The most oft-cited example of this was W. E. Johns' 'Biggles' stories, first published in 1932. Many of the future pilots of the wartime RAF, including the famous 'Dambuster' Guy Gibson, were first introduced to air combat through the adventures of Captain James Bigglesworth. Recent literary studies of the Biggles stories have emphasized their darker aspects, most notably their racism and unsentimentalized approach to violent death. However, for the schoolboys who devoured them in the 1930s, Biggles was an object of unqualified hero-worship.[11] The RAF hierarchy was undoubtedly pleased that such popular cultural renderings of air power emphasized the courage and achievements of fighter aces, whether fictional or real. Until the mid-1930s the RAF placed its strategic emphasis on bombers rather than fighters. However, the lionization of the fighter pilot, who appeared to fight an old-fashioned war of chivalric duelling, facilitated the notion that air power was a 'civilized' form of warfare, the antithesis of the mechanized mass slaughter which characterized the war in the trenches between 1914 and 1918.[12] The bomber, by contrast, with its potential as an instrument of war directed against civilian populations, clearly jeopardized such sanguine understandings of the future of military aviation.

However, in the early and mid-1930s the bomber cast a long shadow over Britain, ensuring that the RAF could not remain untouched by association with the more violent and morally ambiguous aspects of air power. Spectators at the Hendon displays in the 1920s had been exposed to re-enactments of RAF bombing missions, but these had been in the form of mock aerial attacks on 'native villages', tasteless and xenophobic imperial set pieces in which RAF airmen in Arab dress portrayed tribal insurgents. However, during the 1930s the Japanese bombing of Shanghai in 1932, the German Condor Legion's levelling of Guernica in 1937 and Stanley Baldwin's gloomy prediction in November 1932 that 'the bomber will always get through' all suggested that destruction from the skies was now to be the fate, not just of rebellious colonial subjects in Iraq or on the North West Frontier, but of the inhabitants of Britain's cities. Anxieties about future wars characterized by massive air bombardment of civilians boosted the cause of both those who insisted on the need to appease Hitler and Mussolini in the 1930s, and their critics who argued for accelerated rearmament. Unease about the destructive potential of the flyer was also encouraged by the enthusiasm for aviation shown by Europe's fascist leaders. In H. G. Wells' futuristic fantasy *The Shape of Things to Come*, first published in 1935, airmen are initially welcomed as the philosophically literate saviours of civilization, but are quickly revealed to be ruthless fascist strongmen. In an atmosphere of increased queasiness about military aviation, in 1935 the RAF replaced the mock bombing display at Hendon by a mass fly-past of 260 aircraft.[13]

In addition to such ambiguity about the nature of air power, a not inconsiderable section of the public in the 1930s was outraged at the youthful exuberance and apparent levity of the peacetime Royal Air Force. Young flyers shocked the genteel with their adolescent swagger, unkempt appearance, pub-crawling, and noisy sports cars. Aircrew had an especially notorious reputation for reckless driving (usually, although not always, fuelled by heavy drinking), a popular assumption that was so prevalent that insurance companies frequently imposed an additional premium on RAF personnel. Hector Bolitho, who became a RAF Intelligence officer, recalled that in the 1930s the service 'was not popular': 'old ladies rattled their tea-cups in nervous protest when aircraft dived over their lawns. They were antagonized [by] . . . the young pilots, with their fast motor cars, their lively slang and jovial tippling.'[14] The novelist (and widow of a fighter pilot) Jane Oliver, writing in 1944, reminded her readers that it had only been a few years before that, 'to the average citizen . . . these noisy young men were just a nuisance, with their tendency to pick fights on the least provocation, to drive almost continuously to the danger of the public, to break all the comfortable conventions'. In Oliver's novel *In No Strange Land*, the female narrator, Mary, condemns the 'peace-hugging people of England' for placing too high a premium on safety in the 1930s, but predicts that, once war comes, public valuation of the flyer would be transformed: 'Then I thought . . . these young men who kept piling up their cars in peoples' ditches, whose reckless courage was cramped by the law-abiding limits of middle-class life . . . then, in time of terror, the law-abiding people are going to need the lawless ones very badly indeed.'[15] Such sentiments were reiterated in the memoirs of Kay Carroll, the wife of an RAF officer. Writing in 1941, she noted that whereas young flyers were now acknowledged as the 'pick of Britain's manhood', only a few years previously civilians had refused to let their property to RAF officers. Carroll and her husband had frequently been turned away by potential landladies, who seemed convinced that all air-force officers were permanently drunk and that their wives were 'recruited exclusively from the local bars and pubs'.[16] In the 1930s some Britons were awestruck by the glamour and modishness associated with the RAF, others were troubled by their association with a violent total war of annihilation which appeared ever more likely, and a significant number of people felt they were beyond the pale of respectability. Which of these very different estimations of the flyer was to become predominant in British culture remained unclear when war broke out in 1939.

The opening phases of the Second World War offered no immediate clarification on this matter. In the first week of the war the RAF mounted raids against naval bases in Germany which provided good propaganda, even if they were of limited strategic value. From the sporadic dogfights which took place between British fighter planes based in France and German aircraft straying over the Maginot Line in the winter of 1939–40, the British press (especially a war correspondent at the *Daily Mail*, Noel Monks) was able to weave stories of young 'knights of the air'. While the RAF hierarchy was hostile to publicizing the achievements of individuals, ultimately forbidding fighter pilots to give interviews, in March 1940 the press proclaimed the New Zealand fighter pilot Edgar 'Cobber' Kain to be the first 'ace' of the war, after he had shot down five enemy aircraft.[17] However, it was the Royal Navy, rather than the RAF, which was to be the main beneficiary, in terms of public esteem, of the relative inactivity of the so-called 'phoney war'. The pursuit, and eventual scuttling, of the German pocket battleship *Graf Spee* at the Battle of the River Plate in December 1939 was presented as Britain's first major military success of the war. When the German armies invaded the Low Countries and France in May 1940, a number of RAF fighter squadrons fought a tenacious campaign against the aerial component of the blitzkrieg. However, while they exacted a heavy toll from the Luftwaffe, their own casualty rates were high, and the loss of machines even more critical. Eventually, faced with the total collapse of the French army on the ground, and conscious that Britain could not afford to leave its own air defences undermanned, the RAF was brought home.[18] If the RAF was, on balance, pleased with its performance in the Battle of France, the British public were less enthused, largely because of popular understandings, originating from the army but soon adopted by a sizeable section of the civilian population, about the RAF's role in the evacuation of the British Expeditionary Force (BEF) from Dunkirk in late May and early June 1940.

The army believed that the air force had manifestly failed in its duty to protect the vulnerable lines of troops, waiting their turn to be taken off the beaches by the flotilla of ships sent across the Channel to rescue them, from German air attacks. Some soldiers acknowledged that they had seen the RAF in action over the beaches of Dunkirk. Christopher Seton-Watson, an officer in the Royal Horse Artillery, recorded in his diary on 29 May that 'there were several air raids, with British fighters engaged', and that 'the RAF was increasingly visible'. On the following day he observed that, while there were 'a few bombing raids', 'the RAF was much in evidence and there were no casualties on the beach'.[19] It is also possible that soldiers on the ground failed to see British fighters in action because they were intercepting German bombers inland, before they reached the beaches. In addition, air combat might have been obscured from the ground by the pall of black smoke rising up from the burning oil-storage tanks at the harbour.[20] However, such explanations cut little ice with the demoralized and bitter infantrymen of the BEF, who were convinced that the Luftwaffe had been allowed to bomb and strafe the waiting soldiers unmolested. New Zealand fighter pilot Alan Deere was shot down over Belgium and found himself among the BEF during the Dunkirk evacuation. On the naval destroyer taking him back to Britain, Deere was placed in a tiny wardroom, crowded with army officers, where a 'stony silence' greeted his announcement that he was a RAF officer. When Deere jokingly enquired of a young gunner lieutenant: 'Why so friendly, what have the RAF done?', he was told: 'That's just it. What have they done? You are about as popular in this company as a cat in the prize canary's cage.' Deere was infuriated by what he felt to be the army's ignorance, pointing out that twelve of the seventeen pilots in his squadron had been lost during Dunkirk, and that 'for two weeks non-stop I had flown my guts out, and this was all the thanks I got'.[21]

Everywhere they went in June 1940 RAF personnel were abused and even assaulted, not just by soldiers, but by civilians too. RAF flyers found it wise to avoid pubs in army garrison towns such as Andover or Colchester, and in Salisbury, Guy Gibson recalled 'the brown jobs are beating up anything in blue they can see'.[22] When Tony Bartley crashed his Spitfire near Hornchurch in June 1940, he was arrested by the Home Guard and taken to the local police station, an unwelcome response to his misfortune which Bartley attributed, in part, to the unpopularity of fighter pilots in the immediate aftermath of Dunkirk. On 15 July a single Junkers 88 succeeded in bombing the South Wales town of Llanelli, before escaping back to occupied France, unharmed. The citizens of Llanelli, their indignation aggravated by the stories they had heard from soldiers recently returned from Dunkirk, vented their anger against the RAF, barracking flyers unfortunate enough to find themselves in the vicinity.[23] Hostility between the RAF and army persisted well into the remainder of the war. In 1941 Philip Toynbee was stationed with his infantry battalion on the Yorkshire coast, where he was visited by his old friend Esmond Romilly, who was serving in a bomber squadron. There was an awkwardness about their reunion, largely because, as Toynbee later recalled, 'at this time the infantry still regarded the RAF with a gnawing and unconfessed hostility'.[24]

Relations with the navy had also been decidedly frosty in the first nine months of the war. Aircrew were often convinced they had been subject to 'friendly fire' from the navy while operating over the Channel or North Sea. Flight Lieutenant Shackelton, who flew Blenheims and Mosquitoes, remembers at least two aircraft being the victims of 'our somewhat overzealous Royal Navy', and the subsequent violent anger directed towards the navy in his mess.[25] Conversely, the senior service regularly accused the RAF of accidentally attacking British ships or submarines. Such tensions between the RAF and navy were sufficiently well known to form the backcloth to Nevil Shute's novel *Landfall*, set in the winter of 1939–40, in which an Anson pilot appears to have accidentally bombed a British submarine, mistaking it for a German U-boat.[26] As with the tales the army brought back from Dunkirk, it seems likely that civilians with relatives and friends in the senior service might have absorbed a measure of the hostility towards the RAF which such incidents provoked.

However, among the broader population attitudes were to be irrevocably changed in August and September 1940, when the unkempt hooligans of the pre-war imagination or the perfidious dilettantes of Dunkirk were transformed into the glorious 'few'. The flyer came to be idolized by the British public. Initially, this infatuation was directed towards the pilots of Fighter Command, the branch of the service most closely associated with the Battle of Britain. However, it was also soon extended to the RAF's bomber crews. In the anxious period between late 1940 and the autumn of 1942 the threat of German invasion receded, but Allied victory remained far from certain. The campaigns of the army were taking place a long way from Britain, and were not always easy to make sense of by the public at home. This was particularly true of the Eighth Army's war, which amounted to a series of successive advances and retreats across the deserts of Egypt and Libya. The fact that the British army's major military commitments at this time were in distant North Africa and the eastern Mediterranean, while German troops still stood amassed only 20 miles away across the English Channel, contributed to the popularity of Bomber Command. Initially in twin-engined Wellingtons, Hampdens, and Whitleys, and then in the great four-engined heavy bombers, the Lancasters, Stirlings, and Halifaxes, the 'bomber boys' appeared to be the only fighting men regularly taking the war to the heart of the enemy, in their nightly raids over German cities.[27]

True, adulation was not universal. Among those questioned in 1941 by Mass-Observation about their attitudes towards the three armed services was the inhabitant of an English coastal town that had been heavily bombed by the Germans. He was indignant that, while he was forced to hear a lot about the RAF's achievements on the BBC, 'I have never seen a RAF fighter about when the air over our city has been thick with German bombers'. The RAF, he avowed, was 'too conceited'.[28] Nor was the popularity of the flyer entirely spontaneous. The RAF's initial desire not to publicize individuals had given way, during 1940, to a desire to vigorously promote the service through features on glamorous fighter aces in the newspapers, broadcasts by serving pilots on the BBC (the latter being collected in two published anthologies, *We Speak From the Air* and *Over to You*), and invitations to war correspondents to join bomber crews on their missions.[29] A major success in the RAF's publicity offensive was *Target for Tonight*, a 1941 drama-documentary made by the Crown Film Unit, which eschewed professional actors in favour of real air-force personnel. The film depicted the preparation and execution of a bombing raid on Germany. Ironically, given that Bomber Command was still a relatively ineffective force at this point in the war, *Target for Tonight* was a critical and commercial success, possibly because it was one of the first movies to portray Britain taking the offensive against the enemy.[30]

If a jaded few felt the RAF might better be identified as the 'Royal Advertising Force', the esteem with which the majority of the public came to regard the flyboys is obvious from the success of the Spitfire Funds, in which people voluntarily gave money to the government to 'buy' aircraft, thereby creating a practical and emotional tie to the service.[31] It was no less evident in the cataract of popular romantic novels which appeared in 1940–1, with titles such as *Flying Wild*, *A Flying Visit*, *Winged Love*, *Air Force Girl*, and *Wellington Wendy*.[32] 'Never', wrote one disgruntled reviewer, who had been required to wade through these RAF-themed potboilers, 'have I felt that I owed so little to so many.'[33] A second Mass-Observation report on attitudes to the RAF found that, while they had encountered some weariness with excessive media coverage of the RAF, even this muted criticism would immediately be followed by a respondent making clear that: 'There's nothing to touch them in the whole of history.'[34]

A PAIR OF SILVER WINGS: THE CONSTITUENTS OF FLYBOY GLAMOUR

The glamour which attached itself to the RAF after the summer of 1940 is encapsulated in the popularity of 92 Squadron, based at Biggin Hill, which captivated the public with its combined reputation for extraordinary bravery and carefree hedonism. The debonair playboys of 92—especially Tony Bartley, Bob Tuck, and Brian Kingcome—took respite from undertaking up to four sorties a day against the relentless assault of the Luftwaffe during the Battle of Britain in a social scene that was elaborate and extensive. Biggin Hill's proximity to London meant that these young fighter pilots snatched brief periods of leave in the metropolis, where they became a regular fixture of hotel bars, private parties, and nightclubs. They travelled to London in a fleet of fast cars. Bartley owned a twelve-cylinder Lincoln Zephyr coupé, Kingcome an SS 100 racer, and Bob Holland a supercharged Bentley. These types of cars were voracious consumers of fuel, which should have made them unusable at a time when petrol rationing was vigorously enforced by the police and gas-guzzling vehicles had their licences withdrawn. Among the civilian population, those who did not require their cars for business found the acute shortage of petrol made it advisable to garage their automobiles for the duration of the war. The flyboys of 92 Squadron, however, simply filled their cars with 100-octane fuel from the aircraft petrol bowsers, a practice to which their commanding officers turned a blind eye. When police officers came to Biggin Hill to remonstrate with the adjutant about the unlicensed (and potentially lethal) sports cars which RAF officers had been recklessly driving through the country lanes of Kent in the small hours of the morning, they were plied with drinks so that they unintentionally divulged the date of the next police check-up of cars for licensing violations. Needlessly to say, on these days any flyers travelling to London took the bus or train.[35]

The men of 92 Squadron also organized fancy-dress parties and entertained celebrated singers and actors in their mess. They even held dances in their hangers, to the accompaniment of the base's own jazz band, composed of London nightclub musicians who had been deliberately conscripted as ground crew at Biggin Hill by a Fighter Command personnel officer.[36] In October 1940 senior RAF officers became concerned about what many were now labelling 'the 92nd Night Club'. They responded by sending an RAF psychologist to Biggin Hill. After three days of observing, and living with, the pilots, he reported that their riotous leisure activities were having no obvious compromising effect on their military capability. Tony Bartley recalled him telling the Fighter Command hierarchy that 'we were shooting down aeroplanes which was all that mattered, and how we went about it was our affair'. However, the psychologist did also infer that he suspected 92 Squadron's habit of burning the candle at both ends could not be sustained forever. A tough Canadian, Johnny Kent, was therefore dispatched to instil some discipline at Biggin Hill. He began with uniform (or more strictly, its absence), adopting a policy of zero tolerance towards check shirts, suede shoes, red trousers, and pyjamas worn under flying kit. Soon after, fast cars were discouraged, and parties at the manor house which served as the officers' mess at Biggin Hill were scaled down, Kent insisting that female guests be out of the building by 11 p.m.[37] Kent's attempts to curtail some of the excesses of 92 Squadron reflected a shift in outlook among the hierarchy of Fighter Command. At the height of the Battle of Britain an indulgent and permissive attitude was justified by the extraordinary circumstances of that summer, but once the worst of the crisis had passed and the air war became more routinized, the restoration of discipline and formality inevitably followed. However, the general public remained wedded to an affecting image of fresh-faced young men living life to the full in the precious intermissions between active duty, reckless sensualists under constant sentence of death.

In 1941 the painter Cuthbert Orde was commissioned to paint sixty-four portraits of RAF fighter pilots, for a volume which received the RAF's official sanction in the form of a foreword by Air Chief Marshal Sir Sholto Douglas. Among the flyers who sat for Orde was Robert Stanford Tuck, one of the most flamboyant members of 92 Squadron, and a genuine celebrity in the aftermath of the Battle of Britain. Orde's appraisal of his sitter reiterated the myth of the fighter boys in general, and 92 Squadron in particular: 'Everyone knows Bob Tuck: flat-out for fighting and flat-out for parties.'[38] Tuck embodied the carefree insouciance the public expected of the fighter boys. Tony Bartley remembered his first meeting with the Battle of Britain ace. Tuck 'lounged out of his cockpit, a silk scarf draped around his neck, a monogrammed handkerchief drooping from one sleeve. He lit a cigarette in a long white holder, and strolled towards our CO.'[39] Such swashbuckling images of the flyer also became the staple of popular fiction. In C. H. Ward-Jackson's short story 'Mess Ante-Room: 12.30', the narrator describes the flyer Elroy, who is compared to a 'Regency Buck' from the pages of romantic historical novelist Jeffrey Farnol, coolly professional in the air but *bon vivant* on the ground. In one passage Elroy is to be found playing poker with a fellow officer, revolvers on the table 'for atmosphere'.[40] Orde also painted Wing Commander Michael Robinson, another debonair and captivating flyer who was 'to be found, when off duty, mostly in night-clubs, and, when on duty, mainly in the air'.[41] If these were crude caricatures imparted by propagandists, flyers themselves were not entirely blameless for the popular association between the RAF and youthful hedonism. Squadron Leader John 'Chips' Carpenter was one of a number of flyers who had the name of their favourite West End nightclub (in his case, *Chez Nina*) inscribed on the side of their aircraft.[42]

The most beguiling emblem of the flyer's allure was their ashy-blue uniform, with the Flying Badge worn above the right upper jacket pocket. The blue uniforms of the RAF were a dramatic contrast with the drab brown uniform of the army, as resentful army officers knew only too well. Indeed, during the First World War convalescing soldiers had been pleased to temporarily eschew regulation khaki in favour of the distinctive vivid-blue uniforms issued to patients in military hospitals.[43] RAF blue could have distinctly elitist connotations. In E. M. Delafield's fictional diary of provincial life in the early weeks of the war, while modest Serena knits a 'stout khaki muffler' to send to men in the army, the snobbish Society debutante 'works exclusively in Air-Force blue'.[44] However, the RAF's characteristic livery was also associated with both heroism and sexual magnetism, particularly if accompanied by a set of silvery white fabric wings sewn above the heart, signifying that the bearer was an operational pilot. A number of fictional narratives attested to the transformative effect of the RAF uniform on those who wore them. In John Watson's novel *Johnny Kinsman*, Johnny works as a clerk, but yearns to be a journalist. When war breaks out he initially decides to join the army, but one evening meets two friends, Tommy and Dick, who have joined the air force. To Johnny, the two men, both wearing their RAF uniform, possess 'a kind of majesty', and he enviously notes the glances of admiration being directed towards them by women on the street. Johnny decides to abandon his plan to enlist in the army in favour of joining the RAF. Lying in bed, he imagines himself 'walking across the ceiling in the uniform of a pilot of the Royal Air Force'. He admitted to himself that he had little idea of what an RAF pilot actually did when not on leave, but that was less important than how he would be able to impress Chris, his girlfriend. He also thought of 'what all the people in the village would say when they saw him walking along the main street in his uniform. Oh God, make it that he would be a pilot, an officer and a pilot.'[45]

Other novels related tales of young men whose pre-war awkwardness with the opposite sex was banished by the possession of a pilot's wings, transforming them into objects of fascination and desire for the very same women who had previously spurned them. In Alexander Baron's *With Hope, Farewell*, Mark Strong is a young Jewish boy, growing up in the East End of London. He becomes alienated from his working-class parents (especially after a scholarship takes him to the grammar school), but is no less estranged from a middle-class culture riddled with anti-Semitism. Moreover, his infatuation for a young woman, Ruth, remains embarrassingly unrequited. Mark is inevitably jaded and cynical and, working as a clerk in the City, fantasizes about one day becoming a fighter pilot. The outbreak of war allows him to fulfil his dream, and serving as a Hurricane pilot during the Battle of Britain dramatically increases his self-esteem. In particular, it gives him the confidence to resume his pursuit of Ruth who, on seeing him in his uniform, no longer repels his advances: 'He unbuttoned his greatcoat to reach for his small change, and blushed with pleasure as she cried, "Oh, that lovely tunic! And wings! Don't button your coat up. I want to hold your arm and let people see you and pretend you're my property".' Years later a disillusioned Mark, who is having difficulty adjusting to the pedestrian nature of civilian life, retrieves his air-force tunic from a suitcase and delights 'once more in the smooth blue cloth sitting sleekly on his shoulders'.[46]

Lest these narratives appear as mere literary devices, a means to dramatize the themes of male restlessness and female capriciousness, it should be noted that real flyers were equally convinced of the empowering possibilities of their blue tunic and silver wings. Geoffrey Wellum, a member of 92 Squadron, recalled his sense of extraordinary satisfaction and self-admiration, after a pair of wings were first sewn on his uniform.[47] Pierre Clostermann, a French exile who became a Spitfire pilot, shared with the British readers of his autobiography his pride in the mysterious allure of his uniform, 'the colour of your island mists'.[48] Even those who were disabled or disfigured found that possession of an RAF uniform ensured that they remained objects of fascination and desire. Colin Hodgkinson, who lost both legs in a flying accident with the Fleet Air Arm, transferred to the RAF, and credited his new uniform with playing a critical role in his rehabilitation: 'Air Force Blue, at that time the most famous colour in the world . . . I smoothed the wings above my left breast pocket, prinked like a mannequin up and down before a glass. My God! Nothing could stop me now. I was irresistible!'[49] William Simpson, who suffered serious burns to his hands and face after his Fairy Battle crashed in France in May 1940, remembered how women were attracted to 'those silver embroidered wings on the smoke-blue RAF uniform, and the little flashes of coloured ribbon beneath them . . . The uniform was redolent of glamour and courage. Even the breaking of our bodies was accepted as part of success rather than failure.'[50] This notion appears to be endorsed by the memoirs of Joan Wyndham, who left a bohemian background in Chelsea in 1941 to join the Women's Auxiliary Air Force (WAAF). At a Victory Dance in the mess at RAF Watnall in May 1945 she began a passionate affair with Kit Latimer, a Spitfire pilot whose face had been badly burned after his aircraft was forced to make a crash-landing. On first meeting, Wyndham registered the distorting effect Latimer's burns had on his features, but nevertheless concluded that he was 'very good-looking in spite of it'. When, on their second date, the free-spirited Wyndham took the initiative and kissed him, Latimer tells her that he had been too frightened to kiss her, on account of his 'face being so funny'. Wyndham replied that he had a 'beautiful face' and she kissed him again, before dragging him off to an empty tent on the airfield perimeter, where they made love.[51]

For Wyndham, facial disfigurement was less likely to compromise the erotic status of the RAF blue than the absence of pilot's wings from the uniform. When she first joined the WAAF, she was disappointed to be assigned to Fighter Command Headquarters, where their officers were usually ground-based administrators rather than dashing flyers. At a headquarters dance she was distressed that no pilots were present, and that she would have to make do with the sweaty embraces of an assortment of 'pint-size Romeos' and other 'wingless wonders'. She concluded that the 'worst thing about being at Fighter Command is that there are no pilots! I can't describe the effect wings have on a WAAF.'[52] However, much of the public was less fastidious, and appeared less able to appreciate the distinction between flyers and non-operational RAF officers. In the autumn of 1940 Derek Gilpin Barnes, who was serving as an RAF Intelligence Officer, found himself the unintentional beneficiary of a climate in which the British public were 'spellbound' by the achievements of the fighter boys, and longed for opportunities to express their appreciation. Barnes was embarrassed when, espied in his blue-grey uniform, he was mistaken for 'one of the few'. Desperate to abjure homage which he felt he had not earned, he protested that 'I was but a disguised business man who felt privileged indeed to serve the air-crews in my unhazardous, but necessary, capacity of Intelligence Officer'. However, this appeal fell on deaf ears, as elderly men in bars offered him drinks 'and patted my blue back', exclaiming 'Good luck, lad! Shoot 'em down!'[53]

Such adulation of the young men of the RAF cannot be accounted for solely by the successful marketing of the service by the Air Ministry. Indeed, the manufacturing of crude propaganda was unnecessary, when a variety of outside authors commissioned to write about the air force found themselves genuinely impressed by the flyers whom they encountered. A classic example of this tendency was provided by Cecil Beaton, the portrait photographer who was notorious for flattering his sitters in public while savagely detailing their imperfections in the pages of his private journal. In 1941 Beaton was asked by the Ministry of Information to spend several weeks with aircrew from Fighter, Bomber, and Coastal Commands, a sojourn which provided the raw material for some brilliantly candid photographs and a published essay, which waxed lyrical about the qualities of the combat pilots he met. Beaton's diaries reveal that his admiration was, for once, sincere and unfeigned, and it is significant that his book on the RAF was the only written text in which he himself was not to be the central character.[54] At times Beaton's gushing prose style verged on hyperbole. He described a pilot returning from a mission as one who had 'just triumphed over time and space; defied gravity; and soaring into the blue empyrean has attained a means of expression that gives him an elasticity denied to all of us bound to the ground. With this new element at his disposal he has attained exquisite sensations of power and purity.' The flyers were, Beaton asserted, a 'new mould of men', for 'never before in history has our country been saved by so youthful a fraternity fighting with such casual perfection'.[55] However, Beaton's breathless eulogizing, and the way that it accorded with a broader public sensibility, is understandable when it is remembered that, before the war, civilian flying had remained a prerogative of the wealthy. In an age before the arrival of mass aviation and the package holiday, few had had the opportunity of, in Beaton's words, 'sitting on top of the sky'. The fact that the flyer fought his war amidst what Gilpin Barnes called 'the lofty ways of cloudland', a world 'inconceivable to lesser men', only added to the airman's glamorous mystique.[56]

THE FLYER GOES TO HOLLYWOOD

Some flyers undoubtedly welcomed all this attention and adulation. Arthur Gwynn-Browne's novel *Gone for a Burton* was written while the author was on active service, and his acknowledgments testified to extensive assistance from 'innumerable members' of the RAF. One of the main characters in the book, Anthony, a 23-year-old sergeant pilot, is certainly a convincing portrayal, rendered without sentimentality or melodrama. At one point Anthony reflects on the issue of the RAF's glamorous reputation. He confesses that 'I like it. It helps. You're part of the public. You aren't cut off, and if you do something good, you're splashed on the front page and you get an interview.' He concedes that some might regard it as 'vulgar' or 'shooting a line', but insists that 'I don't want to feel I'm a sort of muddy secret and I don't want to wait six months before what I do leaks out'. Anthony recalls his pride at the widespread publicity surrounding a real-life flyer, Wing Commander Guy Gibson, leader of Operation Chastise (better known as the Dambusters Raid) in May 1943: 'I liked seeing his pictures in the papers, he looked a swell type, and I felt grand about it.'[57] Many flyers, however, detested publicity and were embarrassed, even disgusted, by the stories which appeared about them in the press or their portrayal in novels and feature films. They were contemptuous of what they labelled 'drip' or 'Hollywood stuff'.[58]

There was particular hostility towards stories which applied to the flyer the same languages of glamour and hero-worship which were more usually reserved for contemporary stars of the silver screen. RAF aircrew saw the heroes of war movies as examples of how war wasn't, and shouldn't be, fought. In 1942 Pilot Officer Richard Tucker was in South Africa for training when he saw *Ships with Wings*, a British movie celebrating the achievements of the Fleet Air Arm. The film, he concluded, was 'absolute tripe'.[59] Hollywood escapism appeared particularly reprehensible, offering upbeat fantasies which seemed to mock the brutal reality of fighting and dying in the skies. The flyer's war was authentic, Hollywood's war completely phoney. American movies such as *A Yank in the RAF*, starring Tyrone Power and Betty Grable, were viewed by many British airmen with scorn. At the outbreak of war David Niven, by this time a Hollywood leading man, returned to Britain and tried to enlist in the RAF. A recruitment officer curtly told him that 'we don't encourage actors to join *this* service'. Niven turned to making propaganda films instead, although he married a WAAF during the war, and included several Battle of Britain pilots among his choice of golf partners. Moreover, his debonair charm made him an obvious choice to play RAF officers on screen, and he was cast as a flyer in *The First of the Few*, a movie about the origins of the Spitfire (with a prologue and epilogue set during the Battle of Britain) and in the romantic fantasy *A Matter of Life and Death*.[60]

In fact, such was the magnetism of the flyer and the extent of his cultural purchase, that the worlds of screen fantasy and the real war in the air could not be kept separate for long. The proximity of Biggin Hill to London ensured that the base often received visits from celebrity guests. As a result, Tony Bartley became a close friend of screen actors Laurence Olivier (and his wife, Vivien Leigh), Roger Livesey, and Ralph Richardson. When making *The First of the Few*, director Leslie Howard was anxious to capture the authentic atmosphere of a fighter station. Bartley, one of two pilots asked to perform aerobatic sequences for the movie, offered to take Howard and David Niven over to Biggin Hill. At this time the station was commanded by the tough South African, 'Sailor' Malan. Bartley was apprehensive as to how Malan would react to the presence on his base of visiting movie stars. Fortunately, Malan 'had just landed from a fighter sweep when we arrived, and had the blood of a [German] tail gunner splashed over his windscreen, so he was quite hospitable'.[61] Richard Hillary, author of the acclaimed fighter-pilot memoir *The Last Enemy*, was approached by Ealing Studios' maverick director Alberto Cavalcanti with a view to adapting the book for the screen. Ultimately nothing came of the proposal, which was unfortunate since Cavalcanti, as was made apparent in his extraordinary cinematic imagining of a German invasion of rural England in *Went the Day Well?*, had a decidedly unsentimental view of the British war effort, and a candour about the violence that was required to secure victory.[62]

However, Hillary did assist Cavalcanti in making a short film about the Sea Rescue Services. In the period between recovering from a crash which appeared to have ended his career as an occupational pilot and embarking on the writing of *The Last Enemy*, Hillary was sent to the United States, then still neutral, to promote the RAF. Having suffered terrible burns and undergone extensive plastic surgery to his face and hands, Hillary was asked not to speak at women's clubs, lest his terrible injuries encourage isolationist sentiment among American mothers, who might be less than eager to send their sons to Europe to meet a similar fate. If this prohibition temporarily perturbed Hillary, who had seen the American tour as a means to further the rebuilding of his life after his catastrophic accident, an opportunity to restore his self-esteem came from an unexpected source. While in the United States, Hillary had a passionate affair with Merle Oberon, Hollywood superstar and the wife of film producer Alexander Korda. Several nights spent together in the Ritz Towers in New York City did much to restore Hillary's spirits, not to say his stamina, given Oberon had a notoriously intense sex-drive.[63] Another seriously disfigured fighter pilot, Geoffrey Page, visited Hollywood in 1944, where he stayed in the North Alpine Drive home of actor Nigel Bruce and socialized with Joan Fontaine and Ronald Coleman. After the war he returned to Los Angeles and married Bruce's daughter Pauline, with veteran screen character-actor C. Aubrey Smith serving as best man.[64]

Another example of personal interaction between the worlds of the flyer and the silver screen was the marriage of famous bomber pilot and Victoria Cross holder Leonard Cheshire to the former silent-screen Hollywood actress Constance Binney in 1941. Cheshire had been sent to the United States to collect American aircraft and deliver them to Britain. He met Binney during four days leave in New York City, where she introduced him to an intoxicating world of champagne parties, celebrity friends, and high living. Binney was much older than Cheshire, and he later came to regret marrying her after their whirlwind romance. However, as he noted in his wartime memoir, 'the future didn't count for much in those days'.[65] Cheshire's predecessor in command of the elite 617 Squadron had been the famous 'Dambuster', Guy Gibson. In 1943 Winston Churchill, in typically romantic vein, invited a number of the most dashing and heroic figures from all three of Britain's armed services to accompany him to the Quebec Conference, hoping their charisma would create goodwill towards Britain in both Canada and the United States. Gathered on the ocean liner *Queen Mary* as it crossed the Atlantic was an impressive cast of debonair war heroes. From the army there was Orde Wingate, whose combination of a successful campaign of irregular warfare against the Japanese in Burma and brooding mysticism led him to be regularly compared to Lawrence of Arabia. The navy was represented by Lord Louis Mountbatten, hero of *HMS Kelly* and a cousin of the king. The RAF's presence on this propaganda mission was Guy Gibson.

Mary Churchill, accompanying her father, chatted with the young wing commander and was struck by his 'school-boy, cherry-cheeked fair good looks'. So were the American public, for on arrival in the United States Gibson captivated the crowds who turned out to see him. Even the most hard-boiled pressmen were charmed by his boyish face and easy smile. As a result, Gibson was invited to spend two weeks at the home of Hollywood tycoon Howard Hawks. Gibson did more than take advantage of the California sunshine, Hawks's private swimming pool, and unrationed steaks. He talked with Hawks about making a movie about the 'Dambusters' raid. Indeed, there is evidence that Hawks went so far as to commission a script from Roald Dahl, a former fighter pilot and writer, who was now serving as assistant to the British air attaché in Washington, and some have even claimed, with less credibility, that Hawks got as far as building a 300-foot-long model of the Mohne Dam which Gibson's squadron had famously breached. While Gibson's discussions with Hawks came to nothing, Gibson's time in Hollywood did leave a peculiar legacy. On the tour of the United States, Gibson adopted Americanized speech, terming aeroplanes 'ships', cars 'automobiles', and referring to the Mohne Dam as 'the big baby'. This habit persisted on his return to Britain, and his memoir, *Enemy Coast Ahead*, written before the renewal of his operational career and death in 1944, contains several examples of American-style slang, notably his frequent use of the term 'stooge'.[66]

In the following year Tony Bartley was to find himself in Los Angeles, as part of a RAF delegation tour of Canada and the United States. Travelling down Sunset Boulevard, his cab driver, who had been completely silent up to this point, caught a glimpse of Bartley, wearing his distinctive blue uniform, in his rear-view mirror and asked his passenger if he was 'for real or from Central Casting'. Bartley failed to understand the question, but his incomprehension was taken as an indication of authenticity, whereupon the cabbie pulled over at the next bar and bought the young RAF officer a drink. Bartley's unfamiliarity with Hollywood was quickly dispelled in the weeks that followed. He was entertained by Clark Gable, whom he had already met in Britain when the American star was serving with the US Air Force. Another host was Basil Rathbone, star of the Sherlock Holmes movies, an English expatriate and one of the 'social lions' of the British colony in Los Angeles. Rathbone was anxious to preserve the codes of British gentlemanly restraint amidst the vulgar extravagance of Hollywood. When Bartley appeared to be enjoying the attentions of minor screen starlets at Rathbone's cocktail party, the tight-laced host hissed to his guest: 'For God's sake, behave like an officer and don't let the side down, old chap.' However, Rathbone's apprehension that the distractions of Hollywood might spoil the heroic young pilot were disregarded. Bartley made his excuses and left the party, but not before he had set up an assignation at her apartment with Betty Hutton, a comedy actress labelled the 'blonde bombshell' after her performances in *The Fleet's In* and *Miracle of Morgan's Creek*. Bartley eventually lost this 'incendiary blonde' (to steal a title of another of Hutton's films) to Clark Gable, who had the advantage over the RAF flyer of having been both an operational pilot and a major international movie star. However, back in Britain Bartley met the rather more serene and ladylike (if no less glamorous) British screen star Deborah Kerr. In a letter to his parents Bartley informed them that he had met 'an absolute whizz-kid of a girl': 'I'm afraid it's another actress, but, oh boy, what a peach.' Despite being warned by Stewart Granger, another actor whom he had befriended, 'never marry an actress, old boy', Bartley proposed to Kerr, by means of a telegram that he composed with the assistance of David Niven. In November 1945 Bartley and Kerr married in St George's Church, Hanover Square. Their wedding reception at Claridges was attended by an amalgam of film folk such as Alexander Korda, and fighter pilots from 92 Squadron.[67]

Of course, only a tiny minority of flyers ever had the opportunity to meet, let alone marry, a film star. However, in a decade in which cinema-going remained the most significant commercial leisure activity in Britain, it is not surprising that the public often perceived the heroic flyer through referents drawn from the world of the silver screen. Indeed, flyers themselves were no different from other young men of the same age, in that they were deeply imbued with movie culture. When Roald Dahl crashed his Gladiator fighter plane in the Western Desert, suffering head injuries and temporary blindness, he was hospitalized, and cared for by a nurse called Mary Welland. Captivated by Mary's soft voice, but unable to see her, Dahl fantasized that her features were those of Myrna Loy, 'a Hollywood cinema actress I had seen many times on the silver screen', who previously had been his 'idea of the perfect beauty'. When his sight was restored he found Mary to be more beautiful than he had imagined, but she did not sufficiently resemble his favourite Hollywood star to sustain his interest.[68]

Life and cinematic art were often entangled in the life of the wartime RAF. In 1942 the movie *Dangerous Moonlight* was released. It was a highly romanticized tale of a Polish pianist (played by Anton Walbrook) who becomes a RAF fighter pilot.[69] The movie's popularity was associated with its signature theme, a lushly orchestrated piece of music entitled the 'Warsaw Concerto'. It was composed by Richard Addinsell, whose song-writing partner, the entertainer Joyce Grenfell, recalled its particular resonance with the RAF: 'The theme was played by concert pianists, dance-band pianists, and by ear on lamentable canteen uprights throughout the length and breadth of Great Britain.'[70] While entertaining troops in Iraq in 1944, Grenfell met a young airman who intended to play the score from *Dangerous Moonlight* at his wedding, such was 'the magic the piece has over the boys'.[71] For Jean Barclay, a WAAF intelligence officer at the bomber base at RAF Waddington, the 'Warsaw Concerto', which always seemed to be playing on the mess radio during 'the first bitter months of 1942', was to have especially poignant associations. She remembered a flyer who had a passion for the concerto, and who constantly played a recording of it, being killed in a raid on Augsburg. Another memory the film and its music brought was of:

coming out of the camp cinema one early spring evening of 1942 where Monica Campbell and I had been to see *Dangerous Moonlight*. A clear vivid blue evening with Waddington's buildings square and black against a sky that went from blue to pale green, then through golden yellow to palest pink deepening to reds on the western horizon . . . and against the glorious sky an appalling column of thick black smoke rising . . . one of our aircraft had crashed after taking off and all the crew were killed. We had watched the ominous black smoke rising as we stood there petrified and sick with horror. And all the time the wretched music of *Dangerous Moonlight* drumming through our heads.[72]

Fictionalized accounts of the world of the flyer also made reference to the 'Warsaw Concerto'. In C. H. Ward-Jackson's short story 'Squadron Farewell', a grieving WAAF plays the piece at a station concert party, having seen *Dangerous Moonlight* with her air-gunner husband just before he is sent overseas, a posting from which he has failed to return.[73] Significantly, Addinsell's heady score was one of Guy Gibson's choice of favourite tunes when he was a guest on the radio show *Desert Island Discs*.[74]

As will become apparent in the remainder of this book, the flyer's image was rarely allowed to stand unmediated, always being understood in relation to other cultural formations, of which popular cinema was only one example, albeit an important one. What the RAF pilot's association, at either the real or the imaginative level, with Hollywood reveals, however, is not merely the extraordinary allure of the flyer in the eyes of the wider public. It also demonstrates that the men in air-force blue belonged to a much wider world than that of a particularized wartime military culture. Moreover, the connotations of screen fantasy which attached themselves to the wartime RAF suggest that the flyer's place in British culture was a complex amalgam of myth and actuality. In the chapters which follow, the intention is not primarily to cut through myth to reach the 'reality' of pilots' lives, but rather to understand how this complex dialogue between the real and the imagined functioned, and how it came to create the dominant cultural representation of the wartime flyer.

2

A Man's World

As warfare became more impersonal in the modern age, there was increasingly less emphasis on the attributes of the individual warrior. Instead, military psychologists insisted that the 'group personality' of the combat unit was now the critical source of martial prowess. The sense of belonging to a team was therefore actively encouraged by senior military figures.[1] However, male bonding in the wartime RAF was not just about the prerogatives of operational efficiency. The need to connect with one's fellow flyers was felt at a profound and emotional level, and was part of coming to terms with being thrown into a unique environment, a world that was intensely exciting, frightening, and macabre. What was forged was not merely an instrumental affinity based on common professional functions and demarcations, although these inevitably played their part. What emerged was a genuine comradeship, based on shared rituals, leisure activities, language, and a common generational similitude. However, whether such camaraderie translated into what, in less extraordinary times, might be construed as friendship, is more difficult to establish, given that relationships with fellow flyers were often perfunctory and frequently violently curtailed by death. Moreover, male bonding was often compromised by a variety of potential differences. There was rivalry between bomber crews and fighter boys, or between different squadrons within the same command. Class divisions, especially between officers and NCOs, were far from negligible, and, for all its vaunted cosmopolitanism, national, ethnic, and racial differences within the RAF reared their ugly heads at regular intervals.

FLYERS TOGETHER

RAF flyers certainly found a common identity in the service's 'adolescent vigour' and relative lack of formality.[2] Pilots adopted, by army or navy standards, an extremely lackadaisical attitude towards drill and saluting. In 1943 Jim Bailey had been an RAF officer and fighter pilot for four years, when he was ordered to take the salute at a Wings for Victory parade at Kilmarnock in Scotland. As the massed ranks of the local Home Guard, Fire Brigade, Air-Raid Wardens, and Boy Scouts began to march past the plinth on which Bailey stood, he realized, to his amusement, that he had no idea about how to salute properly.[3] Even senior commanders appeared oblivious to decorum or protocol. While conducting briefing sessions, Air Marshal Tedder would sit cross-legged on the ground, wearing his Irwin flying jacket, his wing commanders slumped around him in a circle.[4] Cecil Beaton attributed what he felt to be the matchless 'team spirit' of the RAF to its being 'surprisingly free of conventions'. Beaton noted that the difference between ranks was much less discernible on air-force uniforms than it was in the other services: 'The blue lines on the sleeves are so thin that you have to look twice to notice if a man is a Wing Commander.' By contrast, in the army 'you do not have to look twice to recognize a Colonel'.[5] RAF flyers who had previously served with the army or navy testified to the greater informality which characterized the RAF. Adolph 'Sailor' Malan was an Afrikaner who left the Royal Navy Reserve in the mid-1930s to become a fighter pilot, and one of the leading aces of the Battle of Britain. Malan found the RAF much more hospitable, in contrast to the 'starch-ridden caste system' of the navy.[6] The shabby appearance of aircrew was legendary. A portrait of ten fighter pilots, published in 1942, was unapologetic about the 'wild' and 'scruffy' appearance of many of the Battle of Britain flyboys. One Spitfire pilot, 'Dizzy', wore a moth-eaten tunic, and his hair was never, 'with the exception of a few moments before parties, anything but unruly'.[7] Bomber crews were no less ill-kempt and slipshod. Miles Tripp, aircrew on a Lancaster bomber during the war, and later a middlebrow novelist, recalled his own 'Neanderthal' appearance: 'my hair hadn't been cut for months and I never wore the standard forage cap; my dress was a mixture of flying gear and ordinary uniform topped by the red scarf.'[8]

How different the RAF's culture of informality was to the two senior services was all too apparent in the memoirs of Ronald Sherbrooke-Walker, an army officer sent to liaise with the air force in 1940 in order to create ground defence units (what later became the RAF Regiment). Sherbrooke-Walker was dismayed at the lack of structure and discipline he found at the air bases he visited. For a start, he found the system of officers' ranks in the RAF to be virtually incoherent. The air force seemed to have created ranks which bore little or no relation to the function of the holder. Pilot officers and flying officers did not necessarily fly, flight lieutenants had nothing to do with a flight, and while a squadron leader could potentially lead a squadron, that responsibility was usually taken by a wing commander. Equally perversely, a group captain commanded a wing, and an air vice-marshall captained a group. Sherbrooke-Walker was equally perplexed by the RAF's hierarchy of NCOs, in which technical qualifications such as pilot, observer, or air-gunner were sufficient to entitle a flyer to the minimum rank of sergeant, a privilege which had no equivalent in the army or navy. Confusion over ranking was accompanied by horror at the sartorial slovenliness of aircrew. Disgusted by the spectacle of long hair, 'flapping jackets, the crushed and dirty caps, the undone buttons', he came to the unpalatable conclusion that some RAF officers 'seemed deliberately to set out to be as untidy as possible'. Sherbrooke-Walker's Colonel Blimp-like tirade then moved on to a flyer he spotted with 'an immense pirate's moustache', and officers who wriggled out of defence exercises or failed to carry gas masks. He found it impossible to organize ground defence training, especially when it interfered with 'tea and other pleasant habits'. Sherbrooke-Walker was convinced that RAF bases in Britain had amenities which the army was rarely blessed with, unless they were in barracks: cinemas, libraries, and luxurious mess accommodation. Such high comfort levels led, in his view, to complacency. Sherbrooke-Walker might have had a point. When RAF squadrons were moved on to the continent after D-Day in 1944, they had little idea of how to live in the field. The RAF found it did not know how to pitch tents properly, and RAF cooks, 'parted from their palatial kitchens', failed to deliver good-quality meals when forced to work in outdoor cookhouses.[9] However, the relatively easygoing and irregular ethos of the RAF, which so appalled the 'brown jobs', actually helped foster loyalty to, and identification with, the RAF among its personnel. Lacking the traditions of its two older rivals, Britain's junior service made a virtue of a youthful spirit which happily accorded with its operational pilots, who were often barely out of school or university.

Given their youthfulness, it is not surprising that flyers fostered unit solidarity through schoolboy pranks and practical jokes, played against fellow squadron members, other squadrons, and even civilian authorities. These drew on the traditions of adolescent 'dares' and high spirits associated with the single-sex public schools and grammar schools from which many RAF pilots had only recently emerged. Those who had not been fortunate enough to attend these elite educational establishments would nevertheless have been familiar with the culture of jovial japes from schoolboy adventure stories which, through publications such as the *Magnet*, were devoured by adolescent boys across the social spectrum between the wars.[10] Flyers, on their excursions from base into local towns, would often steal street-signs, or toilet seats from public-house restrooms. On their return journey they would throw rolls of toilet tissue from their speeding cars at other motorists or police officers patrolling on bicycles. Boisterous games in the officers' mess served to both offer relief from the stresses of flying and create a group spirit. Pilots stationed in Malta tested themselves by 'walking the plank', which involved balancing on a short board resting on a rolling log.[11] At RAF Coltishall, Douglas Bader's squadron performed the 'muffin man', where a flyer had to turn, sing, and bend his knees, all the time balancing a pint glass full of beer on his head.[12] At Tangmere there was 'mess rugger' and 'ceiling walking'. The latter involved a group of officers helping to lift one of their number, the soles of his shoes dipped in black paint, in an upside-down posture, so that he could leave his footmarks to create the illusion of someone having walked on the ceiling of the mess.[13] Peter Townsend, who noted how these antics 'put a bursting strain on the tight seams of our mess kit', also revealed that practical jokes were even attempted while in the air. Townsend would fully lower the seat in his fighter plane so that his head was no longer visible in the cockpit. He was able to navigate the aircraft by looking through a gun-inspection panel in the side of the fuselage, so that he could sidle up beside an unsuspecting fellow pilot who, terrified at being pursued by an apparently pilotless aircraft, would panic and take flight.[14]

Camaraderie was also forged over a pint of beer.[15] Heavy drinking among flyers was ubiquitous in the RAF, and was indulged by senior commanders. Guy Gibson asserted that drinking excursions by groups of aircrew helped a flying unit to bond, in a way that would not be possible if a flyer had gone out on his own with a girl for a movie and a quiet drink. Indeed, there were so many references to 'parties' and 'drunks' in Gibson's posthumous memoir that Arthur Harris, head of Bomber Command, felt obliged in his introduction to the book to defend his aircrew from 'outbursts of unctuous rectitude' from readers, pointing out that drinking offered pilots a rare escape from the 'intolerable strain' of combat.[16] Gibson had insisted that, unlike during the First World War, flyers did not drink on the day of missions. However, when on leave, or at the end of a day's operations (for fighter pilots) or on an 'off night' (for bomber and night-fighter pilots), flyers participated in riotously drunken evenings, either in the mess or at nearby public houses. Of course, not all flyers were heavy drinkers. Bomber pilot 'Dim' Wooldridge famously preferred music and poetry to drinking, while fighter ace 'Paddy' Finucane only drank in moderation, lest alcohol impair his senses when in combat.[17] However, few RAF diaries or memoirs do not contain some reference to the consumption of liquor, and many are extremely candid about the regularity with which flyers took the opportunity to become inebriated. Denis Wissler, a fighter pilot, recorded in his diary in March 1940 that he had been to a dance the previously evening and 'got gloriously tight'. After seeing action in France, he returned to Britain in early June 1940 and dined at the Trocadero, where 'I really got completely plastered'. Indeed, Wissler remained drunk for much of the following day, despite his wing commander waking him up with an alka seltzer. In the following month he recorded attending a 'terrific party' in the mess at RAF Debden, where 'everyone got plastered'.[18]

Even memoirs of flyers published during the war itself made little attempt to disguise the RAF's drinking culture. Nineteen-forty-one saw the publication of *Fighter Pilot*, a personal record of the RAF's campaign in France between September 1939 and June 1940. The book was originally published anonymously, but the author was later revealed to be Paul Richey of 1 Squadron. Richey described in detail the drinking excursions to Paris undertaken by members of his squadron while stationed in France. The flyers would set out in the morning by rail, their journey lubricated by a bottle of whisky. Arriving in Paris just before lunch, they headed immediately for the bar at the Crillon Hotel, where they drank heartily until the bar closed at three o'clock. After a brief hiatus, during which they would wander around the shops, they would return to drinking when the bars reopened at five o'clock. Dinner rarely featured during the rest of the evening, the flyers' being content with a champagne supper in one of their rooms at the Crillon. Since Paris cafés closed at eleven, 'it would be early to bed, and late to rise the next morning—but not too late to get quite-nicely-thank-you again by lunchtime'.[19] Squadrons stationed in Britain adopted a local pub, where aircrew would drink up to eight pints an evening each. Pubs such as the Red Lion at Whittlesford, the White Horse at Andover, and the Red Lion at Trumpington were annexed by air-force personnel. At Kirton-in-Lindsay there was a telephone tie-line between the airfield and the nearest pub. At the George and Dragon at West Malling the landlady would call time, but then, 'with a nod and a wink', motion 'her RAF boys' into a back room. Once the general public had left, and the blinds were drawn so as to convince the police the pub had closed, the flyers would return to the bar and continue drinking into the small hours.[20]

Drinking was the most obvious shared leisure pursuit in the RAF, but it was not the only one. Flyers would go to the movies or the theatre, take fishing trips, put on amateur dramatic shows or revues, play cricket or football on spare green spaces on the airfield, or play pool in the mess. Given that flyers often spent a great deal of time waiting to go into action at the dispersal hut, card games were inevitably popular. Flight Lieutenant G. Shackleton recollected that poker was frequently played among Bomber Command crews, although too many men lost money, so that bridge then became more favoured.[21] At RAF Tilstock, Cyril Smith, a wireless operator/air-gunner, found his fellow crew members were 'inveterate gamblers' and 'poker mad'. On a non-operational flight in a Stirling bomber, Smith was horrified when, having taken off and set course, the whole crew—including the pilot, who had placed the aircraft on auto-pilot—disappeared aft into the rest bay to play cards.[22] Male bonding was also fostered through shared rituals, such as dropping empty beer bottles from aircraft during air raids, or urinating communally on a bomber's tail wheel before take off and immediately after landing.

Aircrew also connected through their shared knowledge of the RAF's highly particular verbal idiom. Outsiders were both fascinated and baffled by the flyer's esoteric slang. A 'kite' was revealed to be an aircraft, a 'sparks' a radio operator, a 'popsie' a young woman, a 'brolly' was a parachute, the 'deck' the ground, the 'drink' the sea, a 'tit' the firing button in a fighter plane, a 'grease monkey' a mechanic, a 'piece of cake' a task executed with relative ease. To 'flap' was to get excited, to 'prang' was to crash an aircraft, to 'go for a Burton' was to be killed, and to 'walk out' was to parachute out of a stricken aircraft. When Athol Forbes and Hubert Allen collected the testimony of ten Spitfire pilots who had fought in the Battle of Britain for a book published in 1942, they felt it necessary to append a glossary to help the novice reader comprehend the RAF slang encountered throughout the volume.[23] In fact, the public's fascination with the RAF ensured that many of these terms not merely became familiar (so much so that in movies such as *A Matter of Life of Death* in 1946, or *Angels One Five* in 1952, the audience's acquaintance with the RAF's peculiar patois was simply presupposed), but even entered the vernacular of the civilian population.[24] Some linguists laboured to establish the lineage of air-force argot. An exhaustingly detailed survey of 'slanguage' by Eric Partridge in the RAF's own magazine concluded that several air-force terms derived from the army or navy, but that the origins of many more were difficult to establish with any certainty. To generalize, RAF slang drew equally from the public schools, popular culture (especially American movies and song lyrics), and the service's own technical jargon. A shared language, particularly one which, in Partridge's opinion, exhibited one of the 'charming characteristics of youth . . . the tendency to be original—at times, desperately original', inevitably bolstered a shared identity and the fellowship of those who flew.[25]

This is not to say that male bonding developed and operated in a standard format across the service. Peter Townsend accounted for comradeship among fighter pilots, conversely, in terms of their essential individualism in combat. Discussing 85 Squadron, with whom he served during the Battle of Britain, he argued that while 'we fought wing-tip to wing-tip, each one of us had to fly and fight, and, if need be, die, alone. It was this sense of isolation and solitude in the air that united us so closely on the ground.'[26] For bomber crews, by contrast, it was the interdependence of the crew in the air which was the critical factor. Richard Lumford had been the son of an outdoorsman, a hunter and yachtsman with an obsession about virility and manliness, while his mother went insane and eventually committed suicide. At school Lumford was bullied and marginalized, which left a legacy in his adult life of psychosomatic illnesses and a fear of close relationships, even of the platonic kind. Self-acknowledgment of his homosexuality and an association with the aesthetes while studying at Oxford did nothing to mitigate his low self-esteem. However, war, and the opportunity to become one of the aircrew on a Hampden bomber, transformed him. On missions he was able to submerge his individualism in the 'universal destiny' of the group:

I had always been shy of individual attachments since they were fickle, perishable, and often subject to loss and death. But here it was the spirit of the group—a spirit, individual, deep, born of our love of flight, out of the strange, restless, uncertain days and out of experiences in the air . . . it was this spirit which one learnt to love, and to me at least it seemed more durable than any individual mortal membership.

One suspects that Lumford's fellow crew members might have found such hyperbole embarrassing, and it is unlikely that they would have shared his belief that his crew 'would all die peacefully and gaily if we could feel ourselves part of this Whole'.[27] However, while overdrawn, Lumford's belief in the comradeship of the bomber crew was not mere fancy. Miles Tripp, a much more prosaically minded bomber pilot turned author, compared the bonds between the crew of an individual bomber aircraft to the ties of marriage. On his first day at an operational training unit, the men were sent to a large hanger and told it was up to them to form crews among themselves: 'This arbitrary collision of strangers was basically a marriage market and yet the choice of a good flying partner was far more important than a good wife. You couldn't divorce your crew, and you could die if one of them wasn't up to his job at a critical moment.'[28] Noble Frankland, a navigator and later co-author of the official history of the British strategic air offensive, also likened 'crewing up' to the binding ties of matrimony: 'We were left for a fortnight in which to make a love match, after which marriages were arranged for those who had not done so. My crew was the product of the voluntary process.'[29] For many in Bomber Command, their crew became a self-contained universe, and, as one recent account has characterized it, 'the break-up of a happy crew felt as traumatic as the sundering of a happy family'.[30]

An obvious source of commonality among flyers was their youthfulness. Contemporary portraits and photographs show fresh-faced young men, their incongruously boyish demeanours only partially concealed in some cases by the pencil-thin moustache popular in the RAF. The novelist William Somerset Maugham, who met several flyers while working at the Ministry of Information, observed that 'some of them showed cheeks so smooth that you felt a safety razor was only recently a necessary part of their equipment'.[31] Many RAF aircrew were in command of squadrons before they reached 24 years of age. Those who joined up before the outbreak of war, such as Richard Hillary or Guy Gibson, wrote memoirs in the middle years of the conflict in which they presented themselves as hardened veterans of the air war. However, when Hillary was killed in 1942 he was still only 23, while Gibson, who had completed over 170 regular operations in addition to the famous dams' raid which he commanded, was 26 at the time of his death in 1944. One historian has contended that: 'If the representative Englishman of the First World War was Sub-Lieutenant Rupert Brooke, who was twenty eight and acted as though he were eighteen, the representative Englishman of the Second World War was Colonel Kenneth Widmerpool, who was thirty five and acted as though he was fifty.'[32] This assertion that the Great War poet and the decidedly unheroic character from Anthony Powell's *Dance to the Music of Time* novels typify the generations of 1914–18 and 1939–45 respectively, is not without merit. RAF flyers in the Second World War generally repudiated the naive sentimentalism and overblown patriotism of the type exemplified by Brooke. However, the flyer was not averse to espousing his own varieties of youthful enthusiasm and unaffected idealism, especially in the early parts of his service career.

John Carpenter wrote to his parents throughout his training as a fighter pilot and his time flying Spitfires during the Battle of Britain. His letters are boyish and exuberant, illustrated by drawings and cartoons, and displaying a carefree enthusiasm for all aspects of service life. The deaths of colleagues are noted, but not dwelt on. Instead, Carpenter writes of his pleasure in team sports at the base (he had put his name down for cricket, rugger, tennis, and shooting), flying, and having the opportunity to 'have a go' at the enemy. His relative callowness is revealed in his comments on women and sexuality, being both titillated and embarrassed when kissed by a WAAF at a Christmas party. If Carpenter sometimes sounds like a naive schoolboy this is hardly surprising, since he had entered the RAF straight from school in 1938 (he was, as he proudly reminded his parents, an 'Old Cliftonian'), when he was still only 19.[33] A similar youthful high-spiritedness is to be found in the poignant manuscript diary and scrapbook kept throughout 1944 by John Riley Byrne, a radio operator/air-gunner on Wellingtons and Lancasters. Byrne was not yet 20, still possessed of a gamin captivation with the world of aviation. He hero-worshipped a Canadian bomber captain called Paige ('God only knows how much I wanted to fly with you', he confesses to his diary), and indulged in overwrought adolescent histrionics when faced with the possibility that he might not be selected for aircrew ('If I cannot fly, then death is the only way for me'). He pasted into his scrapbook a photograph of the actor Gordon Jackson, in his role as Fred, the young sergeant air-gunner in the movie *Millions Like Us*, and press cuttings relating to famed aviatrix Amy Johnson, accompanied with gushing marginal inscriptions such as: 'My tribute to a wonderful aviator, Miss Amy Johnson, CBE.' On another page he had copied out, in his own hand, quotations about duty from First World War ace Mick Mannock and about courage by American aviatrix Amelia Earhart. He also glued in his RAF 'Rhythm Club' membership card and other inspirational quotations from Rudyard Kipling. However, in the autumn of 1944 Byrne's scrapbook takes on a more morbid tone. A list of names of Great War aviators—Mannock, Ball, Richthofen, Boelcke, McCudden—is followed by the exclamation: 'They all die.' Byrne's journal entries become preoccupied with the death in action of his comrades on raids over Germany. In December 1944 he entered a list of nineteen aircrew he had known well who had been killed or listed as missing in the previous year. Next to the number 19, Byrne wrote: 'Sgt. Clarke, V.J. W/op My best friend.' It was Byrne's last entry. Two months later he himself was killed on operational duty over Dresden.[34]

The flyer obviously experienced his youth in the most peculiar and testing of circumstances. The possibility that, like John Byrne, his young life could be snuffed out before it even properly began was ever present. If he managed to survive, his youthful freshness and naive idealism were unlikely to have been equally resilient. Lovat Dickson, in his preface to the memoirs of fighter pilot Barry Sutton published in 1942, argued that two years of war had transformed the carefree flyboys of 1939 into 'relentless men', with a steely, implacable determination to destroy the enemy. He reassured his readers that they still possessed 'the hearts and feelings of the boys they still are', but claimed that they had nevertheless become 'the avengers for the wrongs done to mankind'.[35] Tony Bartley concurred with the belief that war had turned schoolboys into men before their time, but he felt that transition was about a lessening, rather than a strengthening, of enthusiasm for fighting and killing. Discussing his fellow fighter pilots during the Battle of Britain, he asserted: 'We were fit and fearless, in the beginning. By the end, we were old and tired, and knew what fear was.'

However, if this was a singular, not to say bizarre, progression into manhood (one in which, as Bartley starkly pointed out, the flyer 'had taken a life before [he] had taken a woman'), it was an evolution shared by the young aircrew of the Royal Air Force.[36] The flyer belonged to a distinct fellowship of youth, albeit one in which youth had been violently deformed by experience.

Such strong generational identification was reinforced by a widespread belief among flyers that they were having to lay down their young lives because of the failings of their elders, who had failed to recognize the danger posed by Hitler and Mussolini in the 1930s. Many flyers expressed a sense of alienation from, and even open hostility towards, their parents' generation. Flying Officer Charles Crichton, stationed in the Middle East, in a letter to his mother, contrasted the talent of his wing commander, a 23-year-old New Zealander who commanded a squadron containing men from half-a-dozen nations, with the failed older generation of 'shining diplomats, ministers, party men and the like'.[37] Fighter pilot Jim Bailey discovered that many ground-based administrative officers were illicitly selling RAF equipment and stores. For Bailey, the moral of the story was clear: 'while younger men were daily risking their necks, a very few of the older ones were making money, sometimes on quite a scale. This gave rise to the notion that war encouraged the exploitation of the young by the old, a notion that was not altogether foolish.'[38] Like one of the characters in Helen Zenna Smith's Great War novel *Not So Quiet*, many flyers had come to the conclusion that 'war was made by age and fought by youth'.[39] In *Enemy Coast Ahead*, Guy Gibson asserted that the cream of the previous generation had died in the fields of Flanders, and that the country had fallen into the hands of mediocrities who, because of their failings, had now obliged another generation of young men to make the ultimate sacrifice. He argued that the only way to prevent the scenario repeating itself was 'to let the young men who have done the fighting have a say in the affairs of State'.[40] This view, that they were all young men being sent to their deaths by an antediluvian social and political establishment, was widely shared, and undoubtedly played its part in reinforcing a common identity among flyers.

What is conspicuous about male bonding in the RAF is that relationships between flyers were simultaneously intense and perfunctory. Male intimacy was based on a shared experience of combat, not on extensive interests in each other's backgrounds or prospects. After writing a condolence letter to the widow of a pilot killed in the dams raid, Guy Gibson reflected that he had referred to the deceased as a 'great personal friend' when he had in fact only known him for six weeks.[41] Indeed, the cinematic adaptation of the Dambusters story, released in 1955, re-created the strange confection of attachment and detachment which characterized a squadron specially formed for one single, specialized mission very effectively. The film portrays the flyers of 617 Squadron welding together in terms of their shared professional responsibilities, not their personal relationships. The camera rarely provides close-ups of any of the pilots, with the exception of Gibson (played by Richard Todd), and the aircrew are usually seen in collective settings, such as dining halls and briefing rooms.[42] Serious affective bonds between men were obscured by a language of understatement or displayed obliquely through teasing humour or play. To borrow a distinction set out in a study of male bonding among Cambridge students in the seventeenth century, what we have here might be better construed as 'comradeship' rather than 'friendship', the latter being more intimate, less ephemeral, and less transient.[43] Ultimately, the fact that friendships were liable to be truncated by death made men unwilling to commit themselves to deep emotional involvement with their fellow flyers.

FLYERS APART: INTERNAL DEMARCATIONS AND THE FRAGILITY OF COMRADESHIP

Official propaganda during the Second World War was inevitably attracted to the potential of the bomber crew as a metaphor for the British war effort. Here, within the body of a single aircraft high over enemy territory, were encapsulated the values of cooperation between men of very different backgrounds and temperaments, without which victory would be impossible. This was certainly the way in which the bomber crew of Powell and Pressburger's wartime propaganda fable *One of Our Aircraft is Missing* were portrayed.[44] In fact, the solidarity and *esprit de corps* forged among the crew of an individual aircraft could be highly conditional, and disturbingly fragile. Significantly, by the 1950s, when the sense of common purpose and national unity fostered by both popular sentiment and state propaganda during the war years had grown increasingly threadbare, bomber-crew narratives became more preoccupied with just how brittle wartime comradeship could be. In 1952 Miles Tripp, who had served in Bomber Command aircrew during the war, produced a novel with the rather sappy title of *Faith is a Windsock*. Drawing on Tripp's own experiences, it told the story of the crew of a Lancaster bomber, A-Able, operating from an airfield in East Anglia during the winter of 1944–5. As their tour of duty drags on, the bonding of the crew in the air, where 'they were united more than blood brothers', is increasingly absent on the ground. Craig, the navigator, feels obliged to join the crew on an occasional outing, but 'his laughter was false' and he yearns for the serenity of home life with his wife and son. Flute, the engineer, prefers to stay in his room, saving up his money so that he can train as a veterinary surgeon after the war. McCoy (an air-gunner) and Hamish (the bomb-aimer) absented themselves from crew parties to pursue women. When the crew of A-Able are required to undertake an additional ten missions at the end of their tour, relations between the men became increasingly fraught. Hamish starts to get testy with Arthur, the wireless operator, and was 'irrationally antipathetic' towards Craig, jealous of the navigator's assurance and happy family life. The crew spend more and more time off-base, finding that, 'so long as they saw little of each other during off-duty hours they could tolerate one another's presence in the air. It was only when they spent any length of time together on the ground that tempers quickly went raw.'[45] Another fictionalized account of bomber-crew relationships published at this time, John Watson's *Johnny Kinsman*, described a similar process of estrangement. Kinsman, a Halifax pilot, becomes aware that his crew were no longer socializing with each other on the ground: 'In the air they were component parts of a machine, welded together, dependent on each other. Perhaps for that reason they had scattered on the ground.'[46]

Even in the air, one should not exaggerate the commonality of an aircrew's experience. If the pilot happened to also be a squadron leader or wing commander, he was inevitably distracted from his obligations towards his crew by the responsibility he had for the rest of the operation that night. Guy Gibson's memoir reinforces the notion of the essential loneliness of the leader, a motif which is foregrounded in the 1955 film reconstruction of the dams raid. In *The Dam Busters* Gibson is also presented as apart from other men, studying maps while they play games in the adjacent mess, a model of self-sufficiency, whose only emotional relationship is with his pet labrador.[47] Semi-detached from the rest of the crew in a more literal sense was the tail-gunner, isolated at the rear of the long fuselage of a heavy bomber such as a Lancaster, Halifax, or Stirling. In *Faith is a Windsock*, Miles Tripp reflected on the 'peculiar sense of isolation' of the tail-gunner. Facing backward, he sat in a bowl of glass and looked out onto sky and earth, without the reassuring sight of the aircraft's wings or engines. The sound of the aircraft's motors was remote, and the intercom provided the only contact with life. Even then, 'the voices of the crew seem distant and it is hard to visualize them'.[48] The tail turret was the coldest position in the plane, and the gunner was obliged to wear more layers of clothing than other aircrew. R. C. Rivaz, rear-gunner on Whitleys and then Lancasters, wore vest, pants, shirt, three pullovers, roll-top sweater, and four pairs of socks, all in addition to the regular tunic, flying clothing, and scarf.[49] The problem was, as J. M. Catford, a tail-gunner on the Lancaster W-Willie, pointed out in his unpublished memoir, that wearing so many layers of clothing (or, later in the war, a heated suit) made the already cramped space of the gun turret even less tolerable.[50] Rear-gunners, in their remote station, often felt quite lonely during missions. In a short story by C. H. Ward-Jackson, Tubby, the slightly overweight tail-gunner on a Halifax, is always relieved to be spoken to by his captain over the intercom, a welcome reminder that he is not completely alone.[51] A particular anxiety for tail-gunners was that, if the aircraft was hit and the intercom failed, he might not hear his pilot's orders to bale out. Rivaz recalled that, flying through heavy flak over Dortmund, he began to feel 'cut off from the others', and wondered what might be happening at the other end of the aeroplane. Fearing that the rest of the crew might have abandoned the aircraft and 'forgotten all about me', Rivaz was greatly reassured to hear his captain's voice over the intercom declare 'bombs gone'.[52] WAAF officer Edith Heap recorded a story which, while certainly apocryphal, testifies to the distinctiveness of the tail-gunner's experience. While serving with

405 Squadron, Heap heard that a crippled bomber had arrived back at base and stopped at the end of the runway. To the astonishment of the ground crews who rushed over to the stricken aircraft, the plane was completely empty, with the exception of the tail-gunner, who fainted 'when he was told that he was the only one on board, everyone else having baled out sometime before'.[53]

Sometimes differences between flyers correlated to institutional demarcations within the RAF. For a start, individual squadrons possessed, or were at least reputed to possess, distinctive cultures. Tony Bartley contrasted 'Sailor' Malan's 74 Squadron with his own 92 Squadron. The men of 74 did not indulge themselves in 'large cars, night clubs or fancy dress', and Malan deliberately kept his squadron as distant from the 'bunch of playboys' in 92 as possible.[54] John Carpenter had been a member of 263 Squadron, stationed at RAF Digby, when he was transferred to 222 Squadron at RAF Kirton-in-Lindsay, on the eve of the Battle of Britain. Carpenter initially found it very peculiar that the fighter boys of 222 did not go and party like their equivalents in 263. They were, he disappointingly concluded, a 'very sober crowd'.[55] Noel Monks, observing the performance of Fighter Command in the Battle of France in his capacity as a war correspondent, noted that 1 Squadron fought in the air as a team, whereas 73 Squadron was more indulgent of individual initiative in combat.[56] These differences between squadrons should not be exaggerated. A change of commander could quickly transform the character of a squadron. It has already been shown how 92 Squadron's playboy reputation failed to survive the arrival of Johnny Kent, while 242 Squadron was transformed from an ill-disciplined and dispirited rabble into a highly effective fighting unit by the mercurial personality of Douglas Bader.[57] Moreover, fatalities ensured that squadrons had a rapid turnover of personnel, and redeployment between squadrons was a regular occurrence, factors which jeopardized the establishment of indelible identification with a particular squadron.

Wartime expansion of the RAF also compromised the service's pre-war tripartite division into the regular service, the volunteer reserve (RAFVR), and the auxiliary service. These three sectors retained distinctive cultures in the 1930s, often, although not exclusively, based on social differences. The officers of the regular RAF were graduates of Cranwell, the RAF auxiliary public schoolboys and university undergraduates who learnt to fly as a gentlemen's hobby, and the RAFVR, a territorial force composed of weekend flyers who worked as shopkeepers, clerks, and salesmen during the week. Those who had enlisted in the regular RAF in the early 1930s were often hostile to those who joined in the service's dramatic expansion in the last years of peace and during the war. Peter Townsend confessed that on returning to RAF Tangmere in 1937, after serving for a time in Singapore, he resented the new generation of pilots who had answered the RAF's urgent appeal in the face of rising international tension. Tangmere was now 'peopled by strange faces, different people with a different style'.[58] Townsend's indignation that the RAF was no longer an exclusive flying club eventually subsided, and he came to embrace the once parvenu pilots as trusted comrades. However, some flyers remained aware of the legacy of differences between the old and the new RAF. Jim Bailey, one of the 'wandering scholars' who abandoned their university studies to join the service in 1939, was ribbed by members of the peacetime air force about the fact that he still did not have to shave every morning. Bailey replied that people grew most hair on the parts of their body that they used the most, a retort which 'kept the half-bald gentlemen with their handlebar moustaches quieter'.[59] There were not only differences between pre-war flyers and wartime recruits, but also distinctions between those who entered the service at the start of the war and those who came later. Those who survived from the first cohort of flyers often felt that younger pilots, who had not served in the Battle of Britain, 'can never know', in Hector Bolitho's words, 'the full passion of belief that holds these survivors of the first battles so close together . . . these who are the few living, in the field of the numerous dead'.[60] William Simpson was a Fairy Battle pilot, shot down over France in May 1940, during which he suffered serious burns to his hands and face. Returning to the service in 1942, after two years of surgery, he was mystified by the most recent recruits to the service, 'a new generation with a new language, a slang that I hardly understood'.[61]

The most obvious institutional demarcation within the RAF was, of course, that which existed between the three commands—Fighter, Bomber, and Coastal. There were inevitably differences between fighter pilots, who usually flew single-seater aircraft, and bomber aircrew, who flew as a team. The artist Cuthbert Orde, who was commissioned to paint portraits of both bomber and fighter pilots, asserted that differences between the two RAF commands should not be exaggerated. While the bomber pilot was trained for 'careful, methodical, and steady flying' and the fighter pilot excelled at 'quick sprinting around the sky', it did not follow that 'the first is a ploughboy and the second a cavalier'.[62] By contrast, Cecil Beaton, assigned to photograph all three commands, contrasted fighter and bomber pilots, even when he was at pains to emphasize that they made an equally significant contribution to the war effort. While bomber crew seemed 'to possess a reserve born of their great responsibility to their crew', fighter pilots were 'the gay, more reckless ones, more temperamental, perhaps a bit selfish'. Whereas fighter pilots were hunters, bomber aircrew, caught in the enemy's searchlights, were the hunted, requiring them to exhibit characteristics 'that differ widely from those required in the other Commands', namely cold-blooded courage and 'calculated calm'.[63] Hector Bolitho, an intelligence officer and editor of the *RAF Journal*, insisted that the members of a bomber crew were placid and silent: 'more like sailors than their fighter brothers.' Such distinctions became a cliché of contemporary fictional representations of the air force. Ken, the fighter-pilot hero of Keith Ayling's 1941 novel *RAF*, was convinced that there were distinct differences between the commands, of both temperament (the bomber pilot was more responsible, since he had his crew members to consider) and physique ('the average bombing pilot is stockier than we are, but that may be because these fellows are fed specially so they can endure the cold').[64] Lord David Cecil saw the fighter pilot as being 'like a greyhound', whereas the bomber was more 'stolid and enduring'.[65] Such physical distinctions were essentially stereotypes. While it was true that bomber crews received extra rations, notably more sugar and butter, to help them withstand the low temperatures encountered on night missions, the slight, almost ascetic, frame of bomber pilot Leonard Cheshire and the stocky rugby-player build of fighter ace Douglas Bader reveal that both commands encompassed a variety of physical, and indeed temperamental, types.

In fact, fighter boys and bomber boys were much more likely to be distinguished by their dress than by their bodies. Members of Fighter Command habitually left the top button of their uniform tunic undone, in what came to be known as 'fighter boy style'. Denis Wissler, on graduating from the Oxfords and Harvards, in which he had received his training, to his first operational flight in a Hurricane in March 1940, recorded proudly in his diary that 'I can now wear the top button of my tunic undone, as is done by all people who fly fighters'.[66] Indeed, this convention became part of the dominant wartime iconography of Fighter Command, featuring in, for example, Eric Kennington's famous 1943 portrait of Richard Hillary. Guy Gibson, a bomber pilot posted to a fighter station, felt that, in contrast to the studied informality of the fighter-boy dress code, he felt like 'Little Lord Fauntleroy'. Gibson himself, using the justification of having served in both Fighter and Bomber Commands, actually adopted 'fighter boy style' in the portrait photographs prepared for propaganda purposes after the dams' raid in 1943. However, this did not imply that he believed in concord between the two branches of the air force. Indeed, Gibson's memoirs not merely observed difference, but recorded rivalry and resentment, between the two types of flyer. Bomber pilots were aggrieved that the public seemed to hero-worship the 'scarf-flapping glamour boys' of Fighter Command, while dismissing bomber crew as mere 'bus drivers'. Off-duty, 'the fighters seemed to have all the fun, walking off with the women and drinking the beer, mainly because their stations were always close to a town, while a bomber base is miles from anywhere'.[67] Bomber pilots' jealousy of the glamour attached to Fighter Command in the public imagination was often compounded by the fact that many of those who eventually became the crew of Wellingtons and Lancasters had initially aspired themselves to fly single-seater fighters. Cecil Beaton noted that it was hard to persuade Initial Training Wing cadets that they were temperamentally better suited to bombers than fighters. 'For some of them', he wrote 'the glamour of a Spitfire and the unbuttoned tunic of the fighter pilot have an allure which blinds their judgment.'[68] In one of H. E. Bates's short stories, Lawson reluctantly becomes the captain of a Stirling bomber, having 'been through all the usual Spitfire complex; all roaring glory and victory rolls'.[69] While most of the tension between fighters and bombers was usually tempered into good-natured teasing, it did not lack the capacity to spill over into fractious violence, as during the infamous intra-service 'battle of the snake-pit'.[70]

FLYERS APART: CLASS, NATION, AND RACE

Male bonding among flyers was not merely compromised by distinctions arising from the RAF's own institutional culture. It was also jeopardized by differences of class, race, and nation which characterized the wider society from which its recruits were drawn. For all its apparent informality, the RAF inevitably reflected a Britain which, in the 1940s, remained stiflingly hierarchical and class-bound. There was a time when historians were convinced that, under the pressures of total war, Britain became a much more egalitarian society between 1939 and 1945. The common sacrifices of the Blitz and the wartime rhetoric of 'fair shares' (most clearly encapsulated in the rationing of foodstuffs and other basic necessities) appeared to suggest increased social solidarity. The contribution of the working classes to the war effort was celebrated in official propaganda and granted its ultimate reward in the promises of a post-war welfare state which would banish the spectres of unemployment, hunger, and ill-health which had haunted the inter-war years. However, in the last two decades historians have been much more sceptical about the extent of social change during the 'people's war'.[71] While there was undoubtedly a new populist standard at large during the war, and official propaganda celebrated what has been neatly termed an 'egalitarian morality', there is little evidence that the gap in incomes and capital ownership narrowed dramatically in these years. Rationing ensured there was a levelling of consumption, but this did not necessarily imply a levelling of incomes. It is true that skilled workers in critically important war industries (for example, aircraft production) appeared to be taking home more in their pay packets than middle-class clerks and even some professionals. However, these higher wages were usually the consequence of overtime or piece work, and wage-earners still lacked the security of employment which had traditionally allowed the middle-class salariat to convert income into capital (and, more specifically, home-ownership). Class conflict continued to erupt at periodic intervals during the war, ignited by issues such as the unequal provision of bomb shelters between the West and East Ends of London during the Blitz, demands for the immediate opening of a second front in Europe to relieve the Soviet war effort in 1942–3, and the escalating crisis in coal production in 1944.[72] While the Labour Party's participation in Churchill's coalition government, and, in particular, the presence of the robustly plebeian Ernest Bevin at the Ministry of Labour, might have suggested official recognition of the working classes' role in the defeat of Hitler, middle-class claims to the social leadership of Britain remained resilient during the Second World War.[73] Even Labour's contribution to the personnel of government featured upper-middle-class professionals such as Clement Attlee, Hugh Dalton, and

Stafford Cripps. If bourgeois predominance in wartime government faced any challenge, it came less from proletarian populists such as Bevin and more from the aristocratic flamboyance and patrician grandeur of Winston Churchill.[74]

So, how did the flyers of the Royal Air Force relate to both the rhetoric and the reality of the 'people's war'? Most discussions of the extent to which the Second World War promoted social change in Britain have focused on the civilian populations of the home front. In contrast, representations and configurations of class in the armed services have received much less attention. The standard social history of the British army in wartime argues that military authorities did demonstrate considerable sensitivity to the fact that Britain's war effort was conducted by an army largely comprised of civilian conscripts, and that there was some attempt to promote the idea of the modern 'citizen soldier', even if the desire of many on the political left to create a modern successor to Oliver Cromwell's 'new model army' was always going to be a pipe-dream.[75] A recent study of British military medicine during the Second World War concurs with this appraisal, revealing that a new generation of military commanders (notably Montgomery in North Africa and Slim in Burma) attached great importance to medical provisions for their troops, thereby mirroring contemporary civilian conceptions of social citizenship, in which the citizen received a 'social wage'—health care, education, guaranteed employment—in return for service to the state.[76] However, such concerns for the individual soldier, while they suggest a modernized vision of paternalism in the British army, do not necessarily have to imply any widespread embrace of meritocracy or social mobility. Officer-selection remained largely confined to the social elites, and, at its most senior levels, the British army was, ironically, more patrician in 1939–45 than it had been in 1914–18.[77] Unfortunately, we still lack an authoritative social history of the wartime RAF. Given that, as we have seen, the air force had often self-consciously sought to distinguish itself from the hidebound traditions of the 'brown jobs', it might be expected that class differences might be less significant among flyers than among soldiers. In fact, as with the civilian population, while official rhetoric downplayed social distinctions within the RAF, in reality class prejudice remained an unsettling presence amid the apparently easygoing camaraderie of the air base.

Wartime propaganda inevitably sought to present the RAF as classless. Cecil Beaton's celebration of the young men who flew identified 'a complete lack of snobbery in the RAF'.[78] Ken, the flyer hero of Keith Ayling's Battle of Britain novel, on meeting his fellow trainee pilots for the first time, observed: 'All England was represented, I calculated, and so it should be.'[79] Cinematic representations of the flyer reflected a broader shift from the celebration of the officer class in films made in 1939 and 1940 to narratives which emphasized mutual respect and cooperation between classes, and which had become the dominant framing of the war on screen by 1943. The portrayal of RAF flyers in *The Lion Has Wings*, made in the opening month of the war, made no concessions to working-class audiences or sensibilities in its focus on well-spoken upper-class young men who gave the impression that they would probably have been more at home drinking Pimms at an inter-war suburban tennis club than piloting the advanced war-planes which featured in the movie.[80] By 1945, in *Journey Together*, a film made to publicize the work of Air Training Command, the RAF was deployed to symbolize wartime egalitarianism and both the necessity, and the possibility, of overcoming class hostility. It accomplished this through the story of two aircrew cadets—Aynsworth, a former public-schoolboy (played by Jack Watling), and Wilton (Richard Attenborough), a RAF mechanic given the opportunity to fly—who transcend social differences to become friends. When Wilton, unlike Aynsworth, fails to become a pilot, he is initially disgruntled. However, serving as a navigator in a bomber piloted by Aynsworth, Wilton succeeds in rescuing the aircraft from a potentially fatal crash and comes to appreciate that all the crew contribute equally to the success of a mission. Directed by the left-leaning filmmaker John Boulting, *Journey Together* insists that competence, not rank, is what matters in the wartime air force.[81] Significantly, later that year saw the release of *The Way to the Stars*, in many senses the first post-war British war film. Here, however, working-class characters are of only marginal importance, the film focusing on the emotional lives of RAF officers. In the 1950s war films featuring the RAF, such as *Angels One Five* and *The Dam Busters*, were even more exclusively focused on middle-class officers, the script for the latter film being provided by R. C. Sherriff, who had already panegyrized an earlier generation of public-school officers in his 1930 stage play *Journey's End*.[82] By contrast, during the war itself, the RAF's war effort was usually cast by the mass media in populist and meritocratic terms.

Indeed, the wartime expansion of the RAF ensured that the social composition of the service was much broader in 1945 than it had been in 1939. As was noted in the previous chapter, the RAF had already launched several schemes to extend its recruitment as Britain rearmed after 1935. True, necessity, rather than the imperatives of social justice, was certainly the mother of invention here. Ironically, in the light of its glamorous wartime reputation, in the early 1930s the RAF had difficulty attracting men of the 'right' social class (in other words, ex-public-schoolboys and graduates of the ancient universities) to apply to Cranwell. RAF commissions lacked the prestige of a commission in an established army regiment. It was obliged to look instead to the products of grammar, council, and even elementary, schools. The Direct Entry Airmen Scheme (DEA) sought recruits among the service's own personnel, while the Service Airman Pilot Scheme (SAP) looked to technicians employed outside the RAF. While the DEA was abandoned in 1937, SAPs continued to be a feature of the RAF. When the RAFVR was created in 1936, it encapsulated a deliberately meritocratic ethos. However, the greatest opportunities for advancement from the less privileged sections of society came during the war itself. Pilots who were killed, captured, or invalided out of the service had to be replaced, and social fastidiousness soon gave way to pragmatism in the selection of aircrew. Contrary to popular myth, therefore, the Battle of Britain was not won on the playing fields of Uppingham but in the draughtsmen's workrooms of Coventry.[83] At the height of the Battle of Britain, in August 1940, the Air Ministry debated the educational qualifications of aircrew and expressed the view that, in view of the seriousness of the situation, initial selection boards should base their assessment entirely on 'the desire of the candidates to fly and fight in the air, a reasonable standard of intelligence and the necessary standard of alertness and character'.[84] While this guideline still allowed considerable scope for the exercise of class prejudice, it is significant that the directive explicitly suggested that failure to have taken the school certificate or having left school before the age of 16 should not automatically disqualify a candidate. Fighter Command in 1940 was certainly an elite force, but it was a more socially disparate military elite than any which had previously existed in Britain.

It was to be in Bomber Command that the broadening of recruitment was to be most effectively realized. After 1941 the twin-engined Hampdens and Blenheims, with their crews of four and three respectively, gave way to the four-engined Halifaxes and Stirlings with their crews of seven. The new heavy bombers not merely necessitated more aircrew, but possessed more complex technology, requiring properly trained navigators, wireless operators, and bomb aimers. An RAF fitter who had been turned down for aircrew in the 1930s by a selection board he resentfully described as 'toffee-nosed', benefited from the creation of a new category of flight crew in the new heavy bombers—the flight engineer—a position whose specialized responsibilities forced the RAF to recruit more flyers with technical, rather than purely academic, qualifications.[85] Indeed, in 1941 the Air Ministry received a concerned memorandum from an anonymous public-school master, familiar with 'the future careers of boys at Wellington', anxious that the mathematics qualification required of aircrew might prejudice the chance of a product of the elite private schools securing a place as an operational flyer. Unable to disguise the class bias which informed his academic judgments, he argued that a maths requirement might make sense for a navigator in a bomber, but not for a fighter pilot, and he concluded his harangue with the demand that 'this "banning" of the humanities from our "corps d'elite" in favour of technicians should be summarily stopped'.[86] Fortunately for the British war effort, on this occasion the old school tie was not allowed to prevail over the technological imperatives of modern warfare and the social prerequisites of a people's war.

Elsewhere, however, a residue of class prejudice remained. When on operations, the special conditions which applied to the flying of bombers ensured social mixing. The lowest rank accorded to a bomber-crew member was that of sergeant, an expedient adopted so that captured flyers received the best possible treatment if they became prisoners-of-war. The specialized and interconnected nature of the roles taken by members of a bomber crew disrupted established lines of command. The pilot of the plane was always the captain, even if he was only a flight sergeant. On missions, an informal tone predominated, reflected in the preference for the term 'skipper'—as opposed to 'sir'—to refer to the pilot. Tail-gunner R. C. Rivaz explained to his wartime audience, 'rank in the air, in a sense, does not count'.[87] However, on the ground things were often quite different. While it was possible for a grocer's son to become a sergeant pilot, who would be in charge of a whole flight crew in a bombing mission over Germany, he might find himself excluded from the officer's mess on his return to base. For, despite pressure from the Canadian government in 1942, the RAF retained the distinction which operated in the two senior services between officers and NCOs. Many former RAF personnel testified to a belief that class distinctions were still far too important in pilot selection. Fred Welding, an estate agent in London before the war, joined the RAF and was sent to aircrew training in the summer of 1940. His letters to his mother from this period reveal his disgust with the poor quality of instruction, and his belief that upper-middle-class recruits were unfairly advantaged. Welding himself failed to be selected for aircrew, and joined the air sea rescue service. He was appalled by the fact that among those who were unsuccessful was a man with thirty hours civilian solo flying.[88]

Even those fortunate enough to become aircrew complained about how class bias impeded their service career. G. Shackleton was initially made a sergeant pilot, because the selection committee 'obviously decided that this ex-Grammar School boy with a London accent would be unlikely to merge into an officer's mess'. In 1941 his Blenheim aircraft took part in a raid on Vaagso in Norway, which required precision bombing from 300 feet. The raid was led by a wing commander and his squadron navigation officer, who were awarded 'a well deserved DSO' and a bar to their DFC respectively: 'unsurprisingly the rest of us received nothing.' A year later Shackleton finally secured his commission, but when his group captain recommended him for a DFC, it was turned down on the basis that the newly commissioned officer did not have sufficient experience for leadership. This assertion was clearly contradicted by the fact that Shackleton had already led formations which included a wing commander and squadron leader. Despite serving in the squadron for twice the usual length of tour duty, he still had no 'gongs' to his credit.[89]

Petty snobbery was not uncommon in the service. George Hull, from Stepney in East London, had been hoping to become a pharmacist when the war intervened, upon which he became a navigator in a Lancaster bomber. In a letter of February 1944 to his friend Joan Kirby, he described how many flyers had been enraged by 'nasty remarks' from a senior RAF officer about 'errand boys and chimney sweeps spoiling aircrew'. The aircrew of B-Baker had protested by chalking 'Errand Boys Make Berlin' on the side of the aircraft before take-off.[90] Some of the worst exhibitions of social high-handedness unfortunately came from celebrated war heroes. The legless fighter pilot Douglas Bader, while he developed a deep affection for the Canadian pilots of 242 Squadron, reflected the class-ridden values of the pre-war RAF in which he had served his apprenticeship, and always valued a 'good school' background.[91] Guy Gibson could be insufferably snobbish, refusing to acknowledge ground staff and even non-commissioned aircrew on occasions.[92]

The discrepancies between NCOs and officers remained the most obvious class division among flyers. True, it was not the only one. Samuel Beaumount was a product of Salford Technical College, where he was trained as a draughtsman. After basic training, he qualified as an observer. However, in 1942 the appearance of the heavy bomber effectively eliminated the position of multi-role observer. His correspondence with his sister Mary from that time reveal anxieties about being demoted to an air-gunner, a position they both felt was no better than being ground staff. Mary, in particular, was concerned that: 'People would wonder what was wrong if you were still flying, but in a lower position', and they were both relieved when he was reassigned as a navigator.[93] However, the NCO–officer distinction remained the most corrosive legacy of both the pre-war RAF and the British class system more generally. It persisted even away from the formal demarcations which were enforced on the airfield. Tony Bartley recalled that in 92 Squadron, when off duty, sergeant pilots and officers lived in 'their own spheres of companionship'. Officers patronized the bar at the White Hart, while sergeants patronized The Jail.[94] Even in adversity, social segregation was maintained. Members of the ranks were more likely to be accused of LMF—Lack of Moral Fibre (a euphemism for cowardice)—than officers. At East Grinstead's 'guinea pig club', where flyers disfigured by terrible burns were literally rebuilt by the pioneer plastic surgeon Archie McIndoe, officers and men were treated together in the legendary Ward Three, but officers still had access to their own recreation room.[95] The distribution of medals in Bomber Command also revealed a social bias. The Distinguished Flying Medal (DFM) conferred for acts of valour and devotion to duty performed by NCOs, was much less regularly awarded than the Distinguished Flying Cross (DFC), the recipients of which were officers. This imbalance was despite the fact that the vast majority—around 70 per cent—of bomber aircrew were non-commissioned.[96] The resentments of many NCOs at such inequalities left a legacy which extended into peacetime. In John Braine's novel *Room at the Top* (1957), Joe Lampton's post-war rivalry with Jack Wales is in some sense a continuation of the wartime dudgeon of the working-class NCO towards the middle-class officer. At one point, Lampton refuses to grow a moustache on the grounds that it would make him look like a former officer.[97]

If, at one level, the wartime flyers of the RAF reflected the continuation of class conflict in the midst of a people's war, at another they also reflected the secure grasp retained by the middle class on the social leadership of Britain in wartime. While it is true that the wartime expansion of the service had broadened the social composition of the fraternity of flyers, the chief beneficiaries of a move beyond the public schools and ancient universities had been the products of grammar schools, technical colleges, and the red-brick provincial universities. In other words, this was a refashioned and more progressive bourgeois hegemony, but it was a bourgeois hegemony all the same. The essentially middle-class identity of most aircrew is thrown into sharp relief if we consider the attitude of flyers to the ground staff who made up 90 per cent of the personnel of most squadrons. Some ground personnel—station managers, intelligence officers, meteorologists, for example—were also officers and shared quarters with their flying equivalents. However, those who maintained the aircraft or the facilities on base were messed and billeted away from flyers, and the only regular contact between operational aircrew and ground crew took place on the runway or in hangers when flyers returned or collected their aircraft. Fighter pilot Paul Richey, possibly mindful of the need to accord with the stipulations of official propaganda, told his readers in 1941 that the fitter (responsible for the engine) and the rigger (who looked after the airframe) were the 'two other members of the crew' of a fighter aircraft. 'The pilot', he insisted, 'depends on these two men, perhaps for his life. The fitter and rigger, on their side, are usually proud of their pilot and would do anything for him. Consequently, there is a great spirit of teamwork and comradeship between the pilots, who are usually officers, and the men . . . in the maintenance section.'[98]

The post-war testimony of former ground crew, however, presents a much less auspicious account of aircrew–ground crew relations. Robert Collins was a mechanic with 443 Squadron, Royal Canadian Air Force (RCAF), a fighter unit based in Britain in the last year of the war. He described the RAF's 'caste system' as being ubiquitous, 'like a sliver under the thumbnail'. At the beginning of the war ground crew passively accepted their lowly status, but by 1945 resentment was becoming more manifest. Over the years of service Collins and his fellow mechanics had discovered that, 'man for man', officers 'were no better than we. Yet, without better education or being air crew, we would never attain their rank, with its better clothes, better food, better pay and its salutes from the lower classes.' Collins conceded there were a few ground crew who were on 'pseudo-chummy terms' with their pilots. However, 'I and most others were not'. He recalled his first meeting with a new Spitfire pilot, 'not much older than I but with the officer's air of confidence, authority and elitism which I envied and resented. I guessed I was as intelligent as he, but felt inferior by the very nature of my job and rank.' When the young flyer tried to engage in some friendly small talk, Collins remained unresponsive to what he perceived as 'the phoney good will of the estate manager towards his field hands'.[99] Collins' visceral level of class consciousness may have been exceptional, but it is certainly the case that flyers displayed a patronizing and high-handed attitude towards ground crew. In RAF slang, ground crew were assigned the derogatory appellations 'erks' or 'grease monkeys'. In C. H. Ward-Jackson's short story 'Airman', a lowly 'erk' shows initiative and courage during an enemy attack on his air base. However, this apparent celebration of an ordinary aircraftsman is undermined by a condescending tone which predominates throughout the narrative. The hero of the story is the son of a farm labourer, 'a bit of a swede . . . happy in any work that was honest and useful', for example, sweeping out the hangers.[100] Even NCOs, whose social origins were usually closer to ground crew than commissioned officers, could be insensitive and discourteous towards their fitters and riggers. A Mass-Observation survey of morale and attitudes in the RAF in 1941 concluded that 'a very frequent source of resentment is the reservation by the ruling classes of practically all the flying jobs for themselves'.[101] That the notion of a people's war was often more a product of government rhetoric than a depiction of social realities was no less true of the flyers of the RAF than it was of the nation as a whole.

There were also differences among flyers on national, ethnic, and racial lines. The wartime RAF was a genuinely multinational service. Hector Bolitho described his visit to an RAF station in the north of England:

What I liked seeing there was the mixture of blood and race among the men working there. I saw an alert little airman from Barbados, darting about under a bomber that had just landed. There were Irishmen, Scotsmen and Englishmen from our own islands, a South African commanding the station, and Australian sergeant-pilot and twenty or more Canadians. A Pole arrived for lunch, and a Czech pilot landed and joined us during the afternoon.[102]

A WAAF intelligence officer at bomber station RAF Spilsby recalled that the aircrew of 207 Squadron contained numerous Australians, New Zealanders, Canadians, several Americans, a South African, a Belgian, a Dutchman, and 'a couple of Jamaicans and a gunner who had, I believe, some Japanese blood in him'; 44 Squadron, which also shared the base, was a Rhodesian squadron, but included flyers from Switzerland and Chile, 'and several other oddments in the way of nationalities'.[103] Non-British flyers can be conveniently divided into three major groupings: volunteers from neutral countries, exiles from Nazi-occupied Europe, and men from Britain's overseas empire. Volunteers from neutral countries were inevitably a diverse and idiosyncratic element within the RAF. A significant contingent of Americans volunteered for service in the RAF in the years before the United States formally entered the war. Eighty-four Americans served in the legendary Eagle Squadron, commanded by Major Chesley G. Paterson, whose achievements were publicized by British propaganda to combat isolationist sentiment in the American heartland. The Eagle Squadron's eclectic cast of characters included William 'Billy' Meade Fiske III, the almost Gatsby-like WASP playboy and former Olympic bobsled champion; Whitney Straight, the pre-war racing-car driver who became a Battle of Britain fighter ace; 'Art' Donahue, a soft-spoken teetotaller from rural Minnesota; and Eugene 'Red' Tobin, a Los Angeles native who, when he was ready to fly, would tell his ground crew to 'Saddle 'er Up! I'm ridin'.[104] American volunteers were celebrated in fictionalized form in American adolescent fiction and in the Tyrone Power–Betty Grable film *A Yank in the RAF*, released in 1941.[105] This Hollywood appropriation of the Eagle Squadron's exploits was, in some senses, fitting. 'Billy' Fiske was married to Rose Bingham, ex-wife of the Earl of Warwick, but also a one-time Hollywood actress, while 'Red' Tobin's civilian flying career had involved ferrying the stars of MGM studios around California.[106]

Other volunteers had a decidedly exotic provenance. Coastal Command included the flyer Benny Benson, a Chilean of English ancestry.[107] Six hundred Argentinians volunteered for the RAF, producing enough qualified aircrew for the creation of 164 (Argentine–British) Squadron, which had the sun motif of the Argentine national flag on its crest.[108] An air transport auxiliary recalled meeting 'Sas' de Mier, a Mexican who served as an RAF air-gunner.[109] Flying Officer Nicky Varanand, who flew Spitfires with 132 Squadron on D-Day was in fact the *nom de guerre* of His Royal Highness Prince Varananda Dhavaj Chudadhuj, nephew of the King of Thailand. Keith Howard Adams (later legendary production designer Ken Adam), a Typhoon pilot in 609 Squadron, had previously been Klaus Heine, a German Jew who had fled Nazi persecution in the 1930s. In addition to the regular stresses of combat, Adam faced the prospect of immediate execution if he was shot down and captured by the Germans, but he also, ironically, had to negotiate the fact that anti-Semitism had become more, rather than less, prevalent in Britain during the war.[110] Eight Irish fighter pilots fought in the Battle of Britain, despite being officially denounced by Eamonn de Valera's government, which adopted a stance of strict neutrality between 1939 and 1945.[111] One of their number was Brendan 'Paddy' Finucane, who became the top-scoring pilot in Fighter Command at the time of his death in July 1942. Finucane came from a family with a long military tradition, but his father had been a staunch republican who had fought against the Black and Tans. In this sense, his career eerily recalled that of Britain's leading First World War fighter ace, Edward 'Mick' Mannock, whose passionate commitment to the British war effort coexisted with a commitment to Irish Home Rule.[112] Despite being a highly disciplined officer, placed in command of an Australian squadron, Finucane was still subjected to the stereotyping of the Irish in British culture which had long presented them as unruly and hot-headed. Sholto Douglas, a senior RAF officer, even in the course of paying tribute to Finucane, still referred to him as a 'rather wild Irishman'.[113]

In a foreword to a novel by Jules Roy, a Frenchman who served with Bomber Command, Air Marshal Robert Saundby characterized the outlook of the airmen who had fled from countries overrun by the Nazis: Free French, Poles, Dutch, Belgians, Czechs, and Norwegians. 'It is hard to find words', he asserted, 'to convey the grim courage and endurance of these exiled men, cut off from their families and friends . . . Their way was the way of loneliness and bitterness, even to heartbreak; redeemed only by a purpose which glowed the more brightly against this sombre background.'[114] The condition of exile imposed additional burdens on these continental European flyers which created a distinct gulf between them and their British equivalents. As will be seen in a later chapter, separation from, and anxiety about, their homeland was believed to account for a particular fierceness in combat, and a tendency to melancholy on the ground, among Polish pilots. If this was a caricature based on mutual cultural misunderstandings between British and non-British flyers, it nevertheless remained the case that exiled aircrew regularly felt semi-detached from the rest of the force in which they served. This is evident in the wartime careers of two Free French flyers, René Mouchotte and Jules Roy. Mouchotte fled France and joined the RAF, flying Spitfires and Hurricanes. His career culminated at RAF Biggin Hill, where he commanded a fighter wing. Mouchotte's diaries are full of references to the agony of separation from his beloved motherland, and his alienation from the apparent nonchalance of British flyers when faced with the loss of a comrade. Flying over London in October 1940, Mouchotte spied the French coast in the distance and, 'without wanting to be emotional, I abandoned myself to a feeling of great sadness and pity'. He was able to correspond with his uncle in the unoccupied zone of France, but this merely aggravated his homesickness, for his uncle continually reproached him for not returning home to tend to his sick mother. Mouchotte quite rightly pointed out that, if he returned, he would be executed by the collaborationist Vichy government as a traitor, an outcome hardly likely to foster an improvement in his mother's condition.[115] However, the young French flyer's anguish continued unabated. In March 1941 he recorded his response to the death of his fellow French pilot Henri Bouquillard, with whom he shared quarters: 'the empty bed and the sudden silence give me an overpowering sense of isolation. Without family and without friends, too, in this land of exile. We drew close enough together to think of each other as brother.' A month later Bouquillard's replacement, Grand-Pere Blaize, was killed, and Mouchotte noted how the remaining French flyers fell into depression. French flyers felt each loss acutely, not just because they were a minority within the RAF, but because they regarded themselves as precariously upholding the spirit of the true France, unconquered, at a time when the majority of their fellow citizens were tainted by accommodation, and even collaboration, with the German invader. The British, by contrast, seemed to regard the loss of their flyers with an unemotional indifference which Mouchotte regarded as incomprehensibly callous. In November 1942 he disclosed his desire to be able to get away from England, to return home where he could 'feel and think French, to get worked up without scruples, without fear of upsetting a coldly dignified atmosphere . . . Some days I find it hard in my English squadron to play my part imperturbably, sometimes I feel stifled, oppressed [by] the difference between the English and us.'[116] Mouchotte was never granted this heartfelt wish, being killed in action shortly after.

Jules Roy became a bombardier in Halifaxes, completing a tour of thirty-seven missions in 1944–5. Like Mouchotte, he kept a diary, but unlike his fighter-pilot compatriot, he survived the war and used his journals as the basis of two highly accomplished novels, *The Happy Valley* and *The Navigator*.[117] In July 1944 Roy found himself flying over France, which 'wears the gaping wounds of recent bombardments and . . . makes one heavy-hearted'.[118] On one occasion he was sent on a mission to bomb a railway junction in northern France. In Roy's fictionalized account of the raid in *The Happy Valley*, his alter ego, Chevrier, agonizes over the logic of having to destroy the enemy at all costs, even if it meant pulverizing his homeland: 'Men who were not his fellow-countrymen were ordering him to drop bombs on his country . . . and he obeyed, not knowing whether he would be treated as a murderer or not when he at last went back home.' Chevrier eventually reconciles himself to attacking his own country by conceptualizing it as an act of solidarity with the French resistance, 'joining forces at last with those men he knew of who had stayed behind in France and were mining bridges, firing petrol pumps and printing illegal newspapers'.[119] However, the great majority of Roy's missions were over Germany, and his diaries reveal his frustration at not being able to see the liberation of France in July and August 1944 with his own eyes, following events at a distance on the radio or on cinema newsreels. Like Mouchotte, Roy was critical of the emotional conventions of British flyers, although his complaints focused less on their stiff upper lips than on their undignified behaviour at air-base parties, where, by the end of the evening, 'food is all over the floor and the drunkards climb on to the stage'.[120]

It should not be assumed that the exiled flyers always allowed the commonality of nationality to transcend other aspects of their identities. Czech flyers in the RAF were particularly riven by serious factionalism. One source of tension was the fact that the cohort of Czech flyers who had come to Britain after 1938 contained a disproportionate number of officers. Faced with an acute shortage of air-gunners and radio operators, it was necessary to block the promotion prospects of NCOs and warrant-officer pilots. Operational losses eventually produced opportunities for advancement, but many Czech NCOs remained bitter and frustrated throughout the war.[121] A second factor—inevitably, for a group of men whose wartime personal histories were framed by the 'betrayals' of Munich in 1938 and the communist coup of 1948—was politics. M. A. Liskutin noted the divisions among his fellow pilots in July 1940 between Czech patriots and communists. He accused the latter, under directives from the Comintern during the era of the Nazi–Soviet pact, of trying to spread defeatist sentiments among the flyers. Even after Germany invaded the Soviet Union in June 1941, tensions remained. Posted to 312 (Czech) Squadron in December 1941, Liskutin found latent hostility between flyers and ground crew, who were often communists and former Spanish Civil War veterans. While these men now wholeheartedly supported the Allied war effort, they incensed nationalist aircrew by their recourse to Marxist rhetoric.[122] Likewise, French flyers embodied many of the political divisions which Nicholas Atkin has revealed in his study of the wider French émigré community in wartime Britain.[123] René Mouchotte, for example, immediately responded to De Gaulle's challenge to the legitimacy of the armistice with Germany signed by Marshal Petain in June 1940. Jules Roy, by contrast, was initially an admirer of the Vichy regime, and, as late as 1943, found it difficult to wholeheartedly commit to De Gaulle's exile government in London. Even while serving in Bomber Command, he was motivated much more by a philosophical quest to test himself against the fear of death than he was by a robust commitment to the cause of the Free French.[124] However, intra-national conflicts should not be allowed to obscure the fact that national divisions were not easily overcome in the wartime RAF.

The most important non-British presence in the RAF was that of recruits from the Empire-Commonwealth. It has been estimated that 46 per cent of aircrew came from the Dominions—Canada, New Zealand, Australia, and South Africa; or, more strictly speaking, from the white settler populations of these countries.[125] The Battle of Britain might have been fought in the skies above 'deep England', over the oast-houses and apple orchards of Kent and the gently rolling hills of the South Downs, but in terms of personnel it was a decidedly imperial affair. Renowned Battle of Britain pilots included Al Deere, a New Zealander, Johnny Kent, a Canadian, and Adolph 'Sailor' Malan, a South African.[126] The legendary 249 Squadron, whose Spitfires and Hurricanes defended Malta in the summer of 1942 against a German adversary that outnumbered them eight to one, was a highly efficient synthesis of an assortment of rugged flyers from Britain, Australia, New Zealand, Canada, and South Africa. Amongst its number was the famous Rhodesian pilot Johnny Plagis.[127] It might have been expected that Commonwealth recruits would have little difficulty integrating into the RAF, given that most of them had volunteered for service out of a belief in the significant ties of kinship and heritage that bound them to the mother country. Ian Douglas Smith joined the RAF as a reflection of his loyalty to the crown and his belief that white Rhodesians were more British than the British themselves.[128] However, relations between British and Commonwealth aircrew were just as likely to be characterized by difference as by affinity. In the first half of the twentieth century the cultures of the white Dominions had increasingly diverged from that of the mother country. Their political autonomy confirmed by the 1930 Statute of Westminster, Australians and Canadians began to present themselves as the fortunate citizens of societies which were less socially restrictive than that of Britain itself.[129] Esmond Romilly joined the RCAF, largely because, as a former communist, he hoped to adopt 'the robust democratic common sense of the New World as a weapon for attacking the traditional conception of military dignity'. When his squadron was transferred from Canada to Iceland, it came under RAF command for the first time. When told to 'inspect their men', a practice unheard of in Canada, Romilly and his fellow officers merely marched straight down the rows of aircraftsmen, without once turning their heads to scrutinize the uniforms and weapons being presented for inspection.[130]

Many Commonwealth aircrew came from nations where attitudes to Britain were characterized by deep ambivalence. French Canadians not merely had to overcome a language barrier with British aircrew, but also a legacy of bitterness between Britain and the Francophone world caused by the British attack on the French fleet at Mers-el-Kebir in June 1940.[131] South Africa was deeply divided over supporting the British war effort. 'Sailor' Malan's status as the RAF's greatest air fighter sat uneasily with the fact that he was an Afrikaner, a section of the South African population who retained a folk memory of resistance to British imperialism during the 1899–1902 Boer War and maintained pro-German sympathies throughout the war.[132] Commonwealth aircrew often exhibited resentment towards aspects of the imperial relationship which confused British airmen, who had assumed they would be cousins-in-arms and unwavering loyal sons of the crown. British flyers were astonished to observe Rhodesian aircrew file off the crown on the Rhodesian lion cap-badge which they sported, an action prompted by their anger at Britain's unwillingness to grant Rhodesia full Dominion status.[133] British flyers were not always complimentary about Commonwealth aircrew. Flight Sergeant 'Bertie' McGarvey revealed in a letter to his cousin that a group of Canadian sergeants 'didn't get such a hearty welcome as they might have done', largely because they appeared to have been permitted to become wireless operators with only half the number of hours training undertaken by the British: 'Some of them couldn't even tap morse at twelve words a minute, while we're doing 23.'[134] While RAF messes became increasingly cosmopolitan, as bomber crew in particular were made up of a mix of Britons, South Africans, and Australians, men from the white Dominions remained distinctive in patois and appearance. Pilot Officer John Byrne noted in his diary that the South Africans and Australians were much more liable to resort to profanities than their British equivalents. As for the Canadians, they appeared to favour extensive jewellery: gold or silver identification bracelets, diamond rings, expensive watches, and gold neck chains.[135]

Britain's imperial ties also brought the non-white into the fraternity of flyers. Given that there was an obvious inconsistency between a war to defend democracy and the continued denial of self-determination to Britain's colonial territories, the British government was obliged to maintain relations with its imperial subjects by refashioning traditional paternalism into the more flexible conception of 'partnership'. This did not imply a challenge to notions of racial difference and racial hierarchy, but it did require, at least at the level of propaganda and public rhetoric, an opportunity for non-white subjects of the British crown to participate in (and be acknowledged as participating in) the fight against fascism.[136] How far, in the course of furthering this end, the RAF was able, or even intended, to overcome (or at least mitigate) racial divisions is, as will be seen, questionable. The use of air power against civilian populations in Iraq in the 1920s exposed an unapologetic racial arrogance within the RAF, which was reiterated in the grotesque re-enactments of the bombing of 'native' villages at the annual Hendon Air Pageant in the early 1930s.[137] Non-white aircrew have been largely erased from the dominant cultural memory of the wartime RAF. It is possible to recover their contribution to the war in the air, but only by the assembling of sources which are piecemeal and incomplete. They often appear as a brief, fleeting reference in the memoirs of white aircrew. For example, Miles Tripp recalled that the tail-gunner of his Lancaster bomber was Harry, a black Jamaican who could swear and fight but also 'appreciate delicacy and nuance in conversation'. However, Tripp believed Harry to be unique, for in his entire period serving in Bomber Command Tripp claimed not to have set eyes on another West Indian flyer.[138] Even when black flyers do intrude into conventional accounts of the wartime RAF, their presence is passed over without comment. For example, a biography of 'Sailor' Malan includes a photograph of Malan with black Jamaican Spitfire pilot Vincent Bunting. However, Bunting fails to feature in the text of the book, despite the fact that one might have expected the question of the relationship of Malan, an Afrikaner, with a fellow flyer who was black to have aroused his biographer's curiosity.[139]

However, non-white flyers, while a distinct minority among aircrew, certainly did make a significant contribution to the war effort, in the face of barely disguised racial prejudice. Exact figures are difficult to establish, but a memorandum prepared for the Air Ministry in early 1945 estimated that around 422 'coloured' men (the blanket term used to include West Indian, West African, and South Asian flyers) had served as aircrew during the war, with a further 3,900 acting as ground crew.[140] Organizations committed to racial equality, such as the League of Coloured Peoples, were keen to promote the achievements of black flyers, while remaining vigilant towards incidents of discrimination and prejudice. The pages of the League's newsletter recorded with pride the granting of a commission to Pilot Officer Peter Thomas from Sierra Leone, the award of DFC and DSO to Flying Officer Ulric Cross of Trinidad, and mourned the loss of Pilot Officer Victor Tucker, a Jamaican fighter pilot with four kills to his credit, lost over France.[141] Official British propaganda (especially that associated with the Colonial Office) was also keen to publicize the activities of non-white colonial aircrew, although this was always circumscribed by anxieties about alienating white settler populations in Britain's imperial possessions. Ulric Cross appeared in the documentary *West Indies Calling*, while a Maori flyer was featured in *Maximum Effort*, a movie about the New Zealand crew of a Lancaster bomber.[142] Given alarm at the apparent increased militancy of Indian nationalism during the war, official propaganda was eager to promote the contribution of South Asian flyers to the conflicts in both Asia and Europe. Air Ministry files on 'Indians in the RAF' reveal that, whereas security considerations usually precluded releasing details about individuals, this stricture was waived in regard to publicity material released for consumption back in India. Among those Indian flyers singled out for publicity purposes were Pilot Officer Shir der Singh, who had taken place in the famous bombing raid on Brest, and Hari Chaud Dewan, who had flown twice over Berlin 'to bomb the very heart of the country which stands as much a scheming enemy of India's future as of this country's'.[143] In October 1940 the BBC broadcast a radio programme, *In it Together*, which featured an interview

with a Sikh flying officer from the Punjab who had joined the RAF after a
pre-war career with Imperial Airways.[144] Such propaganda inevitably sought
to counter attempts by both Germany and Japan to exploit anti-British and
anti-imperial sentiments in India, most notably the creation of Subhas Chandras
Bhose's Indian National Army.[145] Fictional narratives were put to work for
similar ends. The Indian feature film *Burma Rani*, starring the renowned Tamil
actor and musician Hannappa Bhagavatha, involved a downed Indian flyer being
hidden from the Japanese by a young Indian woman in Burma.[146] Inevitably,
Indian flyers tended to be deployed in the defence of India and the campaign
in neighbouring Burma. However, Francis Yeats-Brown, who had served in the
Bengal Lancers before the First World War, reminded readers of his celebration
of the finest traditions of 'martial India' that, at the outbreak of war in 1939, one
hundred Indian students, rather than returning home, had volunteered to join
the RAF. Forty of them became aircrew, and some served in the Battle of Britain.
'Strange', mused Yeats-Brown, 'how few of us know this, either in England or
India.'[147] One of the Indian pilots who took an active part in operations during
the Battle of Britain was Mahindra Singh Pujji, later a prominent figure in
the development of civil aviation in South Asia, whose wartime correspondence
refers to at least twelve named Indian flyers who were based in Britain during the
course of 1940 and 1941.[148]

   If representations of Indian aircrew in British propaganda were largely laudat-
ory, this most likely reflected the degree of anxiety about sustaining imperial rule
in a subcontinent threatened by Japanese invasion from without and nationalist
revolt from within. It may also owe something to British imperial stereotypes
about the 'martial races', in which the attributes of manly courage and fighting
prowess had been assigned to some (although not all) Indian subjects of the
crown, at the same time as such qualities were denied to West Indians and
Africans.[149] The British empire was constituted around a strict racial hierarchy,
in which South Asians were regarded as closest to white Europeans, while black
Africans (and their diaspora) were considered as childlike savages, closer to
nature than to European civilization. The legacy of such distasteful conceptions
was evident in fictional representations of West Indian aircrew. In his novel
Faith is a Windsock, Miles Tripp created a fictionalized version of his wartime
comrade Harry in the character of Jake McCoy, 'a tall, coffee-skinned Jamaican
with high cheekbones and arrogant eyes'. Jake possesses the ability to predict
where the crew's next mission will be, even before the battle order is posted.
Dorothy, the lover of Bergen, the pilot of Jake's aircraft, accounts for this gift
in terms of the 'coloured races' being more supernaturally gifted than whites,
'who've had the primitive bred out of us'.[150] Wing Commander Leslie Kark's
contribution to an anthology of writings by RAF personnel was a condescending
short story about 'Persil', Sergeant Percy Gabriel Montgomery, an air-gunner
in Stirlings, possessed of a 'shining brown body and . . . smiling brown face'.
'Persil', from Grenada, the grandson of a Barbados slave, is presented as brave

but simple-minded, his face filled with wonder when he observes snowflakes for the first time while returning from a raid on Germany.[151]

Racist assumptions were no less evident in confidential assessments of the capabilities of non-white aircrew produced by the RAF hierarchy. A survey of the performance of 'coloured Aircrew' suggested that, overall, non-white trainees attained the same level of success as their white equivalents, and that they possessed the qualities 'necessary to take their place in operational aircrew'. However, the report then shamelessly back-peddled away from this apparent ringing endorsement of the competence of non-white flyers:

In spite of the satisfactory standard of the technical and other abilities possessed by coloured officers and airmen who have qualified as members of aircrew, experience has shown that the appointment of any of this class of personnel as a Captain of Aircraft has not met with success. However good the individual may be the mere fact that he is coloured may induce a feeling of lack of confidence in the members of the crew. It is a matter entirely beyond the Captain's control and though the feeling may only be subconscious, it will tend to lower the efficiency of the crew as a whole.

Conversely, the report also felt that promoting black aircrew to the position of captain might lead 'a coloured airman to regard himself as a privileged person and to show resentment when certain breaches of conduct and behaviour were pointed out to him by superior officers'.[152] In the early part of the war the RAF had actively sought to recruit aircrew from the colonies, but by 1943 it was only interested in enlisting ground staff. This decision not merely reflected the racist assumptions of the RAF hierarchy, but also a desire to appease the Americans, who were troubled by the presence of black cadets among those aircrew being instructed on RAF training schemes operating in the United States.[153]

While black aircrew were certainly better treated than ground crew (who, even when qualified technicians, were assigned to the most menial tasks on the airfield), they did encounter racism, both overt and covert. Billy Strachan, a Jamaican who began his RAF career as a wireless operator on Wellingtons before receiving a commission, claimed, in an interview with another former veteran, the Guyanan Robert Murray, to have never encountered racial discrimination during his time as aircrew. Indeed, while training as an officer at Cranwell, Strachan, the 'little coloured boy from the Caribbean', had the privilege of having a white man, his batman, a 'real smooth Jeeves type' who had previously served King George VI, call him 'sir'.[154] However, some of the other former West Indian aircrew interviewed by Murray told a very different story. Ulric Cross, despite an illustrious wartime career, was convinced that he only received a commission because he was a friend of the West Indian cricketer Learie Constantine, who was a popular celebrity in Britain during the 1940s. Owen Sylvester, a Trinidadian who joined the RAF in 1941 and eventually received the DFM, was regularly victimized by his commanding officer, who kept calling him to his office to reprimand the black captain and warrant officer for incorrect saluting. Sylvester's first meeting with his CO was far from auspicious. With the crew lined up for inspection, the CO first approached the navigator, who was white, and said 'I suppose you're the Captain'. When the navigator replied in the negative, and indicated that the aircraft's skipper was actually the black warrant officer standing next to him, the CO was clearly put out. On a later occasion Sylvester overheard his CO remarking: 'I know how to deal with these people. I have experience of dealing with them in India.'[155] Relations between black colonial aircrew and flyers from the white Dominions were inevitably complex. There were sometimes examples of shared solidarity in the face of metropolitan snobbery and high-handedness. The West Indian pilot Ivor De' Souza had a good-humoured and enjoyable relationship with an Australian squadron of which he was flight commander, while Billy Strachan was recommended for promotion by his white South African CO.[156] However, wartime RAF service sometimes merely exported to British soil the racial tensions between white settlers and blacks which disfigured the imperial periphery. One flyer recollected a white Rhodesian air-gunner who was incandescent with rage when he discovered his fellow aircrew included a black Jamaican rear-gunner, insisting: 'I'm not going to fly with that black bastard.'[157] The colour bar, whose continued purchase at both home and abroad within the British Empire seriously compromised Britain's claims to be fighting a war in defence of freedom, served as yet another impediment to the achievement of a complete and unqualified sense of camaraderie among the men of the RAF.

In her study of masculinity in Britain during the First World War, Joanna Bourke argues that the extent of male bonding among soldiers in the trenches was ultimately shallow and perfunctory. For all the common experience of combat and military culture, most men were still divided by regimental demarcations, the division between volunteers and conscripts, and differences of social class, region, religion, and ethnicity.[158] A study of the flyers of the wartime RAF reveals similar limits to military camaraderie during the Second World War. The RAF's fraternity of flyers was a genuine one, based around their status as an elite group of fighting men, but also rooted in their shared knowledge of a world above the clouds that few others had experienced. However, such comradeship was unable to efface the differences between—to take a few select examples—fighters and bombers, officers and NCOs, or white Rhodesians and black Jamaicans. In this particular man's world, homosociability was fragile and contingent. However, what proved to be the greatest potential challenge to male bonding in the RAF was that the male-only world of the service was never hermetically sealed, and the flyer was fully exposed to the compelling distractions of heterosexual desire, romantic love, and domestic attachment.

3

The Flyer in Love

In *Pastoral*, his 1944 novel about the romance between a Wellington pilot and a WAAF section officer, Nevil Shute boldly avowed that: 'Everybody at Hartley aerodrome was deeply interested in Love, except perhaps the Adjutant and Flight Officer Stevens, and one or two others more than twenty-five years old. For the majority of the Wing, Love was as essential a commodity as petrol, and much more interesting.'[1] It is the contention of this chapter that there is much truth in Shute's characterization. The conceit of the young flyer in love was an important element in the dominant cultural representations of the wartime RAF, and also played a not insignificant role in the subjectivities and sensibilities of aircrew themselves. Moreover, it was not merely when off duty or on leave that the flyer was able to give himself up to affairs of the heart. The presence of female personnel on RAF bases allowed a degree of male–female interaction that was rare in military cultures. However, a study of the romantic susceptibilities of the flyer has implications for the history of masculinity in 1940s Britain which extend beyond the RAF's singular culture. The pursuit of love was not merely a welcome release from the alternating boredom and terror of war. Romantic fulfilment was viewed as a fitting reward for those who had undertaken the obligations of military service: further testimony to the striking contiguity between martial and civilian cultures in the twentieth century.

LOVE'S DISTRACTION

There were those who argued that the business of war left no time for romantic love, or that romance was a dangerous distraction which diminished combat effectiveness. Cecil Beaton, after visiting several air bases in 1941, assured his readers that the flyers of the RAF were habitually accustomed to sacrifice their personal interests in the pursuit of duty. They shouldered 'their great responsibility with a single-mindedness which is almost monastic'. Romantic entanglements would be postponed until 'the big job is over'.[2] Beaton's insistence that these young men preferred the pleasures of flying to flirtation with young women, including those serving on the air base itself (who are completely absent from Beaton's sketch of air-station life) seems unconvincing, to say the least. Indeed, one of Beaton's most engaging wartime photographs is of two uniformed, yet boyish, RAF officers frolicking in a country stream with two young women.[3] However, he was not alone in insisting that the flyers of the RAF represented the finest elements of the British character, not least because they were able to exercise appropriate self-restraint when faced with the siren song of female sexuality. Rom Landau served as a RAF liaison officer with the Polish Air Force in Britain. The contrasts between Polish and British aircrew formed the basis of a reflection on national character published in 1942. What he believed to be the greater sexual restraint of British flyers was presented as a strength, not a weakness: 'When faced with the conflict between the call of duty and the call of sex—often interpreted as a call of love—he fights a far less difficult inner battle than do most of his foreign colleagues.' Landau was confident that Britons would be relieved by this knowledge, since France's pitiful resistance to German invasion in 1940 revealed how 'the submission of professional and even national interests to erotic ones [has] played a tragic part in the life of nations'.[4] Presumably, the Battle of France had been lost in the bedrooms of the Elysée Palace, while the Battle of Britain had been won in the cold showers of Biggin Hill.

Landau's characterization clearly owed more to xenophobia than observation, and few others were willing to present the calls of duty and love as so unequivocally exclusive. However, some flyers adopted a tone of world-weary cynicism which belied their youth, and declared themselves immune to the claims of romantic attachment. Battle of Britain pilot and self-chosen voice of the 'long-haired fighter boys' Richard Hillary boasted to his lover Mary Booker that, despite having had several affairs, he had never been in love, preferring to 'see things straight' rather than be blinded by romance. Hillary's cold-blooded disdain appalled Mary, who retorted that the charm of youth, as she understood it, was that the young always believed themselves to be totally in love.[5] However, some flyers felt Hillary had a point, since the harsh realities of war and the ever-present possibility of immediate physical annihilation made romantic sentimentality seem inappropriate, or even absurd. If the flyer could not guarantee being able to protect himself from the cannon fire of a Messerschmidt 109, he could at least prevent himself being downed, instead, by Cupid's arrow. George Hull, a flight sergeant in a Lancaster bomber, wrote regularly to Joan Kirby, who was serving in the Women's Royal Navy Reserve (WRNS). Hull had first met Kirby through her brother John, who had been killed in an accident while training to be a navigator. Hull clearly felt sufficiently intimate and comfortable with Kirby to share his anxieties, frustrations, and even the profanities of service life. At times his letters were mildly flirtatious, but he held back from an explicit declaration of love. In January 1944 a candid letter confessed: 'I could get a great deal fonder of you if I saw you more often . . . [but] it would not be fair. Not fair to me because it disturbs my peace of mind, unfair to you because what little interest you may have in me might be one day a grief to you equal almost to that which you have lately suffered.'[6] Tragically, Hull's prudence proved to be all too prescient, since he was lost over Germany two months later. If falling in love might compromise the flyer's personal 'peace of mind' or leave a young woman grieving the loss of a fallen lover, it also jeopardized the safety of his comrades. Peter Townsend recalled that fighter pilots were often troubled by the presence of broody or lovesick flyers in their midst, fearing that, now they had someone to care about, they were less likely to take risks for their comrades when in combat.[7] In Nevil Shute's wartime novel *Pastoral*, Wellington pilot Peter Marshall falls in love with a WAAF officer, Gervase. When she rebuffs his declaration of affection, his disappointment in love causes him to lose concentration and, on return from a mission, he crashes his aircraft, narrowly avoiding killing both himself and his crew.[8]

Sweethearts of flyers often found that they faced twin rivals to their attachment: the flyer's love of flying, and the flyer's love of sharing danger with his comrades. Fighter pilot Geoffrey Wellum found himself torn between the claims of his squadron and his girlfriend, with whom he lived in a 'quaint little inn'.[9] Such tensions became a regular motif in RAF middlebrow fiction published after the war. In John Watson's *Johnny Kinsman*, the Halifax pilot hero goes drinking with his fellow crew member, Flying Officer Wakefield, and the latter's girlfriend, Julie. As the evening progresses the two men become increasingly drunk and engage in a maudlin roll-call of lost comrades. Julie, excluded from this mutual lament, finally loses patience and interjects: 'You two have forgotten me. Is this a very private get together or can anyone join in?'[10] In Walter Clapham's *Night Be My Witness*, Johnny Somers finds his love for Anne, with whom he has a passionate affair while training as a pilot, rapidly fades once he joins an operational squadron. Johnny had 'been drugged by war, or fallen too much in love with flight'.[11] Later in the novel the close friendship between Johnny and two other aircrew, Bill and Bruce, is fatally ruptured when Bill falls in love with, and marries, Mary. After Bill is killed, Johnny confronts Mary and cruelly tells her: 'The three of us started together . . . Your trouble is you can't get over the fact that you were never a part of it . . . It was something you could never touch.' When Mary begins to cry, Johnny apologizes and comforts her, although, significantly, he does not retract his harsh words, privately believing 'that what I said was true, as far as I could track the meaning'.[12]

AS ESSENTIAL A COMMODITY AS PETROL

Fighter ace Johnnie Johnson initially shared Richard Hillary's belief that emotional entanglements with women were a dangerous distraction for fighting men. Light-hearted flirtation or casual sexual encounters were acceptable, but love, Johnson resolved, 'must wait until after the war'. However, one night at a party in Norwich Johnson met Paula Wingate, a 19-year-old staff member of the operations room of the Auxiliary Fire Service. Johnson's earlier strictures were abandoned, and after a month-long whirlwind romance they became engaged.[13] Peter Townsend also succumbed to the siren song. Fellow fighter pilot Jim Bailey recalled that, not long after Townsend had asserted that it was impossible to be a good pilot and be married, he shocked Fighter Command by announcing his own engagement.[14] The fictional flyer was also liable to find his initial preference for emotional disengagement impossible to sustain in the face of grand passion. In *Johnny Kinsman*, the Halifax pilot Johnny struggles to deny his love for Julie, convincing himself that it would be selfish to love her while he was 'standing with one foot on either side of the chasm of death while she lay luxuriant in the soft green grass of life, laughing and bright-eyed, free and willing to love, and sure of the rightness of living'. However, he finally confesses his feelings to Julie, who helps restore his self-belief, their love giving him a reason to overcome his guilt that he is still alive when so many of his comrades have been killed.[15] In Nevil Shute's *Landfall* (1940), bomber pilot Jerry persuades himself that it might be advisable to avoid a romantic entanglement with pub waitress Mona: 'Perhaps it was better, after all, to stick to beer.' Mona is equally reluctant to become involved, although her motives are more social than emotional. She fears (in passages in the novel which cast further doubt on the universal subscription to the notion of a 'people's war' in Britain in 1939–45) that working in a pub was an unsuitable background for the wife of an RAF officer. However, when Mona succeeds in proving that Jerry has been wrongfully accused of accidentally bombing a British submarine, their love blossoms and they marry (although the class differences between them can only be overcome by having them relocate to Canada and Mona take up elocution lessons).[16] Nevertheless, once again, the story is one of reservations overcome and love triumphing over war.

While inevitably overblown, the sensibilities dramatized in the middlebrow fiction of Watson and Shute were no less evident in the letters and diaries of real flyers. RAF Wigsley, an actual bomber base in Lincolnshire, seems extraordinarily reminiscent of Nevil Shute's fictional Hartley, if the letters written in 1943 by George Hull to Joan Kirby are to be believed. Scrutinizing the crew of his Lancaster, Hull was convinced that they were all suffering from 'love pangs' of one form or another: 'Roy my twin, is trying hard to get over a bad case of unrequited love . . . Skipper is married as you know. Aussie R/gunner has a much-adored love in Brisbane named Joan whose photograph is enough to rock him, in spite of 13,000 miles of sea . . . Best, the mid-upper gunner, has a Colleen in Ireland, and both the w/op and flight-engineer moan nightly over Ivy and Carol respectively.'[17] Flying Officer Frank Blackman recalled that it was only his daydreams of his girlfriend Mary that prevented him from breaking under the stress of combat.[18]

To say that, for the flyer, surrounded by so much death and destruction, falling in love was an affirmation of both life in the present and hope in the future is obviously a cliché. However, like many clichés, it had a cultural purchase that ensured its regular presence in both fictional accounts of the RAF and in the flyer's own self-fashioning. Also, as a highly imaginative essay on the gender politics of the United States during the Second World War has argued, the promise of romantic fulfilment was presented in both official and popular wartime discourses as a post-war reward for those taking up the obligations of military service.[19] A study of American popular music in wartime has endorsed such claims, demonstrating that the appeal of swing was in its 'homeward gaze', which presented the war not as an ideological or militaristic crusade, but as the defence of personal dreams centred on the women who waited, and to whom the serviceman would ultimately return.[20] An understanding of the masculinity of men of the wartime RAF would therefore be woefully incomplete unless it considered not merely the flyer in war, but also the flyer in love.

At this point, it might be worthwhile briefly reflecting on some problems posed by any attempt to offer a historical analysis of romantic love. For a long time love was regarded as a topic unworthy of serious scholarly investigation. As recently as 1992 Stephen Kern confidently asserted that: 'One of life's deepest mysteries and most powerful emotions has remained one of the darkest corners of history. Most historians dismiss love as an irrational distraction from rational behaviour or an interruption in the course of important events that makes one bow out of history, as when a king abdicated for the woman he loved.'[21] True, in the last two decades new research on the psychology and sociology of emotions has made the academic study of love increasingly respectable.[22] Historians have played a significant role in this transformation, inevitably insisting that love cannot be understood independent of the social and cultural context in which it is experienced. Pioneer studies by, among others, Karen Lystra (of nineteenth-century American love letters), Beth Bailey (of changing courtship practices in the United States between the 1890s and the 1960s), Stephen Kern (of how changing modes of loving are represented in literature and art between the 1840s and the 1930s), and Deborah Field (on romantic love and the limits to the private sphere in Khrushchev's Russia), have all revealed how the meaning and uses of love have varied greatly over time and space.[23] However, this emphasis on historical contingency has had the unfortunate effect of producing a historical literature on love which is sporadic and lacks a shared vocabulary which might facilitate more discussion and interaction between scholars. The continued immaturity which characterizes the historical literature on romantic love is certainly true of studies of Britain in the twentieth century. A dramatic growth of interest in the history of sexuality in modern Britain has aggravated, rather than ameliorated, this problem. We now know much more about the intimate physical experiences of Britons in the last century than we do about their intimate emotional experiences.

There have recently been a few notable exceptions to this scholarly neglect. Marcus Collins has surveyed the rise and fall of theories of mutual love within heterosexual relationships in the twentieth century.[24] Claire Langhamer has used the archives of Mass-Observation to examine the everyday practices of courtship in mid-twentieth-century England. Her research has important things to say about how class and gender informed romantic encounters, emphasizing the continued resilience of social status in the selection of partners, and also revealing that, by the 1940s, women were able to exercise considerable agency in the spheres of love and courtship. While she does consider the issue of subjectivity, Langhamer's predominant focus is on embedded practices, and she has little to say about how an individual's understanding of love might have been informed by the discourses of popular culture, especially the new mass medium of cinema. Moreover, the majority of respondents she discusses were women, and British male attitudes towards love and courtship remain largely obscure. Langhamer's research suggests that we still know surprisingly little about the most important aspect of love: what it actually meant to those who experienced it.[25]

This subjective aspect of the historicization of romantic love is undoubtedly the most challenging. What did the young flyers of the wartime RAF think love was? This apparently straightforward question is confounded by the idiosyncrasies of the individual love affair or, conversely, by a common resort in the language of love to the universal and the timeless which appears to repudiate historical contingency. Love has long been regarded as an incomprehensible force. As Karen Lystra sensibly reminds us, if lovers themselves frequently 'found the experience of love opaque', we should not be surprised to find the historians who study them 'equally bedevilled'.[26] Moreover, falling in love under the shadow of catastrophe inevitably invested wartime love with a particular intensity and drama, which may mitigate against its value as an index of broader social attitudes towards romance and courtship. Langhamer reveals that, across the century as a whole, understandings of courtship were informed by a synthesis of romantic love and unsentimental pragmatism. The peculiar pressures of war clearly offered an alternative vision of love as reckless, thrill-seeking adventure, that could not be expected to easily mutate into a form of emotional commitment which could last a lifetime. However, this should not preclude us from trying to reconstruct the specific cultural apparatus of love which sustained the wartime flyer. We can at least speculate on the broader cultural influences which these men found most useful in capturing and articulating their emotions. For those flyers who were highly educated, or those who were professional authors, their assumptions about love appear to be informed by a popular late romanticism. For all their rejection of overblown language and sentimentalism, these were still men who (as the contributions to anthologies of RAF poetry published during the war reveal) had been raised on the poetry of Keats and Yeats, and the novels of Thomas Hardy.[27] The idiom of popular music may also have had an influence on how the flyer understood love, especially given the ubiquity of radio and gramophone in the mess. Some popular wartime songs, notably 'Silver Wings in the Moonlight', spoke to the specific romantic angst of the airman 'flying high up above' while his lover was 'patiently waiting' below.[28] However, it is likely that it was the silver screen which contributed the most to shaping the sensibilities and practices of love in this period. One contemporary observer testified to a widespread belief that Hollywood had made a major contribution to the art of love in Britain during the 1930s and 1940s: 'It showed boys how to walk with girls, how to pilot them in public places, how to chaff, flatter and rally them. It taught them how to hold a girl, how long and how tight. It familiarized them with looks which mean "I won't be kissed", "I don't mind if I'm kissed", "I want to be kissed", "Stop it, I like it", "I like it, but stop it", and a dozen others.' Many men acknowledged that women would expect their performance of courtship to incorporate the gentlemanly and dashing styles of their screen idols, although they were equally aware that it was important to appear to do this effortlessly, since a young woman might grow restive if her boyfriend was too obviously trying to 'do a Gable'.[29] As we have already noted, the flyer's inherent glamour created a contradictory dialogue with the discourses of Hollywood, but it is difficult not to believe that the young men of the RAF, like so many of their peers, did not have their understandings of love fashioned, at least in part, by the conventions and styles of cinematic romance. The dislocations of wartime possibly allowed them to be among the first young Britons to be able to combine a celluloid notion of love with the opportunity to pursue courtship independent of the oversight of family and neighbourhood.

Some writers have argued that one of the difficulties in mapping male subjectivities in regard to romantic love is that men lacked either relevant vocabulary or sufficient reflexive capability to be able to express their emotions effectively.[30] As will be seen, the flyer was certainly capable of suppressing the feelings of both fear and grief with which he was inevitably tortured. However, letters, diaries, and memoirs composed by the men of the RAF often virtually vibrate with emotion, and can be startlingly frank about the flyer's longing for love. Letters home from Wellington air-gunner Sam Miara regularly resorted to block capitals to emphasize just how much he wanted to be in the arms of his wife again. Even the mildly repressed Lancaster flight sergeant George Hull laid bare his jealousy when it appeared that the object of his affections might be taken from him by the attentions of a rival. The conceptions of love held by such men were rarely sophisticated or profound, but they possessed a heartfelt belief that their romantic entanglements amounted to more than physical attraction and a light-hearted distraction from the war. For all its agonies, love clearly offered a source of hope and comfort amidst a world marked by chaos and destruction.

Certainly, most flyers welcomed the distractions of the fairer sex. As young men, they inevitably possessed a healthy libido. The all-male atmosphere of the mess encouraged the profane and the prurient. Illustrations of aircraft silhouettes, used to facilitate the recognition of enemy airplanes, shared space on the walls of dispersal huts with cheesecake pin-ups.[31] Some of the more lewd RAF songs linked combat with carnality, one popular number exploiting the widespread use in RAF slang of a part of the female anatomy to refer to the bomb-release button in heavy bombers: 'Bombing is like playing with a girlie | Don't press the tit too late or too early.' Blenheim pilot 'Shack' Shackleton recalled that, while practising low flying, he passed over a group of land girls who, toiling in very hot weather, were working topless in the fields. Their exact position was carefully charted, 'so that it could remain as a focal point for many low level flights thereafter'.[32] How far sexual curiosity progressed into sexual adventure and physical consummation is not always easy to establish. The disruptions of wartime certainly led to a temporary loosening of the standards of pre-war sexual morality, and judging from the accounts of young female bohemians such as Mary Wesley and Joan Wyndham, the young flyers of the RAF participated fully in this new climate of increased sexual freedom. Among the many lovers Mary Wesley took in the afternoons to her room in the Ritz Hotel was a Spitfire reconnaissance pilot, the Free French flyer Chris Martell (who arrived with a pair of black silk pyjamas with his initials embroidered on the pocket), and fighter ace Squadron Leader 'Paddy' Green (described by Wesley as 'very beautiful' but unfortunately 'a positive stockbroker' in the arts of love).[33]

However, we should be careful not to exaggerate the extent of sexual promis-cuity among flyers. Confidential Air Ministry health reports provided a useful, if not altogether unproblematic, index of levels of sexual activity among RAF air-crew. The incidence of cases of venereal disease among RAF personnel increased from 8.3 per thousand in 1938 to 11.6 per thousand in 1943. This 1943 figure was an average across the service. Incidences per thousand for 'officers, general duties' were 8.61, for 'officers, other branches' 2.61, for 'aircrew' 12.22, and 'ground personnel' 12.09. This wartime increase in the proportion of personnel contracting VD seems relatively modest, and the incidence during the Second World War was still less than half what it had been in the early 1920s. Of course, such figures raise as many questions as they answer, not least in regard to whether they tell us more about sexual hygiene (especially the use of prophylactics, which were made available to men in the service) than they do about levels of sexual continence. However, they do seem to suggest that the young men of the RAF were no more, and no less, liable to sexual profligacy than the rest of the population in wartime.[34]

Even in its most lascivious manifestations, the flyer's interest in the opposite sex was rarely just about physical gratification. John Sommerfield, a novelist who served as RAF ground crew, recalled that even the bawdiest conversations among pilots were 'touched with homesickness', while 'the lustful images that often floated above the bodies of those on the verge of sleep evoked not only desire but regretful nostalgia'.[35] In Arthur Gwynn-Browne's *Gone for a Burton*, a 1945 novel about Bomber Command written while the author was on active service in the RAF, Anthony, a sergeant pilot, has a one-night stand after a particularly stressful mission, 'a horrible trip'. Anthony meets a woman at a dance, and they absent themselves to a room where she lights the gas fire and undresses: 'It had been so deliberate, somehow, but it had been wonderful all the same. Because there was warmth and stillness; no fear and no heaving.'[36] Other fictional representations of the flyer equated their callow youth not with sexual edification, but with unsullied innocence. Fred, the painfully shy air-gunner portrayed by Gordon Jackson in the feature film *Millions Like Us*, would be an obvious example.[37] Nor should we assume that all flyers were necessarily eager to exploit the erotic allure associated with their uniforms and heroic status. George Hull complained in 1943 about the young women of Lincoln 'offering themselves for the price of a dance ticket and a glass of port . . . it makes me sick'.[38] While sexual desire was clearly a significant element in the flyer's romantic attachments, it rarely operated independent of the broader contexts of affectivity, companionship, and the rituals of courtship.

Inevitably, it was when off duty that the flyer had the most opportunities to pursue the joys and disappointments of affairs of the heart. However, romantic infatuation had the capacity to make its presence felt even on operational duty. In Shute's *Pastoral*, the Wellington pilot Peter Marshall is on a mission when he realizes he has fallen in love with Gervase Robertson. He performs his tasks in the cockpit like an automaton, for: 'All the way from Hartley Magna to Essen and back from Essen to Hartley Magna his mind was only on Gervase. The vast glow of smoke and flame that they saw fifty miles away did not excite him.'[39] Johnny Kinsman, in John Watson's novel, is also over Germany when he sees in his imagination Julie, the former girlfriend of a dead comrade, and the woman who eventually becomes his lover.[40] Some authors reversed this device of flyers daydreaming of their lovers while in the air. In Roald Dahl's short story 'Only This', the girlfriend of a bomber pilot watches his aircraft pass overhead on its way to Germany, and imagines herself in the cockpit at his side.[41] One of the most moving imaginative collapsings of the barrier between the worlds of combat and romantic passion comes in the opening scene of Powell and Pressburger's 1946 cinematic fantasy, *A Matter of Life and Death*, in which Flight Lieutenant Peter Carter (David Niven) falls in love with June (Kim Hunter), an American radio operator on the ground, with whom he converses as his crippled Lancaster bomber goes down in flames over the English Channel.[42]

A Matter of Life and Death was an exercise in flamboyant and stylized romanticism. However, for all their literary licence, such fictional narratives nevertheless spoke to the romantic yearnings of real flyers. Leonard Cheshire confided to the readers of his memoir *Bomber Pilot* (1943) that he once spent the large part of an out-bound flight to the Ruhr thinking about a young woman with 'flaming red hair' who had offered him a lift while he was hitchhiking from his base to the nearest town on the previous evening.[43] Pilots sometimes diverted their aircraft from their scheduled routes so that they could fly over the houses and hotels in which their girlfriends were accommodated. In November 1940 fighter pilot Denis Wissler was frustrated when thick cloud prevented him from performing an unsolicited fly-past over the Ipswich hotel in which his fiancée, Edith, was staying. What invested his failure with greater poignancy was that Wissler was killed in action a few days later.[44] Some flyers looked for tangible ways to transcend the boundaries between waiting and fighting, between love and war. In theory, aircrew were prohibited from carrying photographs of wives or girlfriends when on missions, as they might be of use to German intelligence-gatherers if the flyer was killed or captured.[45] However, few men complied with these instructions, secreting a photograph of their beloved in their tunic pocket or pinning it inside their aircraft. Ossy, the Stirling tail-gunner in H. E. Bates' short story 'How Sleep the Brave', kept with him, in the legs of his flying boots, 'the things that mattered', a revolver, a spanner, 'and the pictures of a young girl, light-haired, print-frocked, pretty in a pale Northern way, taken in the usual back-garden attitudes on Tyneside'.[46] Flyers begged their sweethearts to give them a stocking to wear as a talisman around their neck when in action, a testing request for young women faced with an acute shortage of hosiery during the war.

Far from military service and combat creating barriers of understanding between flyers and their female lovers, the war led young people of both sexes to believe that their generation shared a common experience which eclipsed differences of gender. Many of the paradigmatic literary texts of the First World War had identified a giant chasm which existed between what fighting men had endured in the trenches and the lives of women on the home front. In some cases, most notably the writings of Siegfried Sassoon, it fed a male resentment which regularly lurched into misogyny.[47] However, recent interventions in the cultural history of the First World War have emphasized how many contemporaries were struck less by the differences, and more by the similarities, between male and female experience during the war. Vera Brittain, in her elegy for the lost generation of 1914–18, *Testament of Youth*, published in 1933, insisted that differences of experience between fighting men and their sweethearts were ultimately less significant than the alienation from parents common to both young men and young women.[48] Such a claim required a certain degree of wishful thinking, in that Brittain's unpublished wartime correspondence with her fiancée Roland Leighton revealed that, at the time of his death in 1915, he was making himself less emotionally available to her, becoming increasingly morbid and inward-looking.[49] However, Brittain's belief that the horizontal cleavages of generation mattered more than the vertical partition of gender struck a chord with her readers, and was to be reprised in narratives surrounding the wartime flyer in the Second World War.

In H. E. Bates' story 'There's No Future In It', the supportive and comforting relationship of Kitty, a 20-year-old woman, with a young bomber pilot is counterpoised with the insensitivity and selfishness of her parents, who resent the time she spends with him. Her mother is suspicious of the young flyer's intentions, noting that he looks much older than the 24 years he professes to be: 'Experienced. His eyes look old.' Kitty is 'calmly enraged' by this statement, and retorts: 'He has done things that make him old.' One evening Kitty stays out late with her young lover, in order to help him restore his nerves after a raid during which his aircraft was hit by flak. On her return home she discovers her parents have been waiting up for her:

Her father coughed heavily. 'Does your pilot friend realize that we sit here, waiting?'
    She did not answer.

'We have a right to be considered'.

She stood slowly taking off her gloves.

'You'll agree that he owes us something, won't you?'

She stood thinking of the long flight in the darkness, the hellish flak, the hole in the wing, the shell through the fuselage, the shaky landing . . . Her mind became unsteady with hatred. She looked at her mother. The clean prejudiced hands were motionless on the knitting. Her father with the evening newspaper folded between his fingers stood with his back to the dying fire . . . She wanted to go on speaking . . . She wanted to tell them about the flak, the darkness and the bitter cold, about the way the tracer bullets came in at you so slowly that you could watch them until suddenly they hurled with red frenzy past your face . . . She went out of the room and went upstairs instead.[50]

In his full-length novel *Fair Stood the Wind for France*, published in 1944, Bates returned to this theme. Franklin, the pilot of a downed Wellington bomber, is helped to escape from occupied France by Francoise, with whom he falls in love. His passion for Francoise is not merely physical, but is rooted in a shared generational commonality: 'though French, she was close to his own world: the world of being young on the edge of danger, the experience of running your finger along the thread holding things together and not knowing if or how soon the thread would break.'[51] Bates's novel actually had a number of real-life counterparts, including the story of Gordon Carter, a Halifax navigator who, shot down over France, began a love affair with a French woman, Janine Jouanjean, while on the run. Carter eventually reached safety, but returned to France at the end of the war and proposed to Janine.[52] The motif of generation trumping gender resurfaces in Bates's neglected stage play *The Day of Glory*. The fighter pilot Jack Sanderson, a well-known ace and DFC, falls in love with Julia, because he can confide in her the fears and anxieties he keeps hidden from his mother, Millicent, and uncle, the latter an army colonel and hero of the First World War. Jack fails to make his mother understand why he has decided to call off his engagement to his childhood sweetheart, the selfish Catherine. Unlike Julia, Millicent cannot comprehend how combat has changed her son, and she continues to accept at face value Jack's performances of breezy aplomb.[53] Generational commonality was therefore a significant element in the flyer's pursuit of love, and it was granted even greater stature when the object of his desire shared his experience of service life in the RAF.

LOVE ON THE BASE

The presence of female personnel, in the form of the Women's Auxiliary Air Force (WAAF), created the possibility of romantic attachments developing on the air base itself. At the outbreak of war there had been 1,734 WAAFs, but by 1943 membership of the force peaked at 181,835, accounting for 22 per cent of the RAF stationed in the British Isles. Framing, as this chapter does, WAAFs within the romantic and erotic compasses of the flyer, should not be allowed to detract from the serious achievements of the women in air-force blue. WAAFs worked in a variety of capacities, serving as cooks, waitresses, radiographers, instrument repairers, meteorologists, and mechanics. Some manned barrage balloons or worked as plotters in the operations room. What was little known outside the RAF at the time, largely because of security issues, was the extensive work done by WAAF intelligence officers in debriefing crews after missions.[54] WAAFs were justifiably proud of their contribution to the war effort, and felt that they were an integral part of the wartime RAF, a conviction which appeared to be symbolized by their cap-badges, which (unlike the other two women's services) were almost identical to those of the men they served beside.[55] Much of their work required high levels of skill and responsibility, and it is not surprising that WAAFs resented assertions that they had entered the service merely because of the glamour of the RAF or in the expectation of romantic adventures. The notion that they were there to provide recreational relief for male aircrew rightly rankled, and they were angered by thoughtlessly sexist tags such as 'aircrew comforts'.[56] The memoirs of many WAAF officers harshly condemned those servicewomen who jeopardized an appearance of focused professionalism. Edith Heap was horrified at the blatant and undignified behaviour of a WAAF signals girl, possessed of a 'fantastic figure' and a propensity to attend parties in mufti dress without any underwear. Heap believed her to be 'vastly oversexed and a menace to the boys'.[57] Some wartime propaganda downplayed the romantic possibilities offered by men and women working in such close proximity on air bases, one publication characterizing the relationship between RAF and WAAF personnel as 'pleasant, unsentimental, comradely'. However, even this paean to the platonic life conceded that WAAFs could 'look very attractive, and naturally men prefer it so'.[58]

The RAF hierarchy disapproved of airfield romances, suggesting that even this most casual of all military cultures had its limits, and it actively intervened if the relationship was between a male officer and a WAAF from the ranks. When one pilot flew a WAAF to a dance, sitting on his lap in his single-seater Spitfire, he was court-martialled.[59] In 1943 the Air Ministry received a letter from a public-health official in Westmoreland, who was concerned about RAF orders which forbade commissioned officers from accompanying other ranks in public places such as parks or movie theatres. He cited the case of a young flying officer, 'an exceptionally nice man and a teetotaller', who had been reprimanded by his station commander after being spied in public with a WAAF 'other rank'. The letter concluded with a protest that the spread of venereal disease was hardly likely to be combated by prohibiting young officers from spending time with 'decent service girls'. By forbidding such relationships, the authorities were running the risk of driving young officers into the arms of 'diseased harlots'. The Air Ministry's response to this letter was confused. Some civil servants conceded that the public might feel such a ban smacked of class snobbery, but others were eager to sustain discipline in the service.[60] In November 1943 the Air Council issued a memorandum which required male officers to observe the same attitude and relationship towards airwomen that had always existed between officers and airmen. The association of RAF officers and airwomen was, therefore, 'in normal circumstances to be avoided, particularly in the immediate vicinity of the station' and, if necessary 'in the interests of the service, should be prohibited'.[61]

However, the issue stubbornly refused to go away. Two months later an Air Ministry official expressed his dismay at the habit of some stations holding periodically, 'sometimes weekly', mixed dances for RAF and WAAF personnel of all ranks. The author of this report was anxious that such flouting of the Air Council's stipulations would undermine the authority of WAAF officers over WAAF airwomen. In the subsequent discussion, civil servants appeared open to the possibility of relaxing the rules, but the issue was ultimately fudged when they contented themselves with leaving the matter to the discretion of individual group commanders. Without elaborating on the criteria they might have in mind, they concluded that mixed dances might be acceptable at a 'good station', but harmful at an 'inferior station'.[62] Most WAAFs simply ignored the directive, although they were usually careful to conduct their relationships with officers with discretion.[63] For some, the RAF hierarchy's stance was not merely unfair, but absurd. One evening a wing commander dined with the station commander in the mess at RAF Grangemouth. They were served by an airwoman, Jean Edge, who, without prompting, placed a glass of Guinness in front of the wing commander. The station commander was understandably curious as to how the WAAF had known what to serve him, and the wing commander was forced to offer a rather convoluted, and largely unconvincing, explanation. What he had not wanted to reveal to his fellow diner was that Jean inevitably knew what he liked to drink because she was his wife. She had been selected for officer training, but chose to remain in the ranks, as this allowed her to be more mobile, able to get postings closer to her husband. However, because of the hierarchy's hostility to relations between officers and other ranks, the married couple had been forced to go through the charade of pretending to be perfect strangers.[64]

Other attempts were made to discourage relationships between servicemen and servicewomen, irrespective of rank. Nancy Anderson, a WAAF stationed at RAF Rowley Mile in Suffolk, told her boyfriend that the WAAFs had recently been subjected to a lecture from the squadron padre in which he warned the women not to succumb to 'groundless flirtations'.[65] Edith Heap recalled a similar plea coming from the station doctor, who urged WAAFs 'to save ourselves for Mr. Right'.[66] Nancy Mullet, a WAAF serving at RAF Halton, described how a line was painted around the perimeter of the WAAF living quarters, about three yards from the walls. This was intended to prevent WAAFs canoodling in the shadows with male personnel who had escorted them back to their billet after a station dance.[67] However, in other respects opportunities for interaction between the sexes increased during the war for, from 1943, staff shortages led to the merging of WAAF dining facilities with their RAF equivalents. Moreover, official attitudes were to some extent contradictory. For all the efforts to police romantic and sexual liaisons on the air base, it was also believed that WAAFs should maintain a degree of glamour and attractiveness as a means of raising the spirits of male aircrew. Indeed, during the Second World War female beautification was promoted as a national duty, a vital contribution to the maintenance of morale. Women were encouraged to flaunt their sexuality for the admiration of men as part of their patriotic obligations, not merely through paying attention to dress and make-up, but by posing for home-made pin-up photographs they gave to boyfriends and husbands in the forces. Far from being seen as narcissistic or inconsequential, to have pride in one's personal appearance was vital to the war effort. In the words of one historian: 'Bright lipstick was a symbol of defiance against Hitler as well as against those who regarded it as morally suspect.'[68] The fact that WAAFs were already contributing to the war effort in so many practical ways did not exclude them from the imperative of also looking their best for the boys who flew. Edith Heap was blessed with naturally shiny hair, but if it wasn't 'quite up to scratch', the aircrew with whom she worked on intelligence briefings would demand that she give it 'a good brush and polish'. Flyers, she avowed, liked to return from missions to 'England-home-beauty'.[69]

Attempting to remain alluring while engaged in demanding and stressful work was inevitably a double burden for many WAAFs. Cosmetics were in short supply, as was 'Evening in Paris', the fragrance of choice among WAAFs ('Spare cash didn't run to anything more expensive and desirable', opined Pip Beck, a WAAF in Bomber Command).[70] The wearing of silk stockings by servicewomen was prohibited, and WAAF uniforms had been designed to meet the requirements of function rather than fashion. Joan Wyndham reported in her diary in 1941 that: 'There is not much you can do to make a WAAF's uniform look sexy (apart from pulling your belt in till you can hardly breathe), but jumping up and down on your cap to loosen the brim does help to give it a rakish air.'[71] A Mass-Observation survey of WAAF life in 1941 found that women in the service maintained 'a lively interest in clothes, fashion and general dress matters', and that the wardrobe of the average WAAF was little different to the 'average civvy girl's'. It noted that most WAAFs violated those RAF rules which insisted that hair should remain above collar length or forbade the wearing of nail-varnish.[72] Other WAAFs found ingenious ways to circumvent regulations requiring them to continue to wear their uniforms when off the base. One ruse was to pretend they had heavy colds, requiring them to wear bulky WAAF greatcoats, buttoned to the neck, as they left the station on the way to a dance. Safely beyond the perimeter of the base, they would remove the coats to reveal the civilian dresses they had been wearing underneath.[73]

The testimony of flyers suggests that these efforts at sustaining morale through beauty were appreciated by the men of the RAF. Flyer memoirs are awash with references to 'stunners' and 'lovelies' among the WAAFs. Czech Spitfire pilot

M. A. Liskutin noted that the WAAF parachute section at RAF Catterick was staffed with 'some of the prettiest girls I have ever seen', and was convinced that someone must have deliberately selected 'a team of beauty queens, to help with morale'.[74] New Zealand fighter ace Al Deere recalled 'the bevy of beautiful plotters' who served at the same station.[75] In fact plotters—the women who tracked both enemy and friendly formations with long, croupier-like rakes on a large map table in the centre of the operations room—were regarded as being especially glamorous, a sentiment which inevitably fostered resentment among more regular WAAF clerks.[76] An erotic charge was also brought to the air base by female members of the Air Transport Auxiliary (ATA), whose arrival at an RAF station was always a welcome distraction for male flyers. The ATA was a civilian organization, employing pilots ineligible for active service to ferry aircraft from factories to operational squadrons. The majority of its personnel were elderly amateur male flyers, but it also contained a select, and highly chic, cluster of young women. The ATA uniform was undoubtedly glamorous, combining the dark blue, double-breasted, and gold-trimmed livery of a civilian airline and the single-breasted uniform of the RAF. Many ATA women refused to wear helmet and goggles, and preferred to arrive among the fighter boys with their hair fetchingly wrapped in beautiful silk scarves.[77] The women of the ATA had considerable pre-war flying experience, and some of its members were objects of particular fascination, for example Margot Duhalde, a 20-year-old from Santiago, Chile who, while she spoke little English, had 350 flying hours to her credit.[78] In the early years of the war legendary aviatrix Amy Johnson served in the ATA, and news that she was taking tea after delivering an aircraft could be guaranteed to initiate a stampede of young flyers to the mess. Edgar Featherstone, a flight mechanic at RAF Millom, was one day marshalling a Spitfire which was being delivered to the airfield. The aircraft parked in its allotted space, the cockpit canopy slid back, and the pilot removed the flying helmet. To Featherstone's surprise, 'the head gave a shake and the blonde hair came streaming out in the breeze'. Within seconds a swarm of young male officers appeared from nowhere and rushed over to introduce themselves to this empyrean bombshell.[79] Sometimes the ATA were deliberately used to improve RAF morale. In December 1944 some of the comeliest pilots in the Auxiliary were selected to take a new batch of Mosquitos to a squadron which had suffered heavy losses. The ATA women were encouraged to flirt with the RAF flyers, their orders requiring them to be both 'efficient and pretty, please'.[80]

The ATA's visits were inevitably all too fleeting, but this did not prevent the more persistent, and the more cunning, flyer from seizing the opportunity for romantic dalliance. Tony Bartley recalled the day that a Magister communications aircraft with engine trouble landed at RAF Debden. The aircraft was piloted by Diana Barnato, 'a beautiful female ferry pilot', former debutante, and friend of Gogo Schiaparelli, daughter of the owner of the famous couture dress establishment. The commanding officer at the station, Humphrey Gilbert, deliberately encouraged the ground crew to take as long as possible to locate what was wrong with the Magister, using the opportunity of Barnato's enforced stay at his station to attempt to court her.[81] Gilbert and Barnato fell in love and planned to marry, but, only a month later, Gilbert was killed. Barnato continued to socialize with the fighter boys, spending evenings with them at the 400 Club in London, debating (over a well-made cocktail) how best to deal with getting lost in cloud. In 1944, after a whirlwind romance, she married Acting Wing Commander Derek Walker, a swashbuckling, blue-eyed Typhoon pilot. Soon after, Walker flew to recently liberated Brussels to take up a ground-staff position. By coincidence, Barnato was also in the Belgian capital, delivering a Spitfire required for a photo-reconnaissance operation, and the newlyweds were able to spend some time together. The story was widely covered in the British press, in a highly embellished form, which portrayed the beautiful ATA and the handsome DFC each flying their Spitfire on an unsanctioned 'honeymoon trip to Paris'.[82]

While not part of the WAAF, and an inevitably transient presence in the world of RAF flying personnel, the women of the ATA do, in extreme form, dramatize the need to appreciate the female presence on Britain's wartime air bases, and the consequent effect on the sensibilities of young male flyers. Amidst the heartless materiel of war, Circe was no less present than Mars. Some historians of the allied home fronts have argued that the Second World War saw femininity increasingly defined in terms of sexual attractiveness.[83] If so, such cultural changes made their presence felt on wartime RAF airfields, where a quarter of the personnel were female, most of them of similar age to the young flyers with whom they worked side-by-side. For all the committed professionalism of both female and male servicemen, romantic liaisons between flyers and WAAFs were a familiar component of air-base life, and they feature in the journals or memoirs of both aircrew and WAAF personnel, and in fictional reconstructions produced on page and screen.

Not that the course of true love always ran smoothly. There was a minority of RAF flyers who were decidedly cool towards the presence of women on the base. Pip Beck encountered a pilot at a dance prior to her joining the service. He had initially been agreeably flirtatious, but when Beck mentioned that she hoped to join the WAAF, he immediately registered his disapproval. Beck met him again when they were both stationed at RAF Waddington, and his low opinion of WAAF personnel appeared unchanged. Beck ruefully proclaimed: 'So much for my "Young Gods".'[84] The glamour associated with the RAF in the popular imagination left some WAAF recruits disappointed when they encountered RAF men in person for the first time. Joan Wyndham, a free spirit raised in bohemian Chelsea in the 1930s, hoped that the WAAF might provide the opportunity to seduce a dashing squadron leader. However, as we saw in Chapter 1, her plans were frustrated when she was posted to Fighter Command Headquarters, where most officers were not even pilots, or were 'burnt out cases with nervous tics and alcohol problems'.[85] Marjorie Hazell was ecstatic when informed that her first posting was to be to a Fighter Command station at Croydon. On arrival, however, Marjorie and her friend Joan were horrified to see none of the expected Spitfires or Hurricanes at dispersal. Instead, they were subjected to the less than prepossessing spectacle of an ungainly Oxford trainer lumbering across the grass and, only after some difficulty, succeeding in taking to the air: ' "That wasn't a Spitfire", said Joan reproachfully.' The two young women had in fact been posted to an army cooperation squadron. Hazell became a motor transport driver, and she recalled that after the first few months flyers became commonplace rather than objects of fascination or infatuation: 'The days of awe for a Pilot Officer were over.'[86]

If romance was thwarted by unrealistically high expectations, it could also be foiled by the anxieties concomitant with combat. Every station appeared to possess a 'chop girl', a WAAF whose amorous advances were spurned because it was believed she brought bad luck, all her previous flyer boyfriends having been killed in action. At a post-war reunion of a Lancaster aircrew, George, a former wireless operator, remembered his consternation when he discovered he had danced with a 'chop girl', reputed to have lost five previous boyfriends, at a station dance. He was anxious throughout the whole of the next mission, 'worried lest some supernatural influence working through the medium of a pretty cookhouse WAAF might be stronger than the crew's skills and the other imponderables of survival'.[87] Conversely, WAAFs tried to avoid becoming emotionally involved with flyers they felt were unlikely to complete their tour of duty. Pip Beck once had the eerie experience, when dancing with a pleasant and unassuming Scottish sergeant pilot, of suddenly having a premonition that he was 'for the chop'. Sure enough, he failed to return from his next operation. Superstition often provided an alibi for a more rational solicitude about the risks of embarking on a love affair when air-force casualty figures were so daunting. Pip Beck met an American, Andy, who was serving in Bomber Command. After spending an evening with her at a dance, he contented himself with planting a chaste kiss on her forehead, stroking her hair, and then making a speedy departure. His reluctance to take matters any further was, Beck wistfully recollected, well founded, since he shortly after failed to return from a mission over Berlin.[88]

However, the regular contact between WAAFs and aircrew created the space for everything from mild flirtation to serious relationships, offering the opportunity not just for sexual release, but for the sympathetic comfort and companionship which flyers also cherished. A particular intimacy might develop between flyers and parachute packers. Packers had to have strong hands and wrists, but also had to be highly alert, as one act of carelessness could cost a man's life. A WAAF parachute packer, interviewed in 1942, explained that 'every parachute is a person to me'.[89] In Richard Pape's autobiographical account of a raid on Berlin in 1941, during which his plane was shot down, he relates how he spends the last hour before operations with Blondie, his WAAF lover, who earlier that day had folded and packed his parachute for him. He recalled their laying together on his thick flying coat on some waste ground by the base's bomb dump, stroking 'her small, oval face' and cupping 'her golden hair' in his hands: 'The touch of her soft skin is alive in my senses even today . . . We lay there for a long time. A fighter plane droned across the sky, bringing me to my senses. It was time to part.' The significance of this tender passage is heightened when juxtaposed with the remainder of the book, which is a distinctly unsentimental rendering of the horrors of combat and the privations of a prisoner-of-war camp.[90] In Nevil Shute's *Pastoral*, WAAF officer Gervase and the Wellington pilot Peter Marshall are brought together by a shared love of the countryside, taking walks, picking primroses, and watching badgers play at night. However, Gervase's companionship also extended to acting as a helpmate to the male bonding vital to the performance of Peter's military effectiveness. When Peter's crew become increasingly stressed and fractious, it is Gervase who organizes a fishing trip which reunites them. Love here is not, therefore, a distraction from, but rather an aid to, combat efficiency, 'as essential a commodity as petrol', as Peter's commander characterizes it.[91]

A select number of WAAFs had cemented their closeness to aircrew by actually having the opportunity to be taken up in an aircraft. Pip Beck was smuggled by a Canadian flight sergeant, Cliff, onto his Lancaster during a low-level formation exercise, in clear contravention of RAF regulations.[92] Some WAAFs unsuccessfully tried to persuade pilots to take them on missions. In one extraordinary case, one WAAF actually succeeded. Rosemary Britten was a WAAF intelligence officer with 38 Group RAF. On 24 March 1945 she accompanied the crew of a Stirling bomber which was towing a glider during Operation Varsity, an airborne assault in support of the crossing of the Rhine. The crew colluded in her plan, carrying her parachute and life-jacket, so that, as she approached the aircraft before take-off, she 'merely looked like a love-sick Waff officer bidding a fond farewell to the brave unto the very last moment'. Her regulation aircrew escape kit was supplemented by powder and lipstick, although she refrained from wearing either because she 'wanted to look like a German girl in case of baling out'. The Stirling was hit by flak on the return flight, and had to make an emergency landing at an American air base. When the Americans greeted the appearance of a woman among the crew with consternation, the RAF pilot dissembled by insisting that the RAF regularly took WAAFs on missions with them.[93]

The physical proximity which airfield romances permitted was a mixed blessing, since the contact between, and separation from, lovers was more starkly and regularly juxtaposed than it was away from the base. One of the most affecting images of the Second World War is a photograph of uniformed WAAFs waving off Lancaster bombers as they taxi, in the evening twilight, along the departure runway of a Lincolnshire airfield.[94] WAAFs often drove aircrew to dispersal, so a female presence was registered on the very threshold of embarking on a mission. Miles Tripp described how the pilot of his Lancaster had narrowly avoided crashing their aircraft (which was carrying a full bomb-load) when he performed a dramatic take-off to impress his girlfriend, a WAAF working in the control tower.⁹⁵ WAAFs were also there when the aircraft returned. Jean Smith recorded how she and her fellow WAAF flight mechanics awaited the first lights of returning aircraft at dawn: 'Can one imagine the feeling if a beloved boyfriend was bringing it home? Nearly all the [female] flight mechanics had boyfriends from the air crews. So, there we were brewing up the tea on the stove and waiting.'⁹⁶ Sometimes, of course, they waited in vain. A short story by an RAF sergeant, N. A. Varley, 'They Also Serve', portrayed a WAAF driver, 'tired and very cold', waiting, with her hope evaporating, for a Wellington bomber that has failed to return on schedule.⁹⁷

A select group of WAAFs with pilot beaux were able to follow their missions over the intercom system in the control room at base or headquarters. Pip Beck met Ron Atkinson, an air-gunner from Hull, at a RAF–WAAF dance. When Atkinson was on operations, Beck, who served as an R/T operator, would listen anxiously on the cathode-ray tube for the distinctive accent of his Rhodesian skipper, as their time for return approached.⁹⁸ Some female R/T operators might even exchange cheery banter and risqué remarks with their boyfriends, or engage in what was called 'binding', good-natured flirtation with flyers they might know only vaguely, if at all. The strain of combat could sometimes diminish inhibitions. Joan Wyndham recalled fighter pilots engaging in 'filthy' and facetious comments on air such as: 'What's your name? Where do you come from? Chelsea, eh? Coo-er! Bet you're hot stuff.'⁹⁹ Some flyers, by contrast, clearly felt the presence of WAAFs in the operations room required them to maintain an almost courtly decorum, even in the most trying of circumstances. When Peter Townsend was shot up by a Messerschmidt 110 during the Battle of Britain, he muttered 'Christ', but in a hushed voice, 'as if I had spilled some tea on the drawing-room carpet', so 'that the ladies would not hear'.¹⁰⁰ In the imaginative domain, it was the poetic rather than the profane possibilities of the on-air dialogue between the flyer and a female R/T operator which proved most compelling, featuring in several fictional narratives, not least the famous opening scene of *A Matter of Life and Death*.

WAAFs working in the operations room would endeavour to keep their overwhelming sense of relief under control as they wrote, in the precise manner of a schoolmistress, the large 'M' (for Mission Completed) next to the aircraft code (for example, B for Bertie, or D for Donald) of their beloved's aircraft on the massive blackboard which always filled the back wall of the operations room. In *Pastoral*, Gervase struggles to maintain self-discipline as Peter's aircraft is reported hit by flak. After a night of tension, Peter eventually returns safely.¹⁰¹ Others were not so fortunate, and many an operations room WAAF was to be found stoically writing up her signal log at the end of a shift, in numb shock at the realization that the word 'missing', carefully and dispassionately chalked on the board next to P for Popsie, meant that her friend and lover would not be coming home. Edith Heap became engaged to fighter pilot Denis Wissler, and they scheduled their wedding for 4 December 1940. However, on 11 November, while plotting on the blackboard in the operations room, she heard the cry over the air of 'blue four going down in the sea', which she quickly came to realize was code for the loss of her fiancé's aircraft.[102] The privileged position of being granted a greater access to their lovers than that enjoyed by their civilian equivalents had a tragic corollary for WAAFs: it brought them into closer proximity with their physical annihilation. Heap recalls that the smell of burning flesh from crashes would permeate the airfield quarters where WAAFs were living and working.[103] Joan Hamer visited the RAF chapel on her station to pay her respects to three New Zealanders killed when their aircraft crashed on take-off. Despite being encased in their coffins, she was overpowered by the stench of burnt flesh, a moment of horror she was still able to vividly recall over forty years later.[104] Physical proximity inevitably led to emotional involvement. When the WAAFs stationed at RAF Scampton were informed on the morning after the legendary Dambusters raid that fifty-six men had been lost, they burst into tears, and for days remained in a state of shock. The RAF hierarchy decided to reassign the WAAFs at Scampton to different squadrons, in the belief that the women had become too involved with the aircrews to function efficiently.[105]

One former WAAF, Jean Smith, claimed that aircrew preferred to spend their time with WAAFs rather than civilian women, as 'we knew a side to them that these civilian girls did not'.[106] Jean Wright, a WAAF stationed in the West Country, befriended Stewart, 'a gentle, quiet bomber pilot'. Taking walks along the Cornish coastline, they had serious conversations about the horrors of combat and the moral basis of the war effort. When Stewart was posted to North Africa, they determined to continue these earnest discussions by letter. However, to Jean's distress, her second airmail letter was returned with an official stamp informing her that the recipient was 'missing—presumed dead'.[107] Flyers certainly felt comfortable about sharing their private fears and vulnerability with WAAFs, at a time when they were obliged to preserve a façade of composure and nonchalance in the presence of male comrades, their families, and the wider public. This type of emotional support offered by WAAFs was most pertinent in the hours directly after the return from a mission. Men would frequently spend time with WAAFs during, or immediately after, debriefing, allowing them to 'get things off their chest' before returning to their quarters to get some much-needed sleep. Edith Heap, who served as an intelligence officer, recalled WAAFs regularly consoling men in tears, 'but no one ever mentioned it. These things were sacrosanct.' Heap herself comforted a bomber pilot shaking with nerves, whom she talked to 'rather like one of my horses frightened by rough handling'.[108] The bluff of male stoicism which featured so often in popular representations of the flyer therefore obscured private emoting of which female servicewomen were the only witnesses. Some older WAAFs took an almost maternal interest in aircrew. Joyce Brotherton, an intelligence officer with 207 Squadron, was around twenty years older than the flyers to whom she became a friend, confidante, and talisman. Aircrew insisted that Joyce be present in the caravan at the end of the runway during take-off, in all weathers. Watching their Lancasters depart, she 'felt like the old hen who watches her adopted children when they first become waterborne and sail away from her'. For Joyce, the bomber boys were 'my family'.[109] Even younger WAAFs acted as surrogate mothers, darning socks and ironing shirts, or sewing wings on battledress. By such small acts of kindness, by ensuring the messes were decorated with flowers, or by helping officers from less privileged backgrounds polish up their table manners, WAAFs ensured that the female presence on air bases was as much domestic as it was erotic. Many WAAF memoirs were rightfully concerned that the sexual innuendo which often characterized flyers' banter with WAAFs should not be allowed to obscure the practical and emotional support that servicewomen gave to the men who flew.[110]

It is important not to romanticize the relationships between RAF flyers and WAAF personnel. Heart-rending tales of a dashing squadron leader having his head turned by a fine ankle and a whiff of 'Evening in Paris' at the station dance, or of the shy young air-gunner sharing a love of birdwatching with a cookhouse WAAF, should be set against stories of sexual harassment or embarrassing fumbles in the shadowy spaces under the wings of parked aircraft. Jean Smith recalled the presence of 'predatory' men (married officers being the worst offenders, in her opinion) on her base at RAF Trowbridge. She also noted another darker side to love on the base. Some unmarried WAAFs became pregnant, and tried to induce miscarriages. Others were discharged from the service or were posted to a different station, conditional on giving their baby up for adoption. There was a serious sexual double standard here, in that men merely had to report to their CO that they had got a girl 'into trouble', and they would be posted elsewhere within twenty-four hours, but without further consequences.[111] However, these more unsentimental or squalid aspects of RAF–WAAF relations cannot detract from the fact that the presence of so many women on RAF bases created space for male–female companionship and heterosexual desire to an extent that was rare in military cultures.

That said, the wartime flyer in love tells us something about British masculinity in the 1940s which has implications beyond the highly specific culture of the RAF itself. During the Second World War the British state came to accept that the obligations of wartime service it imposed on its citizens, both male and female (women, after all, were also conscripted after 1942), needed to be matched by the state taking up responsibility for the social well-being of the population once the war was over. The reward for service to a warfare state would be a post-war welfare state, providing material rewards in the form of better schools, houses, health, and work for all. Those who came, by the end of the war, to flesh out these aspirations for social reconstruction into concrete policies and plans saw material improvement as bolstering the rebuilding of family life, the latter secured through an emphasis on the companionate marriage and mutual emotional support between men and women.[112] Love and marriage, as much as a new council house or free hospital care, were the right and reward of the post-war citizen, provided they remained within the domains of sexual continence and heterosexuality. Narratives surrounding the flyer encapsulate both sides of this wartime compact. The flyer in war was the citizen called to duty by the state in defence of the nation. The flyer in love was the citizen anticipating a post-war future in which the reward for sacrifice would be a material security in which romantic love and companionship would flourish. The First World War, and the emasculating effects of the inter-war depression, had appeared to promote a male anger that had sought solace in the compensatory hyper-masculinity of fascism. This time, it was imperative that a world war did not morph into a sex war.[113] Men needed to become efficient killing machines, but it was vital that they should not become so hardened that they failed to successfully reintegrate into post-war society. For this reason, the 'love pangs' of George Hull's Lancaster crew had a political, as well as a purely personal, connotation.

4

Husbands and Fathers

The romantic distractions of the flyer ensured that the wartime RAF was never a closed homosocial world in which masculinity operated independently of a female presence. Moreover, for many RAF men affairs of the heart were to progress to marriage and parenthood. In peacetime these claims of domesticity might have been seen as unremarkable, or would have even been actively encouraged by political and cultural agencies which promoted family life as an essential foundation of social stability. However, in wartime there was inevitably more ambiguity about servicemen maintaining obligations to wives and children which might compromise their commitment to the effective prosecution of the war. Both the air-force hierarchy and flyers themselves wrestled with this potential conflict of interest, while the particular strain which fell on the shoulders of aircrew who were also husbands and fathers was also a regular motif in fictional narratives concerning the wartime flyer. Ultimately, the flyer, for all his participation in a highly specialized wartime service culture, strove to retain a presence in the domestic domain, and indeed regarded family life (albeit one disrupted by the dislocations and privations of wartime) as a necessary antidote to the dehumanizing effects of military discipline and the violence of combat. If such desires were often more aspirational than achievable, the fact that the RAF was predominantly based on British soil during the war ensured that accessing the pleasures of domesticity at least remained within the bounds of possibility. For many flyers, therefore, their masculinity was a complex synthesis of the dedicated military professional and the devoted family man. This observation not merely illuminates our understanding of the wartime RAF, but has broader implications for the history of modern British masculinity, suggesting, as it does, that during the twentieth century the militarization of men and male domestication should not be understood as inevitably exclusive or incompatible.

'NO GOOD IN TIME OF WAR'? MARRIAGE AND MORALE

Many RAF medical officers were convinced that the responsibilities of marriage and fatherhood placed an additional strain on aircrew which negatively impacted on their combat effectiveness. An investigation into 'psychological disorders' among flying personnel carried out in 1942 concluded that 'domestic worries' were a not-insignificant factor in eroding a man's efficiency during a tour of duty. In particular, mental and physical breakdown were often specifically attributed to getting married during the tour, a wife becoming pregnant, and worries over household finances. Medical officers also noted the corrosive impact of wives transferring their own anxieties to their husbands, either through letters or when the flyer was on leave. The investigation conceded that it was important not to generalize, and that the effect of these anxieties depended on the man's attitude (some used them as an excuse not to fly, while others put duty before family) and on 'the wife's personality'. In regard to the latter factor, medical expertise seemed content to follow the conventions of class prejudice, the report insisting that 'in this respect sergeants' wives in general tend to be less helpful than officers' wives'.[1] Roland Winfield, who served as a medical officer with Bomber Command, was particularly concerned that the obligations of marriage jeopardized the companionship among aircrew vital for the effectiveness of the four-engined heavy bombers. Winfield observed that the vast majority of marriages entered into by aircrew while in the middle of a tour of duty 'came unstuck'. Operational flying made such exacting demands on the flyer that his bride required a degree of patience 'born of an understanding and love that few women could reasonably be expected to possess'. Marriages made during a tour either 'took the heart out of the airman or left him with a desperately unhappy and hurt wife'.[2]

Winfield believed that the most successful captains of heavy bombers were those who could focus exclusively on the job in hand, and that it was therefore extremely unusual to come across a high-calibre pilot who could combine his military vocation with an equally successful marriage. RAF commanding officers interviewed for the 'psychological disorders' report made clear their belief that family affairs were sufficiently liable to interfere with combat effectiveness that it would be better if all operational aircrew lived on the station, with their families out of immediate reach.[3] Some station commanders argued that families should be prohibited from living within 30 miles of a base, and that aircrew should only be allowed to go home during periods of extended leave. 'Dambuster' Guy Gibson was anxious about the impact of his aircrew returning home immediately after a mission to the wives who lived around the perimeter of his station. He imagined the flyer turning up the front gate of his cottage, to be met by a nervously exhausted wife who 'would tick him off for not having his scarf on, in the cold of the morning. Something silly, anything to stop her going down on her knees and praying to God to stop him getting into the air any more.' Gibson recommended that flyers should follow his own example of having his wife working at a distant munitions factory, where, blissfully ignorant of whether her husband was on operations that night or not, her stress might be kept within manageable proportions, to the mutual benefit of both herself and her spouse.[4] Sections of the press were also concerned about the risk to military efficiency posed by flyers living 'off-base' with their families. In an article in the *Daily*

Sketch in 1941, Beverly Nichols fulminated against the wives of RAF men who followed their husbands to live adjacent to the air bases at which they were stationed: 'Cannot women realise that flying and fighting and everything that goes with it is a hundred per cent masculine business—a business from which they should isolate themselves?'[5]

Some flyers certainly subscribed to such intemperate sentiments about the disruptive effects of domestic attachments. Richard Hillary was at his disdainful worst when drawn on the subject of men whose odds of survival were so thin choosing to marry and start families. Hillary 'didn't believe that a man with something important to do in this war wanted the responsibility of a wife, more especially if he loved her . . . All he needed was the purely physical satisfaction of some woman, and that he could get anywhere.' He told fellow flyer Colin Pinckney that it was always 'the nonentity, the fellow who was unsure of himself, standing drinks . . . trying to be one of the chaps and never quite succeeding', who chose to marry: 'He doesn't feel himself accepted by the others and somehow he's got to prove himself, so he does it by marrying some poor, clinging little girl, giving her a child to prove his manhood and then getting killed.' Elsewhere Hillary claimed that pilots were 'really only happy' when with their squadrons, as opposed to merely 'content' when with their families.[6] Squadron Leader 'Bush' Cotton, an Australian Hurricane pilot based in Britain, had a romance with a WAAF corporal, Daphne. While the two talked in a 'desultory way' about the future, neither chose to raise the subject of marriage or betrothal. Cotton was convinced that it was vital not to have any ties that precluded giving his full attention to the job in hand. Those flyers who were 'not wholly married' to their job might jeopardize their own life, and the lives of others, by holding back from giving up all to the team with whom they flew and fought.[7]

However, other flyers who were reluctant to commit to matrimony appeared to be motivated less by misogyny or issues of military effectiveness than they were by a compassionate concern for what would become of the women they married and the children they fathered, in the event of being killed in action. Fighter pilot Ian Gleed had become engaged to Pam before the war. Flying across the Channel on an operation over France, Gleed reflected that he 'loved her now more than ever', but he was equally certain that 'we mustn't be married'. In a world in which 'life and death seemed very close together', Gleed felt his priority was to help win the war, and only when peace was restored, endeavour to 'start off a new life with a happy marriage, if I was still alive'.[8] Such perspicacity was, sadly, to prove well founded, Gleed being lost in action in 1943. Pip Beck, a WAAF serving in Bomber Command, fell in love with Cecil, a Rhodesian flyer. Cecil told Beck that he desperately wanted to marry her, but only once the war was over. In the meantime, he gave her a gold ring with her birthstone—'a lovely oval turquoise'—as a token of his commitment. Beck later found out that Cecil's unwillingness to wed had a less honourable explanation: he was already married.[9] Nevertheless, the awareness that their life-expectancy was simply too short to make marriage anything other than a reckless leap in the dark was a genuine consideration for many of those flyers who wished to postpone matrimony until hostilities ceased.

It should not be thought that flyers were always more reluctant to enter into marriage than the women with whom they were romantically involved. Pip Beck recalled that Ron, the air-gunner she had met and fallen in love with while serving in the WAAF, was more eager to marry than she was. When he proposed to her she tried to explain that, at this point in her life, 'romance was all I had needed: marriage was serious and I didn't feel old enough'. Ron felt he was being rebuffed, and 'turned away, hurt and angry'.[10] Decisions over whether to wed obviously reflected the idiosyncrasies and specific dynamics of individual relationships. Moreover, the proximity to physical annihilation could generate a variety of responses, making some couples more cautious, but others more impetuous. Adding an additional level of complexity was the issue of sexual frustration. While popular attitudes to premarital sex in the 1940s could be surprisingly nuanced, many flyers would still have emerged from a civilian culture in which it was presumed that the full physical consummation of a relationship had to await their wedding night.[11] For those flyers who were reluctant to abandon the standards of premarital chastity, but still wished to experience sexual solace with their sweethearts before their lives were cut short by violent death, it seemed imperative that the traditional drawn-out period of courtship be radically curtailed.

The agonizing that could accompany the flyer's decision over whether to marry his girlfriend is revealed in a startlingly candid letter, sent by Pilot Officer Rohan Evans, while he was stationed at RAF Feltwell, to his brother-in-law Roy, in October 1939. Evans clearly felt the need to unburden himself of the anxieties associated with his 'young lass'. He opens his letter by informing Roy that his girlfriend wants to postpone marriage until after the war, which would give her the time to accumulate the money necessary to purchase her trousseau. Evans, on the other hand, fears that he might not survive the war, which was only at this stage a month old, and wanted to ensure that he would have the opportunity to enjoy the pleasures of married life, even if only briefly. That such matrimonial pleasures for Evans would include those of the flesh is obvious from the subsequent section of the letter. He tells Roy that he has 'known my young thing about eighteen months without either of us getting too amorous on the love side', but he concedes that two young people are inevitably 'bound to be influenced physically'. However, while 'I know and she probably has a fair idea of what married life is all about', he also insists that 'we have no intention of finding out before we are married'. Evans speculates on what might be the consequences of his being killed in action: 'Wouldn't she say to herself. . . "Damn it! If only we had been married, I could have given him that love which I so much wanted to give him" (aside from me or my ghost [adding] "And which I so much deserved"). Or would she say that it was lucky she was not married because the wrench would have been greater. I don't think so.' Evans's emotional turmoil over the pros and cons of a wartime marriage was compounded by anxieties associated with social class. Evans was a clergyman's son, but his girlfriend 'comes of very poor parents' and, despite once being 'offered a job on the films' on account of her beauty, was currently employed as a telephonist. Evans reassured Roy that 'she has no social ambition like so many poorer girls with good looks'. He boldly asserted that it was irrelevant 'from which section of life my wife comes', but he acknowledged that his father, 'with his ideas', would never forgive him, and thus it would be necessary to marry in secret.[12] The letter is therefore a useful reminder of the middle-class milieu which produced many RAF officers, and also an indicator of the reactionary social politics which continued to characterize the opening months of the war. However, it also reveals how, in wartime, decisions over whether to marry reflected those singular apprehensions which inevitably accompanied the pursuit of love amidst so much death and destruction.

Fictional narratives also dwelt on the unhappy consequences of flyers irresponsibly taking on marital and familial commitments during wartime. In Walter Clapham's *Night Be My Witness*, bomber pilot Johnny Somers reflects on the fate of 'Young Lockhart, with the bounce and baby grin', a married flyer who had been killed in action. Lockhart had initially refused the entreaties of his 'girl-wife' to come and live adjacent to his air base, since he feared it would bring bad luck: 'And then, one morning, she rang him up from a pub in the village and said she had brought her bags, and he frowned at the telephone and said "All right, darling", and three days later she packed her bags and walked out of that pub for the last time.'[13] In James Campbell's *Maximum Effort*, Mrs. Harrison lets her cottage to a succession of young, newly married officers belonging to a Halifax squadron stationed nearby, all of them 'nice couples, all very much in love with each other'. However, twice she had been forced to hear 'these girl-wives sob quietly' as they packed away their few belongings to leave the cottage, while their husbands rested 'in some unmarked grave'.[14] In a contribution to a volume of poetry by RAF personnel, Anthony Richardson's 'Song to Hymen, 1942' movingly contrasted the joys of a flyer's wedding night at an inn with the subsequent departure from that same honeymoon suite of his now widowed bride:

> My friend's sweet love came into town,
> With a new gay air and a gay new gown;
> We drank at the inn, before he led
> His glad girl-bride to their wedding bed.
>
> His lady left and her gown was black,
> She never smiled, nor glanced she back,
> And she threw as she passed, on a heap of stone,
> The key of a room that love had known.[15]

If the temper of such heartbreaking narratives of the airman's widowed 'girl-bride' was essentially sentimental and melancholic, other literary texts revealed qualities of bitterness and resentment. In *Maximum Effort*, Martin expresses his disapproval of Quilbey, a fellow flyer who had married four weeks previously, and whose wife lived in a furnished cottage three miles from the base on which he was stationed. Quilbey would cycle over to the cottage after every mission, having saved up, as Martin uncouthly observed, the 'pep pills' issued to bomber aircrew to keep them awake on operational duty so that he was 'all fired up' for sex with his wife. Martin was unable to conceal his disgust at the 'couple of love-sick kids', adding that Quilbey had 'no damned right having his wife on the squadron's doorstep'.[16]

In other fictional narratives, some married flyers came to the conclusion that the comradeship of service life and the experience of combat were more emotionally satisfying than the routine domesticity of married life. In H. E. Bates's short story 'How Sleep the Brave', a Stirling bomber crashes into the English Channel, and the crew are cast adrift in a dinghy. The narrator, a 30-year-old flight engineer, lapses into a mesmeric daze, during which he reflects on his relationship with his estranged wife. He confesses that he had been 'glad of the war', because it had given him the opportunity to break from her. The RAF had been a release from their petty squabbling over 'little things like my not cleaning the bath after I'd used it, and the fact that my wife liked vinegar with salmon', an escape from 'the way she spilled powder on her dressing-gown, the silly songs she sang in the bathroom'. Facing the possibility of death in the icy waters of the Channel, the narrator comes to the realization that his marriage had failed because both his wife and himself had been fundamentally selfish, but the story ends with no prospect of salvaging the relationship. Instead, the unselfish camaraderie of his fellow aircrew, as they struggle for survival on the ocean, forms the basis of an alternative, all-male 'family', whose viability has been corroborated in the most extreme of circumstances.[17] Eileen Tremayne's *Four Who Came Back* (1941) was a socially conservative novel, in which the heroes are officers from affluent families and the villain a pregnant working-class ATS typist, who wrongly accuses an army lieutenant of being the father of her child, in the hope of gaining his family's money. One of the novel's numerous overcharged subplots is the relationship between Wing Commander Linley-Frost and his adulterous wife, Myora. On duty in France in early 1940, the cuckolded wing commander finally reaches breaking point, and writes to Myora to demand that she free him from 'this unmoral travesty of our lives which we have called marriage . . . Out here one finds different values for living.' After Linley narrowly survives his plane being shot down, Myora realizes her selfishness and seeks a reconciliation. However, just as they are about to be reunited, Myora is killed in an air raid, and Linley himself dies when a ceiling collapses while he is searching for her body in the still-smouldering ruins of her apartment building.[18]

However, for all these negative appraisals of marriage and domesticity, flyers continued to be attracted to the pleasures and responsibilities of matrimony. Indeed, official attitudes towards marriage among the RAF hierarchy became more accommodating on the outbreak of war. In the peacetime RAF officers under the age of 30 had been discouraged from entering into marriage, out of a belief that the distractions of wives and children jeopardized the creation of a mess-centred squadron spirit. Pilots wishing to marry had to secure the consent of their commanding officers, and if they failed to do so, the flyer would be denied married accommodation and other allowances. However, in the summer of 1939 the number of requests to marry increased dramatically, and station commanders were reluctant to check this rush to matrimony, which was a by-product of the heady mix of excitement and apprehension which characterized the last days of peace. When fighter pilot Pete Brothers approached the commandant at Biggin Hill to tell him he was now engaged, the latter pointed out that the young officer was only 21 years old, and asked Brothers what would happen if he refused to grant permission to marry. Brothers impudently replied that it would therefore be difficult to send the commandant an invitation to the wedding, at which point the senior officer laughed and gave in.[19] Kay Carroll, the wife of a peacetime RAF officer, declared that by the end of 1939 the 'old Anti-Marriage regime seemed to have vanished overnight from the RAF', and that benevolent COs 'practically gave their young hopefuls away, and discussed the brides with animation in the Mess afterwards'. At the base on which her husband was stationed a 'marriage boom' soon started in earnest. Not merely was there 'hardly a bachelor left on the Station', but whenever she went into the Ladies Room there would be a wedding party in progress: 'eighteen-year-old brides all looking exactly alike and dressed almost identically with hair hanging round their shoulders, tiny hats perched over one eye, and long fish-net veils draped over their pretty little faces; black frocks, gossamer stockings and high-heeled shoes.' Their new husbands, she observed, were most likely to be 20-year-old pilot officers, looking pleased and proud, but also a little self-conscious.[20] Wartime weddings were generally rushed affairs, with a honeymoon often snatched on a forty-eight-hour leave pass. However, the RAF displayed a surprisingly sentimental side in relation to flyers who married WAAFs. An entry in the RAF's *Welfare Bulletin* in December 1943 reminded readers that each Command headquarters held a wedding dress which had been presented by the Americans, for the use of WAAFs who preferred not to be married in uniform. This dress could be cleaned and altered according to need.[21] WAAFs were also married in dresses lent by prominent members of high society or the romantic novelist Barbara Cartland, and in one case, a flamboyant Regency wedding costume borrowed from the Gainsborough film studios.[22]

Given how many flyers continued to get married during the war, it is not surprising that many fictional flyer narratives promoted a positive valuation of marriage, and some went so far as to suggest that matrimony might enhance, rather than diminish, men's capabilities as flyers and fighters. In Keith Ayling's novel *RAF*, Ken is initially reluctant to ask his girlfriend, the 'peach blonde' nightclub hostess Viola, to marry him, as he cannot offer her security: 'I can dance with her, joke with her, kiss her—but that's the limit.' However, by the end of the novel Ken, having observed several of his fellow flyers embark on married life in spite of their limited life expectancy, overcomes his reservations and marries Viola.[23] Terence Rattigan and H. E. Bates's unproduced film treatment 'Signed With Their Honour' tells the story of John Quayle, a Gladiator pilot who falls in love with, and marries, a local woman, Helen, during the German invasion of Greece in 1941. In one scene Quayle tells a fellow flyer that he is more proud of marrying Helen than he is of receiving the DFC.[24] In Miles Tripp's *Faith is a Windsock*, 37-year-old navigator Richard Craig finds it difficult to readjust to the masculine world of the base after a period of leave with his wife Margaret, and two children, Tony and Janet. He contrasts the 'discontent' of 'trite noisy arguments' in the mess with the contentment of sitting at home in his 'special chair', with his daughter on his knee and his son poring over his stamp collection. Craig writes to his wife every day without fail, nor does a day pass without him receiving a letter in reply. When he secures a cottage for Margaret and the children close to the base, Craig uses the delays at the dispersal hut to slip away for a cup of tea and cigarette with his wife. Far from seeing his home life as a distraction, Craig believes it is his family which gives him the mettle to go on with his job. He tells Margaret: 'It's a terrific help to have someone like you waiting and praying for me, living for me as I live for you.'[25]

If Craig's uxoriousness might be deemed unrepresentative, not merely because he is a fictional creation, but because he was fifteen years older than the rest of his Lancaster crew, it is surely more difficult to discount those testimonies to the connubiality of the flyer found in a range of contemporary memoirs and pen portraits. Derek Gilpin Barnes, who served as an RAF intelligence officer, recorded the positive change that had overcome a recently married flyer, 'Quixote', after his wedding:

He seemed at once illuminated by an inner glow of serenity and armed with a new determination and thoroughness. 'Funny thing, being married', he said one day. 'S'pose I came into this racket because I loved old England. But if anyone asked me why, damned if I could have told 'em. But now I know'. Then he went suddenly red about the edges of his ears and told me a regrettable story, just to prove there was nothing soppy about him.[26]

Wing Commander 'Sailor' Malan, one of the top aces of the Battle of Britain, told painter Cuthbert Orde, for whom he was sitting, that 'having a wife and son had been of the greatest moral help to him. It gave him an absolutely definite thing to fight for and defend.' Another of Orde's sitters, Squadron Leader 'Boydy' Boyd, extolled, over a large whisky and soda, 'with much sentimentality', the happiness of married life.[27] Even some of the least domesticated flyers were not completely immune to the appeals of the comforts of home. Playboy Peter Bartley had, by 1942, sought solace from the loss of so many of his comrades by renting a cottage on the edge of his airfield, and inviting his girlfriend to come and look after him in this 'haven of peace', to which he would return 'beat and exhausted'.[28] Douglas Bader, the legless Battle of Britain squadron commander, emerges, even in Paul

Brickhill's hagiographical biography published in the 1950s, as a man who, while unquestionably courageous, could be an insensitive bully. His marriage proposal to Thelma Edwards was made with an 'unromantic and irritating directness' (informing her over a meal in a curry house, 'I suppose we can start thinking about getting married now'). Thelma was obliged to watch helplessly as Bader, unable to disguise his glee, was allowed, despite his disability, to return to the service on the outbreak of war as an operational pilot. She was willing to indulge Bader's legendary impatience and swashbuckling hyper-masculinity, not merely out of compassion for his terrible injuries, but also because, as the product of an RAF family herself, she had an insight into the masculine cultures of the service to which both her father and husband belonged. Bader was certainly not an easy man to live with. Shot down over France, and taken prisoner, he did not return to England until the end of the war in Europe. No sooner was he reunited with Thelma than he endeavoured to get a posting to operations in the Far East. However, such breathtaking insensitivity did not preclude him from regularly inviting Thelma to join his fellow officers in the mess, or from taking a low-flying detour over their house on his return from missions to reassure her that he had made it home safely.[29]

Home and family clearly provided flyers with much-needed relief from the severity of military life and the horrors of the killing zone. However, such welcome mitigation has to be set against the difficulty of maintaining the responsibilities and obligations of married life while wearing the uniform of a service which demanded absolute commitment in the prosecution of the war effort. The guilt engendered by this clash of commitments is revealed in a typescript memoir written in the 1990s by a Yorkshire newspaper editor who became a sergeant observer flying Mosquitoes. In 1936 Gordon Lang married Marjorie Scarf. Three years later, while Lang worked as a sub-editor on the *Manchester Evening News*, Marjorie gave birth to a daughter, Valerie, but the delivery was botched and the baby girl was soon diagnosed with cerebral palsy. In his memoir Lang admonished himself for what he had come to regard as his selfishness in becoming an operational pilot in December 1941, at the age of 30. For acceptance by the RAF not merely meant leaving Marjorie to cope on her own with a handicapped child. The Langs now had to pay off their mortgage on a bungalow bought before the war and fund Valerie's treatment on meagre RAF pay. The letters the couple exchanged became vitally important. Marjorie would report on Valerie's progress, while Gordon would offer advice and support. Sometimes, however, underlying tensions would be revealed. On one occasion Gordon accused Marjorie of being insufficiently supportive of his war work, an outburst for which he later felt genuine remorse, acknowledging not merely all that Marjorie was doing for their daughter, but how solicitous she was of his needs as well, sending him money she could ill afford to spare, looking after their home, and even doing the laundry he posted to her every week: 'She deserved better of me!'

Unusually for a flyer's memoir, Lang's recollections are much more preoccupied with his marital and domestic obligations than with his operational career, and the fact that he shot down a Junkers 88 bomber and a V-1 flying bomb is only granted cursory attention. However, it is difficult not to conclude that Gordon Lang was being unnecessarily hard on himself. Out of the eleven weeks leave he was given during his RAF service, he only missed going home on one occasion, despite the fact that each trip involved 300 miles of rail travel. He also used all his initiative to ensure that he was not posted overseas. When his pilot requested a transfer to the Mediterranean, Lang found another navigator who wanted an overseas posting, and the two crews effectively swapped. Gordon Lang's story reveals the continued resilience of the claims of marital domesticity, even in the midst of a total war.[30] Similar testimony came from Kay Carroll, who disclosed how domestic concerns could not be repudiated, even when flyers were on operations. She felt the majority of civilians failed to appreciate the prosaic private lives which lay behind the spectacular achievements of the flyer in combat. Far from being carefree and 'aloof from earthly cares', the young RAF officer, when setting out on a lonely patrol, was 'probably thinking of just the ordinary homely things that you or I think about as we pursue our daily round. Whether the puppy's skin trouble will clear up, or whether he ought to take him to the vet tomorrow . . . Whether Betty has remembered that the Simpsons are coming in after supper, and has ordered in some beer, or whether he'd better bring a few bottles down from the Mess when he gets back.'[31]

Marriages made in the heightened emotion and urgency of war often proved to have insufficiently robust foundations to survive long periods of separation overshadowed by danger and loneliness. Flyers, no less than other servicemen, came to dread the notorious 'dear John' letters, in which a wife might confess marital infidelity or ask for a divorce. Bomber pilot Johnny Somers, in *Night Be My Witness*, unequivocally declares that 'the only certain thing I knew about the war' is that 'there was no happiness in letters. Their only news was disaster.'[32] The glamorous public image of the flyer often raised romantic expectations which were cruelly exposed in the more prosaic environment of routine domestic life. A working-class factory worker who married a flight sergeant from Cornwall was horrified when she discovered that his family were not the gentlemen-farmers she had imagined, but were rough hill farmers, living on the edge of poverty. At her first dinner at her husband's family farm, she was unable to conceal her disappointment when she saw 'my glamorous airman was wearing a baggy pair of trousers, and a crumpled jacket' that had been kept hanging on a nail on the back of the door, waiting for its owner's return 'to his Hill-Billy family'.[33] Those women who had married RAF career officers had not merely to deal with general household responsibilities, but with maintaining a lifestyle appropriate to the upper-middle-class status of their husbands. Kay Carroll's 'log of an Air Force officer's wife' provides a rare insight into the trials and tribulations of 'keeping up appearances' in the RAF in the immediate pre-war and early war years. Since officers were often moved from one posting to another at short notice, wives were regularly preoccupied with finding new accommodation—in official officer's quarters, rented houses, or rooms in private hotels—or the packing and unpacking of possessions. On one occasion Carroll had to move into new quarters the very same week she was due with her second child. No less than civilian middle-class wives, Carroll was particularly exercised by the 'servant problem'. Carroll's husband had a daily batman, whose wife would come in to cook if they were giving a party, and a thrice-weekly charwoman. Later, she also employed a nanny to help with her two children. However, she complained at not having a live-in maid and bemoaned the fact that, by the war years, it was much more difficult to find domestic servants among the daughters of RAF fitters or mechanics. Problems associated with accommodation and domestic help were inevitably aggravated during the war, although wartime wives were saved some of the more elaborate rituals of pre-war service life, most notably 'calling upon' the wives of officers newly arrived at the base, a practice which was discontinued as the RAF expanded into a less intimate, and frankly less socially fastidious, institution.[34]

Less socially privileged wives faced rather different challenges, not least the double burden of managing the household and the obligations of conscripted service in either factories or the auxiliary services. In some cases, husband and wife both served in the air force. Sam and Doris Miara were a Jewish couple from Cardiff who gave up their home and garment business and volunteered for military service in 1938. Doris became a corporal in the WAAF, while Sam served as an air-gunner on Wellington bombers in the Middle East and North Africa. Sam's letters to his 'darling Dolly' are replete with declarations of his love and affection (he often repeatedly scrawled 'I love you' in block capitals at the bottom of the page), and his concern for her well-being after she announces she is pregnant with their child. As the birth becomes imminent, Doris leaves the WAAF and returns to Cardiff. Sam, who reveals virtually nothing about his fears for his own safety in both his letters to his wife and his personal diary, is alarmed when he receives news that Cardiff has been bombed by the enemy in early 1941. In fact Doris was safe, and it was to be Sam who was tragically killed in a raid on Derna three months later.[35] The fact that women were also conscripted, or were liable to be the casualties of air raids directed at British cities, meant that the domains of the domestic and the military cannot be straightforwardly dichotomized in the lives of flyers, a contention this chapter will explore more fully in due course. Certainly, some authors concerned with rendering the lives of the flyer in fictional form, notably H. E. Bates, were struck by the dramatic irony that it was their wives and children, rather than the flyers themselves, who might succumb to physical annihilation delivered from the skies. During the latter stages of the Battle of Britain, the elation of a fighter pilot at cheating death at the hands of a Messerschmidt 109 roaring out of the sun on a cloudless summer afternoon might be tempered as night fell. Looking northward from his station in Kent, he would be able to spy the red glow on the horizon that marked London's nightly agony during the Blitz, and he might anxiously speculate on whether his wife and child had reached the comparative safety of an air-raid shelter before the firestorm started. In Bates's 'How Sleep the Brave', Allison, a radio operator, is described as possessed of 'a kind of cancerous emptiness on his face', after his infant daughter is killed in an air raid. A fellow crew member recalls how much both Allison and his wife had longed for a child, and 'how its responsibilities excited them'. Instead Allison, his clothes plastered white from the debris, 'walked out of his bombed house with all his excitement, his joy and his responsibilities compressed into a piece of dead flesh in his hands'.[36]

If Bates's story focused on the loss of a child, other flyer narratives celebrated the pleasures and pride of fatherhood. In 'Four Enemy Aircraft Were Destroyed', a short story by C. H. Ward-Jackson, Lofty, a Hurricane pilot stationed in Egypt, takes more pleasure in news from home about his son's first day at school than he does in shooting down two Italian aircraft.[37] Flying Officer E. Roberts's story 'Airmen at Home' describes a flyer showing off his 'infant prodigy', Michael, to a fellow officer. The child's tentative first steps are proudly compared to flying solo for the first time, his unsteady legs to an aircraft's undercarriage, and his arms, outstretched for balance, to the wings of a plane.[38] Real flyers displayed similar emotions. For Peter Townsend, the birth of his son Giles in 1942 was a symbolic compensation for the lives he had taken in action. After months of destroying life, 'I now found, before my eyes, a life that I had actually created'.[39] One pilot, Alf Denney, spent his time between operations writing a fairy tale for his daughter, which was later published as *The Fairy Who Lost Her Wings*.[40] Unmarried or childless flyers were no less capable of affection and kindness towards children. Guy Gibson was devoted to his niece, and even the uncompromisingly unsentimental Richard Hillary dedicated a section of *The Last Enemy* to a group of evacuated children whom he and his fellow pilots befriended while on leave in Scotland.[41] In Roald Dahl's semi-autobiographical short story 'Katina', a 9-year-old girl is adopted by a squadron of fighter pilots in the last days of the campaign in Greece in 1941, becomes a human mascot at their base, but is tragically killed in a bombing raid.[42]

Acknowledging the significance of marriage and fatherhood in the lives of RAF aircrew not merely contributes to a more rounded portrayal of the wartime flyer. More broadly, it makes an important contribution to the historiography of masculinity in modern Britain. In his pioneering study *A Man's Place*, John Tosh argued that domesticity was central to masculinity in nineteenth-century Britain: 'In an age when, in the estimation of Victorians, economic and social advance reached unprecedented levels, the men credited with these achievements were expected to be dutiful husbands and attentive fathers, devotees of hearth and family.' True, Tosh detected increased ambivalence about male domesticity after the 1870s, not least because imperial expansion seemed to require a return to the old association between manliness and adventure.[43] However, literary scholarship in the 1970s had suggested that it was the outbreak of the First World War which really interrupted the domestication of the male. According to influential authors such as Paul Fussell and Eric Leed, male combatants, estranged from their families on the home front, developed new and intense forms of male bonding which they believed to be more authentic and substantial than relationships with mothers, wives, and children.[44] This narrative has, in the last decade, been disputed by historians who have moved away from a narrow focus on alienated poets and novelists such as Siegfried Sassoon, Robert Graves, and Wilfred Owen, to the letters and diaries of ordinary soldiers. Joanna Bourke demonstrated that wartime male bonding was ultimately fragile and contingent, and did not survive into peacetime. Indeed, most servicemen yearned to return to their families, bolstered by political and cultural agencies which saw domestic emotional ties as vital to the stability of the masculine personality. During the war itself, letters reveal that 'home remained the touchstone' for men who 'returned gratefully, and happily, to the domestic fold'.[45] Michael Roper has reminded us that unmarried soldiers still wrote regularly to their mothers, requesting news of their families.[46] Nicoletta Gullace has pointed out that, during the Great War, 'the popular image of "Tommy Atkins" was of a gentle, clean-living family man, rather than the vulgar (if also brave and patriotic) imperial soldier celebrated in the pre-1914 poetry of Rudyard Kipling'.[47] To date, the relationship of servicemen to domesticity during the Second World War has received much less attention, although Sonya Rose has suggested that the capacity to be 'home-loving' was an important component of the complex amalgam of the ordinary 'everyman' and the 'soldier hero' which constituted hegemonic masculinity in Britain between 1939 and 1945.[48]

A study of the wartime flyer concurs with works such as these, and bolsters their insistence that the domestic domain remained a critical reference-point in the lives of men, even when they were sequestered from that world and placed in the overwhelmingly all-male environment of military service. Indeed, the lives and worlds of feeling of RAF aircrew provide plentiful evidence that home and front, far from being distanced and antithetical, were intrinsically and intimately interrelated. Recent research in the fields of modern French and German history has provided some useful models of how distinctions between military and domestic cultures might be collapsed or transcended. Stephane Audoin-Rouzeau found wives and families to be the second most common topic of discussion in French trench newspapers.[49] Marcus Funck, in studying the everyday regimental life of the late imperial German officer corps, and noting in particular the important role played by wives in the social life of the barracks, came to the conclusion that 'the contours of the stereotypical dichotomy of gender roles—hardened, invulnerable masculinity here and domestic femininity over there—becomes unclear'. The regiment was conceptualized as an extended family comprised of officers and their families.[50] Of course, this was a highly specific military culture, based on aristocratic conceptions of the officer as being a courtier as much as a warrior, which failed to survive the emergence of military professionalization in the twentieth century. However, it does reflect a harmony between the military and the domestic which has broader purchase in the history of masculinity. Both Birthe Kundrus and Thomas Kuhne reveal how, in the era of the two world wars in Germany, soldiers developed a flexible usage of the term 'comradeship'. Camaraderie was not merely about the fraternity of fighting men, but could extend to wives and mothers on the home front. Soldiers often addressed their wives in letters as 'my dear comrade', thereby allowing, even if only at the discursive level, the blending of home life into the world of the war front. Conversely, soldiers might attempt to re-create 'family life' in the all-male environment of the trench or bunker, decorating their living quarters with flowers and photographs of their real families.[51] Christa Hämmerle's investigation of German soldiers' letters in 1914–18 demonstrates the complex emotional and practical interconnectedness between home and war fronts.[52]

Historians of modern Britain have been less innovative in their investigations into the relationship between military and domestic spaces, although Joanna Bourke's study includes an intriguing discussion of how soldiers in the Great War, in the absence of women, were obliged to take on 'feminine' and 'domestic' tasks such as cooking, washing, and mending, and Michael Roper's analysis of the letters exchanged between First World War soldiers and their mothers also suggests some of the complex ways in which the 'maternal' and the 'military' were allied, especially at the psychic level.[53] The culture of the RAF during the Second World War certainly seems to be one in which the distinctions between military and domestic worlds were regularly transgressed. The creation of an alternative all-male 'family' among the crew of a heavy bomber or the celebrated fraternity of fighter pilots did not preclude a sincere lionization of marriage and home life. For the married flyer, domesticity represented, to borrow John Tosh's pertinent definition, not just a place of residence, or even a set of obligations, but 'a profound attachment: a state of mind as well as a physical orientation'.[54]

WAITING WIVES

Having said this, what made the RAF so distinct, of course, was that so many of its operations took place not overseas, but out of airfields on British soil. As a consequence, the worlds of the military and of the family were often in close physical proximity. Families of aircrew often lived in hotels, inns, or rented cottages adjacent to air bases. Bomber crew would return from a night over Germany, have a hearty breakfast, enjoy a brief nap, and then cycle out to their rented cottage for lunch with their wife and children. At some stations, such closeness made it possible for wives to be invited to the mess for dinner several times a week. Derek Gilpin Barnes recalled that Quixote's wife was entertained at the base on nights when her husband was on operations. This not merely helped to distract her from anxieties over her husband's safety, but also provided a welcome feminine and domestic presence for those men who were not flying that evening. 'On these occasions', Barnes effused, 'a man might find, not only relief from the eternal conversation and atmosphere of the anteroom, but a fragrance of scent and powder and something of the very essence and grace of "home".'[55] Peter Townsend recalled that even during the most intense days of the Battle of Britain, when fighter pilots were confined to base and lived and slept beside their aircraft, families would come to wish their men well, waiting for them by the perimeter fence. Since most of Fighter Command's combat missions in the summer of 1940 took place over English soil, the war for Townsend was, in every sense, 'a strangely domestic affair'.[56] A subplot to the 1952 feature film *Angels One Five*, a film applauded for its accuracy by several RAF veterans, is the story of Section Controller Barry Clinton and his wife Nadine, who live in a bungalow on the perimeter of the fighter base. The bungalow is hit by a bomb during a German air raid, and the final image of the film is Nadine standing in the ruins of her home, as the camera pans away to show the airfield runway laid out immediately behind her, a powerful visual rendering of the contiguity between combat and domestic life in the world of the flyer.

In one of his famous 'Postscript' radio broadcasts, J. B. Priestley sang the praises of an airman's 'pretty young wife', who lived as close to the airfield as regulations permitted so that her husband could dash out at lunchtime to see her. In the evenings she would listen to his flight departing on a bombing raid, and then in the morning, 'above the loud beating of her heart, count the planes that have come safely home'.[57] Cecil Beaton asserted that wives living in the vicinity of an aerodrome knew instinctively when their husbands were on operational duties: 'They know, as if an electric current were running through them, when there is need for uneasiness, and they know, too, when they can relax and cast off the pall of anxiety that hangs over them.' Some wives claimed to be able to distinguish the engine sounds of individual aircraft, and used this facility to ascertain whether their husband was taking part in a mission, and whether he had returned safely.[58] Other wives relied on less visceral means. Married aircrew were not supposed to be able to let their wives know when they were on operations. Once they had received their briefing, no private phone-calls were allowed. However, Edith Heap recalled that at several bomber stations flyers might surreptitiously slip out of camp and call their wives from a public telephone box.[59] The ability to actually witness the departure and return of their loved ones from missions was a double-edged sword for RAF wives, in that it might facilitate reassurance, but could also heighten fear and vexation. During the Battle of Britain it was even possible to watch one's spouse in combat in the skies overhead, although, possibly fortunately given the already fraught nerves of service wives, aerial dogfights were frequently too fast and furious to be fully legible from below. Nevertheless, Kay Carroll castigated the insensitivity of those on the ground who treated watching dogfights as a pastime. She asked the public to imagine the feelings of the wives of these fighter boys, 'watching their husbands dive again and again to the attack, heavily outnumbered, while around them in the streets people cheer and catcall and thoroughly enjoy themselves'.[60]

If some wives watched, almost all waited. In her study of the Great War correspondence between Vera Brittain and her fiancé Roland Leighton, Carol Acton asserts, with some justification, that 'waiting' was the 'most universal . . . women's war experience', but that it had been excluded from the dominant collective memory of the First World War because it was narrated through private sources, notably women's personal letters and diaries, which have been deemed liminal to the official record of the conflict. Acton contends that Brittain's image of herself as a 'waiting woman' and her close emotional involvement in Roland's life as a combatant expose the inadequacy of an analysis of war which polarizes the experiences of men and women. Instead, Brittain's letters demonstrate how a woman's perception of her own experience was rooted both in her sense of herself as a female non-combatant, and in her relationship with her male counterpart in the front line.[61] Narratives surrounding the waiting wives of aircrew in the Second World War would seem to endorse this plea to consider the connectedness, rather than the separation, between men's and women's war stories. Such interdependence was particularly true of the spouses of Bomber Command aircrew who lived in close proximity to their husband's bases. Wellington pilot Ken Batchelor lodged with his wife 'Micky' in a pub in an isolated Suffolk village, three miles from RAF Honington where he was stationed. Ken usually phoned his wife in the late afternoon to say he would soon be taking off, although he was unable to tell her more over the phone, and Micky was left to imagine the specifics of her husband's mission. Micky generally retired to bed early and tried to read, but she was inevitably distracted by terrifying thoughts of Ken crashing in the sea or being taken prisoner. In the hours before dawn she heard the drone of returning bombers, but there were too many aircraft to count the separate engines. Micky had to endure another hour of torment, until Ken was finally in a position to call and confirm that he had returned safely. Micky Batchelor endured this condensed gamut of emotions on repeated nights for a period of six months, at the end of which, to their considerable relief, Ken completed his tour of duty and took up a ground appointment.[62] Tragically, not all couples were rewarded with such a happy ending. Instead of the reassuring phone-call from an exhausted husband as the sun was rising, some wives awaited the visitation of the commanding officer's wife, bearing the news that her husband's plane was missing. Whether they ended in the joyful reunion of husband and wife or the tragedy of widowhood, the experiences of women such as Micky Batchelor were a familiar part of the RAF story during the Second World War, However, in contrast to Carol Acton's characterization of Vera Brittain's 'waiting' as part of an 'unofficial' war story, in 1939–45 the figure of the flyer's waiting wife had a cultural purchase which not merely transcended the shared private histories of the couples concerned, but extended well beyond the service itself. Indeed, it became a motif in a number of popular fictional depictions of air-force life, not least in two acclaimed works by the playwright Terence Rattigan.

The appearance of Rattigan, a homosexual and lifelong bachelor, in a discussion of marriage and domesticity might initially seem eccentric, even outlandish. However, Rattigan possessed an unquestionable gift for dramatizing structures of feeling among the British upper-middle classes at mid-century, a social formation from which RAF officers were still disproportionately recruited. Moreover, he also had first-hand experience of both the public and the interior lives of the flyer. When war broke out, Rattigan was despondent. Having failed to repeat the success of his 1936 theatrical sensation *French Without Tears*, and suffering from chronic writer's block, he consulted his psychiatrist, Keith Newman. Newman told him to enlist in the RAF, arguing that service life might become the basis of artistic inspiration.[63] Rattigan trained as an air-gunner and wireless operator, and joined the crew of a Coastal Command Sunderland flying boat. On a flight to Freetown in West Africa in 1942, Rattigan's aircraft had to ditch in the ocean after suffering engine failure. On evacuating the stricken aircraft, Rattigan was eager not to lose an air-force exercise book which contained the manuscript of a play about RAF officers and their wives, entitled, at this point, 'Next of Kin'.[64] When the play was brought to the West End stage, with the new title of *Flare Path*, the reviewers offered only qualified praise. In the *New Statesman*, Roger Manvell accused Rattigan of not having the courage to give the play a tragic ending, while Ivor Brown in the *Observer* felt he had delivered only a competent compromise between a routine war comedy and a battlefield tragedy.[65] However, the play clearly touched a chord with wartime audiences. In a letter to his parents from the officers' mess at RAF Lough Erne, Rattigan expressed his pleasure at the excellent returns for *Flare Path*, and announced that five studios had already approached him about the film rights.[66] Clementine Churchill was able to persuade her husband to make a rare visit to the theatre to see the play, the premier declaring it to be 'a masterpiece of understatement'. What is particularly significant about the huge popularity of *Flare Path* is how positively flyers and their families responded to Rattigan's reconstruction of their lives and sensibilities. On its opening night, at the Apollo Theatre in London (where it eventually ran for a subsequent 678 performances) on 13 August 1942,[67] the audience was dominated by the wives of aircrew who were so moved by what they had seen on stage that they made no effort to conceal their tears. Air Chief Marshal Sir Charles Portal, Chief of the Air Staff, summoned Rattigan (in his RAF uniform) to his box to offer his congratulations. Pilot Officer John Riley Byrne attended a revival of the play at a provincial theatre in Grimsby in 1944, scribbling on his playbill: 'Really wizard show!'[68] A slightly more reflective, but equally positive, appraisal came from an officer from Rattigan's own squadron. This flyer had initially been upset that Rattigan had 'taken our secrets and is now putting them out in public'. Later, he had come to realize that the dramatist was not exploiting the men he served with, but rather was demonstrating to the world how flyers and their kin lived their lives and fought the war. However, while Rattigan had been 'quite right to do this', it was still something of a shock 'to realize that he had seen so deeply into us'.[69]

Few today would consider *Flare Path* to be among Rattigan's greatest dramatic achievements. However, its commercial success contributed to ensuring that the image of air-force wives anxiously awaiting the return of their husbands from a mission became a prominent constituent in representations of the flyer in the wartime popular imagination. Deriving its name from the lines of flares which lit airfield runways at night for the benefit of returning aircraft, *Flare Path* takes place in the residents' lounge of the Falcon Hotel in the fictional town of Milchester in Lincolnshire. Close to an air base, the hotel is frequented by bomber aircrew and their wives. Peter Kyle, an actor who is now based in Hollywood, has come to persuade his former lover, Patricia, to leave her husband, Flight Lieutenant Teddy Graham, whom she has married after a brief wartime romance. Peter succeeds in getting Patricia to admit she is still in love with him, and she promises to ask Teddy for a divorce. Teddy is called off on a surprise mission, and on his return confesses to Patricia how frightened he was on the raid. Patricia decides she must stay with Teddy, and Peter quietly slips away, having determined to return to the United States. The play sets up some rather hackneyed dramatic oppositions. Patricia must decide between duty and sexual desire. Peter's Hollywood artificiality (Teddy says of actors: 'they never seem to do or say anything naturally. They're always thinking of an invisible audience') is contrasted with Teddy's unassuming heroism. The working-class characters, the air-gunner Dusty Miller and his wife Maudie, are one-dimensional caricatures, and the Polish flyer, Flying Officer Count Skriczevinsky, is equally lacking in credibility. And yet the extraordinary stresses endured by the waiting wives of flyers are successfully rendered in Patricia's shifting moods during the long night, as she waits for Teddy to return from operations. At times she seems fully integrated into service culture, using the same vernacular as her husband and his fellow flyers: referring, for instance, to the 'shaky do' Teddy has endured. However, there are also moments when she confesses to impatience with 'polite Air Force understatement', and the studied nonchalance of flyers facing possible death. When the landlady, Mrs Oakes, sets up a breakfast table for the returning flyers to dine with their wives, before she has even confirmed whether all the men have returned safely, Patricia declares the neatly laid buffet to be 'horribly smug and complacent'. The play also celebrates domestic attachment and marital affection, even under the shadow of the grim reaper. Squadron Leader Swanson cannot resist reading out a passage from the mess 'suggestion book' which refers to Teddy's repeated references to the joys of married life while relaxing with his fellow officers:

Suggested that Flight-Lieutenant Graham shall in future be permitted to mention his wife's name not more than ten times per diem; and that on each subsequent mention of the said wife's name—to wit, Patricia, or Pat, Paddy, Paddykins, and other such nauseating diminutives—over and above the allotted ten times per diem, Flight-Lieutenant Graham shall forfeit to all officers within hearing a pint of beer.[70]

In 1944 Rattigan began work on an outline for a film script about the relationship between British and American flyers. His first typescript treatment, entitled 'Rendezvous', proposed the story of an RAF fighter base which is later taken over by the USAAF. The action focuses on the interaction between British and American personnel during the period of transition. At this point, Rattigan's plot outline contained no female characters whatsoever.[71] However, the appeal of the waiting-wives narrative, which had contributed so much to *Flare Path*'s success, quickly came into play. By the time 'Rendezvous' had become the 1945 film *The Way to the Stars*, Rattigan had reshaped his outline into a screenplay which foregrounded the marital and domestic attachments of the flyer.[72] In *The Way to the Stars* a bomber pilot and poet, David Archdale (Michael Redgrave), is killed, leaving a widow, Toddy (Rosamund John), to raise his infant son alone in a hotel near the airfield where he was stationed, and where officers socialize between missions. David's fellow officer, Peter (John Mills), breaks with his girlfriend, Iris, fearing the responsibility of leaving her a widow too. However, Toddy tells Peter that, if she had her time over again, she would have made exactly the same choice, and Peter reverses his decision and proposes to Iris. Far from emphasizing the separation between the worlds of male combat and female domesticity, the film collapses any distinction between the two. There are no combat sequences in the film, merely scenes in which both flyers such as Peter or wives such as Toddy reveal a common stoicism when faced with the death of a husband or comrade. Both accept the inevitability of David's death, and, in typical Rattigan fashion, suppress the rage against loss that might be expected of those grappling with grief.[73] As an artistic project, *The Way to the Stars* has stood the test of time better than *Flare Path*, largely because Rattigan sensibly excluded working-class characters and focused on the undemonstrative middle-class emotional culture he knew best, and which was later to form the subject of his most celebrated works, *The Browning Version*, *The Deep Blue Sea*, and *Separate Tables*. A reviewer in *Monthly Film Bulletin* declared: 'No other film has so subtly and so truthfully portrayed the life of the airman in war.'[74] However, taken together, *Flare Path* and *The Way to the Stars* provide an eloquent testimony to the ordeal of the women who waited on the perimeters of Britain's airfields during the Second World War.

MARRIAGE, WRITING, AND FLYING

Carol Acton's plea to consider the 'connectedness' of male and female war stories seems particularly germane in the case of one wartime marriage in which a flyer and his wife shared a passion for both writing and flying. On 5 August 1940 Flight Lieutenant J. L. Rees was killed in action during the Battle of Britain.

He was better known in the literary world by his *nom de plume*, John Llewellyn Rhys, under which he had published a series of short stories and novels about the RAF, which he had joined in 1935. His widow Helen, whom he had married in 1939, was also an author, who wrote under the name Jane Oliver. In 1941 Oliver edited and published a series of posthumous short stories by Rhys, and subsequently wrote two semi-autobiographical novels. Rhys's stories and Oliver's novels both dealt with the sometimes problematic, but ultimately mutually enriching, relationship between love, marriage, and the passion for flight. Rhys and Oliver first fell in love when they discovered they had shared enthusiasms for both literature and aviation. They spent hours sitting on Hampstead Heath or in little country pubs, with Rhys explaining the intricacies of a 'flick half-roll' or a 'rocket loop', while Oliver corrected the spelling on the manuscript of one of his stories. Aeronautical metaphors, not to say clichés, flourished in their love letters, Rhys telling Oliver that 'we shall be as two pilots flying wing-tip to wing-tip, who, for all their nearness and understanding, can only communicate by clumsy and laborious effort'.[75] In Oliver's *In No Strange Land* (1944), the RAF flyer, David, confesses to his fiancée Mary that she is the one person 'I can feel the absolute truth of . . . I can see by your eyes that it's true. They're like the lights of the home aerodrome when you've been lost in a fog.'[76]

However, both Rhys and Oliver were concerned that the experience of combat might create an unbridgeable chasm between men and women. Rhys's short story 'England Is My Village' celebrates an intense male comradeship which transcends even death. Robert, a bomber pilot killed over Germany, finds himself transported back to his mess, where he is reunited with all his fallen comrades, including 'Nails, who got his on the first show, and Dick, who went down in flames, and Thistle his second pilot, and Badger, who was lost in the North Sea in December'. Badger greets Robert with a smile: 'We've been waiting for you.'[77] Oliver's *The Hour of the Angel* is the story of a young airman, Robert, and his wife Moira. Moira feels alienated from the 'clannish' culture of the air force, resenting the fact that while, as Robert's wife, she had a claim on the courtesy and kindness of his fellow flyers, 'as a person' she remained 'an outsider'. Her unwillingness to join her husband and his comrades when they drink at a local pub is indicative of a more substantial gulf between Moira and Robert:

Moira didn't care much for drink. She'd never needed it . . . She'd never been sick with fright, lost out over the sea in fog with the engines spluttering and the petrol low . . . She'd never been so lonely in the terrible beauty of the night sky that the voice of the wireless operator at base, prosaically giving a bearing, was like that of a brother in hell. She'd never needed the warmth of the Mess, the blessedness of solid earth, the goodness of the friends who'd share their last pint with you for the sake of so many other things they had also shared.

Robert becomes tortured by anxiety that his marriage to Moira is impoverishing his loyalty to his comrades, and compromising his effectiveness as a flyer.

However, when his engine catches fire on a routine flight, and Robert is forced to bale out, images of both his fellow pilots drinking in a local pub and of Moira preparing breakfast in their London home flash through his mind like 'the slides of a magic lantern'. In a moment of epiphany, he realizes that his love for his wife and loyalty to his comrades are not antagonistic, but complementary. Indeed, 'the further he was taken by the corporate emotion of comradeship the further the balancing swing could take him towards the individual passion which expressed his personal need for a kindred creature to love and protect'. Robert finally yields to 'the full violence of his love for Moira', abandoning his previous concerns that surrendering to such longing was reckless when it was highly probable that he would soon be killed in action. The 'most precious possession' he takes with him on a mission is the memory of the simple domestic pleasures he enjoyed with Moira when they lived in a country cottage in the last summer of peace. These were 'the things for which he must fight with his last breath because they lay warm at the heart of every man's life'. Robert is killed in a flying accident, but, in an epilogue which reflected a belief in mysticism which both Rhys and Oliver shared, Robert and Moira are reunited after death, the strength of their love superseding material reality, 'as an airman transcends the maze of conflicting road and railway lines, and flies, by dead reckoning, straight for his goal'.[78]

The marriage of John Rhys and Jane Oliver was clearly, to some extent, exceptional. As has been seen, waiting, rather than writing, was a more common experience for those women who were married to RAF aircrew. However, their story is nevertheless emblematic of the broader theme of this chapter: that we should understand male and female wartime experiences during the war, not as polarized and antithetical, but as complementary and conjoined. For married flyers, the pleasures and the responsibilities of family life continued to exercise a powerful effect, one which was only slightly tempered by male comradeship and the prerogatives of military duty. In the midst of the life-and-death struggle in which the Royal Air Force was engaged between 1939 and 1945, home remained the place where many men's deepest needs were met. The fact that the immediate post-war decades saw the apogee of the companionate marriage and the home-loving 'family man', is therefore not surprising, anticipated as it was in both the private and the publicized yearnings of the wartime serviceman.[79] As Graham Dawson has pointed out in his study of imperial 'soldier heroes', the 'manly world of adventure' and the 'domestic, romantic world of male–female relationship' have always been intrinsically linked.[80] However, whereas Dawson detects that link at the level of the unconscious mind, the relationship of home and front among men of the wartime RAF was immediate, apparent, and grounded in the material realities of the letter from home or the cottage on the airfield perimeter. For all his fearsome reputation as a warrior, and for all his genuine emotional attachment to the fraternity of those who flew, domesticity remained a fundamental constituent of the masculinity of the flyer.

5

The Flyer and Fear

If the romantic and domestic attachments of the airman reveal one aspect of how masculine identities were forged at the intersection between individual subjectivities and social norms, the flyer's relationship to fear provides insight into another. As Joanna Bourke reminds us, 'of all the emotions in combat, fear was the most dominant'.[1] Fear, even if generated by an external trauma such as war, was always understood in terms of individual anxiety and personal vulnerability. However, the common experiences of combat meant that the way fear was registered in the minds, and on the bodies, of flyers could often be remarkably similar. Moreover, the RAF's hierarchy approached fear as a collective problem, a challenge to military morale, discipline, and fighting effectiveness which could spread like a virus through a whole fighting unit. This chapter examines how fear was understood by both individual flyers and the medico-psychological experts brought in by the RAF authorities to help regulate the emotional lives of their aircrew. Its primary focus is on how flyers coped with the stresses associated with both flying and combat. It recovers the diversions they sought, the ameliorations they pursued, the superstitions they were wedded to, and the personal rationalizations of their macabre situation that they fashioned for themselves. Ultimately, all these strategies worked, at least at the most rudimentary level, and rates of mental breakdown among aircrew were surprisingly small. On the one hand, discussions within the RAF about how to overcome fear reflected the specific dynamics of air warfare, in particular the required balance between individualism and teamwork, or between physical strength and temperament. On the other, a discussion of the courage or cowardice of the Second World War flyer illuminates the broader question of how manliness was defined in Britain in the first half of the twentieth century. Manly courage remained a vaunted standard of normative masculinity, but it was defined in terms which were nuanced and appropriate for the citizen-soldier in the age of mass democracy.

CAUSES AND EXPLANATIONS

The source of the fear experienced by wartime flyers is obviously not difficult to locate. RAF aircrew were a group of healthy young men who faced the imminent danger of serious wounding or complete annihilation. It is almost superfluous to point out that they served in active offensive roles, were repeatedly exposed to great danger, and that many of them faced almost certain death. However, what RAF aircrew were also aware of, either from personal observation or the testimony of comrades, was that the specific complexion of aerial warfare ensured that death might come to the flyer in myriad forms. The advanced technology which made the wartime fighter or bomber the ultimate modern fighting machine also created the possibility of a variety of terrifying and violent ways in which aircrew might meet their demise. For a start, piloting an aircraft was a potentially dangerous activity in its own right, even in a non-operational context. As Chevrier, the hero of Jules Roy's semi-fictional Bomber Command memoir points out, even if there had been no war the professional airman would still not have been able to eliminate the risk of flying. A former airmail courier, Chevrier rationalizes volunteering for the air force by insisting that 'it was not war that had killed all those friends of his whose bits and pieces he had helped to pick up on the slopes of the hills'.[2] In the 1930s insurance companies had been unwilling to offer policies to RAF aircrew, given the hazards of flying, even in peacetime. Indeed, this practice of excluding flying risks continued in some places during the war itself, with the unfortunate result that some companies refused to pay out when flyers were killed in action, a scandalous situation which led to protests from the Air Ministry and questions in the House of Commons.[3]

During the war 8,305 Bomber Command aircrew lost their lives in non-operational flying.[4] Most non-operational fatalities took place during training, when insufficient experience, overconfidence, or a simple lack of aptitude could prove fatal. A regular element in the memoirs of fighter pilots is reference to the loss of comrades who were not even granted the opportunity to prove themselves in combat. Richard Hillary was sitting through a lecture on armaments at a training airfield in Scotland when he heard the wailing scream of an aircraft, followed by a distant crash. A cadet pilot had fainted at the controls of his aircraft. The recovery services 'did not find much of him, but we filled up the coffin with sand and gave him a grand funeral'.[5] Peter Townsend recalled an equally gruesome training accident, a mid-air collision which killed two instructors and two cadets, whose mutilated bodies had to be recovered from trees and neighbouring fields to be reassembled, 'as best they could', for burial.[6] Geoffrey Wellum was horrified at the loss of a fellow cadet, killed after stalling his Harvard trainer. He had been prepared for the possibility of one of his cohort failing to make the grade and suffering the ignominy of being thrown out of the service—what was termed in RAF slang 'the bowler hat'. What he had not anticipated was the likelihood of being killed even before they reached an operational squadron.[7] The Czech flyer M. A. Liskutin remembered that the urgent need to replace men lost during the Battle of Britain produced a dangerously accelerated training regime during the summer of 1940. Liskutin was one of thirty pilots enrolled on a fighter conversion course at RAF Grangemouth.

At the end of six weeks' instruction six flyers had been killed. Of these, one flew into his girlfriend's house, one crashed into a hill, and another collided with the flying target during air firing.[8] Hector Bolitho, who was a close friend of many Battle of Britain pilots, claimed that: 'Death had already become their companion when they were training . . . The experience of death was not new to them when the war began. It was merely intensified and made more horrible.'[9]

If death in training was not unusual, on operations it was clearly ubiquitous. Life expectancy in the wartime RAF could be brutally perfunctory. During 1941 Wing Commander Athol Forbes edited ten first-hand accounts of Spitfire pilots who had fought in the Battle of Britain. Despite their average age being only 21, by the time Forbes's collection appeared in print in early 1942 three of its subjects had already been killed in action.[10] Miles Tripp recalled 'a little tragedy' that was posted on the notice-board of his Lancaster bomber squadron. Under the heading 'New Arrivals', seven names were listed, while directly below were the same seven names, this time listed under 'Missing in Action'.[11] At one point in 1942 RAF bomber crews had a no more than 10 per-cent chance of surviving a full tour of operations. David Stafford-Clark, a medical officer attached to Bomber Command, emphasized the panoply of dangers faced by the aircrew of a heavy bomber on a night raid over Germany. There was:

danger from the enemy, from sudden blinding convergence of searchlights accompanied by heavy, accurate and torrential flak, from packs of night fighters seeking unceasingly to find and penetrate the bomber stream; of danger from collision, from ice in the cloud, from becoming lost or isolated, from a chance hit in a petrol tank leading to a loss of fuel, and a forced descent into the sea on the way back . . . There was no single moment of security from take-off to touchdown.[12]

The austere categorizations adopted by the Air Ministry in its official lists of 'causes of death' of aircrew (fatalities being listed under one of the following headings: multiple injuries with fractures, multiple injuries with burns, fractured skull with other injuries, multiple missile wounds, generalized burns, drowning, carbon-monoxide poisoning) failed to do justice to the full repertoire of the grim reaper, which was as prolific as it was gruesome.[13] Hit by a cannon shell, a fighter pilot's head would immediately be turned into a bloody pulp which would cover the inside of the cockpit canopy. Bomber aircrew could be literally sucked out of an aircraft by a slipstream rushing through the hole blasted in the side of the fuselage by an anti-aircraft shell. A flyer, clambering out of his stricken aircraft, might find his parachute had burnt away and would fall to earth at speeds of over 100 miles an hour, before his body was finally split open on impact with the ground. Bomber crew whose parachutes did open, and who landed on German soil, were occasionally murdered by lynch mobs of civilians angered by the destruction of their cities and incited by Nazi propaganda which referred to bomber crews as 'gangsters'.[14] Sometimes it was the elements, rather than the enemy, that struck the fatal blow. As the tail-gunner on a Lancaster,

J. M. Catford, testified, at altitude bombers would become covered with ice, lumps of which, thrown off the propellors, would crash through the aircraft's perspex side panels, seriously injuring or killing the pilot or bomb-aimer on the other side.[15] Bomber crew also faced the risk of being bombed by other RAF aircraft in formation above them. A WAAF intelligence officer noted that aircrew paid particular attention in briefing sessions to the bombing heights they were assigned for that evening's raid. A pilot was eager to discover whether he was to be on the lowest height band and have bombs dropped on him from above, or was 'one of the lucky ones' who had the chance of dropping his load on the unfortunates below him.[16] In John Watson's novel, Halifax pilot Johnny Kinsman is told a story by a fellow flyer which involves a pilot who had to fly back from the Ruhr without either a navigator or maps. When Kinsman enquires as to what happened to the navigator, the story's narrator takes ghoulish delight in discomforting his listener: 'An incendiary [bomb] from one of our own aircraft chopped his head off over the target area. The blood spurted out of the chap's body and ruined the maps.'[17] Even reaching the apparent safety of a home airfield was no guarantee of survival. Many aircraft crashed while attempting to land, and in one celebrated case a distracted flyer walked into the still-rotating propellor of the aircraft from which he had just disembarked, and was decapitated.

Given that the manner of death could not only be grotesque, but also unpredictable, it is perhaps surprising that many flyers were convinced that the specific circumstances of their death had already been revealed to them. Some were certain their demise would come through being trapped in a burning plane, others had premonitions that they would drown in the Channel or were fated to be the victim of a malfunctioning parachute. In some cases the fears of flyers were highly particularized, for understandable reasons. Harry Levy, an air-gunner on a heavy bomber, had a very specific anxiety about baling out of his aircraft over German-occupied Europe. If captured by the enemy, his position would be substantially different to that of his fellow aircrew, for his Nazi captors would 'surely know from looking at me that I was a Jew'. Levy's worst fears were almost realized when he was shot down and became a prisoner-of-war in Stalag VIIIb in Silesia, from which he subsequently successfully escaped.[18] A Czech Jew, Heinz Zeigler, who became a rear-gunner on Wellingtons, and whose father died in Theresienstadt concentration camp in 1943, adopted the name Henry Zetland, in order to disguise his origins if he was shot down.[19] Short of death, the air war could conjure up countless other horrifying prospects to disturb the self-possession of even the most phlegmatic flyer. The most prominent fears in this regard were of disfigurement caused by cockpit fires or the loss of limbs through cannon fire, crashes, and in some rare cases high-altitude frostbite.

In addition to the dread of death or disability, there was also what might be termed 'fear of fear'. Cecil Beaton suggested that flyers who suffered mental breakdown were victims of an inner conflict between the instinct of self-preservation and 'the social code of a fighting unit'.[20] The fear of being killed was often less acute than the fear of being thought a coward by one's comrades, with all the consequent ostracism that might follow. Another version of this tension between private emotional disposition and public expectations of personal conduct arose in relation to rookie pilots, who were forced to confront the dramatic disparity between the fearful reality of combat and the romantic myths of aerial warfare which had encouraged them to join the service in the first place. If the sources of fear were varied and complex, the manifestations of anxiety were equally diverse. Of course, strictly speaking fear is a subjective feeling which is invisible to the historical eye. However, the symptoms of anxiety and trepidation were all too evident in the behaviour and physical condition of aircrew. Fear expressed itself as moments of sheer, blind terror—for example, a flyer simply refusing to climb into the cockpit of his fighter plane—or as a slowly corrosive nervous strain, betrayed through increased testiness or insomnia. Miles Tripp claimed that, among Lancaster aircrew, fear was widely felt but never openly expressed. Nobody listening to the interchanges on the intercom between the seven members of a bomber crew on an operational mission would have been able to ascertain 'that fear was the eighth passenger on board'.[21] However, even if flyers operated a veto on verbal acknowledgment of fear, perceptive observers were aware of the terrors that gnawed away at aircrew, not far beneath the surface. Lord David Cecil observed that:

So dangerous a life inevitably leaves its mark on the nerves. The airmen preserve a rigid appearance of imperturbability and good spirits; but one soon begins to realize that they are living in a state of tension. The newspaper picture of the laughing aviator, carelessly risking his life, is not really a flattering likeness. It is no compliment to a man to say that he is too insensitive to know when he is in danger. Anyway it seemed to me a false picture. Going down to the airfield with a group of men about to start on night operations, one notices that through the mask of self-control their eyes gaze out serious and preoccupied.[22]

Fellow flyers were, of course, even more likely to recognize that the apparent nonchalance of his comrades was largely feigned. Fighter pilot Ian Gleed described how, while waiting to go on a mission, his fellow officers and himself attempted to play billiards in the mess, but 'none of us could hit a thing. . . It was surprising to me that we didn't tear the cloth'.[23] Geoffrey Wellum appraised the behaviour of fellow Spitfire pilot Brian Kingcome while they were waiting at dispersal. Kingcome ostensibly appeared relaxed, reading and sucking a matchstick. However, 'on second thoughts' Wellum reflects, 'when did he last turn a page? I watch quietly and he doesn't.'[24]

Nervous strain was betrayed by changes in mood and behaviour. During the Battle of France, fighter pilot Paul Richey became increasingly short-tempered and had difficulty sleeping.[25] Medical officers surreptitiously monitored flyers in the mess for the first signs of strain: men becoming restless, peevish, laughing too much or talking too loudly. Waking frightened and sweating from nightmares was another danger signal.[26] Even more apparent were the physical manifestations of stress. As Joanna Bourke reminds us, repressing the inward consciousness of fear was insufficient, since 'the body would betray itself through its respiration, circulation, digestion and excretion'.[27] Even if they insisted they were able to carry on, flyers could not escape the physiological signs of their fear and anxiety. Aircrew developed various psychosomatic conditions, including sweaty palms, freezing, diarrhoea, shortage of breath, nervous tics, or violent and spontaneous jerking of the tendons. Jim Bailey recalled that fighter pilots would hold their tea-cups at an angle, so as to hide a shaking hand.[28] On the return from one particularly traumatic raid on Berlin, Guy Gibson suffered an outbreak of what RAF nurses termed 'bomb happy', a type of shock in which the flyer shook uncontrollably. Later, the heavy responsibility of planning the 'Dambusters' raid meant that, on the eve of the mission itself, Gibson was beset by a disfiguring carbuncle on the side of his face.[29] Peter Townsend was also subject to facial sores as a consequence of becoming overstrung with flying.[30] Mental strain was often aggravated by physical fatigue. Normally, the human eye sees objects as inverted until the brain performs its natural function of reversing this image. However, the brains of seriously fatigued flyers were too tired to perform this readjustment, and a pilot would be left with the disconcerting effect of suddenly seeing everything upside-down.[31] French fighter ace Pierre Clostermann reminded non-flyers that manoeuvring an aircraft required considerable physical strength or agility, and that he was prone to severe pains in the arm and shoulder throughout his operational career.[32]

Nervous and physical exhaustion usually became most obvious as a tour of duty or a campaign progressed. In his short story 'Death of an Old Man', Roald Dahl takes his reader inside the head of a fighter pilot who has been on active service for four years. He recalls that initially he had found combat flying exciting and rewarding. Over time, however, fear

creeps closer and closer, like a cat creeps closer stalking a sparrow, and then when it is right behind you, it doesn't spring like the cat would spring; it just leans forward and whispers in your ear . . . At first it whispers to you only at night, when you are lying awake in bed. Then it whispers to you at odd moments during the day, when you are doing your teeth or drinking a beer . . . and in the end it becomes so that you hear it all day and all night all of the time.[33]

David Stafford-Clark identified a similar pattern of cumulative deterioration in morale among the bomber crews he examined, although he also detected a slight stabilization at the end of a tour. In the first three to five trips of a thirty-sortie tour the flyer's morale was sustained by initial courage and determination. Between the eighth and sixteenth sorties even the most stolid flyer went through a period of crisis, manifested in acute physical symptoms of stress, in which he realized what he was really up against, at a time when the completion of the tour seemed almost unattainably distant. If they made it through this stage, aircrew could then 'expect a relatively stable period until the end of the tour, when the cumulative toll of mounting stress, physical exhaustion and fatigue produced the last of the three critical periods'.[34] Certainly, at the end of Guy Gibson's second tour he broke down and wept.[35] Paul Richey, landing at Hendon aerodrome at the end of the air campaign over France in June 1940, was unable to control his feelings any longer and burst into tears.[36] However, for all these frequently observed patterns of stress becoming more acute over time, on a more hour-to-hour basis fear also had a habit of reaching critical proportions at unexpected times and in unexpected places. Guy Gibson felt that bomber aircrew faced the highest levels of stress in the hours immediately before, rather than during, a mission, standing around in the crew rooms as they awaited the vans that would take them out to their aircraft. Unable to stand still, the flyer laughs 'at small jokes, loudly, stupidly': 'Your stomach feels as though it wants to hit your backbone . . . Sometimes you feel sick and want to go to the lavatory.' Gibson insisted that he 'always felt bad' until the door of the aircraft was closed and its engines burst into life: 'Then it's all right. Just another job.'[37] René Mouchotte reflected in his diary about the complex patterns of trepidation felt by the fighter pilot. He claimed that he had never, even for a moment, experienced 'a reflex of fear' or 'some sort of apprehension' while in the air. However, prior to take-off he would be agitated, inspecting his plane scrupulously and breaking out in a cold sweat if he discovered even the slightest defect.[38] Blenheim pilot G. Shackleton confessed that he had been more frightened when he was caught up in an enemy air raid on London during his leave than he had ever been while in combat.[39] Some fears might seem, with the privilege of hindsight, ungrounded or even inexplicable. Chief among these chimeras was a widespread belief that flyers were being endangered by the handiwork of saboteurs and fifth-columnists operating on Britain's airfields. Despite all evidence to the contrary, some aircrew were entirely convinced of this threat from within. A Blenheim pilot claimed to have discovered corroboration that the oxygen connection on his aircraft had been tampered with prior to a mission. Bill Beverley was certain that a bombing raid on Cologne in 1940 had proved disastrous because mechanics on his airfield had disclosed that night's target in a local pub frequented by German spies.[40]

Psychologists have long recognized that the degree of fear experienced by an individual or group is rarely in a straightforward correlation to the degree of peril to which they are exposed. Wartime flyers demonstrated this adage—the so-called 'snake puzzle'—perfectly.[41] Life expectancies among bomber crew were, by and large, longer than they were for fighter pilots. However, wartime psychological investigations found that bomber aircrew consistently demonstrated higher levels of fear than fighter pilots. The reason for this disparity is not too difficult to ascertain. Fighter pilots, in sole control of highly manoeuvrable aircraft, could maintain the myth of being in control of their own fate. Bomber crews, on the other hand, were flying in slow and cumbersome aircraft, often under instructions to fly in a direct and unwavering path, in tight formation. An article in the *British*

Medical Journal in 1943 related the story of a flyer who had been traumatized by his inability to see his targets or witness the effect of his bombs when serving as a light-bomber pilot during the Battle of France. However, when the very same pilot was transferred to fighters during the Battle of Britain he appeared rejuvenated by the ability to engage the enemy in close, intimate conflict. It was easier to cope with the strain of dogfights, in which one could play the role of hunter or hunted, than with the impersonal and inexorable danger of anti-aircraft fire, which left the flyer feeling passive and overwhelmed. In other words, fear often had more to do with the presence or absence of personal agency than with an objectively defined degree of danger. While combat fears were ubiquitous, the anxieties of fighter pilots appeared to have been subdued by their belief that they possessed an ability to fight back against an enemy they could see. By contrast, combat trauma among bomber aircrew much more closely matched the patterns of neurosis which characterized twentieth-century warfare as a whole. The modern battlefield, dominated by long-distance killing by means of heavy ordinance or the machine-gun, was a domain in which the enemy was invisible and the weaponry of war highly impersonal. The resultant stripping away of the individual agency which had been associated with hand-to-hand fighting became the major cause of anxiety neuroses in combat. Such responses were most dramatically demonstrated in the trench warfare of the western front in the First World War, but a similar sense of immobility and helplessness was to be experienced by bomber crews (especially those in the most cramped and inactive positions, such as rear-gunners) in the Second World War.[42]

In order to ascertain more precisely how fear and stress impacted on the lives and, more specifically, the combat efficiency of flyers, the RAF hierarchy looked to expertise from the psychiatric realm. From 1914–18 onwards, the sheer scale of mental breakdown engendered by modern warfare, and the fact that military authorities were dealing with fighting men who were volunteers or conscripts rather than regular soldiers, made it increasingly difficult to sustain nineteenth-century beliefs that the expression of fear in combat was simply cowardice, a failure of willpower or character. During the Great War pioneers of psychoanalysis such as W. H. R. Rivers began to promote the idea that the phenomenon of 'shell shock' required consideration of the unconscious, as well as the conscious, mind. This is not to say that traditional conceptions of the relationship between fear and manliness did not persist. Rivers's therapeutic response to neurasthenia in fighting men was only made available to officers, and ordinary soldiers who displayed the symptoms of fear were regarded as simple malingerers, and treated much less indulgently. However, despite the uneven and incomplete impact of psychoanalytic theory in Britain in the first half of the twentieth century, by the Second World War the military authorities had come to believe that the professional services of psychiatry were essential to the war effort.[43] Indeed, the definitive history of British military medicine during the war reveals that by 1942 army psychiatrists were increasingly being appointed to forward areas, despite the scepticism of regimental officers.[44] Military medicine now sought to discipline the emotions, and not just the bodies, of fighting men.

In the air force, the relationship between psychiatric expertise and military morale seemed particularly close. Data relating to stress among wartime aircrew often provided the basis for broader post-war reflections on the effects of fear and anxiety on the individual personality. For example, David Stafford-Clark served as a Unit Medical Officer with the RAF during the war. His experiences of treating stress among over 4,000 operational aircrew was utilized at length in his post-war writings, most notably his best-selling *Psychiatry Today*. In particular, Stafford-Clark argued that flyers demonstrated three stages of accommodation to flying stress during a tour of duty, which matched the three stages of physiological response—alarm reaction, adaptation, and exhaustion—exhibited by laboratory animals in experiments conducted by Hans Selye, the leading proponent of what was to become termed 'general adaptation syndrome'.[45] Other psychiatrists who had served in the RAF drew very different conclusions from their wartime case studies, arguing that the complexity of human emotion revealed in air combat made experiments based on laboratory animals of dubious relevance. However, irrespective of the uses to which they put their wartime observations in the post-war years, during the war itself the priority of psychiatrists working with RAF personnel was simple: to return men to operational duty. The predominant concern of the RAF psychiatrist was the morale and efficiency of the military unit, not the emotional well-being of the individual. Joanna Bourke's assertion that military psychiatrists comfortably worked within, and helped reinforce, structures of regimentation and discipline in the services is applicable to the wartime RAF.[46] Miles Tripp recalled that medical officers in Bomber Command were more concerned with helping men overcome fatigue than with dealing with the longer-term effects of psychological tension.[47] The use of psychiatric counselling for men suffering stress could often be highly perfunctory, or even non-existent. Despite his extensive interest in the psychology of aircrew, Roland Winfield, who served as a medical officer in Bomber Command, still felt the best antidote to insomnia among flyers was the physiological regulation of sleep and wakefulness through oral medication.[48]

However, despite the fact that psychological expertise was deployed unevenly and incompletely, with a predominant emphasis on group morale rather than a humanitarian concern with the individual patient, medical officers' reports into the psychological conditions of wartime aircrew provide valuable insight into the way flyers experienced fear and anxiety. At the very least, they provide an official and collective perspective which complements the informal and individual responses to stress which constitute the majority of this chapter. In 1942 two specialists in neuropsychiatry who had joined the RAF at the outbreak of war, Air Vice-Marshal Sir Charles Symonds and Wing Commander Denis Williams, initiated a study of the incidence of psychological disorders in RAF flying personnel. Drawing on the observations of both medical officers and flying-instructors in the field, the subsequent report was submitted to the Air Ministry in early 1946. The report represented both the best and the worst of the Whitehall bureaucracy which framed its composition. The idiosyncrasies and sheer messiness of the emotional lives of flyers remained largely invisible, in a document which saw human frailties in strictly functional terms. Mental breakdown was simply another technical problem that required the application of professional expertise and the austere and unruffled civil-service mind. The authors of the report clearly saw their task as pinpointing the signs of potential mental breakdown among flyers, and suggesting how they might be remedied. The priority of the report, and of the unnamed medical officers who feature in it, was to return the neurotic flyer to duty as speedily as possible. Human sympathy was a commodity in very short supply throughout this document, whose pragmatic instrumentalism regularly veered into heartlessness.[49]

Despite the report's title, there was little stomach for delving too deeply into the unconscious mind. Two military psychiatrists in the USAAF who produced an analysis of war neuroses among American flyers at this time felt they had discovered a psychopathology which was peculiar to the men who flew. In their view, for most people, 'the child's dream of omnipotence' was abandoned on reaching adulthood. However, the flyer was able to revert to this infantile state of supremacy, feeling himself to be the master of space and time by virtue of the aircraft which served as his 'supertoy'. Wanting to master one's environment through flying was, the USAAF report insisted, a perfectly healthy instinct. However, it could also offer compensation to those with feelings of marked inferiority, acting as 'the perfect prescription for those that are weak, hesitant or frustrated on earth', especially men with a predisposition to exhibitionism.[50] The Air Ministry report, by contrast, had less desire to put the flyer on the couch in order to recover the unconscious neurotic drive which attracted them to flying in the first place. Instead, attention was directed to the observable signifiers of flying stress, which were divided into two categories.

First were changes in behaviour detected by others, particularly squadron and station commanders. These included increased excitability, irritability, or truculence, weight-loss (one medical officer reported a loss of fourteen pounds in 100 operational hours), an inability to concentrate, increased smoking and drinking, and a tendency to dwell in conversation on casualties. Over the target, a stressed flyer might be unduly cautious or, conversely, more liable to take risks. Others revealed underlying strain by returning to base before reaching the target, excusing themselves on the basis of defects in the aircraft (such as failure of the intercom or a fall in oil-pressure) that were trivial or imaginary, the latter scenario proving to be sufficiently common that one station commander visited each aircraft before take-off in the company of the engineering officer to restrict the opportunity to cite mechanical failure as a justification for abandoning a mission.[51] Second, there were men who approached medical officers with physical ailments—eye-strain, sinus trouble, ear-ache, vomiting, or mild dyspepsia—which had no real foundation. In conversation with the doctor, these men would then confess to the fear or stress which had produced their physical symptoms. The report concluded that men who tried to use their physical symptoms to be taken off duty were much less likely to fly again than those who went to their commanding officer and honestly admitted that they could not carry on. However, in all cases the medical officer's primary response was to tell his patient that his fears were not peculiar to him alone: 'This helps them greatly, and even if their symptoms don't go, they carry on.'[52] Carrying on, not seeking a cure, was clearly the dominant concern for those who drew on psychological expertise to confront the nervous strain of the flyer.

The authors of *Psychological Disorders in Flying Personnel*, in isolating the factors which determined a flyer's ability to cope with stress and fear, placed their dominant focus on what they termed 'extrinsic factors', environmental variables which they confidently predicted could be modified or eliminated in order to improve morale and endurance. Bomber aircrew's ability to 'carry the load', it was believed, was dependent on the degree of confidence they possessed in their fellow crew members. Station commanders reported on 'the disintegrating effect' of an anxious flyer on the rest of his crew. Air-gunners were considered to be particularly liable to complain and affect the others, but the effect of an 'unsuitable captain' was regarded as the most grave. In one case, an experienced air observer who had never previously exhibited signs of strain went on a freshman pilot's first two raids and vomited each time. When his captain was changed, he was never sick again. Good leadership was deemed to be critical to morale. The most desirable qualities in a squadron leader was that he possess operational experience, and should have personal knowledge of the crews. It was advisable for him to go on occasional operations in order to show he appreciated the hazards his men faced, in particular when losses had been heavy and morale low. However, the authors of the report were anxious that the commander, while being friendly towards his crews, should not appear too kind or sympathetic, and reiterated the necessity of hardness and discipline, 'not giving an inch where duty is concerned'.[53]

While there was a consensus over the value of confidence and leadership, the commanders and medical officers interviewed were in less agreement about the relationship between the specific tempo of operational flying and patterns of nervous strain. Most of those consulted felt that, for bomber crew, three consecutive nights of operations was too much to bear. Two nights on, followed by one night off, was seen as best, but some felt two nights on and two nights off allowed greater possibility of sleep and social relaxation. Few favoured the idea of flying on alternate nights, as it left no time for relaxation. It was felt to be beneficial if a tour of duty mixed up easier and more heavily defended targets. Novelty also had something to recommend it, with many crews expressing weariness at endless missions to bomb Brest or Essen. Seven days was widely felt to be the optimum period of leave, with general disapproval being expressed at the notion of a ten-day furlough, which would leave a flyer disconnected from what was happening in his squadron. Some of those interviewed pointed out the particular problems of overseas aircrew who, clearly unable to return home, required country clubs and other venues during their leave periods. Recognition of effort was also believed to bolster morale, although the award of decorations was regarded as less valuable than the receipt of praise from commanding officers. Finally, a loss of confidence in their aircraft was a significant factor in flying stress. One commanding officer claimed: 'The men are faddy about their aircraft, and if something goes wrong which they can't understand they get very depressed and anxious.'[54]

Where disagreement among the expert witnesses really emerged was in regard to determining the point beyond which even the most disciplined and resilient flyer needed to be taken off operational duty. The report conceived an 'operational limit' in brutally instrumentalist terms, defining it in terms of 'to secure a man's return for a second tour [of duty] with unimpaired efficiency'. The challenge for those who framed RAF policy and practice was that equity and discipline required a tour of duty to be constituted of a fixed minimum number of operations, but that the idiosyncrasies of how stress was experienced by aircrew suggested flexibility needed to be exercised. For example, if the operational limit for day bombers was set at twenty missions, was it better to take off a flyer who was beginning to exhibit signs of serious stress after only seventeen missions, in the hope that a period of rest would ensure he returned for a second tour? Or should he be forced to see out his tour of duty, at the risk of permanently breaking down and putting his life, and that of his fellow aircrew, in jeopardy?[55] Discussions within the Air Ministry rarely resulted in an agreement on this issue. Moreover, defining a tour solely in terms of the numbers of missions failed to account for the fact that not all missions were alike. Bomber Command missions deep into the heart of Germany clearly produced greater levels of strain among aircrew than raids over France or the Low Countries. However, when the Air Ministry attempted to convey such concerns to RAF commanders in the field, they were given short shrift.

For example, in January 1943 Air Vice-Marshal Bottomley, assistant chief of the Air Staff, wrote to Arthur Harris, the commander-in-chief of Bomber Command, after the investigation into a pilot classified as a 'waverer' highlighted the problem of how to define an 'operational sortie'. Bottomley noted that an operational tour in Bomber Command was set in general terms at 200 hours, but that in practice the length of a tour was determined largely on a sortie basis, the accepted standard usually being thirty operational sorties. As far as Bottomley could ascertain (a trawl through the ministry's filing cabinets failing to turn up an official statement), Harris had been defining a completed sortie as one in which the aircraft had bombed the designated target. What troubled the air vice-marshal was a recent case in which a bomber had been engaged in combat over the North Sea during the outbound phase of its mission, resulting in its bombs being jettisoned. The relevant squadron commander had determined that this was therefore not a completed mission, and would not count towards the aircrew's tally of missions on their tour of duty. Bottomley felt this was manifestly unfair, given that the aircraft had been hit five times by cannon fire, during which 'the crew may have undergone more than the average stress', and insisted 'that it would be reasonable to count the flight [as] an operational sortie'.[56] The Air Ministry received a furious and indignant response from 'Bomber' Harris, who declared himself

most unwilling to do anything to foster the idea that our crews are under some description of Trade Union contract to carry out a certain number of carefully defined operational missions, after which they are free, at any rate for a fixed period, to take no more part in the war . . . No other service could or would tolerate for a moment the notion that in war time its officers and men are not entirely at the disposal of their commanders.

Harris argued that flyers had 'no presumptive right to rest from operations', and he denounced the 'exaggerated solicitude' of Bottomley's letter.[57] In the midst of his fury, Harris had a point. The maintenance of discipline surely required that squadron commanders be left to make the ultimate judgment on whether a crew had completed an operational sortie or whether they were just offering an excuse for failure to complete a mission. Most aircrew felt their commanders operated their discretion in this regard fairly, and without prejudice.[58]

HOW FLYERS COPED

Given that the RAF hierarchy predominantly understood mental strain in terms of morale, combat efficiency, and discipline, how did the flyers themselves cope with stress? How do we explain their extraordinary resilience, given that official responses to their anguish (even those deploying psychiatric knowledge) were often far from flexible or humane? Considering the extraordinary demands made on these young men, and the omnipresence of the 'silent passenger', how do we account for the fact that the incidence of psychological breakdown among flyers in the wartime RAF was less than 5 per cent? Many flyers sought a personal rationalization of their macabre predicament. At the extremes, one could either convince oneself that 'it won't ever happen to me' or that 'it will definitely happen to me'. Richard Hillary usually adopted the former stance. On his first day in combat he was certainly more preoccupied with the fact that he was likely that day to kill for the first time, than with the possibility that he himself might be killed: 'I knew it could not happen to me.' As the Battle of Britain progressed, he confessed that he did begin to think more about death in the abstract, but 'once in the air, never'.[59] Others, faced with the prospect of death, familiarized themselves with it, and accepted its inevitability to such an extent that they effectively regarded themselves as already dead. Such a stratagem could, according to one Lancaster aircrew, generate 'a wonderfully liberating feeling'.[60] Some flyers, when off-duty, saw little point in refraining from perilous escapades which in more regular circumstances might have been deemed reckless and foolhardy. We have already noted how the playboys of 92 Squadron ran their fast cars on potentially lethal aviation fuel. Leonard Cheshire described a pilot, Andrew, who, 'not satisfied with trouble in the skies', bought himself an MG sports car, and 'because he was asking for it, ended by breaking the car up'. Another former comrade of Cheshire was Beau, who once responded to a dare from a young woman by inscribing her initials on the back of his hand with a lighted cigarette.[61] George Bell, a medical officer at RAF Kidlington, was regularly summoned from his bed to the mess by a concerned bartender, who simply informed him on the telephone that: 'Sir, they're at it again.' 'They' in this instance referred to a number of battle-hardened Australian pilots whose mess games became increasingly irresponsible as the night went on. Bell usually arrived in time to halt the culmination of their evening of fierce mischief, an idiosyncratic game in which the head of one unfortunate flyer was placed against a dartboard while his comrades, from a distance 'which could vary considerably', tried to pin his ears to the board with a flurry of lobbed darts.[62]

Even those who lacked such a reckless streak could be no less resigned to the need to simply live for the moment. Some, like the fictional Johnny Kinsman, welcomed the fact that in the RAF one did not have to plan or even to think: 'All you had to do was to live.' Detachment, and the ability to desensitize, were valuable assets in the struggle against fear. When Kinsman's Halifax bomber is hit on a raid and Geordie, the mid-upper gunner, is killed, Kinsman 'felt nothing. Except relief. It was Geordie who was dead, and he was alive.'[63] Real-life flyers echoed such sentiments. In a diary entry in October 1944, bomb-aimer Jules Roy confessed his growing insensitivity to the loss of his comrades: 'A crew disappears and each one calculates in his own small way the happy results for himself as if the departed had bequeathed him their boots. The missing are effaced from this world with prodigious ease. One more crew gone to destiny's bag, one more crew, and you are still safe.'[64] There was rarely time, or inclination, to grieve. Wing Commander Athol Forbes candidly admitted to his wartime readers that, 'when a chap doesn't come back, we don't grieve over him. If we did that we'd go completely nuts in no time. We just think he's been posted to another squadron in a hurry and hasn't had time to say au revoir.'[65] Of course, this apparent indifference to the death of comrades was part of the mythology of the wartime RAF, a cliché with sufficient cultural reach that it could be satirized in Danny Kaye's Hollywood rendering of James Thurber's classic American short story, 'The Secret Life of Walter Mitty'.[66] However, many flyers would have agreed with the assessment of Battle of Britain ace 'Sailor' Malan that 'sentiment was sapping', and that it was better to build an emotional cocoon around oneself.[67] After the sixth of his comrades had been killed, fighter pilot Jim Bailey went away and wept, but from that point on he found he 'had reached that degree of sadness which could no longer touch me; the delicate instruments which recorded this emotion were now wrecked'. In future, his response was no longer the *Sturm und Drang* of grief, but merely a dull feeling of hollowness.[68]

Whatever these men felt when their friends and comrades died, there was a virtual veto on the verbal expression of loss. Death, if mentioned at all, was referred to flippantly, its sting drawn by recourse to euphemism, notably the RAF slang expression to have 'gone for a Burton'. The light-heartedness of the flyers, their underplaying of deep emotion, were ultimately intended to domesticate the terror which threatened to shred their nerves completely. John Pudney's verse 'The Bomb Dump' contains a telling phrase in regard to the attitude of flyers towards life and death: 'and fun shall be our cloak.'[69] Pudney's most famous wartime poem, 'For Johnny', was deployed in the film *The Way to the Stars*, a movie which implied that the stoical acceptance of danger and death by RAF flyers could serve as an epitome of the qualities of emotional restraint and understatement which supposedly constituted the British national character. Small gestures and veiled words, not rage or tears, became a common motif in the popular representation of RAF aircrew. However, as Cecil Beaton recognized, 'the realisation of their proximity to danger is never far removed from the minds of these men, in spite of their easy grace of heart'.[70] Moreover, not every observer was certain that emotional self-control and detachment were the best means of dealing with combat stress. A study of 1,000 WAAFs who were suffering from psychiatric problems discovered that women were more likely to display 'overt emotional upset' rather than an emotional trauma masked by physical symptoms. This was attributed, in the far-from-enlightened gender politics of the time, to 'the socially acknowledged and permitted emotionalism of women' which made physical symptoms superfluous.[71] By contrast, male flyers, subject to sterner public emotional standards, were unable to talk about their fears, and were given no other recourse than to reveal their nervous strain through physical symptoms that left them incapacitated.

Was it possible that the legendary stiff upper lip of the flyer actually made mental breakdown more, rather than less, likely? If few wanted to pursue this question further during the war, it is also important to appreciate that it was not just public codes of masculine emotional restraint which contributed to the flyers' reluctance to put their feelings of fear and loss into words. They might well have been concerned that, once they gave verbal expression to those feelings, it would no longer be possible to keep them under control. Paul Baumer, the hero of Erich Maria Remarque's classic novel of the First World War, *All Quiet on the Western Front*, explains why it is he is unable, while on leave, to tell his family about the reality of life in the trenches: 'it is too dangerous for me to put these things into words. I am afraid they might then become gigantic and I be no longer able to master them. What would become of us if everything that happens out there were quite clear to us?'[72] However, while there were undoubtedly those who agreed with this sentiment, there is substantial evidence that wartime flyers, while they were reluctant to open up about their fears in front of comrades, were willing to confide in others, most notably women. We have already seen how aircrew disclosed their fear and grief to WAAFs on the bases at which they were stationed. Guy Gibson was only able to maintain his public composure during his long Bomber Command career by privately breaking down in tears in the arms of Margaret North, a nurse at the RAF hospital at Rauceby.[73] Mary Wesley, who counted several RAF heroes among her numerous wartime lovers, contrasted the willingness of Second World War flyers to open up about their feelings to her with the reluctance of her father to disclose the strains of combat to her mother while he had been serving in the First World War. Her pilot paramours would regularly confess to Mary: 'I'm sorry I'm being so bloody and so rude, but I'm scared witless and I've got to go back on ops. tomorrow.'[74]

Respite from stress lay not merely in the comforting arms of a lover. Ameliorization could also come in the form of a glass of beer or a handful of pills. The contribution of heavy drinking to sociability and bonding among aircrew has already been discussed. Hector Bolitho tried to reassure his wartime readership that flyers drank only to celebrate the fact that they were alive, 'never to stimulate false ecstasy or drown depression'.[75] However, many of the officers interviewed for the Air Ministry's 'psychological disorders' survey noted a distinct correlation between increased drinking and rising levels of stress among flying crews.[76] Some flyers clearly found that drinking helped, if only temporarily, to obliterate the distressing memory of the mission they had just completed and the dread of the sortie to come. Another artificial mood-enhancer which flyers had access to was benzedrine. RAF medical officers regularly distributed 'wakey wakey' pills to aircrew (and WAAFs) who were suffering from fatigue. For many flyers benzedrine became virtually addictive. Doctors were only supposed to allocate the pills for use on missions (especially long-range bombing raids, where wakefulness was obviously a requirement for combat efficiency). However, often little effort was made to regulate the supply of benzedrine, and flyers became skilled at obtaining additional quantities of the stimulant, which they then hoarded and used to sustain their energies during off-duty parties. Flyers undoubtedly welcomed benzedrine's positive impact on their endomorphins. Joan Wyndham, who describes an off-duty culture in which both aircrew and WAAFs regularly took benzedrine while partying, recorded in her diary: 'I really love the clear, cool feeling in my head, and the edge of excitement it gives to everything you do.' However, excessive use of benzedrine often resulted in over-stimulation and subsequent mood swings. As Wyndham conceded, 'you certainly can neither eat nor sleep when you are on them, and you cry a lot'.[77] In Mary Renault's novel *The Charioteer*, Laurie Odell is at a party in London when he meets Bim, a fighter pilot who is high on benzedrine and has not slept properly for a week. Bim's artificial restlessness is all too obvious, leading one witness to suggest that what the flyer really needs is 'bromide and twelve hours sleep'.[78] Some flyers also put themselves at serious risk by combining the drug with alcohol. Tony Bartley recalled a party in the officers' mess at RAF Hornchurch in May 1940, in which Spitfire pilot Bob Holland 'gobbled his benzedrine, washed down with whisky and took over the upright [piano]'.[79]

While senior officers occasionally sought to control access to benzedrine or to curtail heavy drinking, generally they were willing to indulge their aircrew, providing combat capability was not compromised. It was recognized that the ability to seek diversion was crucial to flyers' ability to cope with what otherwise would be intolerable levels of strain. However, the RAF hierarchy was often decidedly slow in providing recreational facilities on air bases which could allow men to find distraction from fear. This was a particularly important issue at RAF bomber bases, which were often, especially in Lincolnshire, remote from large towns. It was not until 1942 that a Directorate of Air Force Welfare was created in the Air Ministry, which in turn urged the creation of Station Welfare Committees, composed of the station commander, chaplain, catering officer, education officer, entertainments officer, a senior WAAF officer, and the physical-fitness officer. In 1943 the Directorate began publishing a monthly bulletin, which gave advice on creating leisure activities on and around air bases. Station Welfare Committees were encouraged to distribute large-scale maps to personnel interested in hiking, to talk to local landowners about securing places for men to go fishing, or to set up cycling clubs. Suggestions were made on how to arrange plays, cabaret shows, or dances on the base, with detailed guidance on how to cover cement floors in hangars so as to make them more suitable for dancing (RAF personnel had complained that they resulted in worn shoe leather and slowed the tempo of the jitterbug). The Directorate also entered into schemes with manufacturers to provide gramophone records at a discount rate, and with the National Gallery to loan artworks to messes.[80] However, some bases remained woefully lacking in leisure facilities.[81] The letters of George Hull, a navigator in Lancasters, regularly dwelt on the inadequacies of RAF Wigsley in Lincolnshire. 'Pigsley', as he called it, was 'a dunghill', and the only diversion on offer was to 'get sozzled every night'. Forays into Lincoln were little improvement, given the lack of cultural outlets in the town (Hull was a music lover) and what the disenchanted airman believed to be open hostility towards the RAF from local bartenders and café proprietors.[82]

Relatively few flyers believed that their fears would be mitigated by earnest subscription to the abstract notions of God, King, and Country. In June 1940 *The Times* published 'An Airman to his Mother', which purported to be a posthumous letter from a flyer, who had asked that his commanding officer forward the epistle to his mother in the event of him failing to return from a mission. The officer, it was claimed, had been sufficiently impressed by the sentiments expressed in the letter that he sought the permission of the downed flyer's mother to publish and publicize it. The letter contained an elevated patriotism which might be more readily associated with 1914 than 1940, and certainly suggested that the young man had been unacquainted with the lacerating critique of such sentiments in the war poetry of Siegfried Sassoon or Wilfred Owen. The young flyer counselled his grieving mother not to be sad, for he would have died doing his duty to the British Empire, and defeating 'the greatest organized challenge to Christianity and civilization that the world has ever seen'. His sacrifice will not have been in vain, for 'I shall have lived and died an Englishman. Nothing else matters a jot.' The propaganda value of this letter from a 'loving son' was obvious, especially in the immediate aftermath of the fall of France, where its sentimentalized patriotism and somewhat priggish tone was less jarring than it was to become in the more cynical and war-weary years which followed.[83] However, how far the letter matched the outlook of the majority of the men who flew is doubtful. Good patriots they undoubtedly were, but happy martyrs, who would die for their country without regret, they certainly were not. Eric Rawlings, an air-gunner killed over Germany in 1942, also left a letter for his parents, to 'keep as a remembrance in case anything should happen to me'. Like the letter in *The Times*, Rawlings assured his parents that he knew 'what I am fighting for'. However, he identified this not in the inflated rhetoric of public duty to nation or the defence of western civilization, but in the more modest, yet ultimately more convincing, private obligations to 'the things which I revere and esteem most in the world—my family and my home'. 'I'm fighting', Rawlings insisted, 'so that in the future people will have the chance to live as happily as we all did together before the war without interference.'[84] John Sommerfield, a writer who worked as ground crew during the war, contrasted the 'realm of official announcements, patriotic exhortations and newspaper articles', which declared that flyers had not died in vain because they had been fighting to preserve the British way of life, with the 'submerged, undocumented, inarticulate world' which constituted the emotional responses of real flyers. In this more intimate, private world, men's feelings were 'sterile, undirected', characterized by a fundamental helplessness in the face of fate.[85] Roland Winfield, who served both as a medical officer and as aircrew in Bomber Command, argued that pride in a job well done—'putting your bombs exactly where they'd hurt most—fair and square in the centre of the target, regardless of all opposition'—was more likely to sustain a flyer's peace of mind than pride in one's country.[86]

Establishing how far religion may have alleviated the fear and anxiety of the flyer is problematic. While there may have been tokens of a religious revival during the war, albeit ones which ultimately failed to slow the relentless march of secularization in Britain in the twentieth century, very few memoirs, diaries, or letters of flyers make reference to religious belief, in either formal or informal terms.[87] Even Leonard Cheshire, who after the war became a devout Catholic and renounced materialism in favour of a profound spirituality, made no reference to God in either his conversations with comrades or his wartime memoirs.[88] There were obviously chaplains on RAF air bases, but compulsory church parades were attended under duress, to the accompaniment of catcalls and whistles.[89] One progressive chaplain, John Collins, abolished compulsory worship at the RAF camp at Yatesbury, and replaced it with a small discussion group, composed of a number of keen Christians. However, Collins was only too aware that most military chaplains were usually second-rate figures who had been pushed into the armed services by bishops, eager to remove mediocre or troublesome clerics from their dioceses.[90] The reminiscences of Jewish flyers such as Ken Adam and Harry Levy seem to imply—although they are never explicit on the matter—that their world-view was essentially secular.[91] Of course, a lack of evidence of religious observance need not indicate a lack of private religious faith. However, despite frequent resort to the analogy of 'God is my co-pilot' in the wartime sermons of prominent men of faith, such as Archbishop of Canterbury William Temple and Sir Stafford Cripps, there is little to suggest that flyers were possessed of a particularly religious sensibility.

Nevertheless, this did not mean that they did not look to other supernatural powers to offer reassurance and allay fears. Flyers, no less than sailors, could be intensely superstitious. Cecil Beaton noted that aircrew were extremely reluctant to use the word 'goodbye'.[92] In Miles Tripp's Lancaster, the pilot, 'Dig', would not fly without his hat, which had to be placed in a niche behind his head in the cockpit with the peak facing forward, while the wireless operator, George, insisted on carrying his girlfriend's brassiere on missions. Tripp himself flew with an extensive range of good-luck tokens, including a silk stocking, a badge given to him by a member of the women's land army, a pink chiffon scarf, and a tiny elephant sculpted from bone.[93] These same tokens also feature in Tripp's novel *Faith is a Windsock*, where they are in the possession of Hamish, the bomb-aimer. When Flute, the flight engineer, contemptuously refers to this 'frightened and miserable pagan practice', Hamish points out that these tokens of good fortune were also keepsakes of the friendships, loves, and associations he had left behind.[94] It was not uncommon for flyers to place their childhood teddy-bears in their aircraft, while Porgie, a fictional airman in Walter Clapham's *Night Be My Witness*, carried a soft doll which had been given to him by his cousin.[95] The crews of Lancaster bombers in 50 Squadron insisted on the ritual of listening to a recording of the Andrews Sisters performing 'The Shrine of St Cecilia' in the mess before each mission, and it was considered 'extremely unlucky' not to have been in attendance.[96] Some flyers became anxious or depressed if they lost a good-luck charm. Battle of Britain fighter pilot Ian Gleed once turned over his quarters in a desperate search for the gold St Christopher mascot medallion which normally hung around his neck: 'I didn't at all relish flying without it.'[97]

Even those, such as Alan Deere, who professed not to be superstitious were not willing to tempt fate. Deere, as a New Zealander, had a Kiwi insignia painted on the side of his Spitfire. However, after a mid-air collision a fellow pilot recommended he remove it, as it clearly had not brought good luck, pointing out it was probably inappropriate to have the image of a flightless bird on the fuselage of an aircraft. Deere reluctantly concurred, and eliminated the offending emblem.[98] There was no guarantee, of course, that an insignia, charm, or mascot would necessarily provide positive kismet. Air-gunner John Byrne purchased a velvet teddy-bear, whom he named Barker, as a mascot for his crew. Six months later, while Byrne was attending an interview for a commission, the rest of his crew went on a mission and were reported as missing in action. In his diary Byrne solemnly noted: 'Barker went [on the raid] also. But apparently even that didn't save them.'[99] However, flyers continued to testify to the efficacy of superstitious practices. Such insistence aligned them with the mass of the British population during the war, a Mass-Observation survey in 1941 revealing that 86 per cent of women and 50 per cent of men admitted to observing superstitions.[100] Moreover, psychiatric experts such as David Stafford-Clark avowed that ritual superstitions played a valuable part in maintaining morale: 'The man who flew with his girl-friend's stocking really believed it would protect him against flak and enemy fighters.'[101] Leonard Cheshire felt survival was ultimately down to luck, pointing out that flyers he knew who 'had never made a mistake' had lost their lives, while he, despite 'the many times that through sheer stupidity and carelessness I had literally asked to be shot down', had escaped unscathed.[102] However, the recourse to superstition suggested that most flyers believed less in luck than in fortune, a minor distinction, but one which at least allowed them to reclaim some sense of agency, even when perched on the edge of oblivion.

COURAGE AND COWARDICE

Fear among flyers was predictably entangled with questions of courage and cowardice. While some enlightened figures appreciated that these two terms might be better understood as points on a shared continuum rather than as incompatible opposites, the wartime RAF believed it could still make a clear distinction between valour and funk when evaluating the behaviour of flyers in combat situations. An act of bravery could be recognized through bestowing military decorations and honours which confirmed that the recipient's gallantry was unimpeachable. Conversely, receipt of the appellation of Lack of Moral Fibre (LMF) unequivocally marked out the disgraced flyer as a shameful recreant, who would be stripped of his wings and either reassigned to the most menial of ground-crew duties or discharged from the service entirely. In fact only 0.4 per cent of aircrew were ever charged with LMF, possibly because senior officers preferred to give men who had refused to fly or perform duties in the air a second chance to redeem themselves.[103] However, the notion of LMF, and its grave consequences for masculine self-respect, definitely impacted on the way flyers understood, regulated, and displayed their fear and stress. Miles Tripp argued that bomber aircrew preferred to continue to fly long after 'their nerves were in shreds' rather than risk being accused of LMF. What made the prospect of LMF so appalling was the humiliation of being regarded as inadequate to the pressures of combat, 'in a country totally committed to the winning of the war'. A man who shirked his duty in this context would inevitably become a pariah, 'an insult to the national need'.[104]

However, it is not always that easy to establish whether a flyer had been cowardly in combat. An air-gunner who temporarily left his station when under fire from flak or enemy night-fighters might find that his misdemeanour had gone unreported, covered up by his fellow crew members, and never to be spoken of again. For fighter pilots, air combat was fast and furious, and it was not always clear what was going on. Those who had served as war correspondents in both world wars regularly contrasted the rapid speeds and manoeuvrability of the Spitfire and Hurricane with the air aces of 1914–18, who had 'chugged across the channel at 90 miles an hour'.[105] Ian Gleed emphasized the difficulty, as a combatant, in making sense of the brief, frenetic dogfights which characterized the Battle of Britain. In his first engagement Gleed found he had run out of ammunition, and broke off from 'the scrap'. He then found himself alone, lost in fog, convinced he was the sole survivor, a conviction which was only dispelled when he finally found his way back to his home airfield, where he discovered that most of his fellow flyers had also returned safely.[106] In the midst of such confusion it was, in theory, possible for a flyer to absent himself from the action once he had made his initial attack. Battle of Britain ace Al Deere reflected on this possibility in his post-war memoirs. He felt confident that, up until the minute the battle was joined, a pilot who was 'inclined to cowardice' would find his fears contained by the censorious eyes of the other flyers in his formation. It was 'immediately subsequent to his first attack that the opportunity occurs for the less courageous to make their getaway without seeming to avoid the issue'. Deere was frustrated that it was, in practice, extremely difficult to prove that a particular pilot had not pulled his weight. After the initial attack, it was 'almost impossible' to determine with certainty the actions of any one pilot, even if (and Deere claimed that this had indeed happened during the war) 'a watch has been set on a suspect'. While Deere was troubled by the disciplinary implications of it being all but impossible to establish 'positive proof of cowardice' among single-seater fighter pilots, he also acknowledged how easy it was for fear to gain the upper hand:

I know only too well the almost overpowering urge to either break off an engagement, or participate in such a way as to ensure one's safety, when surrounded and outnumbered. On many an occasion in July [1940] I had to grit my teeth and overcome fear with determination in just such circumstances or, alternatively, when I became temporarily isolated from the main battle, to talk myself into going back. I refuse to believe that there are those among us who know no fear.[107]

Deere's insistence that fear was natural, and that what was important was to overcome it rather than deny its existence, is vital in reconstructing how flyers understood notions of courage and cowardice. In the nineteenth century military manliness was defined in terms of stoic endurance and the forbearance of pain.

Unconscious reactions to danger were ignored, or believed to be capable of being suppressed by the qualities of 'character' which had been shaped on the playing-fields of England's public schools. While such unreflective codes of manly stoicism proved surprisingly resilient in the twentieth century, it seems difficult not to agree with Michael Roper's claims that the impact of total war on a mass conscript army in 1914–18 permitted more nuanced understandings among the military (and society as a whole) of fear and courage. Faced with the sheer scale of horrors arising from the mechanized slaughter of the Western Front, it became obvious that, in regard to quelling fear, 'willpower alone was not enough'. Fear, it came to be believed, needed to be managed, not repressed or channelled into strenuous activity. The most famous advocate of this new approach was W. H. R. Rivers, whose psychotherapeutic regime for shell-shocked officers at Craiglockhart in the last years of the Great War included among its celebrity patients the war poets Siegfried Sassoon and Wilfred Owen. Rivers's reputation has been the source of much controversy. While he maintained an ambiguous relationship to Freudian ideas, Rivers sought to help his patients recover by forcing them to overcome emotional repression, to testify to the traumatic experiences which the ideal of manly stoicism insisted that they should forget. While Rivers's ideas were not universally approved, it is certainly the case that, by the Second World War, military authorities were more ready to accept that nervous sensibilities had to be acknowledged, and could not be hidden behind an increasingly tremulous stiff upper lip.[108] Courage and fear came to be understood as not mutually exclusive, and even Lord Moran, Churchill's physician and a figure often identified with the last hurrah of Edwardian manliness (and especially the notion that cowardice was a failure of will), could concede in 1945 that courage was a limited fund, which could easily be used up, without hope of restoration.[109] By the Second World War most military leaders agreed that they could no longer rely on their ranks containing large numbers of men with 'natural courage', in other words, men who were simply insensitive to danger. The 'threshold of fear', they believed, had fallen steadily since 1914. Courage in the Second World War was to be understood, not as unreflective fearlessness, but as the conquest of fears that were openly acknowledged.[110]

Not merely was this notion one which registered with both flyers and those promoting their achievements to a broader public. The possession, as opposed to the denial, of heightened sensibility was celebrated as an essential quality of the national character at war. When John Strachey, the former communist politician who had become a public-relations officer in the wartime RAF, came to write an introduction to Ian Gleed's Battle of Britain memoirs in 1942, he asserted that the most exciting thing to emerge from the book was the fact that the young flyers of Fighter Command 'felt frightened', which he believed was 'their ultimate claim to glory'. For, if they had been 'Nazi or Japanese robots', indoctrinated and dehumanized into 'actually liking death and destruction', then their success would have been 'incomparably less remarkable'. Instead, they were 'just young

Englishmen with the same dislikes, likes, hopes, fears and expectations as the rest of their generation'.[111] Senior RAF officers actively discouraged exhibitions of reckless bravery, particularly in Bomber Command, where teamwork and the disciplined and systematic implementation of highly specific objectives were seen as much more desirable qualities. 'Bomber' Harris publicly declared that 'any operation which deserves the V[ictoria]C[ross] is in the nature of things unfit to be repeated at frequent intervals'.[112] Roland Winfield defined valour, not as 'the impulsive, isolated act done in an instance that may, or may not, win the Victoria Cross', but as the capacity to carry out 'a continuous and sustained course of action that requires the highest degree of skill in the face of gross physical hardship'.[113] Leonard Cheshire, writing in 1943, recalled that while at training school he still maintained an image of the flyer as a heroic individualist. However, he had subsequently come to appreciate 'that bombing is technical, a matter of knowledge and experience, not of setting your jaw and rushing in'. The critical factor in combat efficiency was not individual valour, but collective resolution and cooperation among the crew.[114] A year later Cheshire was actually to receive the VC, but significantly the 'date of act of bravery' in the official citation was given as '1940–1944'.[115] In other words, the award was for four years of sustained fortitude, not a specific deed, which reflected Harris's belief that the cumulative pressures upon bomber crews required a redefinition of how gallantry was understood and honoured.

Fighter pilots, it might well be assumed, had more opportunities to engage in acts of individual courage and heroism. Barry Sutton, a Hurricane pilot in the Battle of Britain, wrote in 1942 that, while the war in the air since 1939 had not seen the 'glorious tournaments of the heavens' which had characterized aerial combat in 1914–18, it had managed to retain many of the features which had made air fighting in that earlier conflict 'fundamentally a match between men'. Sutton felt reassured by the fact that death for the fighter pilot 'only comes by the superiority of one's adversary in honourable contact'. The Spitfire or Hurricane pilot did not have to reckon 'with the chance shell or bomb which may blast him to eternity; he reckons with a man armed as he is armed, and with whom he must come to grips before the issue can be decided'.[116] Richard Hillary longed to be a fighter pilot, because it promised the possibility of war as it 'ought to be, war which is individual combat between two people', and he regularly compared flying a Spitfire in combat to the duellists of centuries past.[117] However, the fighter pilot, like the duellist, was most likely to succeed if he remained cool, composed, and precise. Paul Richey had begun the Battle of France 'rushing about the sky like a madman', but by the end of the campaign he had come to appreciate the importance of keeping his brain 'coldly clear' as he held an enemy aircraft in his sights: 'You'd think an aerial combat was a hot-blooded, thrilling affair, but it isn't.'[118] The Battle of Britain's leading ace, 'Sailor' Malan, concurred with this assessment, telling one interviewer that: 'Courage these days is a minor talent. No man is braver than the rest. The civilian fighters in London—the air raid wardens of Coventry or Plymouth—these men do things under fire which we fighter pilots can only regard with awe. A fighter pilot doesn't have to show that kind of courage. Unreasoning, unintelligent blind courage is, in fact, a tremendous handicap to him. He has to be cold when he's fighting.'[119]

In tandem with the decline in the wartime RAF of an identification of courage with an instinctual fearlessness was the recognition that physical strength was an unreliable indicator of potential valour. Malan felt that steady nerves counted for as much as a good constitution, pointing out that 'a pilot's fitness was not the same as a boxer's'.[120] This is not to say that the air force did not contain its quota of stockily built 'hearties'. Douglas Bader had been a rugby player before the accident in which he lost his legs, while William Rothenstein painted the portrait of a 'hefty' New Zealand wing commander who, in his flying kit, looked like a reincarnation of 'one of Drake's captains'.[121] Another artist, Cuthbert Orde, felt that most of the fighter pilots he painted had an 'inherent toughness', by which he meant that they possessed physical and mental strength in equal measure. Paul Richey, he observed, was a good example of how 'the heart and the physique equally balance, and the combination is proclaimed in the build and the demeanour'. However, Orde also painted Peter Townsend, whose slight frame and obvious sensitivity made him appear more like a tortured poet or painter than a highly decorated fighter ace. Orde noted that Townsend had made himself ill through overworking, 'an example of the heart being too strong for the physique'.[122] However, it was generally agreed that an individual's physical attributes were of little value in gauging a man's courage or martial capabilities. Indeed, Noel Monks offered the example of Flying Officer Peter Walker, a fighter pilot during the Battle of France, whose 'fair, delicate appearance and his shyness were in startling contrast to the fierceness with which he tackled the enemy'.[123] Spitfire pilot Jim Bailey asserted that the 'big, imposing men . . . burly fellows with big voices', were more likely to succumb to LMF than the 'small, insignificant clerk'.[124] The novelist Somerset Maugham was taken aback when he discovered that legendary fighter pilot Ian Gleed was 'quite a little chap, not more than five foot four, I should guess'.[125]

The unwillingness to equate physicality and courage created a space in the wartime RAF for men who possessed potentially 'feminine' attributes or sensibilities. Cecil Beaton recorded his meeting with 19-year-old bomber pilot Hughie Tring, 'the son of a clergyman, aesthetic looking, with strong, rather feminine features, lean, with the long well-formed hands of a violinist, and the dark quiet voice of a scholar'. Beaton could scarcely believe that this gentle, almost androgynous figure was strong enough to handle a huge four-engined Stirling heavy bomber.[126] Intelligence officer Derek Gilpin Barnes provided a gushing pen portrait of a pilot he nicknamed 'the Black Prince', who possessed 'a dark, saturnine face . . . aristocratic nose; stern yet beautiful lips . . . he was distinguished by the most sensitive and flexible hands . . . They were the hands

of a violinist, of a conjurer, of an orchestral conductor.' However those delicate
hands, far from compromising his combat effectiveness, allowed him to fly
his Hurricane 'like an artist... Like a lover, beneath whose enchanted touch
that three-ton aeroplane would swim into heights of achievement beyond the
designer's dreams.'[127] The wartime RAF was also home to many gay flyers,
for example, the fighter pilot and alleged lover of Noel Coward, Billy Drake,
men whose bravery in combat ensured that their association with normative
masculinity remained publicly secure, despite their private sexual orientation.[128]
Courage among flyers was comprehended in terms which were flexible and
latitudinarian, as befitted a service which was, by the war's end, largely composed
of men serving only for the duration, whose values were ultimately those, not of
a military culture, but of the civilian society to which they would one day return.

A discussion of fear and courage among wartime flyers suggests that British
masculinity in the 1940s was still in transition. Edwardian constructions of
stoic manliness still informed the way the RAF hierarchy and flyers themselves
addressed issues of stress and anxiety. However, psychological understandings of
masculine behaviour, and a more nuanced approach to men's emotions, were
also in evidence, albeit in association with a continued priority being given to
the maintenance of discipline and combat effectiveness. At the level of individual
subjectivities, flyers attempted to cope with fear through a variety of diversions,
ameliorations, alibis, and rationalizations. At one level, they succeeded in the
management of their anxiety. The precise incidence of psychological casualties
in the wartime RAF is difficult to determine, the total number of LMF cases
providing only a haphazard guide. Nonetheless, studies which have appropriated
the neuropsychiatric ratio indexes widely used by ground forces during the
Second World War have concluded that rates of mental breakdown in the
RAF were remarkably low.[129] However, the strain on flyers was both real and
relentless, as their shaking hands, violent nightmares, facial sores, and the resort
to benzedrine and alcohol made only too clear. Young men who, only a few
years before, in the words of John Sommerfield, hadn't 'yet started to take
their jobs seriously, who go to musical comedies and come away humming the
choruses', were now prematurely aged.[130] As Tony Bartley said of the Battle of
Britain 'few', to whose illustrious company he himself belonged: 'We were fit and
fearless, in the beginning. By the end, we were old and tired, and knew what fear
was.'[131] The constant battle against fear was not merely about the requirement
to maintain appropriate public masculine standards. It was a struggle which also
had to be ceaselessly fought at the level of the private self. Fear may possess a
cultural history, but, in the case of the wartime flyer, it also tells us something
about how the individual human personality accommodated itself to an age of
catastrophe.

1. Flyboy cosmopolitanism: (i) A. O. Weekes of Barbados and Flight Sergeant C. A. Joseph of Trinidad, two West Indian members of the Bombay Squadron (IWM Department of Photographs CH 11478)

2. Flyboy cosmopolitanism: (ii) Indian Air Force officers chatting with Lady Runganadehan and her daughter at a British Council reception, 1943 (IWM Department of Photographs CH 10521)

3. Love on the base: two WAAFs wave off a Hurricane pilot (IWM Department of Photographs Album 66)

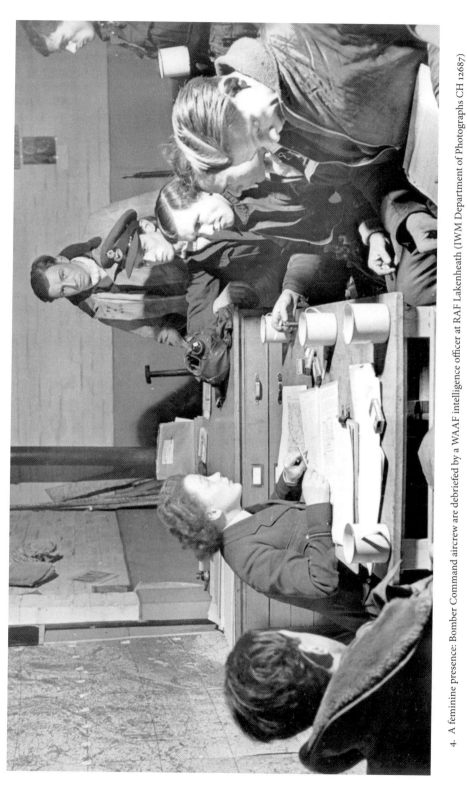

4. A feminine presence: Bomber Command aircrew are debriefed by a WAAF intelligence officer at RAF Lakenheath (IWM Department of Photographs CH 12687)

5. The flyer married: Group Captain Al Deere and his new bride, Joan (RAF Museum)

6. Waiting wives: publicity photograph for Terence Rattigan's play *Flare Path*, Apollo Theatre, London, August 1942 (V&A Images/Victoria and Albert Museum, London)

7. 'The heart being too strong for the physique': portrait of Wing Commander Peter Townsend
by Cuthbert Orde, 1941 (RAF Museum)

8. The false flyer: John Mills as Flight Lieutenant George Perry in *Cottage to Let* (1941) (British Film Institute/London Features International)

9. The flyer as playwright: Terence Rattigan in RAF uniform, photographed by Paul Tanquery (V&A Images/Victoria and Albert Museum, London)

copyright Marc Bryan-Brown Photography

10. 'A masterpiece of harmony and power': Spitfires at Sawbridgeworth, Hertfordshire, 1942 by Eric Ravilious (Imperial War Museum Department of Art LD 2125)

11. Homicidal Hun-hater or man of feeling? Wing Commander Guy Gibson reading in a poppy field near RAF Scampton, July 1943 (IWM Department of Photographs TR 1125)

12. The flyer-poet confronts the supernatural: David Niven as Flight Lieutenant Peter Carter in *A Matter of Life and Death* (1946) (British Film Institute/Granada International)

6

A Darker Blue

Provided he did not succumb to a complete breakdown, the flyer's struggle with fear failed to diminish his heroic stature among the British public. Civilians either took the feigned nonchalance of aircrew at face value, or, if they were privy to the extraordinary stresses which these young men faced, saw their hard-won triumph over terror as yet another reason why they deserved to be treated with such reverence and adulation. However, there were some flyers who might be potentially excluded from this widespread idolization of the men in air force blue. These flyers who, for one reason or another, were felt to be inadequate to the standards of heroic masculinity, can be placed under three broad categories. First were aircrew who were mutilated and disfigured, either through the loss of limbs or severe burns. Instead of adoration, these men found that their wounds were likely to produce responses of disgust or sympathy, both of which degraded their masculine self-esteem. Second was the flyer who was psychologically maladjusted or emotionally defective, a figure who was surprisingly common in a range of novels, plays, and films produced during the war and immediate post-war years. In these fictional narratives flyers appeared as amoral womanizers, selfish narcissists, and emotionally immature husbands or lovers. Third, crossing the boundary between the fictional and the real, were men who used the RAF's glamorous and heroic status as a cover for activities which were nefarious or even pathological. Some, such as serial killer Neville Heath, exaggerated and embellished their air-force service record, while others had no right to wear the air-force blue at all, being either fantasists or enemy spies. The damaged flyers, flawed flyers, and false flyers who are the subject of this chapter, while featuring in the lives of real flyers and in cultural representations of the RAF in a relatively minor key, speak to a broader ambivalence about the wartime flyer, particularly his complex relationship to both sensibility and savagery, an issue which will be explored more fully in Chapter 7.

BROKEN BODIES AND BURNT FACES: THE WOUNDED FLYER

In a powerful critique of the euphemisms which surround the language of military conflict, the literary critic Elaine Scarry has reminded us that the 'main purpose and outcome of war is injuring', in which men seek to triumph over their enemies by the blasting, burning, and rending of human tissue.[1] If death guaranteed removal of one's opponent, permanently disabling him through wounding came a close second in terms of military effectiveness. In the twentieth century the number of permanently disabled servicemen increased dramatically. As weaponry became more deadly and effective, the ability of military medicine to treat wounded men also improved, through innovations in wound ballistics, vascular surgery or anaesthesia, and due to more effective methods of evacuation of casualties to medical facilities behind the lines, where they could receive more intensive treatment. Therefore, a higher proportion of severely wounded men survived than had done in the past.[2] Given this, one might have expected the relationship between disabled servicemen and the broader population to have been largely affirmative and accommodating. In fact, like Sophocles' wounded warrior Philoctetes on his lonely island, the disabled serviceman of the Second World War found that he inspired responses of fear and pity, both of which subverted his status as a valorous man of honour and action. Like all those who are physically disabled, limbless or badly burnt servicemen appeared freakish and menacing to the able-bodied, who preferred to turn away from broken bodies which reminded them of the fundamental insecurity of their own corporal integrity. The disabled serviceman's understandable bitterness and anger seemed to enhance his unnatural monstrosity. Pity was just as unwelcome as revulsion, for it risked the creation of a masculinity that was fatally compromised.[3] If being a man meant not being either a child or a woman, disability raised the spectre of both infantilization and feminization. In the First World War handicapped British ex-servicemen had shared hospital facilities with children crippled by accidents or infantile paralysis. Women were expected to help in the rehabilitation of men disabled in war, but they had to ensure that this was achieved while remaining deferential to masculine authority, even when the man in question lacked full bodily potency and manly presence.[4] Public sympathy for the disabled serviceman was, moreover, highly conditional. Deborah Cohen has shown that limbless British veterans of the Great War were only likely to secure philanthropic attention if they eschewed bitterness and remained cheery. Since no one appeared to want to support a malcontent, a depressive, or an amputee resentful at the loss of a limb, they were obliged to perform the role of the 'jolly paraplegic', a worthy successor to the 'brave Tommy' of wartime. Only through good cheer and public fortitude would they be allowed to maintain that their manhood had been strengthened, rather than obliterated, by their horrific injuries.[5]

Of course, wounds did not inevitably have to result in a compromised or abject masculinity. Injuries sustained in combat could also bear testimony to manly heroism, what American novelist Stephen Crane famously (albeit ironically) titled 'the red badge of courage'.[6] However, those RAF flyers who suffered severe wounds, in which bodies were literally dismembered or misshapen by fire, found the experience traumatic and a major challenge to their self-esteem and understanding of themselves as men. This is only too obvious from the narratives of wounding and recovery surrounding five wartime flyers—two who lost limbs (Douglas Bader and Colin Hodgkinson) and three who were disfigured by severe burns (Richard Hillary, William Simpson, and Geoffrey Page)—whose stories may be seen as parables of remasculinization. Of these five, the names of Bader and Hillary are well known, if not legendary. However, placing their stories in juxtaposition with the rehabilitation narratives of less well-known figures allows us to appreciate that the process by which war-maimed flyers renegotiated their masculinity was complex and protracted. In particular, it becomes clear that, for all their insistence on a self-generating return to full manhood, medical expertise, the camaraderie of the hospital ward, and the esteem of women were all to play a critical role in making the disabled flyer 'whole' again. It is certainly true that the recovery of manhood by the physically damaged flyer was not merely physically agonizing, but was more emotionally anguished than the conventional narratives which emphasize fortitude and stoicism among those who were wounded, and acceptance and admiration among the wider public, would have us believe.

Douglas Bader is undoubtedly the most well known disabled flyer of the wartime RAF. However, he was possibly also the least representative. For a start, his terrible injuries had been sustained, not during the war itself, but as far back as 1931. A career officer in the peacetime RAF, Bader had been giving an unofficial demonstration of his skill at aerobatics when he had lost control of his Bulldog biplane, resulting in a crash-landing in which the young flyer lost both his legs beneath the knee. In the years which followed Bader doggedly sought to adapt to life with two artificial legs, and, as war approached, used his contacts in both the air force and the Air Ministry—what Bader himself termed 'the old chums act'—to return, not merely to the RAF, but to flying duties. Given the acute shortage of qualified pilots during the Battle of Britain, Bader was soon given command of his own squadron, and by September 1940 was in charge of an entire wing, composed of five squadrons. Bader was a swashbuckling figure, his exuberance on the ground and contempt for danger in the air proving inspirational to the men he commanded, who were, on average, almost ten years younger than he was. Cuthbert Orde, who painted Bader's portrait soon after the Battle of Britain, described him as 'the embodiment of willpower and aggressiveness', and lauded his 'unruly, unyielding, extravagant spirit'. However, Orde also conceded that Bader was undoubtedly 'not the easiest type to cope with'.[7] Bader was a controversial figure in the wartime RAF. While the public was enthused by the widely publicized exploits of a (at that time unnamed) legless fighter ace, many of Bader's comrades, subordinates, and superiors came to loathe a man they regarded as an insensitive bully. When he publicly intervened in tactical debates among senior commanders over the efficacy of the so-called 'big wing' (effectively assembling fighters en masse to attack German bomber formations) in the late summer of 1940, he was widely accused of both megalomania and insubordination. Former fighter pilots interviewed by Patrick Bishop acknowledged Bader's undoubted courage, but remained troubled by his bombastic nature and fondness for self-promotion and publicity.[8]

While Bader has been the subject of several biographies, these have provided only limited insight into how his physical disability might have impacted on his masculinity and sense of self. Paul Brickhill's best-selling *Reach for the Sky*, first published in 1954, verged on the hagiographical. Its cinematic adaptation, released in 1956, secured Bader's heroic reputation, being the most successful film exhibited in Britain since *Gone With the Wind*. Bader himself had been involved in the film's production, but he was also fortunate that the actor chosen to play him, Kenneth More, provided a sympathetic and attractive rendering of the flyer's personality, emphasizing not just breezy ebullience, but also a quiet tenderness.[9] Among later biographers, 'Laddie' Lucas had been a fellow pilot and one of Bader's 'old chums' for forty years, while Robert Jackson was a close friend in the last decade of his life.[10] Inevitably, therefore, these biographers tended to essentially reiterate Bader's own unreflective public personality, in which his ultimate triumph over his catastrophic injuries, and his understandable desire not to become an object of pity, often meant that his disability itself was almost kept out of sight. In *Reach for the Sky* we are encouraged, with obvious justification, to admire Bader's ability to swing a golf-club without losing his balance, to clamber into the cockpit of his Hurricane unaided, or extricate himself and parachute out of a Spitfire that was going down in flames over France. In other words, the focus is on the process of overcoming disability, not on the fact of disability itself. Indeed, the virtual erasure of the mutilated body from *Reach for the Sky* means that the reader is then bizarrely startled by an occasional reference to Bader, at the close of a day spent in combat, 'taking off his legs to go to bed'.

It is possible to recover, from the official versions of Bader's life, clues that would allow us to develop a more nuanced understanding of the relationship between disability and masculine subjectivity in regard to this legendary figure. *Reach for the Sky* can sometimes betray the extent of Bader's anxiety in attempting to restore his masculinity when his conception of manliness had been so closely associated with physicality. Before his accident Bader had played cricket, rugby, and hockey. He also boxed, his muscular five-foot ten-inch frame providing the perfect body for a middleweight fighter. It is therefore significant that one of the few setbacks in Brickhill's narrative of triumphant and inexorable recovery comes in an episode when Bader is taken by a friend to watch the Harlequins play at Twickenham: 'In that hour Bader felt more bitterly than ever before the loss of his legs. All his old friends were playing and it really hurt.' On returning home, Bader vowed to never go and see another rugby match.[11] The passages in the book dealing with his courtship of his eventual wife, Thelma, also reveal private apprehensions about his disability which he sought to conceal behind a public breeziness. He was only willing to actively pursue Thelma once he had been fitted with his artificial legs, and could walk into the restaurant where she worked as a waitress, his stumps camouflaged 'with full-length trousers and no crutches'.[12] Reading between the lines also suggests that Bader's re-entry into the RAF in 1939 involved a further challenge to his masculine self-esteem. Before his accident Bader had been a highly proficient pilot, but he was now faced with returning to the air in aircraft which were dramatically more advanced than the flimsy biplanes in which he had flown almost a decade earlier. A fighter-plane cockpit now possessed not twenty, but a hundred instruments and knobs, and Bader had to adapt to features such as flaps, a constant speed propellor, brakes, and retractable undercarriage. Moreover, while the Battle of Britain ended up being remarkably similar to the dogfights of the First World War, from September 1940 onwards RAF tactics changed dramatically and Bader had to adjust to a less individualistic form of aerial combat.[13] Underneath the external confidence, the loss of his legs only further aggravated Bader's restless insecurity, and, as even his highly sympathetic biographer conceded, his aggression and competitiveness betrayed a desire for reassurance that went back to his childhood. However, such potential opportunities for exploring Bader's masculinity and how it was refashioned to incorporate the ongoing trauma of dismemberment remain little more than intriguing exceptions in a story which, in the spirit of its subject, celebrates bluff stoicism and eschews introspection. At the very end of *Reach for the Sky* Brickhill reminds his readers that 'Bader's war goes on unsung and unceasing to be won anew each day'. Unfortunately, we are granted virtually no access in his book to the emotional and psychological dimensions to that daily struggle with disability.[14]

By contrast, the autobiography of another limbless flyer, Colin Hodgkinson, was much more forthcoming in this regard. Like Bader, Hodgkinson had been a public-schoolboy whose poor academic record had been compensated for by his success at sports. At the Nautical College at Pangbourne, Hodgkinson boxed and played both cricket and rugby. His prowess on the playing-fields led him 'to attach a disproportionate value to physical power, something for which I was to suffer later'. His father had been a pilot in the Great War, and Hodgkinson, having initially joined the navy, began training in the Fleet Air Arm.[15] However, on the eve of the outbreak of war the aircraft in which he was training crashed after a mid-air collision with another Tiger Moth, and Hodgkinson's right leg was smashed to a pulp, while his left ankle and foot were shattered as if run over by a steamroller. The right leg was immediately amputated above the knee, but his surgeons prevaricated over what to do with the other leg. In the meantime Hodgkinson had read a newspaper article about Douglas Bader, and he became determined that he too should become an operational pilot. Indeed, Hodgkinson realized that if a legless man wished to be in the front line, flying was the sole option. Only in an aircraft might tin legs be as good as natural ones, and the cockpit of a Spitfire or Hurricane 'was the one place where he could fight the war sitting down'. However, having made this determination Hodgkinson was aware that he had some serious obstacles to overcome. His situation was certainly very different from Bader's. Bader had been a regular officer in the RAF, whereas Hodgkinson had been merely a midshipman under training in the FAA. Bader had hundreds of hours of flying experience to his credit when he crashed, whereas Hodgkinson had only completed fourteen hours in the air, all in training aircraft. Bader was well connected in the RAF, whereas Hodgkinson knew nobody. Most critically of all, Bader had been a natural pilot, whereas Hodgkinson's experiences in training had been less than encouraging. Indeed, he confessed that 'my bowels turned to water every time I climbed into a Tiger Moth'. Hodgkinson agonized over how, 'diminished and disabled', he could come to terms with flying when, while still 'fit and whole', he had never been on terms with it at all: 'And then, suddenly, I knew that it was not a question of coming to terms with flying but with myself. To prove to myself that I could still be a man among men I had to get into the war, and in a fighting role.'[16]

Hodgkinson's plan was to get back into the FAA and then transfer to the RAF and fly Spitfires against the enemy. Only then 'would I feel that I had restored myself in my own eyes'. Hodgkinson became obsessed with the Spitfire, talking about, dreaming about, and making models of this 'symbol of my regeneration'. A major impediment to his desire to fly again was the fact that his left leg might never heal, and that he would be left a total invalid, unable to operate an aircraft. Hodgkinson therefore insisted that the left leg be removed below the knee. Hodgkinson's wartime story was remarkably similar to Bader's. First was the painful struggle to adjust to walking on two artificial legs, followed by his efforts to convince the relevant authorities that he be allowed to become an operational pilot, then came a distinguished career as a fighter pilot, and finally, as with Bader, he was shot down and captured by the Germans. However, what makes Hodgkinson's memoirs more engaging than Brickhill's celebratory life of Bader is that 'Hoppy' (as he came to be nicknamed by his fellow flyers) was candid and reflective about how being a double amputee impacted on his sense of himself as a man. He was open and honest about his fears of how, as a legless man, he would be able to negotiate the small, yet necessary actions of living, such as getting in and out of the bath, walking downstairs, or making love. He was frank about the fact that, even as a successful operational pilot at RAF Tangmere, he was never to be fully at ease in the air. He feared crashing into the sea, where his tin legs would undoubtedly cause him to drown, and he initially filled them with ping-pong balls in the hope that they would offer flotation in the event of ditching in the water. However, he had to abandon this expedient when the balls exploded at high altitude.

Moreover, while Bader had been decidedly insensitive towards the feelings of his wife, gleefully welcoming every opportunity to seek out danger in the air, Hodgkinson seemed more conflicted over how his desire to reclaim his manhood through combat might have created unnecessary anxieties for his family. In particular, he felt that he had betrayed his mother, who had never wanted him to follow his father's career and become a pilot: 'I knew that I had made her suffer, doing what she had instinctively warned me against.' He agonized over telling his mother that he was returning to flying, lest she use her knowledge of his own sense of guilt to dissuade him. 'How could I persuade her', he mused, 'that my going back to flying was the only lever of my self-regeneration, that without that achievement I could not feel myself a man?' Hodgkinson was desperate to reassure his mother, a woman of distinctly pacifist inclinations, that 'I didn't want glory. I was using the war, and through the war, flying, as instruments to sculpture me into the shape of man I believed I should and could have been.' The use of the verb 'sculpture' is pertinent here. For, as Hodgkinson himself was only too aware, his artificial legs did not so much restore his original body, or even the illusion of it, as fundamentally refashion it. Before his accident Hodgkinson had been an imposing six feet one inch tall, with a broad, muscular physique. Walking with tin legs required heaving from the hips, which made a disabled man liable to tip over if his torso was too far from the ground. As a consequence, Hodgkinson's height was reduced to five feet ten. His original shoe size—a ten—would also have to be reduced if the artificial legs were to be light enough to operate effectively. Hodgkinson now found himself wearing size eight shoes, which gave his feet a dainty appearance in marked contrast to the clumping extremities of the pre-war hearty.[17]

Hodgkinson's masculine rehabilitation was accomplished not merely through the test of war. Women too were to play a critical role in the restoration of his manhood. After the first amputation, his girlfriend 'Baba' proved to be a less than heartening visitor to Hodgkinson's hospital bedside. Her horror at his injury and unwillingness to continue a relationship with a crippled man was sufficiently patent that Hodgkinson felt obliged to release her from any obligation to him. While 'Baba' had been little more than a 'pleasant distraction' for Hodgkinson prior to his accident, the fact that she had so readily recoiled physically from the thought of his injury left the crippled airman troubled. He had a tendency to be shy with women anyway, which he tried to obscure with the 'bottom-slapping approach' of the virile, 'no-nonsense' type of male performance. Now, with the loss of his legs, he ruefully contemplated, the pursuit of sex and romance would be even more problematic. An initial remedy was provided by some of his comrades, shortly after he re-entered the FAA. After a dance, a fellow officer set Hodgkinson up with a blonde, who seduced him on the back seat of a car parked outside the dance hall, an experience that was all the more positive for the fact that the woman in question was completely unfazed by his tin legs. Indeed, Hodgkinson came to the conclusion that women cared less about physical disablement than he had anticipated. His memoirs suggest that his disability was no impediment to pursuing what he termed 'the amorous blandishments of war'. While stationed at RAF Coltishall he had an affair with Claire, a glamorous and cultured WAAF officer. Hodgkinson explicitly confirmed how the opportunity to be 'the recognized cavalier of this pretty, witty, much sought-after woman' contributed to the restoration of 'the masculine confidence my disability had undermined'.[18] If Hodgkinson credited women with a key role in facilitating his recovery, though, not all severely wounded aircrew were equally appreciative and complimentary. As we shall see, in some narratives of the damaged flyer women were to be presented not as allies in, but as impediments to, the process of masculine regeneration.

At one point during his convalescence Hodgkinson had met another flyer engaged in a protracted struggle to attain physical and psychological rehabilitation, the badly burnt fighter pilot Richard Hillary. If Douglas Bader was the war's most famous limbless flyer, Hillary has come to epitomize the flyer disfigured by fire. This status is largely a consequence of his autobiography *The Last Enemy*, first published in 1942, and the subsequent interest shown in both his life and writing from prominent literary figures, ranging from Arthur Koestler in the 1940s to Sebastian Faulks in the 1990s.[19] Hillary's literary reputation will be considered in the next chapter. At this point, the focus will be on how Hillary's response to disfigurement provides insight into how badly burned flyers understood, and sought to reclaim, their masculinity. If Hillary's account, published in wartime, ultimately presented his injuries as an ennobling experience, or at least an exemplary fable of the sacrifices required to triumph over the enemy, the post-war memoirs of Geoffrey Page and William Simpson suggested a more turbulent and problematic renegotiation of manhood by men who had suffered horrific burns. First, however, it is necessary to establish the broader contexts of these individual stories of recovery. It has been estimated that around 4,500 allied airmen suffered serious burns during the Second World War. Most were caused by enemy machine-gun or cannon fire puncturing an aircraft's fuel tank, causing highly inflammable fuel to leak back into the aircraft, where it would combust when struck by bullets. Fighter pilots, seated immediately behind their main fuel tank, were especially vulnerable to having the full force of their fuel literally exploding in their faces. The result was what came to be known as 'airman's burn', in which faces and hands suffered whole thickness burns, in other words, burns in which all skin tissue was destroyed, including hair follicles, sweat glands, and even nerve endings. A pilot wearing full kit was, in theory, protected from serious scorching by his clothing and goggles. However, in the stifling heat of the cockpit of a Spitfire or Hurricane during the Battle of Britain, most pilots found the temptation to dispense with the prescribed leather Irvin jacket and gloves, and fly effectively in their shirt-sleeves, irresistible. The consequences of exposing so much vulnerable flesh to intense, dry heat or flame inevitably proved catastrophic. Many of these fighter boys whose faces were burnt away were treated in Ward Three of the Queen Victoria Hospital at East Grinstead, by the legendary plastic surgeon Archibald McIndoe. However, the vast majority of burned airmen actually came from Bomber Command, and three out of the four

RAF burns units—Cosford, Rauceby, and Ely—were situated in the Fens or Lincolnshire, areas in the country closely associated with the strategic bombing offensive. Long-distance missions required large fuel tanks, which significantly increased the risk of burns for bomber aircrew.[20]

Before 1939 most victims of severe burns had died almost immediately, but during the Second World War medical advances meant that most survived. The pre-war survival rate had been so insignificant that treatment had been primitive and often counter-productive, particularly the use of coagulation treatments which hindered circulation of the blood and led to infection and gangrene. McIndoe insisted that the 'one-stop' use of tannic acid was simply inadequate for the scale of burns suffered by many flyers, and he adopted protracted, labour-intensive techniques which involved repeated surgery, regular immersion in saline baths, daily changes of dressings, and the use of skin grafts. McIndoe became a hero to all the flyers who encountered him in Ward Three. His brusque emphasis on the practical aspects of their recovery was welcomed by men who were unable to stomach pity. He deliberately sought to insinuate beauty among the freakishly deformed faces and hands of his patients, employing attractive nurses and having fresh flowers placed in the ward on a daily basis. McIndoe was also sensitive to the fact that, while they required continuous care and attention, burnt flyers were rarely bed-bound, and so he endeavoured to ensure they did not become bored, by organizing outings to social events in East Grinstead and even the West End of London. Recovery was also aided by the camaraderie of the ward, where black humour and practical jokes abounded. The creation of the 'Guinea Pig Club', with its own magazine featuring cartoons, poems, and short stories, provided an institutionalization of the spirit of shared suffering and courage which existed at East Grinstead. Outside the ward, McIndoe appreciated that his patients' rehabilitation might be accelerated if it could be yoked to widespread public esteem for the RAF. He was able to get the RAF to declare that burnt airmen were still on 'active duty' during their convalescence, which permitted them to continue to wear RAF battledress, with all the associations of glamour and heroism which the public had attached to the distinctive blue uniform.[21] A recent study of the military backdrop to McIndoe's work at East Grinstead argues that the RAF believed that the terrible wounds suffered by burned airmen were a visual rendering of the burden they had borne on behalf of their service, and the country as a whole, and that, in return, they should be entitled to the best medical care and most conscientious rehabilitation efforts available. This contract was also one between the disfigured flyer and society as a whole, in which the civilian population publicly recognized the sacrifice of those who had suffered so appallingly on their behalf.[22] It is certainly true that the RAF made no effort to hide its most disfigured casualties away from public exposure, but rather encouraged such men to actively circulate in the civilian community, so as to remind non-combatants of their responsibility to those who had fought. However, individual narratives of burned airmen suggest that their reintegration into a wider society was not entirely unproblematic, and that these disfigured flyers could succumb to understandable feelings of alienation, bitterness, and violent anger.

McIndoe himself testified to the detrimental impact of disfiguring injuries on the mentality of a young flyer. 'A fighter pilot', he told a friend, 'can't help being vain because the girls all swoon round him like a honey pot . . . Think what it must be like for that young man to go back into the same circle with his face burned to bits. One minute has changed him from a Don Juan to an object of pity—and it's too much to bear.'[23] This statement seemed particularly appropriate in the case of McIndoe's most famous patient. Richard Hillary had not merely been extraordinarily handsome before he baled out of his burning Spitfire in September 1940. His attractiveness to the opposite sex had become a vital part of his own sense of self, and the possibility that he had lost his looks was to be a major test for him. His vanity now had to cope with hands which looked like claws, a face which was a shiny patchwork of burnt skin, and eyes which lacked eyelashes and produced an involuntary glare reminiscent of a chimpanzee. As his editor at Macmillan, Lovat Dickson, indicated, Hillary was one of those disfigured men for whom 'the sense of beauty lost was so heartbreaking that they suffered in spirit damage which could never be repaired'.[24] In fact, as fellow Guinea Pig William Simpson pointed out, while burns and plastic surgery had combined 'to play strange tricks with his face', Hillary was—by East Grinstead standards—only slightly disfigured, and was able to return to active service, being killed on operational duty in 1943. It often took three years or more to reconstruct the faces of men without noses, ears, eyelids, chins, and even lips to a semblance of normality, and some remained forever grotesquely misshapen. Hillary ironically termed Ward Three the 'Beauty Shop', but Simpson was eager to establish that what the burned flyers received was not, in the strictest sense, cosmetic surgery. McIndoe's priority was to patch men up and get them back to their squadrons as quickly as possible: 'Personal appearance was not as important as flying fitness.'[25] McIndoe was, in some senses, learning on the job, and some of his early skin grafts were not entirely successful, the seams of each different skin patch visible on the rebuilt face of his patients. Restored eyebrows often gave the impression that they had been carelessly stuck on, often at some considerable distance from, or at a peculiar angle to, the eyes themselves. It was usually impossible to fully restore muscular movement to faces frozen by fire, and many flyers were unable to register a smile or a frown, sometimes incapable of even winking or blinking. All these men were clearly aware of their potential monstrosity, and while the population of East Grinstead rapidly accommodated itself to the presence of so many disfigured flyers in their midst, excursions by McIndoe's patients to London often exposed them to looks of horror, pity, and repulsion.[26] As one author has trenchantly commented, there is an undeniable poignancy in seeing a proud man like Hillary rendered so dependent and vulnerable, 'without even a skin to protect him'.[27]

So how did flyers whose faces were made grotesque by fire come to terms with their ghastly facial dilapidation? In *The Last Enemy*, Hillary presented his wounding as the catalyst to the reorientation of his character. During his agonizing treatment Hillary suggested that he underwent a transformation, from a selfish and cynical egoist to a more reflective, mature man who had come to understand the war as a moral struggle against evil. His disfigurement, therefore, served as 'a sign of the weightiness of war's ends'. Hillary's newly acquired humility was specifically linked to the horrifying change in his appearance. During a hospital visit, his mother bluntly tells him: 'You should be glad that this had to happen to you. Too many people told you how attractive you were and you believed them. You were well on the way to becoming something of a cad. Now you'll find out who your real friends are.' However, the real moment of epiphany comes at the close of *The Last Enemy*, when Hillary helps fire-fighters remove the injured from a bomb-damaged house near Liverpool Street station. He administers brandy to a woman whose child has been killed in the raid. She thanks him, and then, looking at his ravaged face, remarks: 'I see they got you too.' In this instant, Hillary, 'with awful clarity', finally attains self-knowledge: 'Great God, that I could have been so arrogant!' Hillary had discovered his kinship with mankind, a sudden sense of anguished love for his courageous compatriots and, beyond that, the human race more generally.[28] In the words of Lovat Dickson, who provided an extravagantly sentimental gloss on the final chapter of *The Last Enemy* in his 1950 biography of Hillary: 'with all his heart and soul he yearned to deserve now this companionship that had been offered to him. Not to lie in hospital, and with undergraduate wit tease the nurses; not to sit in night-clubs, battle-scarred in the latest mode, and with sardonic quips belittle humanity . . . but to submerge his suffering in that which all humanity had to bear, and to earn the right to share in its nobility.'[29] Realizing that the woman in the blitzed house had recognized his mangled face as a badge of a common, shared sacrifice, Hillary sought to return to combat. In fact, Hillary's conversion was less straightforward and sincere than *The Last Enemy* would have us believe. A fellow patient at East Grinstead, Geoffrey Page, tersely told Hilary that, while: 'You write of being an irresponsible undergraduate before the war, then, as a result, you change, and, presto, here you are, a different person . . . In my opinion, you're still as bloody conceited as ever.'[30] Certainly, Hillary later admitted that the exchange with the woman during the air raid was entirely fictitious. Hillary's diaries also reveal much more anger and fiery impatience during his time at East Grinstead, where he was not always regarded as the most agreeable of patients.[31]

Moreover, if Hillary's memoir insists that he was able to overcome his grief at his own disfigurement through a broader process of personal revaluation and near-spiritual enlightenment, it also contains references to other, less rarefied, contributions to his ultimate rehabilitation. Particularly significant was the discovery that, for all his terrible wounds, Hillary's sexual allure had not been extinguished. In the immediate aftermath of his accident Hillary joked that, like an old man of 60, carnal pleasures in future would be confined to eating and drinking. Over dinner in a London restaurant, he assured Tony, a fellow patient, that: 'We are free of the lusts of youth.' Tony was sceptical, insisting that youth, 'with all her temptations, trials and worries', would catch up with them again. Hillary was being disingenuous, for on an earlier stroll through Ravenscourt Park he had 'passed one girl' whose 'lips were soft, her breasts firm, her legs long and graceful. It is many a month since any woman has aroused me, and I was pleased. I smiled at her and she smiled back, a nice friendly smile.'[32] If Hillary looked to women as a means to confirm the reconstitution of his manhood, he certainly was not to be disappointed. He developed an intimate friendship, which may or may not have at one point become a full-blown love affair, with Denise, the former fiancée of his dead comrade Peter Pease. As has already been noted, he had a passionate intrigue with Merle Oberon when visiting the United States to promote *The Last Enemy*. In the last year of his life he entered into a frenzied romance with the famously beautiful divorcee Mary Booker.[33] By contrast, the memoirs of two other patients at East Grinstead imply that the psychological recovery of burned flyers was often frustrated by a demoralizing rejection at the hands of the opposite sex.

William Simpson was trapped inside the burning cockpit of his Fairey Battle bomber, after it crashed in France in May 1940. He was eventually pulled clear by his fellow aircrew, but not before suffering severe burns. After treatment in hospital in German-occupied France Simpson was left with a lumpily scarred face, a reduced nose with only one nostril, no eyelids on his left eye, and hands which were no more than stiff, pointed talons. While awaiting repatriation from Vichy France (it was clear Simpson would never be able to fly again), he befriended Yvonne, a prostitute and Resistance worker, a 'burning brunette with an animal sexual magnetism'. Simpson did not feel romantically inclined towards her, but she gave him 'a sense of manhood again', and he respected her intense patriotism and courageous desire to evict the Germans from her homeland. On returning to Britain, Simpson was treated by McIndoe at East Grinstead, where Simpson acknowledged his appreciation of the surgeon's deliberate recruitment of the most fetching and glamorous nurses.[34] However, the feminine affirmation of his continued manhood which Simpson most desired was to be denied to him. Flying back to Britain via neutral Portugal, Simpson could only think of how he would now be reunited with his wife, Hope, whom he had married on the eve of war. He was explicit that it was 'of great importance to me to have proof that women cared nothing for scars and crippling wounds provided that the essential manhood in a man's spirit—and presumably also in his body—was unimpaired'. He was devastated, therefore, at Hope's initial horrified reaction to the extent of his injuries. She had braced herself to find him badly wounded and scarred, but with a distinguished limp or a romantically Nelsonian empty sleeve or striking dark patch over an eyeless socket. She had not prepared herself for him to be 'smelly, offensive, streaming at the eyes, dirtily bandaged and clumsily disabled'. 'From that moment onwards, no matter how gallantly she tried . . . there was no way back into my heart.'[35] This staggering blow to Simpson's self-confidence was only finally exorcised when he later married Monica, one of the nurses in Ward Three. However, with a candour about the psychological wounds of disability which echoes the sensitivity of Colin Hodgkinson's memoir, Simpson refused to conceal how his new wife had to tackle his violent temper, brought on by the day-to-day frustrations of trying to complete household tasks with only limited facility in his hands. What allowed Simpson and Monica to develop a less exacting and more companionate marriage was the birth of their children, in 1945 and 1949. As Simpson himself disclosed, he had 'a psychological need to see before my eyes children of our own that were physically normal . . . able to do all the things that I could not do myself—flowers of my seeds grown out of my own ashes'.[36]

Like Simpson's account of his journey back to full manhood, Geoffrey Page's memoir also ultimately ends on an upbeat note, with Page's marriage to the daughter of Hollywood actor Nigel Bruce, which was related in Chapter 1. However, for all Page's breezy good humour and repudiation of self-pity, his autobiography does at times disclose the anger and bitterness which could accompany disfigurement. Page received severe burns to the face and hands after his Hurricane's fuel tank received a direct hit from a German air-gunner during an engagement with an enemy bomber formation in August 1940. In the early days of recovery Page drifted in and out of consciousness. At one point he was able to discern a nurse by his bedside. Her 'attractive face' remained in focus for only an instant, but, unfortunately, just long enough for Page to register her look of revulsion at the swollen lump of flesh that had once been his face: 'At that point I hated her and I hated myself with the illogical reasoning of a drunken man.' For Page, this was to be merely the first of a series of setbacks associated with rejection by women. Soon after, 'one of the prettiest girls I'd ever seen' came to help with Page's dressings. Attired in the colourful uniform of a VAD Red Cross nurse, she 'personified the wounded warrior's vision of the ideal angel of mercy'. However, she was unable to hide her horror and loathing at the sight of the patient's scorched flesh. 'From the depths of my soul', Page lamented, 'I longed for Beauty to cast me a friendly glance, even if it came in the shabby guise of pity, but the first impression remained constant.'[37]

Professional nurses were less likely to be so squeamish, but Page found their detached professionalism no less upsetting. On one occasion he raged at a ward sister's apparently cruel treatment of a flying officer, whose wife had waited for seven hours to get a telephone call through to the ward, only to be told by 'the bloody bitch' that patients were not allowed to receive private calls. A nurse who helped Page undress before surgery was officious and aloof: 'Love seemed dead and all that was left was this unfeeling woman in these chill surroundings. Nothing but pain lay ahead.' On release from hospital, Page's first tentative sexual encounters lacked the self-affirming quality which had characterized those of Hodgkinson or Hillary. On his first excursion to London, Page's sister set him up with a young woman who attempted to seduce him in her apartment after a dinner-dance. However, no sooner had they jumped into bed than an air raid began, and the noise of the anti-aircraft fire frightened Page: 'I could not raise an eyebrow, let alone any other part of my anatomy.' In time, Page's experiences with the opposite sex became much more positive. On a goodwill lecture mission to the United States in 1944 Page socialized with Joan Fontaine (his ideal of 'English feminine beauty personified') and spent several days in the company of 'an indescribably lovely young actress'. However, what really animated Page's recovery was his desire to return to combat flying, which he succeeded in doing in 1942. Page was, unlike Hillary, less interested in rejoining the war as a moral obligation than he was in seeking the opportunity for revenge on the Germans for his terrible wounds. In his hospital bed he vowed he would shoot down one enemy aircraft for every one of the painful and protracted operations he had endured at East Grinstead. On return to operational duties, as a Mustang pilot, Page confessed that he had gloated over the 'scenes of hideous violent death' he had meted out: 'Vengeance was mine, and I was enjoying every moment of it . . . my years in the hospital had not been in vain.'[38]

The efforts of Bader, Hodgkinson, Hillary, Simpson, and Page to restore their manhood from the wreckage of their mangled and misshapen bodies therefore reveal a range of subjective responses to the process of physical and psychological reconstruction. Personal pride, the professional expertise and unsentimental humanity of surgeons such as McIndoe, the camaraderie of the hospital ward, the possibility of returning to active service, and an increased appreciation of how the sacrifice of their youth and looks was warranted by the moral righteousness of a war against evil: all of these elements played their part in these narratives of reconstitution. So did women, although, in the cases of Simpson and Page, they seem less immediately auspicious than they do in the stories of Hodgkinson and Hillary. Fictional accounts of the disabled flyer are equally ambivalent with regard to the relationship of women to the recovery of manhood.[39] In H. E. Bates's novel *Fair Stood the Wind for France*, Franklin, a Wellington bomber pilot shot down over occupied France, is obliged to have his left arm amputated by a doctor working for the French Resistance. While recovering, he thinks of his girlfriend Diana back in Britain, 'with her bleached blonde hair and reddened fingers and her clear breasts that seemed purposely uplifted'. He ruefully concluded that Diana was essentially a superficial person, who would reject him once she saw his terrible injury. Before his last mission Diana had hoped that Franklin would soon receive the DFC: 'She would have liked me with the medal, he thought, more than without the medal; but not without the arm.'[40]

However, Diana's perfidiousness is not merely contrasted with the solidarity of Franklin's fellow aircrew, but also with the tenderness and bravery of Francoise, the female Resistance fighter with whom he falls in love. Their first kiss is a vital act of regeneration: 'Lying there, touching her arm, feeling the good warm flesh, so tender and smooth . . . he felt new life flow into him . . . that there was nothing he could not do if he wanted to do it enough.' However, whatever the restorative qualities of Francoise's love, it is his desire to return to the war which is the motor of his rejuvenation. Like Geoffrey Page, Franklin wanted to channel his sorrow at the loss of his arm into fighting 'in a new way, positively, harshly, with the bright anger of new purposes'.[41] In these narratives, both fictional and real, the reclaiming of manhood by the damaged flyer, even when it requires the intervention of women, usually involves the ultimate reassertion of conventional gender categories. William Simpson was unique among the figures considered, in that his injuries were too extensive for him to return to combat, so marriage and fatherhood came to be the most appropriate ciphers of his remasculinization. By contrast, the others were able to restore their manhood by reclaiming their status as warriors. In the 1957 novel *Eve at the Driving Wheel*, an RAF pilot who lost his leg during the war stays at home to manage the household while his wife pursues her career as a Grand Prix racing driver.[42] Few visions of the damaged flyer were willing to accommodate such overt emasculation, and it is perhaps significant that the author of this novel was a woman, Moie Charles. However, Charles's novel does hint at the potentially compromised status of all those flyers whose bodies had been violently dismembered or monstrously refashioned by fire.

FLAWED FLYERS AND FALSE FLYERS

Such portrayals of the disabled flyer in novels and films were relatively rare. Much more common was the fictional flyer who was emotionally or psychologically damaged. For all the RAF's heroic status, there are a surprisingly large number of literary and cinematic texts from the war and, especially, immediate post-war years which feature flyers with decidedly flawed personalities. In September 1945 a play premiered on the London stage which featured one such vision of the emotionally stunted flyer. In Warren Chetham Strode's *Young Mrs Barrington*, 27-year-old Squadron Leader Martin Barrington returns from service in India to his parents' home in Kingston-on-Thames at the ending of hostilities. Here he is reunited not merely with his siblings and widowed mother, but also with his wife Jo, whom he has not seen since their honeymoon four years previously. During their years apart Jo has been working in secret intelligence, during which she developed a close friendship with her boss, Colonel Renwick. While Martin, who had been awarded the DFC during the war, is hero-worshipped by his mother and sister, Jo is alienated by his apparent narcissism and insensitivity. Jo confides to her friend Mary that 'he's enjoying being a hero very much. But you can't live for ever on admiration.' Whereas the war has changed Jo, Martin appears immature, without cares and responsibilities, content to get through life by means of the 'little boy charm' which Jo had once found endearing, but which now seemed shallow and embarrassing. She becomes increasingly frustrated at Martin's apparent inability to comprehend what 'this hellish gap' in their lives has meant to her. His selfishness manifests itself in his failure to take any interest in Jo's wartime achievements (Mary pointedly tells him: 'Everyone's made a fuss of *you*...Don't you think that Jo might feel a bit out of things?'), and in his decision to invite along the rest of his family to what was supposed to be a holiday alone with his wife in Cornwall. When Jo disappears, Martin is convinced that she has run off with Colonel Renwick, and he confides to Mary that his apparent superficiality is a consequence of his need to bury his feelings during his time as a pilot: 'I've spent this whole bloody war stopping myself being sentimental. You've got to—you can't fight—if you are. You'd crack up.' Mary tells Martin that he needs to have the courage to reveal his emotional vulnerability to Jo. When he hears that Renwick is ill in hospital, he finds Jo and takes her to him, fully aware that, in so doing, he risks losing her to the other man. Renwick recovers, leaving Martin and Jo to agree to sort out their problems, staying at a remote hotel well away from the rest of his family.[43]

Another stage play performed in the very same year, H. E. Bates's *The Day of Glory*, also featured a young flyer returning to his family home, in this case on weekend leave. Jack Sanderson is a well-known fighter ace, and, like Martin Barrington, a recipient of the DFC. Jack has come to inform his parents that he is calling off his engagement to Catherine, whom he has known since childhood, and that he is now in love with Julia. In contrast to Catherine, who hopes to use Jack's fame to rise up the social ladder, Julia is able to empathize with the trauma Jack suffers in combat. Unlike Martin Barrington, Jack does not try to conceal his fear and guilt through a spurious performance of carefree bravado, at least not when alone with the woman he loves. However, even in Bates's sympathetic rendering of the young flyer, Jack, like Martin, is not immune to the potential narcissism which might result from the continuous idolization bestowed on a war hero by his family and the wider public. His mother sees him as the modest and gallant warrior, who appears uncomfortable with all the press attention engendered by his exploits. Julia, however, is more perceptive, noting that, 'when everyone else has gone to bed, he'll come down and cut out all the pictures of himself he can find. Then he'll stick them all in a nice little album and look at them all night in bed.'[44] Even the most heroic of fictional flyers could, at times, be surprisingly shallow.

Martin Barrington and Jack Sanderson were, however, essentially sympathetic characters, their imperfections excused, at least to some extent, by the stresses of living under constant fear of death or dismemberment. A much more discomforting rendition of the emotionally inadequate flyer can be found in James Campbell's middlebrow novel *Maximum Effort*. Flight-Sergeant Shern Douglas is a brash, insensitive, and mercenary exploiter of women, promising them love when he is only really interested in sexual gratification. He strings along two women at the same time, Terry in York and Loraine in London, before they both tire of his habitual mendacity. 'Easy living' is Douglas's 'only formula'. As Terry's friend, Sue, observes, Douglas might be handsome, but he is ultimately superficial, 'like a flashy piece of rolled gold. Scratch it, and the glitter comes off to reveal the base metal underneath.' Douglas is not entirely beyond redemption. Kiwi, a fellow pilot, accounts for Douglas's callous behaviour in terms of the strain of operational flying, which required him to build up a 'fine steel barrier' to hide his real feelings. Retreating behind this barrier, Kiwi insisted, Douglas had allowed 'a completely false self' to take over. Douglas comes to discover that, in spite of himself, he has genuinely fallen in love with Terry, and when his attempt to convince her that his feelings are more than mere lust fails, he compensates by proving himself skilful and courageous in combat. However, the novel ends on a downbeat note, with Douglas being forced to acknowledge the shallow amorality of his life, going so far as to conclude that it would have been better for everyone if he had been killed in action.[45]

An even darker imagining of the emotionally defective flyer is provided by the 1950 feature film *Cage of Gold*. Wing Commander Bill Glennon (David Farrar) had been a Battle of Britain hero, Judith May (Jean Simmons) his schoolgirl admirer. After the war they meet again, both changed by the intervening years, Judith physically, Bill morally. Despite his exemplary war record, Bill has deteriorated into a cruel wastrel who exploits women in his search for an easy life. He tricks Judith into marrying him, and then absconds with her money and jewels. Believing him dead, Judith marries a kindly doctor, Alan Kearn (James Donald). However, Bill suddenly reappears and attempts to blackmail Judith, but his sordid scheme is thwarted by Kearn's devotion to his wife. Kearn is superficially dull and pedantic, but essentially sincere and altruistic, in contrast to Glennon's superficial magnetism, which is merely a cover for his selfishness and brutality.[46]

The notion that the glamorous allure of the flyer, if stripped away, might reveal an emotionally stunted or dangerously self-absorbed personality beneath was one which attracted some of Britain's most accomplished literary figures during the late 1940s and early 1950s. In Elizabeth Taylor's first novel, *At Mrs Lippincote's* (1945), the RAF officer Roddy Davenant is hero-worshipped by his cousin, Eleanor. However, as his wife Julia has come to realize to her cost, Roddy may be a 'man of action' and a 'leader of men', but he understands little of the real world. He is cold and condescending, intolerant of those he deems 'weak and unsuccessful'. A control freak obsessed with appearances, Roddy 'wanted love only where there was homage as well, and admiration'. His failure to offer his wife even a morsel of emotional sustenance is highlighted by a passage in which his commanding officer gives a copy of *Wuthering Heights* to Julia, an act of tenderness and sentimentality which is implicitly contrasted with the actions of her emotionally stunted husband. Even Eleanor eventually comes to recognize Roddy's failings, disgusted by her discovery that he has a mistress, but no less appalled by the fact that he seems more concerned that the affair may jeopardize his service career than he is about its impact on his marriage.[47]

It was Terence Rattigan, however, who was responsible for the most well known literary rendering of the self-indulgent and emotionally inadequate flyer. In his wartime play *Flare Path*, the integrity and fair play of Flight-Lieutenant Teddy Graham triumphs over the artificiality and superficiality of the actor, Peter Kyle, who fails to persuade Teddy's wife to run off with him. However, ten years later, in his acclaimed 1952 drama *The Deep Blue Sea*, it is the ex-RAF pilot Freddie Page who is the superficial character, his raffish charms failing to compensate for an inconsiderate and vacuous personality. When, impatient at his continual failure to return her passion, his lover Hester Collyer attempts suicide, Freddie is completely out of his depth, confessing to a friend: 'My God, how I hate getting tangled up in other people's emotions. It's the one thing I've tried to avoid all my life.' Freddie's use of the same RAF slang which had been celebrated in *Flare Path* ('How's tricks?', 'smashing job', 'too bloody silly, old boy', 'knocked me ruddy flat') now appears anachronistic, frivolous, and inappropriate—'idiotic', in Hester's words. Freddie's verbal limitations clearly symbolize his emotional deficiencies. Freddie has taken to drink because, according to Hester, 'his life stopped in 1940. He loved 1940, you know. There were some like that.' When Freddie finally abandons Hester, fleeing to South America, he concludes his letter with the phrase: 'Sorry to have caused so much bother', which, as her estranged husband William, observes, 'has a nice ring of RAF understatement'. The flyer's legendary nonchalance, far from being praiseworthy, here serves as a hostile witness to Freddie's self-absorption and masculine cruelty.[48]

While Taylor and Rattigan explored the literary potential of the flawed flyer, other texts concerned themselves with what might be termed the false flyer. Several filmmakers were attracted to the idea of confounding the preconceptions of their audiences by having the glamorous blue-grey uniform of the RAF serve as a cloak for activities that were nefarious and malign. Such a conceit was sanctioned by official anxieties about civilian complacency over security matters, once the immediate threat of invasion had passed in 1940–1. What better way to remind the public of the need to take seriously the danger posed by spies and 'fifth-columnists' than by suggesting that even those wearing the heroic livery of the flyboys should not be considered above suspicion. One of the more preposterous narratives which emerged from this intersection of official paranoia and dramatic licence was the 1942 feature film *Squadron Leader X*, directed by Lance Comfort. Eric Portman played Erich Kohler, a Luftwaffe pilot who is sent, in RAF uniform, to bomb the Belgian city of Ghent and then to bale out, so that he can convince the local population that British pilots are being sent to bomb non-military targets. Unfortunately, Kohler lands on the roof of a family of resisters, who arrange his escape to England. Unwilling to risk revealing his true identity, Kohler has little choice but to go. In England, Kohler adopts the name

Squadron-Leader Standing, and seeks out Barbara Fenwick, a fifth-columnist he had been romantically involved with before the war. When Barbara betrays him to Scotland Yard, Kohler steals a British aeroplane and tries to return to Germany but, ironically, is shot down by a squadron of German Messerschmidts.[49] The *Monthly Film Bulletin* lauded Portman's performance, insisting that he succeeded in combining 'the reserve of the Englishman, the cruelty of the German bully and the latter's inherent cowardice quite brilliantly'.[50] However, the film lacked any element of surprise, since Kohler's identity is known to the audience from the beginning. Moreover, while audiences might have been mildly disorientated by the fact that Portman had previously appeared as a conventional RAF hero in the previous year's feature *One of Our Aircraft is Missing*, he had also portrayed a brutal Nazi villain in *49th Parallel*, the story of a renegade U-boat crew on the run in Canada which had been the top money-maker at the British box office in 1941. Moreover, Portman's screen persona possessed a tense edginess which meant that moviegoers were rarely surprised when his character was revealed, as it was in many of his films, to be pathological or murderous.[51]

By contrast, another film featuring a false flyer was more imaginative in its casting, which possibly ensured that its eventual denouement was much more discomforting to those who saw it. After receiving his DFC from the king at Buckingham Palace, Spitfire pilot and Battle of Britain hero Ian Gleed decided to spend some leisure time in London before returning to his base. He had lunch at the Savoy, dinner at Grosvenor House, and finally spent 'several happy hours' at Wyndham's Theatre, watching a performance of what he described as 'a grand play'.[52] The drama in question was Geoffrey Kerr's *Cottage to Let*, in which Dimble, a spy for the Germans, plots to abduct leading British inventor Jon Barrington from his Scottish home in a submarine, while making it appear that the boffin has defected to the enemy. Dimble murders Barrington's assistant Trently, but is eventually exposed as an enemy agent, and his plans are thwarted when the U-boat intended to convey Barrington to Germany is sunk. A minor character in the play is George Perrey, a young RAF sergeant-pilot, who has recently given up drinking out of fear that he might accidentally divulge confidential information about a new fighter plane he is test-flying. In one scene Dimble appears to get Perrey drunk, causing him to reveal the secrets of the experimental aircraft. In fact, we later learn that what Perrey has told Dimble is intentionally misleading and bogus, and that it is his aircraft which successfully bombs the German submarine.[53] *Cottage to Let* was very quickly adapted for the screen, although with a revised plot. Dimble is now a British agent, working to identify and apprehend a German spy known to be operating close to Barrington's laboratory. Moreover, Perry (who has been promoted to a flight lieutenant, and had the second 'e' dropped from his name) has a larger role in the film, and is played by John Mills, whose boyish attractiveness and good-natured charm made him an excellent choice for the part of the charismatic young flyer. In the film Perry is injured, and is being cared for by Helen,

Barrington's daughter. Perry uses his glamour and good looks to woo Helen and to gain the admiration of an evacuee, Ronald. Perry mocks the apparently pedestrian masculinity of Barrington's assistant Trently, ridiculing the fact that, while of service age, he is wearing spectacles and a laboratory coat when he ought to be in uniform. However, it ultimately emerges that, while Trently is doing secret research vital to Britain's war effort, Perry is bogus, a German spy attempting to steal Barrington's new design for a bomb-sight. Perry is eventually brought to justice by Trently and Ronald, appropriately in a shoot-out in a fairground hall of mirrors, which horribly distorts the handsome features and unbefitting uniform of the counterfeit flyer.[54]

In the 1947 comedy film *Holiday Camp*, Joe Huggett (Jack Warner) and his family encounter Squadron Leader 'Binkie' Hardwick (Dennis Price) while on a seaside vacation. Hardwick attempts to ingratiate himself with Joe's daughter Joan and her friend Angela, making ample use of his good looks, expensive clothes, and apparently heroic war record. Joe is repelled by Hardwick's flashy manner, and becomes suspicious at the inconsistencies in the stories the former squadron leader relates about his wartime exploits. One evening Angela tells Binkie that she wants to spend the evening with Joan, who has been on her own all day. In an instant Hardwick's breezy manner gives way to a disturbing harshness, as he violently grabs her wrist and demands that she does not leave his side. When Hardwick tries to strangle another guest at the holiday camp he is arrested, and revealed to be Geoffrey Baker, the schizophrenic 'mannequin murderer', whose twisted mind had persuaded him that he could only show love to women by killing them.[55]

If the inclusion of the sinister Hardwick in what was otherwise a routine screen comedy may seem a little bizarre, it was at least topical. Less than a year before *Holiday Camp* was released, in June 1946, a young man with a fresh complexion, pale blue eyes, and fair, wavy hair had checked in to the Tollard Royal Hotel in Bournemouth, under the somewhat improbable name of Group Captain Rupert Brooke. Brooke was glamorous and charming, happily flirting with young women on the sea front and impressing the hotel's more senior residents with anecdotes of his heroic deeds in the wartime RAF. He enchanted 19-year-old Doreen Marshall with a combination of his war stories and his compelling blue eyes. When, a few days later, it was announced that Doreen had disappeared, Brooke went to the police to offer assistance, alerting them to a suspicious-looking man he had seen Doreen engaged in conversation with. His affable manner, however, failed to deflect a sceptical police officer, who realized he had seen Brooke's face before, in a photograph of a man wanted in connection with the recent killing in London of Margery Gardner, whose violent death had appeared to be the result of a sadomasochistic bedroom escapade which had got horrifyingly out of hand. Shortly afterwards Brooke was arrested, after Doreen's mutilated body was found on Bournemouth beach, the victim of a relentlessly frenzied attack which recalled the infamous Whitechapel murders.

Group Captain Brooke was, in reality, Neville Heath, one of the most notorious murderers of the twentieth century, whose trial and execution in the autumn of 1946 captivated the British public.[56]

There was a miniscule element of truth in Heath's impersonation of the gallant RAF flyer. He had served in the air force before the war, but had been court-martialled and dismissed in 1937. During the war he joined the army, where he was again court-martialled, for being absent without leave. He managed to abscond from the troopship carrying him back from Egypt to Britain, and enlisted in the South African Air Force. His operational duties only amounted to a single mission in October 1944, piloting a Mitchell bomber over France while seconded to the RAF, and in 1945 he was court-martialled once more, this time for wearing medals to which he was not entitled. An incorrigible liar and impostor, Heath spent the months immediately after the war seducing wealthy women and then extorting money from them.[57] What became evident after his arrest was that he was not merely a con-man, but also a sexual sadist. If the more prurient aspects of his trial became a tabloid sensation, what was particularly compelling about his story was how this cruel maniac had so successfully employed the cover of the easygoing and heroic airman. In the words of one of Heath's biographers, 'the chivalrous and charming group captain had become the ripper with a knife in his hands'.[58] For a public which had invested so much in believing in the virtuous and heroic qualities of the flyer, the fact that their esteem could be so ruthlessly exploited by an amoral psychopath was unsettling, to say the least.

The Heath murders and films such as *Cottage to Let*, therefore, offered a warning: appearances could be deceptive. It wasn't just criminals who impersonated flyers. A plain-clothes police officer investigating the violation of licensing regulations at the See-Saw Club in Hove pretended to be a dashing RAF hero, so as to get on friendly terms with one of the women who ran the establishment. The result of this subterfuge was that the See-Saw Club lost its licence, despite the defence lawyer's assertion that the police officer had acted in 'a most un-English manner'.[59] If the RAF's blue uniform could be a cloak for mendacity or malevolence, its absence did not necessarily imply a failure to meet the standards of manly heroism which the flyer embodied in the popular imagination. In the 1944 Gainsborough screen melodrama *Love Story*, pianist Lissa (Margaret Lockwood) meets Kit (Stewart Granger) while convalescing from a serious illness in Cornwall. Given that this young, ostensibly fully fit man is not in uniform, she initially concludes that he must be a coward or a skiver. In fact, she comes to discover that he is a fighter ace who is going blind, but who has chosen to hide this fact as he fears pity. Through Lissa's love he develops the confidence to take on a risky operation which restores his sight, rejoins the RAF, and in the final scene is proudly wearing his uniform and pilot's wings once more.[60] Conversely, during the Battle of Britain illustrated-magazine advertisements for Brylcreem hair gel employed the image of a handsome young man in RAF uniform, his longish and uncontrolled hair made neat and shiny by the 'perfect hair dressing'. The desire of an established manufacturer of hair-care products to exploit the popularity of the young flyers of the RAF in the summer of 1940 was understandable, if a trifle cynical. However, what was bizarrely ironic was that the male model used in the advertisement, 'Tony' Gibson, was not merely not a real pilot, but was actually an anarchist member of the Peace Pledge Union, who was at the time serving a term in prison as an unregistered conscientious objector. When Gibson had posed for the advertisement, in 1939, he was wearing a regular suit, and the RAF wings had been added on a year later.[61] Trying to disentangle real flyers from false flyers was clearly a process fraught with difficulty and confusion.

The presence of damaged flyers, flawed flyers, and false flyers in British culture during the 1940s is an uneven one. By and large, these dark and uncomfortable visions of the flyer tended to belong to the margins of both public experience and popular imagination, although this chapter has revealed that they were not entirely insignificant. Moreover, it appears that, while the public became familiar with the real-life stories of a select number of physically disabled flyers, those flyers whose flaws were psychological rather than bodily were more likely to be encountered in the fictional narratives of novelists, playwrights, and screenwriters. While the RAF hierarchy appeared to have had little desire to minimize the exposure to the public of the severely disfigured flyers treated by McIndoe at East Grinstead, the psychiatric facility for disturbed aircrew at RAF General Hospital Matlock was in an isolated site on the Derbyshire moors, and the lives of those aircrew who were treated there remains, even now, highly obscure. In the 1950s actor Kenneth More was lauded for his performances as both a physically broken flyer (Douglas Bader in the screen adaptation of *Reach for the Sky*) and an emotionally defective flyer (Freddie Page, in the original stage production of *The Deep Blue Sea*).[62] Significantly, while the former involved the portrayal (albeit idealized) of a living person, the latter was an entirely fictional creation. However, whether real or imagined, these damaged flyers, flawed flyers, and false flyers projected a series of decidedly discomforting, not to say menacing, visions which were at odds with the glamorous and heroic status of the men in air-force blue. Such contradictions anticipated a broader ambivalence, among the public and the men of the RAF themselves, as to whether they were chivalric knights of the air or merciless agents of violent destruction.

7

The New Achilles? Literature, Technology, and Violence

The identity of the wartime flyer was characterized by a pronounced instability, which arose from the difficulty of reconciling two conflicting visions of masculinity. The flyer was often presented as sensitive and reflective, a gentle and chivalrous warrior, possessed of the sensibility of a poet or philosopher. However, elsewhere the flyer appeared as a cold-blooded killer, an uncompromising instrument of righteous vengeance against the enemy. Such apparently contradictory images of the man-at-arms were, of course, far from novel, and certainly not exclusive to the RAF. The vast majority of the men who undertook military service during the Second World War were either conscripts or volunteers 'for the duration'. Given that they would, at the conflict's end, be returning to civilian life, the public needed to be reassured that the wartime serviceman had not lost his capacity for humanity amidst the brutality and violence of war. However, it was equally true that no one was in any doubt that Britain was engaged in a savage war of survival, in which the enemy should be shown no mercy. Representations of the wartime flyer incorporated both of these very different interpretations of the qualities of manliness required of the fighting man. RAF personnel were fully familiar with depictions of the flyer as either a man of feeling or a heartless butcher, and their own self-fashioning frequently involved a dialogue with one, or both, of these divergent masculine archetypes. Moreover, these two contradictory images of the flyer became entangled with two other apparent binaries.

First, there was a discrepancy between the airman's unapologetic philistinism, observed by many air-base visitors, and the idealization of the flyer as a cultured aesthete, the latter conceit sanctioned by the presence in the wartime RAF of a number of accomplished artists and writers. Second was the contradiction between the association of flyers with a chivalric past (both historical and legendary) and the fact that their role as fighting men was mediated through the aeroplane, the mid-twentieth century's most potent emblem of scientific modernity. In the nineteenth century Karl Marx, dwelling on the cultural consequences of industrialized warfare, had queried: 'Is Achilles possible with gunpowder and lead?'[1] Such concerns about the redundancy of chivalry were obviously even more pertinent in the era of the interceptor fighter and the heavy bomber. In fact, cultural understandings of the wartime flyer revealed the resilience of age-old genres of martial masculinity which shrouded the violence of combat with the more congenial mantles of honour, modesty, and courtly refinement. However, this association of the flyer with the qualities of the 'gentle warrior' was to be jeopardized by the RAF's role in the slaughter of Germany's civilian population in the area-bombing campaign of 1940–5. In the light of the firestorms of Hamburg and Dresden, was the flyer a sensitive poet or a savage psychopath? This question vexed contemporary observers, and even the men who flew themselves, more extensively than we might suppose.

PHILISTINES OR POETS?

The fact that RAF aircrew waged war thousands of feet above the earth, in a world unfamiliar to the rest of humanity, inevitably raised expectations that the flyer would be possessed of a sensibility that was both exotic and poetic. Derek Gilpin Barnes, watching crews in the anteroom in his capacity as an RAF intelligence officer, proclaimed that 'they ride the highways of a strange and lonely world forever denied to the landsman. Behind their resolute eye live pictures inconceivable to all who do not pursue their calling amidst these lofty and ephemeral scenes.'[2] It is perhaps not surprising, therefore, that some commentators were desperately disappointed to discover that men who had seen such extraordinary things should, on firm ground, turn out to be inarticulate and prosaic. Expecting the flyers to be suitably ethereal and visionary, they were distressed to find them earthy and practical. Richard Hillary noted that the public were disappointed when the fighter pilots they met turned out to be withdrawn and uncommunicative.[3] The artist William Rothenstein was concerned 'to find how slight was the acquaintance with English literature among most officers' at RAF Leuchars. He was equally appalled by the fact that, in officers' messes, reproductions of Old Masters were usually hung too high to be properly seen, while 'prints of alluring ladies, taken from the illustrated reviews, are carefully pinned up at eye level'.[4] Rothenstein was forced to conclude that the flyer was more likely, through his heroic deeds, to inspire than to author profound works of literature or art, reassuring himself that: 'If they know little of poets, have not such men themselves been the subjects of great poetry?'[5] Other visitors to RAF bases were equally horrified at flyers' apparent indifference to high culture. In 1942 James Lees-Milne toured Blickling Hall in Norfolk, a Jacobean stately home which was serving as a temporary officer's mess for a nearby air base. He found that priceless antiques had been broken and ancient glass smashed by over-exuberant young flyers, acting merely 'out of devilry'.[6]

Critics of RAF philistinism were staggeringly insensitive to the fact that men facing violent death might have sought solace in mindless frivolity rather than highbrow edification. A Mass-Observation respondent at one RAF base protested in 1941 that fighter pilots awaiting the call to scramble were merely slouching in armchairs, rather than engaging in serious reading.[7] In fact, men whose lives were characterized by an endless cycle of boredom and anxiety inevitably preferred light music and pulp fiction to the more demanding products of high culture. At one point, the National Gallery created a scheme to loan paintings in its collection to RAF messes for the duration of the war.[8] However, significantly, these works of art were not insured, and RAF stations were told they would be liable for any damage caused by service personnel. Far from being a forum for the contemplation of fine art or a suitable place to undertake some serious reading, most RAF messes were dominated by the blaring of the wireless set, on which the volume was deliberately set high, the dial usually turned to a station offering big-band music and popular ballads, rather than to the intimidatingly earnest output of the Third Programme. In the relatively informal culture of the wartime RAF, flyers often seemed to take a mischievous delight in eschewing the highbrow in favour of the populist, the cheesy, and the escapist.[9] Other flyers felt that cultural refinement compromised their status as practical, tough-minded professionals. 'Sailor' Malan's official biographer insisted that the South African became a fighter pilot 'not for aesthetic reasons', but because of an instinctive knowledge that this was the job for which he was best suited, and that, indeed, 'imagination did not burden him unduly'.[10]

However, flyboy philistinism has to be set against an association of the flyer with poetry, literature, and art that went back to the formative days of aviation. Literary flyers such as D'Annunzio and Saint-Exupéry had insisted that manned flight was transforming aesthetics. Being able to rise above the clouds would allow artists to liberate themselves from the chains of tradition and mediocrity.[11] At a more mundane level, the dramatic growth of the wartime RAF ensured that it encompassed many men who were either connoisseurs or practitioners of high culture. Pilot Officer Michael Scott, a preparatory schoolmaster turned Blenheim navigator, recorded in his diary how, in his free time, he sought solace in the music of Schubert, Haydn, Tchaikovsky, and Mahler. The harmonious rhythm of Bach's sonatas for piano and violin, he insisted, 'soothes the nerves'. In a diary entry which reveals how flyers frequently traversed the boundaries between the profane and the refined, Scott boasted how he had, that evening, won seven shillings while playing poker in the mess, but had then returned to his room to listen to Brahms's Trio in B, Opus 8.[12] WAAF Edith Heap recalled that there were always classical-music lovers among the flyers she knew, notably some Australian aircrew who 'had beautiful voices and sang opera'.[13] Navigator George Hull confided to Joan Kirby that music offered compensation for the hardships of war: 'Hitler may rave, Churchill inspire . . . but Beethoven stands alone, unchallenged and never to be imitated.'[14] Squadron Leader John Wooldridge, a much-decorated Bomber Command pilot, was also renowned as a classical composer, who had studied with Sibelius.[15] In terms of the dramatic arts, playwright Terence Rattigan's RAF service has already been discussed. There were also numerous classically trained actors, both established and upcoming, among RAF aircrew; for example, Denholm Elliott, who left RADA to become a Halifax wireless operator. However, given the lack of facilities on air bases for the performing arts, reading remained the dominant form of highbrow cultural consumption. It was an activity that extended well beyond the obvious candidates, such as Oxford-educated officers like Richard Hillary or Jim Bailey. Pilot Officer Richard Tucker, a Halifax bomb-aimer, was the autodidact son of a wheel-tapper from Leyton. His letters reveal that his literary tastes were initially decidedly populist. However, while flight-training in South Africa he progressed from *Gone With the Wind* to *Greenmantle* and *Rebecca*. By the time he reached an operational squadron he had embarked on *Bleak House*, having, as he proudly disclosed to a female correspondent, 'gone all highbrow and started on pukka literature'.[16]

Where there were readers, there were inevitably to be found writers. Paul Fussell's characterization of the soldiers of the Great War—that, as beneficiaries of the expansion of state education in Britain at the turn of the twentieth century, they were 'not merely literate but vigorously literary'—might well be equally applied to the flyers of the Second World War.[17] Michael Scott's papers, retrieved after he was killed on an operational sweep over the North Sea in 1941, contained drafts of several short stories and poems. If Scott never made it into print, other budding authors were more successful. In H. E. Bates's play *The Day of Glory*, Diana Sanderson, on hearing the exploits of Pilot Officer Radwanski, asks the Polish fighter pilot: 'Aren't you going to write a book about it? Everyone in the Air Force writes a book.'[18] It is certainly true that one survey of wartime literature asserted that RAF flyers were more prolific authors than either soldiers or sailors, even if most of their writings lacked serious literary merit.[19] By 1942 a number of instant fighter-boy memoirs of the Battle of France and the Battle of Britain had already appeared, most notably David Crook's *Spitfire Pilot*, Ian Gleed's *Arise to Conquer*, and Paul Richey's *Fighter Pilot*. These were highly readable, and remarkably honest, given the constraints of wartime censorship and propaganda. However, they were clearly written in a hurry, by men still on active service, and they lacked a reflective dimension which might have allowed them, in the words of one literary critic, to 'reach beyond action to meaning'.[20] Ian Gleed genuinely desired to become a serious writer after the war, befriending the novelist William Somerset Maugham and other figures of the London literary scene, but was tragically killed in action in 1943.[21] In addition to these (embellished) memoirs, other authors penned works of fiction or poetry. True, the wartime RAF produced few accomplished novelists. It was to be the short story which would emerge as the most effective literary medium for conveying the RAF's war to the public in fictional form. If the works of C. H. Ward-Jackson and John Rees are now long forgotten, those of H. E. Bates and Roald Dahl have fared much better, and remain in print to this day.

Reviewing a number of 'war books' in November 1941, Tom Harrisson, the head of Mass-Observation, claimed that one of the reasons why the war in the air had received more attention from authors than other aspects of the conflict was the enlightened stance taken by the Air Ministry, which, unlike the War Office and the Admiralty, had appreciated the value of encouraging service personnel to write.[22] Indeed, the Air Ministry's public-relations department employed several leading literary figures, including the poets Henry Treece and John Pudney, as well as R. F. Delderfield, at this point a struggling playwright, but later to become a highly successful middlebrow novelist, whose post-war historical family sagas featured RAF flyers as leading characters.[23] The Air Ministry made a particularly astute decision in appointing Hector Bolitho to edit the *RAF Journal*. Bolitho was a writer and royal biographer from New Zealand with extensive contacts in the literary world. In his three years as editor he was able to secure the services of writers as eminent as George Bernard Shaw, J. B. Priestley, Eric Linklater, Clemence Dane, and David Garnett. Bolitho also proved to be a generous promoter of talented freshmen writers in the service, most notably Richard Hillary.[24] Lesser-known RAF writers who were discovered during the war featured in *Slipstream*, a published anthology of short stories and poems edited by two squadron leaders.[25] RAF servicemen who wished to become authors could be confident that the air-force hierarchy would indulge their literary ambitions, seeing RAF fiction or memoirs as a particularly effective medium for publicizing the achievements of the men who flew. Arthur Gwynn-Browne was still on active service in the RAF when he wrote his Bomber Command novel *Gone For a Burton* in 1942–3.[26]

In July 1941 H. E. Bates, who in the 1930s had been a relatively successful novelist of Midlands life and had already published the first stories featuring his popular protagonist Uncle Silas, was taken to lunch by Harald Peake, director of RAF Public Relations at the Air Ministry. Peake made the author an offer that was unprecedented in the history of the British armed services: Bates would be commissioned into the RAF strictly as a short-story writer. Bates initially had reservations, not least his anxiety that he 'knew nothing of flying, flying men, aerial combat, bombers or fighters'.[27] However, in a series of short stories about Bomber Command, written under the pseudonym of Flying Officer X, Bates was to succeed in capturing the essence of the wartime RAF more successfully than any other writer.[28] In part his success was down to careful observation—'eavesdropping', as he himself termed it—conducted at the bases he visited to research his stories. Many of Bates's characters were directly based on flyers he befriended. For example, an Australian pilot, Geoff Heard, was the inspiration for the short story 'The Young Man from Kalgoorlie', which featured a youth living on a remote sheep-farm in Victoria whose parents hide from him the news that war has been declared for almost a year, until he finally discovers their subterfuge and enlists in the RAF. Bates also wrote in an economical, descriptive style, 'clear and vivid in its pictorial simplicity', which was appropriate to the RAF's preference for understatement and its hostility to inflated bravado. The Flying Officer X stories were enormously popular with both critics and readers, although their author's only financial return was his RAF officer's wage.[29]

For his next literary project involving the RAF Bates sensibly took the precaution of securing the services of a new literary agent and an advance from his publishers. *Fair Stood the Wind from France* was a full-length novel about a downed Wellington pilot's escape through occupied France, after he loses an arm and falls in love with a French woman working for the Resistance. While the novel lacked sophistication, it was no simple romantic melodrama. Franklin, the leading character, was a flawed hero, prone to self-interest and violent jealousy, and the novel's happy ending belies an otherwise prevalent tone of disillusionment and bitterness.[30] Given the commercial success of *Fair Stood the Wind for France*, it is perhaps not surprising that Bates continued to return to the RAF as the subject for his writing on several occasions in the years that followed. *The Cruise of the Breadwinner* was a novel which included a flyer shot down in the North Sea; the stage play *The Day of Glory* featured the doomed fighter ace Jack Sanderson; while in the novel *The Purple Plain*, the suicidal Forrester, a flight commander on an isolated Burma airstrip, begins a love affair with a local woman.[31] If critics have been, at best, lukewarm about Bates's ultimate literary calibre, his contribution to the representation of the RAF in wartime British culture is unquestionable.[32] Moreover, his writings were popular with RAF aircrew themselves. One can imagine that Bomber Command flyers, in particular, who sometimes tired of the publicity and glamour attached to the fighter boys, were delighted to have found, in Flying Officer X, a literary champion of their own. Significantly, Michael Scott, the young Blenheim navigator and aspiring author, struggling to refine his own prose style, confided to his diary that in a recent short story he had composed 'the influence of H. E. Bates is strong, but, I hope, not too obvious'.[33]

While Bates was a non-combatant member of the RAF, several wartime airforce authors served as operational aircrew. Flight Lieutenant John Rees (whose marriage to fellow author Jane Oliver was detailed in Chapter 4) was killed during the Battle Of Britain, but a collection of his short stories, published under his pseudonym of John Llewellyn Rhys, was published posthumously in 1941. In her preface to the compilation, his widow argued that the strain of constant and exacting operational flying had granted Rees a heightened sense of perception which furthered his development as a writer. 'The discipline of his work in the air', she declared, 'gave to his writing something of its austerity and mysticism.'[34] A mystical motif was also to be found in the short stories of Roald Dahl, who, after initial training in Africa, succeeded in cramming his lanky six-foot-six frame into the tiny cockpit of a Hurricane, and became a fighter pilot in the campaigns in Libya and Greece in 1941. After being sent to Washington as assistant air attaché, Dahl began to write for the first time.[35]

His first ten short stories were all based on his RAF experiences. 'Madame Rosette' related the distractions of two flyers on leave in Cairo, while 'A Piece of Cake' detailed the nightmare of being shot down, a fate which had actually befallen Dahl in North Africa. Some of his stories, most notably 'They Shall Not Grow Old', in which a Hurricane pilot flies into a strange cloud and disappears for two days, anticipated Dahl's later interest in the supernatural, while in 'An African Story' we encounter his celebrated predilection for the bizarre and the grotesque (during training in Africa, a fledgling pilot's inattention while practising low flying results in him decapitating a giraffe), which was to be a central, if controversial, feature of his post-war success as a writer of children's fiction.[36]

The most famous writer-flyer was obviously Richard Hillary, whose fiction-alized memoir *The Last Enemy* has long retained a reputation as one of the few literary works produced in Britain during the Second World War to have achieved an enduring degree of profundity. In fact, a detailed appraisal of its strengths and weaknesses from a literary point of view reveals a distinct uneven-ness of quality. The famous epiphanic ending discussed in the previous chapter certainly seems contrived and unconvincing. However, Hillary's book did say something vital. It not merely provided a moving articulation of the sensibilities of the 'lost generation' of young men who fought and died in the Battle of Britain, but also served as a broader parable of suffering and sacrifice in war.[37] His lengthy recovery from the serious burns he suffered in September 1940 gave him the opportunity for reflection denied to other literary fighter boys like David Crook and Paul Richey. Moreover, Hillary had literary pretensions that were much more substantial than those of his fellow flyers who authored instant memoirs of 1940. On the dust-jacket of the first edition of *The Last Enemy*, Hillary identified himself as 'a writer who happened to be a pilot, not a pilot who happened to write a book'.[38] While touring the United States, Hillary met Antoine de Saint-Exupéry and, for all his protestations that he was possessed of an 'alert philistinism', *The Last Enemy* reveals that he had read Auden, Eliot, and Pound as a student at Oxford.[39] However, Hillary was tortured by the fact that his literary acclaim was wrapped up in his success in celebrating the fellowship of flyers, and yet, in becoming a famous writer, he had (as one astute commentator has observed) placed himself beyond 'the circle of their downbeat comradeship'. Desperate to rehabilitate himself in a service culture which was suspicious of anyone who appeared to be 'shooting a line', Hillary felt obliged to return to operational duties, despite his extensive injuries.[40] His subsequent death in 1943 reinforced his public reputation as a latter-day Philip Sidney, but also prevented the fulfilment of his post-war literary ambitions.

'It should be added that no war poetry can be expected from the RAF . . . the internal combustion engine does not seem to consort with poetry.' Such was the solemn estimation of Robert Graves, made at the close of a BBC broadcast on 'War Poetry in This War', which aired in late 1941.[41] Graves pronounced with the authority of both a leading figure in the British literary establishment, and a celebrated poet of the First World War, who, together with Siegfried Sassoon and Wilfred Owen, had served as a lyrical witness to the bloody futility of trench warfare, by which he had been both appalled and strangely beguiled.[42] It is true that the RAF failed to produce an outstanding verse writer during the war, certainly nobody of the talent and status of soldier-poets Keith Douglas, Sidney Keyes, or Alun Lewis. Despite the fact that more subaltern air-force officers died in the Second World War than their army equivalents in 1914–18, this time round the slaughter of the flower of their nation's youth failed to inspire a poetry of indignation and pity of the calibre produced on the Western Front a quarter of a century before. Such a disparity can be quite easily explained. In the Great War, bitter disillusionment had been an inevitable consequence of initial expectations that the war would be heroic and noble. By contrast, the young men who joined the RAF during the Second World War, conscious of the fate of their predecessors in 1914–18, had adopted a pose of studied cynicism from the very beginning.[43] Philip Toynbee, in his memoir of writer and bomber pilot Esmond Romilly, noted how, in 1939, the convention was to distrust anything reminiscent of the extravagant sentiments and high emotions that had characterized the public mood in 1914.[44] However, this did not preclude many flyers from composing verse, nor did it prevent a regular association of the men of the RAF with poetry in the wartime popular imagination. In general, young poets found it relatively easy to publish their work during the Second World War. At a time of shortages, poetry was a genre of writing which made less demands on print and paper than the novel. Verse could also be more readily composed, and read, than prose in the brief intermissions between military duties.[45]

Graves's broadcast prompted a response in the letters page of the *Listener* from Keidrich Rhys, a pseudonym of William Jones, Welsh writer and editor of *Poems From the Forces*, who disputed the notion that poets who had joined the RAF had not chosen to write about their flying experience.[46] Rhys alerted readers to an anthology of the poetry of flight compiled by three flight cadets at the RAF College at Cranwell before the war.[47] Early in the war the posthumous verses of Flying Officer D. N. Weir, DFC, were collected and published after he was killed in action. For all their obvious poignancy, Weir's poems possessed only limited literary merit. Tom Harrisson was convinced that they had never been intended for publication, and he expressed his revulsion that private poems, 'of the sort produced by every adolescent', had been raked out, merely 'because a man dies in action'.[48] A more worthy literary enterprise came in 1944, when John Pudney and Henry Treece, both attached to the publicity section of the Air Ministry, edited an anthology of poems by thirty-three RAF personnel, ranging from squadron leaders to flight sergeants and ground crew. The editors' hope was that their volume would demonstrate 'that a man may fight and yet keep his soul, that a poet is a poet whatever he is called on to face'.[49] Treece was an important figure in poetic circles during the 1940s. He promoted the career of Dylan

Thomas and founded the New Apocalypse movement, which rejected both the political didacticism of the 'Auden set' and the poetry of surrealism, in favour of a direct relation with the actual world. During the war he joined the RAFVR and attained the rank of flight lieutenant. While his poor eyesight prohibited him from flying, he completed a course as a navigator and served as an intelligence officer.[50] When transferred to the Air Ministry, he worked closely with John Pudney, a poet and former writer-producer for the BBC. Pudney lacked Treece's radical poetic agenda, and his verses were at best banal, at worst dangerously close to maudlin sentimentalism. However, Pudney's epitaph on a downed pilot, 'For Johnny' ('Fetch out no shroud | For Johnny-in-the-cloud | And keep your tears | For him in after years') became one of the most oft-quoted poems of the entire war. Pudney believed that a 'tense compression of poetry' was the most suitable style in which to render the sensibilities of the wartime RAF, and the popularity of his verse with both flyers and the broader public suggested this view was widely shared.[51]

'For Johnny' and another Pudney poem, 'Missing', featured in the 1945 movie *The Way to the Stars*, allowing an affective element to infiltrate a narrative which otherwise celebrated verbal understatement and emotional restraint. The film also demonstrated how, even if the quality of poetry produced by the air force was rarely exceptional, the notion of the fictional flyer-poet had captured the imagination of the British public during the war. *The Way to the Stars* had been scripted by Terence Rattigan, who was also responsible for co-authoring, with H. E. Bates, a film treatment (the movie was never made) entitled 'Signed With Their Honour', in which Quayle, a Gladiator pilot, quotes Byron to the Greek woman with whom he has fallen in love.[52] However, the most powerful rendering of the cult of the flyer-poet is Powell and Pressburger's cinematic fantasy *A Matter of Life and Death*. In his highly theatrical opening speech, Flight Lieutenant Peter Carter (David Niven) recites a verse by Marvell to an initially bewildered, but subsequently captivated, female radio controller, as his Lancaster crashes in flames. Carter's obvious devotion to high art and a self-conscious chivalric yearning reveal him as the antithesis of the philistine flyer. Later in the film we discover that Carter is himself an accomplished poet, who had composed his first poem at 15, an 'intense, sentimental affair, inspired by the prettiness of a friend's sister'. Having published his first volume of verse at 19, Carter had gone up to Oxford, 'where he had read copiously and written more poetry, only to be wrenched away at the age of twenty-two by mankind's greatest madness'.[53] For all the flyer's legendary emphasis on understatement and hostility to overblown expressions of emotion, he could also be imagined as a sensitive, indeed lyrical, man of feeling and imagination.

Even if most flyers would have found the flamboyant romanticism of *A Matter of Life and Death* a little too much to take, the published memoirs of wartime airmen are rarely completely immune to the compelling romance of the clouds. Richard Lumford, who served as aircrew in Wellington bombers, described how the lives of pilots 'were bound up, not merely emotionally, imaginatively, but in down-to-earth activity, with cosmic Nature—sun, stars, moon, clouds, wind, ice and magnetism and the poles . . . the strangeness and splendour of this airy kingdom'.[54] Such overblown lyricism might have been expected from a man who had been a noted aesthete at Oxford in the 1930s, and was a self-proclaimed disciple of Walt Whitman. However, such leaps of poetic fancy can also be found intruding into what were otherwise decidedly hard-edged autobiographical narratives. Jim Bailey avowed that, above the clouds, he was 'lifted out of the common philosophy', allowing him to become 'elemental, purged of all but the greater emotions'.[55] Geoffrey Wellum's account of a mission with 92 Squadron includes a description of how, 'climbing steadily through the late-afternoon haze, the sun, red and rather angry looking, throws its last rays on the gently swaying aircraft, bathing them in a brown golden colour'. Wellum also recalled that his memories of August 1940 revolved 'around dawns. Pink dawns, grey dawns, misty, rainy and windy dawns, but always dawns; first light. Shadowy Spitfires and quietness in the tent as we doze and wait.'[56] A fellow veteran of the Battle Of Britain, in equally elegiac mode, recalled on a BBC radio programme:

that what remains most clearly in my memory is not the sweating strain of the actual fighting, not the hurried meals, the creeping from bed at dawn, not even the loss of one's friends; but rather those odd stolen moments of peace in the middle of all the pandemonium—the heat haze lying lazily over the airfield while we sat munching a piece of grass, waiting to take off; the curiously lovely moment of twilight after the last Spitfire had landed, after the last engine had been switched off . . . the moment when the evening lay spread out against the sky, giving for an instant a mocking glimpse of stillness and peace.[57]

Another fighter boy, scrambling into his cockpit at sunrise, was struck by 'the sparkle of the sun on the grass reflected by the dewdrops. Somehow one can't help wondering in these last moments of earthliness with all the beauties of nature around, just how many [of his fellow flyers] are to see them again.'[58] Bomber aircrew were less liable to wax lyrical about the dawn, given that the sun usually rose just as they were crashing into bed after returning from their night missions. Their poetic descriptions were reserved for the moon and the stars, or the mysterious patterns made in the night sky by anti-aircraft flak or the distant glow of the burning cities to which they were headed.[59] Roland Winfield described 'the sinuous beauty of the coloured tracer which slowly climbs in the sky in stately spirals in the way that snowflakes whirl at you in a snowstorm'.[60] In finding beauty amidst the violence of combat, the flyer, even if rarely self-consciously, stood in a long tradition (of which earlier twentieth-century exponents had been Ernst Jünger and Edmund Blunden) of integrating war into nature to create what has been termed a 'military pastoral'.[61] However, where flyers were most likely to abandon their understated nonchalance in favour of poetic hyperbole was not in recalling the beauty of the sunrise or the sublime terror of cloudland. Where the laconic flyer proved most lyrical was in regard to his aircraft, especially if he was fortunate enough to pilot the legendary Spitfire.

MEN AND MACHINES

The flyer was simultaneously an emblem of modernity and a recollection of heroic conflicts from the distant past. The airman's combat experience was inseparable from science and machinery: not merely the aircraft he flew, but the technology of radio, radar, navigational aids, and ballistics with which it was associated. In John Pudney's poem 'Dispersal Point', James is a pilot who flies:

> with a surgeon's glance
> Grave and discriminate, [to] enforce the dreams
> Of mathematic theory.[62]

Bomber crews, in particular, engaged throughout their missions in a series of intricate tasks, resembling those of an engineer or a skilled craftsman in a workshop. To appropriate Robert Wohl's characterization, bomber aircrew were 'technicians, the prototypical figures of a democratic and industrial war'.[63] Subject to factory-like discipline, they were participants in a highly mechanized form of warfare which appeared to leave little space for traditional conceptions of heroism. In Arthur Gwynn-Browne's novel *Gone For a Burton*, the air-gunner, Roy, comes to appreciate that the true worth of his skipper, Anthony, lay in his solid mastery over the mechanics of his aircraft, rather than in any airy gallantry: 'there was nothing heroic, for instance, about a brake pressure gauge. The bubble sextant and indicator of the rate of climb were unmoved by ecstasy . . . flying was not a flashy thing but a serious business.'[64] Fighter pilots were no less aware of their dependency on advanced technology. The memoirs of Peter Townsend reveal that, at the beginning of the war, fighter pilots still relied overwhelmingly on instinct, using road and railway lines to navigate their way home.[65] However, by the middle years of the war radar and other advanced tracking devices were increasingly being resorted to. During the Battle of Britain the desperate need for pilots left little time for training, and flyers were forced to rely on a combination of improvisation and their innate qualities rather than technical competence. However, for the remainder of the war aircrew received the comprehensive instruction appropriate to taking responsibility for the complex and technologically advanced fighting machines they piloted.[66] Novels and films portrayed the flyer and the scientist collaborating in the development of new technology, ensuring that the former was fully associated in the popular imagination with scientific modernity. Jerry, the hero of Nevil Shute's novel *Landfall*, test-flies experimental aircraft and offers advice to the scientist, Legge.[67] In the film *The First of the Few*, Geoffrey Crisp (David Niven) serves as test-pilot to the aircraft designer R. J. Mitchell (Leslie Howard), as the latter develops a revolutionary new fighter aircraft which becomes the Supermarine Spitfire, while in *The Dam Busters* Guy Gibson (Richard Todd) provides practical assistance and moral support to the 'boffin', Barnes Wallis (Michael Redgrave), whose unorthodox 'bouncing bomb' serves as a means of demolishing the great dams of the Ruhr valley. Crisp was a fictional character, but the cinematic relationship between Gibson and Wallis was based on fact, although official secrecy demanded that the legendary inventor be identified merely as 'Jeff' in the memoir Gibson completed before his death in 1944. Significantly, Gibson insisted that the success of the British bombing offensive was not just attributable to 'young men with guts', but also 'to science'.[68] Gibson and Wallis thereby personified the fruitful marriage of theory and action.

However, while the air war was conducted through the medium of machinery, flyers invested their aircraft with personal, and even aesthetic, qualities, which meant that they were never regarded as merely functional 'tools of the trade'. Flyers often referred to their aircraft in language which was romantic and lyrical, rather than technical and instrumental. This tendency was particularly true of those who flew the legendary Supermarine Spitfire fighter, regularly described by its pilots as 'beautiful', 'lovely', or 'noble'.[69] 'Sailor' Malan conceded that the Spitfire was 'obviously a killer', but, nevertheless, also a 'perfect lady', with 'trim sweet lines'.[70] The Spitfire was not entirely beyond criticism. Some flyers found it a difficult aircraft to land, given its narrow wheel-base, while its very long nose obscured the pilot's visibility on take-off. Some fighter pilots preferred the rugged and sturdy Hurricane to the more delicate Spitfire.[71] However, for the great majority of flyers their relationship with the Spitfire can best be characterized, as it was by Czech pilot M. A. Liskutin, as 'love at first sight'.[72] During his inaugural flight in a Spitfire, Geoffrey Wellum admiringly noted that the very shape of the aircraft's wing was 'a thing of grace and form . . . Curved leading and trailing edges, not a straight line anywhere'. Awaiting take-off, he likened the fighter's beautifully proportioned lines to a thoroughbred racehorse at the starting line of the Derby.[73] After his first encounter with the Spitfire, French fighter pilot Pierre Clostermann was even less inhibited in investing his aircraft with a sensuous corporeality: 'How beautiful the machine seemed to me, and how alive! A masterpiece of harmony of power, even as I saw her now, motionless. Softly, as one might caress a woman's cheeks, I ran my hand over the aluminium of her wings, cold and smooth like a mirror, the wings which had borne me.'[74] Richard Hillary insisted that even dull camouflage could not conceal the 'clear cut beauty' of the Spitfires and the 'trim deceptive frailty of their lines'.[75]

In combat, the Spitfire, its infatuated pilots maintained, was more than a mere machine. It was animated, courageous, and gracefully lithesome, qualities which were no less apparent to those on the ground. H. E. Bates, watching the Battle of Britain unfolding over the skies of Kent, likened the agile manoeuvrability of the Spitfires to silver moths engaging in a celestial ballet, while novelist Mary

Renault declared that they were as 'pretty and brisk as minnows in the high clear air'.[76] Even the cynical mechanic Robert Collins, for all his hostility towards the officer caste who piloted the aircraft he serviced, found his 'blood tingled' when he was assigned to a Spitfire squadron: 'every red-blooded boy of my generation worshipped the Spit. Lean and racy . . . it seemed poised as though about to soar, even when silent on the tarmac.'[77] The Spitfire was a triumph of engineering, as was evident from the fact that it continued in service, in various upgraded versions, throughout the whole war. However, its curved elegance and fluency in flight ensured that even the most prosaically inclined flyers testified to its aesthetic appeal. As the character of Geoffrey Crisp, the test-pilot turned station commander, points out to a group of Battle of Britain fighter pilots in *The First of the Few* (in a sentence whose phrasing concisely, if unintentionally, encapsulates the synthesis of the technical and the romantic), the Spitfire 'was designed by an artist'.

Of course, not all aircraft possessed the style and finesse of the Spitfire. Jim Bailey, flying the sluggish and weirdly designed Boulton Paul Defiant (a two-man fighter plane lacking forward-firing fixed guns), envied those fortunate enough to pilot the 'more fluent' Spitfire. Bailey was soon transferred to a Spitfire squadron, but later in the war flew the Beaufighter, an aircraft he came to regard as a formidable destroyer, but still 'a clumsy brute'.[78] It is rare to find bomber aircrew writing of their aircraft in the same language of love which characterized the Spitfire pilot. If the decidedly uncouth four-engined bomber was to be celebrated, it was inevitably for its ruggedness and endurance, not for beauty or elegance. J. C. M. Gibb, one of the contributors to the *Air Force Poetry* anthology, described the bomber as an 'ungainly blackened brute . . . | With wings and breast unfeathered, | Milkless and destructive all'.[79] However, there were occasions on which bomber aircrew could be decidedly lyrical when appraising the qualities of the aircraft they flew. George Hull compared his Lancaster, A-Able, to 'a beautiful woman to be taken care of, treated with respect. She's strong and reliable, never grudging . . . obeying the stern rigours of circumstance with grace and efficiency . . . Her manner is self-assured and sophisticated.' On her return from a mission, his aircraft 'points her aristocratic nose towards England', her 'vivacious flight' sustained by her four Merlin engines, which 'sing in tune and harmony'.[80]

While fighter pilots tended to conceptualize their war as one in which the individual could still feel that he had freedom of action and could control his fate, bomber aircrew demonstrated much more definitively the fact that the flyer was ultimately a man disciplined by technology. In a powerful passage in Antoine Saint-Exupéry's *Flight to Arras*, the celebrated writer-flyer detailed how the airman and his machine became inextricably linked in flight:

all the instruments that were an encumbrance while I was dressing have now settled into place and acquired meaning. All that tangle of tubes and wiring has become a circulatory network. I am an organism integrated into the plane. I turn this switch, which gradually heats up my overall and my oxygen, and the plane begins to generate my comfort . . . the plane is my wet-nurse. Before we took off, this thought seemed to me inhuman, but now, suckled by the plane itself, I feel a sort of filial affection for it. The affection of a nursling.[81]

While generally purged of such quasi-Oedipal associations, wartime RAF flyer memoirs registered a similar sense of flyer and aircraft becoming a single, merged entity. Geoffrey Wellum referred to feeling 'at one' with his fighter plane, while Pierre Clostermann and his Spitfire 'made an integral whole together'.[82] Fictional narratives by RAF personnel reiterated such notions. John Sommerfield drew on his experience as a groundcrew mechanic in describing Phil, a Spitfire pilot, who having clambered into his cockpit and put on his flying helmet, 'didn't belong to us anymore. Once in the seat, with the air screw turning and a great torrent of sound pouring away from it, he became someone else, someone remote and inhuman, the brains of a machine.'[83] In one of Roald Dahl's short stories, 'the body of the Spitfire was the body of the pilot, and there was no difference between the one and the other'.[84] To some observers, the mechanization of the flyer's body appeared so advanced that the human presence in the aircraft had been erased completely. Official war artist Paul Nash claimed that he had first become attracted to the Battle of Britain as a potential subject when he realized that 'the machines were the real protagonists'. For, while 'vast human forces were involved', their operations were both directed mechanically and they 'themselves assumed increasingly a mechanical appearance. Pictorially, they seemed to be unimportant compared with the personality of the machines they employed as weapons, for, so powerful were these agents of war, that once set in motion they soon dominated the immense stage.'[85]

However, not all those who witnessed the dogfights which took place over south-east England in the summer of 1940 saw them exclusively as an epic conflict of machine versus machine. Many observers felt that, ironically, the Battle of Britain had seen machines renewing the romance of war. Significantly, Pierre Clostermann had compared the synthesis of man and machine he had experienced when flying a Spitfire to 'a rider and his well-trained steed', an analogy which potentially recalled the chivalric knights of the Middle Ages.[86] Lord David Cecil, after visiting several air bases, found the RAF, on the one hand, 'modern and organized and scientific in the very highest degree', while on the other it recalled 'the personal warfare of medieval knights'. For, while a warplane, with its paraphernalia of technical equipment, was 'necessarily scientific', it held, at most, a handful of men (and, if it was a fighter, only one), and hence the 'individual quality of each airman counts more than the individual quality of each soldier or sailor'. This essential individualism, this spirit of 'free gallant adventure', ensured that air warfare was 'a reversion to that of an earlier day'.[87] Cecil had in mind the courtly chevaliers of the Hundred Years War, or those who had manned the 'timbered hulks at Trafalgar', but other historical and mythical analogies were regularly employed at this time. Geoffrey Wellum likened his fellow fighter pilots in the summer of 1940, flying against superior numbers of enemy aircraft, to the swashbuckling Elizabethan 'sea dogs'—Hawkins, Grenville, Frobisher, Raleigh, and Drake—who had turned back the Spanish Armada.[88] Roald Dahl compared the dramatic air battle over Athens on 20 April 1941, in which he took part, to the heroic encounters of classical antiquity, such as Thermopylae or Marathon.[89] The opening credits of Laurence Olivier's cinematic adaptation of *Henry V*, released in 1944, dedicated the film to the 'Commandos and Airborne Troops of Great Britain', an appropriate citation in the year of D-Day and Arnhem. However, the film-treatment notes of Alan Dent, who worked with Olivier on adapting Shakespeare's play for the screen, revealed that the filmmakers expected (and encouraged) the British public to detect another recent analogue to the outnumbered English bowmen who had triumphed at Agincourt. 'Surely', Dent insisted, the triumph of Henry's 'band of brothers' was 'comparable with Britain's hour in the autumn and winter of 1940, when a "pitiful few" during the Battle of Britain went up into the skies, hour after hour, week after week, and kept a powerful invader at bay. These modern warriors of the skies were worn too—tired, nerve-wracked, but they had that same courage and won the day as King Henry and his soldiers won theirs centuries ago. The parallel is very significant.'[90] If Dent's focus was on the potential value of such contemporary affinities for the marketing of Olivier's film, he was nevertheless articulating a comparison that had considerable purchase among the British public. Men of the wartime RAF seemed to have embodied the apparently opposed qualities of the aesthetic and the technological, the romantic and the scientific, the traditional and the modern. The flyer both represented the transformation of warfare through machinery in the twentieth century, and a yearning to return to the apparently more individualistic, and heroic, martial endeavours of the historical and mythical past.

SAVAGERY AND SENSITIVITY

'This is not a troubadour's war.' This remark, addressed by the mysterious Robert Kelway to his lover Stella Rodney, comes from Elizabeth Bowen's unsettling novel of the London Blitz, *The Heat of the Day*.[91] Robert clearly had a point. A total war, in which mechanized mass warfare had replaced individual combat, and in which little attempt was made to discriminate between soldiers and civilians, appeared to be the very antithesis of the traditions of gentlemanly chivalry celebrated by the lyric poets of the Middle Ages. Indeed, conventional wisdom insists that chivalry, born in the legendary court of King Arthur, and subsequently revived as part of the fashioning of a new social elite in the nineteenth century, had already been laid to rest a generation before Stella and Robert, characters in a novel characterized by dislocation and disorientation, had been obliged to come to terms with a new form of warfare in which home front and battle front were increasingly indistinguishable. Chivalry's demise had come about between 1914 and 1918, when young men, eager to match the ideal of the gentle, courteous warrior, had found themselves instead confronted by the industrialized slaughter of the Western Front.[92] Recently, however, the view that chivalry failed to outlast the horrors of the Great War has been called into question. Joanna Bourke has pointed out that military authorities continued to encourage the language of chivalry as a means of checking demoralization, realizing that it permitted the fighting man to shroud the violence he was required to enact under a mantle of honour and fellowship.[93] Allen Frantzen also argues for continuity rather than dramatic disjunction, demonstrating that the Crusades and the Hundred Years War remained important reference points during the First World War, finding their way into the iconographies of postcard illustrations, recruiting posters, and war memorials. However, in contrast to Bourke, Frantzen asserts that such cultural resilience was less to do with chivalry's ability to hide men's violence from them (and from the public), than with its ability to justify the logic of military reprisal. The soldiers of the Great War, no less than medieval knights, believed they were fighting a holy war, seeing themselves as both instruments of righteous vengeance for insults to sacred beliefs and institutions, and Christlike sacrificial victims.[94] Frantzen's thesis has proved controversial, but his insistence on the continued significance of chivalry in cultural understandings of the fighting man in the twentieth century clearly has particular pertinence in regard to representations of the flyer.

Even those who had accepted that the dream of the courtly warrior had died amidst the mud of Flanders conceded that there were one or two exceptions during the Great War which proved the general rule. T. E. Lawrence's irregular warfare against the Ottoman Turks in the Levant seemed to recall the chivalric warriors of the past, an identification reinforced by its exotic setting and association with the feudal honour codes of the Arabs whom he led, and whose customs he (albeit partially) adopted. Lawrence ultimately proved to be a flawed hero for those who wished to retrieve from the brutality of modern warfare a narrative which recalled more congenial traditions: his admission to having ordered the killing of Turkish prisoners-of-war at Tafas certainly failed to accord with the expectation that the chivalric warrior would be courteous and considerate towards his vanquished enemies. However, when Lawrence died in 1935 his tomb, designed by his friend and acolyte the artist Eric Kennington, was modelled on the medieval recumbent effigies of crusader knights.[95] The other exception was aerial warfare. Chivalry was seen as widely relevant in regard to the war in the air between 1914 and 1918. The exploits of fighter aces such as Manfred von Richtofen, Albert Ball, and James McCudden were presented as analogous to the individual combat of jousting knights. First World War pursuit pilots appeared to represent the finest traditions of chivalry and fair play, letting an adversary fly home safely if his guns had jammed, entertaining a captured enemy flyer in the mess, or respectfully dropping a wreath over an enemy airfield to honour a fallen opponent. In fact, the reality of the 1914–18 air war was significantly less prepossessing. Gentlemanly airborne duels, and the nobility and romance they suggested, were rare. Most of the great fighter aces owed their success to being cold-blooded killers, who preyed on sluggish reconnaissance aircraft. However, operating as they did, high above the sordid world of the trenches, ensured that these airmen were linked in the popular imagination to older, more noble, traditions. The appellation 'knights of the air' spoke volumes, and these early flyers were often reluctant to shatter the illusions of an adoring public.[96] Cecil Lewis, in a book widely read by aspiring young flyers of the next generation, described being a fighter pilot as equivalent to 'the lists in the Middle Ages, the only sphere in modern warfare where a man saw his adversary and faced him in mortal combat, the only sphere where there was still chivalry and honour'.[97] Moreover, as Linda Robertson has established, the boosters of aerial warfare in the inter-war years encouraged identification of the flyers of the Great War with the ancient standards of chivalry in order to foster the notion that aviation offered a clean and civilized approach to warfare. Such rhetoric was, of course, disingenuous, given that the purpose of air power was increasingly being conceptualized by its proponents in terms of demoralizing the enemy through the deliberate bombing of civilian populations.[98] However, in the 1920s and 1930s the Great War flyer, like Lawrence of Arabia, appeared to be an honourable exception to the mechanized slaughter that had come to characterize modern warfare.

The Second World War flyer benefited from being seen as the heir to these 'knights of the air'. In August 1940, at the height of the Battle of Britain, literary scholar and critic C. S. Lewis published a short essay arguing for 'the necessity of chivalry'. Lewis, an expert on medieval literary romance, argued that to be chivalric required a man to possess, in equal measure, ferocity and meekness, bravery and modesty. The knight of Arthurian romance was 'a man of blood and iron, a man familiar with the sight of smashed faces and the ragged stumps of lopped-off limbs; he is also a demure, almost a maidenlike, guest in hall, a gentle, modest, unobtrusive man'. Lewis saw in Malory's Lancelot 'the one hope of the world', an ideal that had to be aspired to, lest humanity fall into two sections—those who were unable to prevent their ferocity in war from spilling over into brutality, and those whose meekness rendered them cowardly milksops, unable to stand up to the fascist aggressor. 'Happily,' Lewis proclaimed, 'Lancelot is not yet irrecoverable':

To some of us this war brought a glorious surprise in the discovery that after twenty years of cynicism and cocktails the heroic virtues were still unimpaired in the younger generation and ready for exercise the moment they were called upon. Yet within this 'sternness' there is much 'meekness'; from all I hear, the young pilots in the RAF (to whom we owe our life from hour to hour) are not less, but more, urbane and modest than the 1915 model.

For Lewis, the wartime flyboys implied that 'there is still life in the tradition which the Middle Ages inaugurated'.[99] Some observers found that the flying gear of RAF aircrew created a startling physical resemblance to the Arthurian ideal, or at least to its more recent rendering in nineteenth-century Pre-Raphaelite art. William Rothenstein painted the portrait of a young pilot 'of fine appearance', who came to his sitting 'wearing a helmet of a kind I had not hitherto seen, which gave the appearance of a knight from one of Burne Jones' tapestries'.[100]

The chivalric attributes of the flyer were further reinforced by an association with T. E. Lawrence. Eric Kennington, who was commissioned to paint the portraits of many prominent RAF flyers, found that Lawrence's combination of bravery and humility was 'very much alive in the wartime RAF'. He was pleased to discover that many flyers were already familiar with Lawrence's account of the Arab revolt, *Seven Pillars of Wisdom*, while others asked Kennington to supply them with copies of *The Mint*, Lawrence's autobiographical account (at this point still unpublished) of his years spent anonymously in the RAF in the 1920s.[101] However, for all these chivalric connotations, flyers by and large were eager to disassociate themselves from the romance of war. Even Richard Hillary, who, through his friendship with Kennington, was captivated by the cult of Lawrence of Arabia, adopted a tone of coarse scepticism in *The Last Enemy*.[102] Noel Monks, the war correspondent who reported on a Hurricane squadron during the Battle of France, observed that fighter pilots were 'too hard-headed and practical' to display the chivalry which he believed had been in evidence during the air war of 1914–18. If a pilot's guns jammed in 1940, his opponent was unlikely to be magnanimous. This time round, the flyer expected to pay for the misfortunes of war with his life. 'As for the victor flying over the victim's squadron and dropping a note of condolence,' Monks made clear, 'the Hurricane boys will have none of that.'[103] When, in 1942, Douglas Bader was shot down over France, he was entertained by Luftwaffe officers in their mess, and a request was made through the Red Cross to the RAF to supply a new artificial leg to replace the one which he had been forced to leave behind while parachuting out of his stricken aircraft. However, if such *noblesse oblige* echoed the spirit of 1914–18, it is significant that, when the RAF dropped Bader's replacement prosthetic leg over St-Omer airfield, they also took the opportunity to discharge a cluster of bombs onto the German fighter aircraft parked on the runway.[104]

The failure to successfully contain the flyer within the chivalric tradition disclosed a broader ambiguity. There was a potential opposition between the flyer as sensitive and urbane and the flyer as a heartless killer. Was he a lover of flight, or a lover of war? Contemporary responses to this question could be unsparingly unsentimental. Lord David Cecil, for all his heroic idealization of the men of the RAF, was still adamant that: 'The airman's task is destruction . . . To shroud its true character in a cloud of idealizing sentiment is shocking as well as impertinent.'[105] If this was the case, would it still be possible, as Hector Bolitho claimed of fighter pilot John Simpson, to be 'a man who had killed the enemy without losing the gentleness of his own spirit'?[106] Flyers themselves were fully aware of this disconcerting dilemma. Peter Townsend joined the RAF in the mid-1930s, and was initially revolted by the shift in emphasis at the outbreak of war from flying to destroying the enemy. The idea of flying as a means to kill 'went against all that flying meant to me—the joy, swift and clean and sensual, of living'. However, by the end of the Battle of Britain 'a terrible change' had come over Townsend, who now found it possible to slay the enemy without remorse.[107] Another fighter pilot, Paul Richey, also quickly overcame his initial distaste at the act of killing, confessing to the 'savage, primitive exaltation' he felt as he watched a German bomber he had fired at become enveloped in flame.[108]

The literary critic (and former marine pilot) Samuel Hynes has argued that most flyers' narratives do not reflect on the killing of individuals in combat, but talk instead, in more abstracted terms, about the death of planes: 'In a battle of machines, it's the machines that are hit, stagger, fall to earth. It's their deaths that are visible and dramatic. The men who are in them die invisibly.'[109] Indeed, Peter Townsend claimed that he never saw a single corpse throughout his RAF career, the demise of his victims masked by being encased within their aircraft.[110] However, aerial combat did allow, even if only for a dramatic instant, flyers to register the impact of their machine-gun or cannon fire on individual human bodies. A Spitfire pilot in the Battle of Britain might have seen the perspex canopy of an enemy fighter plane suddenly turn a shocking shade of crimson as the head of the pilot inside was split open by a burst of machine-gun fire. Or a burning airman could be spied struggling to clamber out of his aircraft, finding his parachute had burnt away, before tumbling to earth at high speed. Ian Gleed riddled a German Junkers 88 with machine-gun fire, and watched as 'three black objects fly out from the top. Bodies. I was close enough to see them somersaulting. No parachutes open.'[111] 'Bogle', one of the 'ten fighter boys' profiled by Athol Forbes and Hubert Allen in 1942, described the sight of a gunner in a Dornier bomber, which was already in flames and beginning to dive, stuck in the aircraft's underneath escape hatch: 'poor devil, he couldn't get in or out, and his legs. . . flailed about wildly as he tried to release himself.' Bogle initially feels guilty, even physically sick, at the thought that he is the agent of this man's certain death. However, he reminds himself of the 'people down below, wives, young mothers, kiddies, huddled in their shelters', and fires a round of bullets into the pathetically wriggling body of the trapped airman.[112] For some flyers, their bloodthirstiness was more personally grounded. Flying Officer G. A. Stillingfleet, an RAF pilot stationed on Malta, in a letter to his clergyman father, related his grief at the death of a civilian friend, 'a kind-hearted, contented orange grower', strafed by a low-flying Messerschmidt. The following day Stillingfleet saw the charred and mangled remains of a German pilot: 'the awful sight did not make me sick. I had very little pity towards him.'[113] As we saw in Chapter 6, Geoffrey Page, the Battle of Britain pilot who had returned to operational duty after a prolonged and painful recovery from disfiguring burns to his face and hands, pursued the enemy in a spirit of personal vengeance, and 'felt my blood boiling with the exultation of our recent killings'.[114] In a total war of uncompromising annihilation, the distinction between the flight-lover and the war-lover became increasingly difficult to sustain.

Bomber aircrew faced particular challenges in regard to killing, guilt, and remorse, since their nightly missions inevitably resulted in the deaths of German civilians. The area-bombing offensive remains a highly controversial topic, with historians divided not merely over its morality, but also about its military effectiveness. This is not the place to revisit these debates.[115] Rather, what it is necessary to consider here is how far Bomber Command's campaign to comprehensively devastate Germany's cities, and the consequent killing of women and children, impacted on representations and self-understandings of the wartime flyer. The answer is much more nuanced than polemical presentations of bomber aircrew as either war criminals, or brave men scapegoated by an embarrassed military and political establishment, would lead one to believe. In the decades after the Second World War many former members of Bomber Command were distressed to read memoirs by leading wartime fighter pilots who argued that they could not have managed to live with themselves if their war experience had required killing innocent civilians, rather than enemy combatants. Bomber aircrew responded, with justified indignation, that fighter pilots had never raised this distinction during the war itself, and were now cynically attempting to distance themselves from their fellow flyers at a time when both the government and the public were beginning to feel that the strategic bombing campaign had seriously compromised Britain's claims to have fought a 'good war'.[116] During the war itself bomber aircrew had little opportunity, or desire, to visit the issue of air-power ethics. The demands of operational life discouraged excessive reflection. Many reassured themselves that they were attacking economic targets, such as a docks, a railway yard, or a specific factory, rather than the broader civilian population. However, debriefing sessions would have revealed the fact that their bombs rarely fell on assigned targets, and the predominance of incendiaries in the bomb-loads of Lancasters and Halifaxes made it obvious that the intention was to unleash firestorms that would rage indiscriminately through the old residential centres of Germany's cities.[117] However, any sense of unease was likely to be overridden by pride in the successful completion of a mission, and the enormous relief at having escaped the hail of flak and night-fighter cannon to which every bomber was subjected while over the target.

Bomber crews can certainly be excused for their apparent indifference to the moral debate about carpet bombing which intermittently took place among politicians and churchmen in Britain during the war. Critics of the bombing campaign were unrepresentative and peripheral figures. Richard Stokes, the Labour MP who condemned the 'filthy task' young flyers were being obliged to undertake, was an unpopular maverick.[118] George Bell, the bishop of Chichester, was a much more respected figure, but his protests failed to convince the rest of the Anglican establishment, who remained—as they had done for most of their history—unwilling to risk conflict with a state to which they were institutionally wedded.[119] When interviewed by the Roman Catholic priest and veteran pacifist Gordon Zahn in the 1960s, clergymen who had served in the wartime RAF insisted that judging the morality of air-force policy had not been part of their job as chaplains.[120] Those critics, like Vera Brittain, whose pacifist beliefs led them to bemoan the consequences of bombing, not only for its victims on the ground, but for those who inflicted this suffering from the skies above, would have seemed self-righteous or seriously naive.[121] The views of Stokes, Bell, or Brittain certainly found little resonance among the broader population. Indeed, surveys of attitudes towards the ethics of aerial bombing revealed that Bomber Command members were generally less bellicose than the rest of the population, their outlook more likely to be characterized by fatalism, or even melancholy, than by hatred.[122] Mass-Observation found less desire among aircrew for 'reprisal raids' against German cities than among civilians. For the bomber boys, enacting retribution seemed less salient than 'the craftsman's delight in a well-aimed bomb'.[123] Cecil Beaton recorded that bomber pilots failed to exhibit any overt hatred of the enemy, regarding Lord Beaverbrook's flippant reference in a speech to 'beautiful bombs' as decidedly tasteless.[124] Jules Roy, the French writer and Halifax pilot, insisted that he had the right to massacre people on the ground, not merely because he himself could so easily be shot down, but also because he was fighting to defend western civilization from an unscrupulous opponent. However, in a diary entry for October 1944 he expressed his disgust at a British newspaper which had published a photograph of a German child in tears and the 'tragic face' of a German woman staring at the ruins of her home, accompanied by the caption: 'Your Turn Now.' 'This', Roy protested, 'is where I am out of step with public opinion.' He felt unable to 'share with those who have suffered, their joy at seeing others suffer. Whether friend or foe, any child in tears upsets me, and with the best will in the world I can find nothing noble about bombing.'[125]

There are also several recorded instances of bomber aircrew wrestling with a troubled conscience, although this was usually in regard to a specific mission, rather than the area-bombing campaign as a whole. For example, Jo Capka was piloting a Wellington destined for Wilhelmshaven, when he took the opportunity, on his own initiative, to drop a single bomb over an undefended German town. 'Immediately after,' Capka recalled, 'I felt a complete and utter swine. I had probably wiped out innocent people—Germans, yes, but sleeping peacefully in the firm belief that there were no military targets in the town.' However, he then attempted to excuse his action: 'Why should they sleep when I was risking death every night?' Significantly, he then continued his mission to bomb Wilhelmshaven, 'legally and without regrets'.[126] In May 1943 Willie

Lewis told the skipper of his Halifax bomber that he was uneasy that their designated target was Wuppertal, a city overflowing with refugees. Lewis believed he was being asked to commit 'deliberate murder', and he had 'a good mind not to come'. Lewis ultimately fell into line, fearing an LMF charge, although he vowed to no longer deceive himself that he was fighting a clean and respectable war: 'we are only mean bastards taking orders from a bunch of hypocrites.'[127] Peter Johnson, a squadron leader and Lancaster pilot, had been in the RAF since the 1930s. In the last year of the war he came to have growing doubts about both the efficiency and the morality of the bomber offensive. In a letter to his lover, Shelagh, Johnson candidly revealed his agony that he had become 'a murderer, a killer of women and children'. He suppressed his uneasiness over the controversial raid on Dresden in February 1945, believing that the firestorming of this historic city was necessary to aid the advancing Soviet armies. However, a month later he seriously considered refusing to fly when he was ordered to bomb Würzburg, a small town in Bavaria which Johnson was convinced was of no military or strategic value whatsoever. After the war Johnson became a prominent critic of what he regarded as a 'permanent stain' on the honourable record of British arms.[128]

There are fleeting glimpses in RAF memoirs of isolated, but meaningful, moments of remorse among aircrew, although such finer feelings for their civilian victims were, inevitably, balanced by equal concern for their own lives and those of their comrades. As Les Bartlett's Lancaster climbed away from base in the winter of 1943, 'I said my prayers, for forgiveness for the killing of innocent people with my bombs, and for a safe return to base'.[129] However, even the most sensitive flyers rarely succumbed to a prolonged anguish of guilt about the morality of bombing. Leonard Cheshire had the persona and appearance of a theology student, and was intellectual, highly introspective, and genuinely compassionate. After the war he became a prominent pacifist and founder of the hospice movement which is named for him. However, it was not until he witnessed the dropping of the atomic bomb on Nagasaki that Cheshire found his conscience troubled in regard to his participation in the destruction of Germany from the air. During the war itself he had been a ruthlessly effective bomber commander, who wished to show the enemy no mercy.[130]

At the opposite end of the spectrum to the conscience-stricken flyer, there were some aircrew who displayed a decidedly bloodthirsty approach, revelling in the destruction they were meting out to the enemy. This was particularly true of those who had seen comrades killed or whose home towns had been blitzed. In an graphic passage in his 1943 memoir, which revealed both that aircrew were fully aware of the effect their bombs were having, and that the wartime reading public were clearly much less squeamish about the ethics of bombing than their post-war successors were to be, the tail-gunner R. C. Rivaz appeared to relish the opportunity to speculate on the violence his aircraft had unleashed on the citizens of Germany. As his Whitley returned to base, 'the fires would still be burning in Cologne, where there would be a lot of suffering and misery'. 'That', Rivaz acknowledged, 'is what we had intended':

Our target had been a large factory, and a lot of nightshift workers would have been working there: there would be people dead or dying . . . there would be people burned there. Some people might be alive . . . living with broken bones, unable to move, and with crushed and mangled bodies pressed against them . . . with nothing but the stink of rubble and putrefying flesh for company. There would be people with arms and legs blown off . . . and people with their stomachs blown open . . . and people with half their faces blown away. They might have to wait hours or even days until they were found; unable to help themselves and wishing they could die . . . yet afraid to die. Some would be badly burnt and would die: others would not die, but would be crippled and scarred always.

If Rivaz seemed to be delighting in the suffering of others, he sought justification in the imperative of avenging dead comrades: 'All these [terrible] things I had seen when our own aerodrome was bombed.'[131] Roland Winfield, the psychiatrist who served as a medical officer with Bomber Command, was once asked by a group of medical students whether the kind of men best suited to becoming heavy-bomber pilots would be 'destructive psychopaths'. Winfield's response was unequivocally in the negative. He pointed out that fulfilling the duties of bomber aircrew required 'sustained determination', and that without that quality, 'all the destructive psychology in the world would be of no avail'.[132] Nevertheless, the bomber pilot was never able to entirely free himself from an association with indiscriminate destruction which was only rarely applied to fighter pilots. Richard Hillary, in typically provocative vein, asserted that, while for the fighter pilot killing was done with cool dignity and without pettiness, the bomber pilot was prone to the 'dangerous emotion' created by repeatedly acting out 'that childhood longing for smashing things'.[133]

  It is true that wartime literary and cinematic representations of bomber aircrew rarely betrayed such darker undercurrents. The bomber boys of Terence Rattigan's *Flare Path* or H. E. Bates's 'Flying Officer X' stories were humble and good-natured, those of *The Way to the Stars*, sensitive flyer-poets. One controversial history of the bombing of Germany has accused RAF aircrew of seeing themselves 'as gods, hurling bolts of lightning down upon the vileness of the enemy'.[134] Even without the additional biases created by patriotism, propaganda, and censorship, Rattigan and Bates, who had observed bomber pilots at first hand, and were captivated by their apparently easygoing professionalism, would have undoubtedly found it impossible to even countenance the possibility that these self-effacing young men might be subject to a 'Jupiter complex'. Even less surprisingly, fictional wartime narratives provided little or no space to contemplate the sufferings of German civilians. A rare exception was Roald Dahl's short story 'Someone Like You', in which two drunken aircrew speculate on the character, and even physical assets (observing a curvaceous female at the bar, one airman asserts that 'I bet I've killed lots of women more beautiful than that one'), of the civilians they have killed.[135] After the war, when the extent of casualties among non-combatants (especially children and the elderly) in the bombing raids on Germany became fully apparent, fictional narratives became more preoccupied with the bomber pilot's status as an agent of merciless destruction. Shern Douglas, in James Campbell's *Maximum Effort*, upsets his girlfriend Terry with the savagery of his response to her expression of sympathy for children being killed and maimed in mass raids: 'I want to see every town and city in Germany in flames and their inhabitants blasted into dust.'[136] During the war literary and cinematic renderings of the flyer had often presented him as a sensitive nature-lover. In the film *Tawny Pipit*, a recuperating airman, Jimmy (Niall MacGinnis), helps save a rare songbird from extinction, while in Nevil Shute's novel *Pastoral*, Peter Marshall watches for foxes and badgers in the woods adjacent to his aerodrome.[137] However, in Miles Tripp's *Faith is a Windsock*, published in 1952, the Lancaster pilot Bergen is walking through a field with his navigator, Craig. Bergen picks up a fledgling thrush, which had fallen from its nest: 'With a quick movement of his right hand Bergen flicked the bird's head from its body; he threw away the lifeless bundle of warm down as a thin stream of blood spurted from the severed neck. He grinned, not cruelly, but with the delight of a good sport. The unexpectedness of this action made Craig's stomach turn in disgust.'[138] The significance of such intimations of the murderous potential that lay beneath the meek exterior of the bomber pilot should not be overstated, but neither should they be entirely disregarded. True, one of the dominant post-war cultural representations of Bomber Command, the 1955 movie *The Dambusters*, celebrated the bravery, dedication, and skill of those who flew the heavy bombers. However, it is highly significant that the mission lionized in this particular narrative was a one-off precision raid carried out, in the face of overwhelming odds, against a legitimate economic target, rather than the carpet bombing of a densely packed urban centre.[139]

While bomber crews' implication in the death of innocent civilians created a potential challenge to the notion of the flyer as the epitome of chivalric forbearance and humility, there were other subcultures within the wartime RAF where (according to both fictional and non-fictional accounts) the flyer's function as a killing machine was even more explicit and unapologetic. Memoirs frequently refer to the particular bloodthirstiness of Polish pilots, who had escaped German occupation to fight in the RAF, and whose lives now seemed almost exclusively preoccupied with securing vengeance on the Nazis for the brutal destruction of their homelands and the rape and murder of their loved ones.[140] Hector Bolitho noted how a Polish fighter pilot would be aloof and silent in the mess, apparently indifferent to the chatter of other flyers around him, 'nursing the bitter memory of Warsaw and the perpetual sorrow of separation from his children and wife. The only way he could answer these feelings within himself was with moroseness when he was on the earth and terrible hatred when he was in the sky.'[141] Some flyers recalled Polish fighter pilots machine-gunning helpless enemy aircrew who had parachuted out of their aircraft. When informed by the RAF hierarchy that such behaviour contravened British standards of fair play and they were to desist at once, Polish airmen adopted an alternative technique of flying close to the parachuting flyer, thus creating a slipstream that ripped away his parachute canopy, leaving the unfortunate German to plummet to his death.[142] Polish bomber pilots—or at least their fictional counterparts—could be equally candid about their desire for vengeance. In a short story by C. H. Ward-Jackson, a guard-room sergeant observes a Polish bomber crew taking their dog Mischka on missions, and then attaching miniature bombs carved out of wood to his collar to commemorate each raid he had participated in.[143] In the Mills and Boon romance *WAAF into Wife* the hero is Count Cziskiwhzski, a Polish bomber pilot whose eyes light up when his squadron is detailed for raiding Germany. He becomes involved in a passionate affair with WAAF Mandy Lyle, but their courtship is interrupted by his single-minded desire to wreak revenge on the Germans. When Mandy complains that he would rather be dropping bombs on Germany than spending an evening with her, the count does not immediately deny it, but ponders the suggestion 'as though it deserved his most serious consideration'.[144]

Polish flyers' obsession with the fairer sex was widely attested to. Rom Landau, who worked as a RAF liaison officer with Polish pilots, noted that they discussed women 'at great length, openly, seriously, both lyrically and descriptively, as a connoisseur might talk of wine or beautiful statues'.[145] Many British women welcomed the attentions of Polish airmen, who were famous for their courtly manner, and seemed much less inhibited about expressing their feelings in regard to love and sex. One WAAF recalled that, with Polish flyers, 'you knew that the fellow saw you as a woman and wanted you', a refreshing quality when contrasted with the more furtive and embarrassed approach to sex offered by many of their British equivalents.[146] However, references to the Polish flyer's obvious charms was never entirely free of insinuations of violence or danger. When fighter pilot Jack Sanderson introduces his Polish comrade, Radwanski, to his mother in H. E. Bates's play *The Day of Glory*, he jokes: 'Be careful, mother. He'll probably tell you that you look sixteen and then ask you to elope with him.' Radwanski's other name, he warns her, 'is Bluebeard'.[147] While Polish airmen were certainly seen by British women as exotic and romantic, especially after the release of the feature film *Dangerous Moonlight*, in which Anton Walbrook played a handsome pianist from Warsaw who joins the RAF, their sexual magnetism was often described in almost feral terms, implying that their cold-blooded callousness in the air might be no less evident in the bedroom. Joan Wyndham dated several Polish airmen while she was serving in the WAAF, finding their 'ice-cold green eyes' and 'wolf-like charms' difficult to resist. However, she also conceded that their sexual advances were often uncouth and unwelcome, and that on some bases WAAFs were obliged to use their hat-pins to deal with what today could only be classified as sexual harassment.[148] In Watson's *Johnny Kinsman*, the Polish pilot, Dilewski, takes his new girlfriend to Blackpool and, without consulting her first, rents only one room, speaking 'of his appetite for her in the same way that he spoke of his appetite for food'.[149] A widespread belief among British women was that Polish flyers had been known to bite off the nipples of women during lovemaking, so incapable were they of restraining their violent passion, either during sex or during combat.[150]

If such myths betrayed the power of a rather distasteful national stereotyping, they also revealed a broader anxiety that the flyer, for all his glamour and potential as a man of feeling, was ultimately a violent agent of destruction. If the flyer was superman, then he might be as capable of an unimaginable crime as he was of unbelievable heroism. In the 1930s the aviator had often been identified in the popular imagination with fascism and authoritarianism. The airmen of H. G. Wells's futuristic fantasy *The Shape of Things to Come* arrived as the philosophically literate saviours of civilization, but were soon revealed as narcissistic fascist strongmen.[151] In Rex Warner's *The Aerodrome*, written during the 'Phoney War', air-force pilots are presented as the sinister embodiment of the fascist man of action. The novel's hero, Roy, admires the 'undeviating precision' and charismatic good looks of the air-force personnel who populate an airfield near his village. However, on being recruited into the service Roy discovers that the airmen are callous and authoritarian technocrats, whose brutal discipline and ability to rise above the earth has encouraged them to believe that they were 'a new and more adequate race of men', who aimed to smash 'the servility of historical tradition' by means of a coup against a government which was in sway to the 'money-makers and sentimentalists'.[152]

Needless to say, such associations of the flyer with fascism rapidly diminished after the Battle of Britain. By the time Warner's dystopian parable was published in 1941, he felt obliged to include a prefatory disclaimer, insisting that he had 'the utmost affection and respect' for the RAF.[153] However, some residual anxieties remained. Kim, the air-gunner in Arthur Gwynn-Browne's *Gone For a Burton*, is hostile to a Britain which left him rotting in the slums, and dedicates himself to the RAF, a genuine community which was the antithesis of 'drivelling democracy'. In discussion with his skipper, Kim argues for the RAF as a model for a post-war society, in which everything, even child-rearing, would be under the control of the state.[154] John Pudney had a long discussion with a young pilot on a troopship in the Mediterranean about a newspaper article which had described the RAF as 'potential fascists'. The airman protested that 'we don't live by force, that we want ordinariness, houses, peace, like everyone else'. Pudney agreed that the RAF was 'too imaginative, too objective', to be 'the fascist nursery which some frightened people seem to fear'.[155] Poet and literary editor John Lehmann published some of the earliest writings of Richard Lumford, a pilot officer in the RAF who idealized the 'godlike pilot fraternity' and the 'dream of an elite in the air'. One reader, a soldier, wrote to Lehmann angrily denouncing Lumford's 'manufactured sense of otherworldliness—detachment—aloofness—superiority', and predicting that 'such pseudo-Promethean young men' would be a danger to democracy after the war. In fact Lumford was an acutely sensitive man, who viewed flying as a means to commune with nature and valued the companionship of his fellow flyers as an antidote to his low self-esteem. As Lehmann perceptively observed, Lumford lacked the self-confidence to be a fascist superman.[156] However, there would always be potential unease about the godlike sense of omnipotence that might be fostered in young and impressionable men who were literally able to raise themselves above the mass of humanity.

The public persona of Wing Commander Guy Gibson, hero of the 1943 'Dambusters raid', encapsulated the potential contradiction between flyer as ruthless killer and flyer as man of feeling. Accompanying Churchill on a visit to the United States in August 1943, the master bomber was asked by the prime minister to tone down references in a speech to his personal pleasure at the number of casualties caused by the raids he had led against German cities. Even Churchill, hardly a shrinking violet, feared that Gibson might appear too bloodthirsty. Gibson, an animal-lover, appeared genuinely distressed at the thought that thousands of farm animals or household pets might have been drowned after the dams raid, but expressed no remorse for the deaths of civilians caused by the Allied bombing offensive.[157] In an unpublished section of his autobiography he unapologetically admitted to having on one occasion ordered his crews to drop their bombs indiscriminately across a German city, in order to avenge the death of the mother of one of his NCOs, killed in an air raid on London.[158] Gibson often appeared as a ruthless monomaniac, driven by a deep loathing of the Germans, and intolerant of those who did not share his unremitting aggression. Crews who returned with their bomb-loads found themselves the objects of Gibson's formidable wrath.[159] However, while many in the RAF regarded him as a homicidal 'Hun-hater', the wing commander's celebrity, Victoria Cross, boyish good looks, and deep blue eyes made him something of a matinee idol in the eyes of an adoring public, an object of hero-worship to adolescent boys and of sexual magnetism to young women. Moreover, for all his unapologetic belligerence, Gibson could also be found telling his cousin that, when reading *Hamlet*, 'sometimes the words are so beautiful it makes my heart ache', or having his photograph taken in a field of poppies reading the *Morte d'Arthur*, the very epitome of the gentle *parfait* knight.[160]

These contradictory images of Gibson testify to the heterogeneous identity of the wartime flyer. The masculinity of the men of the RAF was characterized by a distinct elasticity, which allowed it to encompass a number of seeming opposites—the bellicose and the pacific, the philistine and the poetic, the traditional and the technocratic—and ensured its appeal to the widest possible spectrum of the British public. Depending on context, the 'civilian' or the 'military' aspects of the flyer's identity could be emphasized more, either in the writings of those who observed and dramatized their lives or in the self-fashioning of the airmen themselves. However, as the end of the war approached many sought reassurance that it would be the gentle and compassionate qualities of the flyer which now came to the fore, as he sought to reintegrate himself into the civilian society he had left six years previously.

8

Coming Home

In the final chapter of Miles Tripp's semi-autobiographical novel *Faith is a Windsock*, the crew of Lancaster A-Able find, much to their surprise, that they have survived the war. However, their sense of relief is tempered by melancholy at the unravelling of the ties of comradeship and by anxiety at what the future might hold. They faced 'uncertainty, readjustment and resettlement, words cumbersome in sound and meaning'. 'Damocles' sword', Tripp asserted, was 'twisting in shape to a question-mark.'[1] How flyers coped with the return of peace is the theme of this final chapter. Many found the transition taxing and problematic, regarding civilian life as a banal sequel to their wartime adventures. Some sought imaginative ways to recreate the camaraderie of service life, while others drifted into a life of antisocial behaviour or criminality. However, the great majority, as might be expected from the conspicuous roles played by heterosexual romance and domesticity in the identity of the wartime flyer, eagerly embraced the return to hearth and home. A significant majority of former flyers attempted to draw on their wartime exploits as inspirations for post-war careers in public life, either at Westminster, or—in two high-profile cases—in the twilight years of Britain's overseas empire. Most were content with a life of calm anonymity. Finally, a return to civilian life also provided flyers with more time than they had been permitted during the war itself to reflect on those comrades who had failed to survive the war. Through private memory and public commemoration, the dead were to remain a powerful presence in the lives of those they left behind.

BUMPY LANDINGS: THE FLYER'S FRAUGHT RETURN TO CIVILIAN LIFE

Tripp's novel had insisted that, as long as the conflict was still waging, no flyer had been able to even begin to conceive of what life after the war might be like:

Somehow life had always been centred around the excitement of op[eration]s., and always would be. The strange taste of cigarette after hours of chewing gum, the smell of aircraft dope, glycol, cordite, overheated flying-suits, cleaning oil, barley-sugar taste, rum, octane tang, bacon and egg before and beans after, coke-fumes from the stove, the feeling of toes spreading in the spacious warmth of flying-boots, cold silk gloves, bulky layers of clothing, three days stubble shaved off for the soft cheek, careless love. Life had always been like this, very vivid, very present, fullest pleasure from the most trivial happening.[2]

Speculating about the post-war world seemed foolhardy, given the high probability that the grim reaper would intervene before the war had reached a conclusion. Richard Hillary claimed in a radio interview in 1942 that his fellow fighter pilots dreaded the prospect of having to give up the excitement and comradeship of the RAF in favour of a return to the humdrum existence of 'bowler hats, rolled umbrella and the eight-thirty to town . . . They know what it means to live, but will they know how?'[3] By contrast, in the same year Paddy Finucane, the then top-scoring pilot in Fighter Command, told an interviewer that he was looking forward to the end of the war and settling down with his fiancée.[4] Ultimately, the fact that Finucane appeared more optimistic about his post-war prospects than Hillary proved irrelevant: both men were to be killed in action soon afterwards. It seemed wiser not to plan ahead. As Tony Bartley, Spitfire pilot and member of the notoriously hedonistic 92 Squadron, put it in a letter to his father during the Battle of Britain: 'If the Germans don't kill us, the party at the end of the war certainly will.'[5]

Bartley initially believed that he would never be able to return to a conventional life after his wartime experiences. However, by 1945 he was exhausted by war and was more than ready to capitulate to marriage and family life.[6] Now that the guns had fallen silent, most flyers were glad to bid farewell to the fraught excitement of combat and the discipline of service living. As the RAF scaled down to a peacetime service, flyers ceased to be men joined together by the shared exposure to aerial combat, the communal living-space of the mess, the shared culture of practical jokes or service slang, and the commonality of the grey-blue uniform. They returned to regular jobs, to the rewards and tribulations of family life, to what they could not help but regard as 'ordinary' lives. On their return to their homes and families some flyers wrote to their former comrades, and stayed in contact with them by letter, and in later years by telephone, for the rest of their days. But most did not, as memories of the war years gave way to new routines, new interests, and new obligations.

The great majority of ex-RAF personnel, like their equivalents in the army and navy, successfully merged back into civilian life. However, this is not to say that the consolidation of family life after the disruption of wartime was entirely unproblematic. There is evidence, for example, of serious resentment among some women at the loss of autonomy they suffered when their husbands returned from military service in 1945.[7] Marriage-guidance literature from this period reveals a reluctance among some returning servicemen to give up the all-male camaraderie of military life, and popular literary and cinematic texts disclose (especially in the genres of the adventure narrative or war story) male ambivalence towards the responsibilities and pleasures of domesticity.[8] It is likely that former flyers were just as subject to feelings of disorientation and restlessness as other ex-servicemen. We need to be aware that the successful readjustment of flyers would have been dependent on the family situations these men left, and the ones they returned to, once demobilized. Also, those who were able to pick up the threads of their pre-war lives were likely to be older men, many of whom had already established their families and civilian careers. By contrast, many flyers had still been boys when they joined the service. Since it had been the war that had shaped their passage into manhood, now they faced the challenge of being required to return to a civilian society of which they had no adult experience. Returning veterans in 1945 appeared to display little of the hatred, bitterness, and barely repressed violence of the men who had come home from the trenches in 1918. However, we should not assume that an absence of public anger necessarily indicates a deficiency of private angst or disenchantment. The problem here is one of evidence. Most of the diaries and memoirs of wartime flyers (whether published or deposited in archival collections) abruptly stop with the ending of hostilities, and so we have only limited evidence of how individual airmen coped with the return to home and family. That overwhelming majority who settled back into civilian life with relative ease have tended to leave little trace in the historical record. By contrast, the minority who found readjustment difficult, or even impossible, have left us with extensive testimony, and were also to prove a popular subject in post-war fiction and cinema. While not representative of former RAF flyers as a whole, such narratives of the alienated ex-airman do have significant historical value, revealing, as they do, that some of the qualities of the flyer celebrated in wartime culture—notably his capacity for comradeship and his spirit of adventure—appeared less germane in Britain during the immediate post-war years.

A number of flyboy memoirs reveal a definite ambivalence at the news that the war in Europe had finally ended. Pierre Clostermann recalled that he had no desire to join the exhilarated crowds in the streets of London on VE Day. In his mess no one spoke, let alone sang, and one angry airman threw a bottle at the radio set which was broadcasting the celebrations in the capital, in protest 'at all this noise, at all those people shamelessly parading their sense of relief and deliverance before us'. Clostermann took up his aircraft for one last flight, only to break down in tears at the prospect of never flying again. He switched off his engine for the last time, and clambered out of the cockpit: 'when my waiting pilots and my mechanics saw my downcast eyes and my shaking shoulders, they understood and returned to the Dispersal in silence.'[9] The announcement of Germany's surrender simultaneously delighted and alarmed Jim Bailey. He believed he had developed night-fighting into an art, and now his brushes and paints were to be taken way and his commissions rescinded.[10] An unexpected sense of malaise at the war's end among some bomber crews was hardly ameliorated by Churchill's notorious failure to refer to the achievements of Bomber Command in his tribute to the British war effort in his Victory in Europe broadcast on 13 May 1945.[11]

A representative tale of post-war disenchantment is provided by Flight Lieutenant J. M. Catford's account of his life in the years immediately after
demobilization. Catford had been a Lancaster tail-gunner. After retiring from
the RAF at the end of the war, he went back to his former job in the City.
He was made to feel welcome by old friends and colleagues, but he could not
escape the feeling that 'time was passing on leaded wings'. He yearned for the
excitement of his life in the RAF, feelings which were only made bearable by
the fact that many other veterans, with whom he worked, felt exactly the same.
'Each day', Catford recalled, 'we used to gather in the staff restaurant, and
over coffee and cigarettes, we'd relive and re-fight the war.' By 1949 Catford
decided the only way to overcome such restlessness was to enlist for voluntary
part-time service in the RAF Volunteer Reserve (RAFVR). However, even this
expedient proved unsatisfactory, as he was denied the opportunity of returning
to flying. In the jet age the air-gunner was already obsolete.[12] Former WAAF
Edith Heap, who had her own problems adjusting to civilian life in the two
years after 1945 (she felt 'life was slow and dull', and she no longer 'spoke
the same language' as her family, who had been isolated from the war in the
Yorkshire Dales), confessed to a distinct empathy for George Frederick Beurling,
the Canadian fighter ace who, she believed, finding post-war life unfulfilling and
pointless, 'eventually flew himself into the deck in despair'.[13] In fact the cause
of Beurling's death in an air crash in Italy in 1948 was never fully established,
and it has been claimed that his aircraft was deliberately sabotaged. However,
'Buzz' Beurling certainly typified the disaffected ex-flyer. Returning to Canada
at the end of the war, he found it impossible to adapt to civilian life and, in the
aftermath of his marriage falling apart, he had, immediately prior to his death,
been contemplating offering his military expertise to the air forces of either Israel
or Nationalist China.[14]

Such real-life narratives of ex-flyers' reintegration into civilian life had their
literary and cinematic equivalents. Some of the more spectacular fictionalized
examples of the maladjusted ex-flyer—Freddie Page in Rattigan's *Deep Blue Sea*
or Wing Commander Glennon in *Cage of Gold*—have already been encountered
in Chapter 6. To these celebrated archetypes of male estrangement can be
added a supporting cast of alienated ex-flyers. In Maurice Edelman's novel *The
Happy Ones*, former bomber pilot Roger Metcalfe is a self-pitying 'adolescent'
figure who runs a somewhat sordid air-freight business.[15] In the noirish thriller
They Made Me a Fugitive, the ex-flyer Clem (Trevor Howard) drifts into the
twilight worlds of gangland and the black market.[16] The hero of *Escape*, a
film based on a play by John Galsworthy, is Matt Denant (Rex Harrison), a
former squadron leader who accidentally kills a detective in Hyde Park while
protecting a woman from being wrongfully arrested. Convicted of manslaughter,
Matt is sentenced to imprisonment in Dartmoor. Labouring under a sense of
injustice, he mounts an escape across the moor, during which he is befriended
by Dora (Peggy Cummins). The two fall in love, and eventually Dora succeeds

in persuading Matt to give himself up. The film ends with Matt being driven back to prison, knowing that, once he has completed his sentence, he will be able to settle down to a happy married life with Dora.[17] If *Escape*'s fable of fraught peacetime readjustment concluded with the possibility of domestic happiness, we should register David Gerber's caution (in his study of the classic Hollywood drama of returning veterans, *The Best Years of Our Lives*) that formulaic happy endings cannot be allowed to mask darker subtexts, for beneath the surface 'lurk the ominous messages about veterans' anger, bitterness, violence, alcoholism and personality disorganisation that were part of the discourse of the veteran's problem'.[18] Moreover, many of these fictional texts featuring ex-flyers were less willing to countenance the possibility of an ultimately successful reintegration.

Some former airmen found it difficult to cope with the break-up of the all-male camaraderie of service life. Richard Lumford pined for the 'warm physical proximity of the mess' or 'the friendly smile of a fellow pilot as he got into his aircraft', which stood in stark contrast 'to the bleak and competitive civilian world'.[19] As a homosexual, Lumford could not look, as heterosexual flyers could, to marriage and fatherhood as consolation for the loss of the comradeship of the wartime RAF. Indeed, life for gay men in the immediate post-war years was distinctly uncomfortable, given the homophobic temper of the popular press and the increased victimization of male homosexuals by the police and the courts.[20] As the high-profile trial of Michael Calvert, former commander of the irregular forces in Burma, revealed, even celebrated war heroes were not to be exempt from this official persecution of the gay community.[21] Feeling increasingly desperate, Lumford underwent a disastrous session with a female psychoanalyst, the failure of which he attributed to his 'nervous distrust of women'. A more successful remedy for his emotional despair came in the form of a sojourn in a Benedictine monastery, where he welcomed the 'sense of participation in a super-earthly reality' and the 'intense group-feeling and loyalty' which reminded him of happier days in the air force.[22] Former master bomber Leonard Cheshire tried to re-create the sense of community and common purpose of military life through Commandos for Peace, a land-settlement scheme for veterans on derelict airfield sites.[23]

Other flyers longed less for their former comrades than for the excitement of flight. Some joined the expanding civilian airline sector after the war, or set up their own charter flying businesses in Australia or Canada. A small number of former RAF personnel, including Colin Hodgkinson, made money in the late 1940s by illegally smuggling black-market goods (perfume and stockings for wealthy clients, brandy for the restaurant trade) into rationing-beset Britain from the continent, using discarded RAF aircraft.[24] One Halifax crew used the opportunity provided by the repatriation of refugees across Europe by air to set up a complex black-market operation. In Brussels, while preparing to collect liberated Greek prisoners, Cyril Smith and his fellow aircrew sold tyres in order to purchase bottles of sweetening tablets. On arrival in Athens, a local population desperate for supplies of saccharin for use in the manufacture of soft drinks was willing to exchange Leica cameras for these artificial sweeteners, which, in turn, Smith was able to sell in either Brussels or London.[25] Another group of flyers, faced with the prospect of immediate demobilization, simply collared the Mosquitoes and Beaufighters they had only recently been flying on operations and flew them to Israel, where they were gratefully received by a fledgling air force fighting a war of national survival against its Arab neighbours.[26]

A few flyers stayed on in the RAF, although they were often disappointed by the mundane nature of peacetime service life. Many former wartime aircrew were inevitably disillusioned by the fact that, in the age of the jet engine and atomic bomb, air battles were decided by merely 'pressing buttons'.[27] Even the celebrity test-pilots who flew the new generation of jet aircraft coming into existence in the late 1940s and early 1950s lacked the élan of the wartime flyers. Despite having been a distinguished fighter pilot during the war, jet test-pilot Neville Duke 'looked and talked'—according to Philip Gibbs, who met him in 1952—'like a scientist rather than a typical pilot . . . because of his quiet way of speaking and manner, without "dash" or any touch of self-dramatizing'.[28] Duke's supersonic exploits, conducted in white overalls and a white helmet whose design was derived from American football (rather than the old-style leather flying-cap), and accompanied by detailed note-taking and statistical data, anticipated the stolid era of space exploration to come rather than recalling the dashing recent history of the wartime RAF.[29] The year 1952 saw the release of a feature film about test-pilots, *The Sound Barrier*, directed by David Lean. In the film, former Battle of Britain ace Tony Garthwaite (Nigel Patrick) is killed, largely because he is an inspired amateur, lacking the intelligence to handle modern technology. By contrast, the most successful test-pilot is the uncharismatic Philip Peel (John Justin), a methodical and measured technical expert.[30] Terence Rattigan, who wrote the screenplay, recounted meeting real test-pilots at Farnborough. They were, he concluded somewhat dolefully, 'quiet young men, absolutely unlike the types I had known during the war'.[31] The identification of the flyer with technology, which had been tempered during the war by a continued association with the chivalric tradition, had now become virtually absolute, and in the process the glamour of flight seemed to have been largely forsaken.

Many of the narratives of qualified, or failed, reintegration into civilian life reflected a nostalgia for the all-male fellowship of service life or a yearning for a more robust vision of masculinity, untainted by association with the domestic or the feminine. However, in one—albeit highly idiosyncratic—case the flyer's problematic readjustment to the post-war world culminated not in the recovery, but in the renunciation, of his masculinity. A few years after the end of the war a shameless Lothario was attempting to impress a young woman by pretending to be an ex-fighter pilot. He had reached the part of his repertoire in which he described how he had once been obliged to force-land his Spitfire at high speed. It was at the point at which he was explaining that he was unable to lower his flaps because his hydraulics had been shot away, that his female listener interjected to ask why his Spitfire appeared to be so radically different from all the others in service, which had pneumatically operated flaps. His imposture exposed, the false flyer slunk away with his tail between his legs.[32] The woman who had delighted in leading him up the garden path, before so artfully tripping him up, was Roberta Cowell, who, until relatively recently, had been a man, a former racing-car driver and wartime Spitfire pilot. During his time in the RAF Robert Cowell (as he then was) was already aware that, deep down, he possessed a feminine nature. However, outwardly he frantically sought to show the world how assertive and hypermasculine he could be. After being shot down, Cowell spent time in a POW camp, where several homosexual prisoners took it for granted that he was one of their own. Cowell, however, spurned the advances of those he scorned as 'pansies'. On demobilization, Cowell found his sense of disorientation intensifying. A visit to an analyst revealed that he possessed what at the time was identified as a 'woman's psychology', and his body betrayed increasing evidence of hermaphroditism (on one occasion his squash partner, a former wing commander, observed: 'You know, you really ought to wear a brassiere'). Cowell's memoir presents his decision to start a career in the dressmaking business as the first, tentative, public admission of the growing predominance of his feminine side. At the end of the decade he underwent hormone treatment and surgery to become a woman. In stark contrast to those ex-flyers who lamented the loss of the male comradeship of the mess-room or the dispersal hut, Cowell asserted: 'Once medical science had shown me that I was basically and fundamentally female I could hardly be expected to be artificially masculinised and continue to live a miserably unhappy life amongst a sex to which I now knew I did not really belong.'[33]

A less exotic, but no less particular, story of failed readjustment was that of Czech and Polish pilots who returned to their home nations. Here they discovered, to their horror, that the newly installed Stalinist regimes, far from welcoming them as anti-fascist heroes, condemned them as 'bourgeois narcissists', or, as the Cold War intensified, imprisoned them as alleged western spies. Fighter pilot M. A. Liskutin returned to Czechoslovakia in August 1945, with his English wife Daphne, whom he had married in 1942. He joined the new post-war Czech air force, and had the bizarre experience of flying both ex-RAF Spitfires and the Mezek, a Czech-built variant of the Messerschmidt 109. However, as pro-Soviet elements became more powerful in Czechoslovakia, ex-RAF flyers became a source of embarrassment to those who sought concord with the USSR. It was feared that those who had served in the RAF might bring western ideological 'infection', or would rival the Red Army as the venerated heroes of anti-fascist liberation. Liskutin found himself under secret-service surveillance, and was dismissed from the air force. Official directives dictated that he could only seek alternative employment in the 'approved' sectors of agriculture, forestry, and coal-mining. Liskutin escaped to Vienna, before returning, with his family, to a life of exile in England.[34] Another Czech flyer, Jo Capka, had piloted Wellingtons, Beaufighters, and Mosquitoes, and married Rhoda, a WAAF, before a serious crash required him to undergo facial reconstruction under the care of Archibald McIndoe. At the end of the war he returned to Czechoslovakia, but after the communists came to power he was accused of collaboration with a foreign power and imprisoned. He was released and, after strenuous diplomatic efforts, in 1957 was allowed to return to Britain, where he was reunited with Rhoda.[35]

Many Czechs and Poles decided it was wiser not to return home in the first place, but found themselves regarded in post-war Britain, no longer as heroes, but as undesirable aliens now that they sought work and housing.[36] The legendary Polish fighter pilot Jan Zumbach was sufficiently disenchanted to move to Africa, where he created a number of mercenary air forces.[37] A more propitiatory alternative to both communist persecution and British ingratitude was adopted by former Polish bomber pilot B. J. Solak, who, interested in issues of faith and spiritualism, travelled to Nepal in order to discover more about eastern mysticism.[38] Other post-war repatriations were equally problematic. Australians, New Zealanders, South Africans, and Canadians returned to nations which were all, to different degrees, turning away from the imperial motherland, on whose behalf these young pilots had just been laying down their lives. Black ex-aircrew from the Caribbean discovered that their exemplary war service was insufficient to shield them from the racism of colonial administrators. Some former West Indian RAF personnel were initially repatriated, but they almost immediately returned to Britain, in flight from the parlous state of the Caribbean economy and in response to metropolitan appeals for overseas manpower to alleviate Britain's post-war labour shortage. Some of these peripatetic former flyers flourished; for example, bomber pilot Billy Strachan, who found his civil service career stalling soon after his return to Jamaica. Back in Britain, he took evening classes in accountancy and law and qualified as a barrister. However, most West Indian RAF veterans were completely unprepared for the violent hostility they were to encounter from white Britons, now that they had returned as permanent immigrants.[39]

The open antipathy experienced by Polish, Czech, and West Indian flyers was, however, exceptional. As a rule, whatever their own personal problems of readjustment, relatively few flyers found the society to which they returned manifestly hostile towards their wartime achievements. While there was some post-war queasiness about the ethics of the strategic-bombing offensive, the bravery and dedication of former Bomber Command aircrew was never called into question. As for the fighter boys, the continued resilience of the Battle of Britain in post-war British culture ensured that their revered status remained unimpeachable. As the popularity of RAF memoirs and popular histories was to reveal, unlike many veterans in other times and other places, ex-flyers had certainly not returned to a civilian culture which was callously uninterested in hearing about their triumph and tragedies. As Pierre Clostermann prepared for demobilization in 1945, he watched his aircraft being decommissioned and his airfield being dismantled, events he compared to the departure of a travelling circus from a small town:

The Big Show was over. The public had been satisfied. The programme had been rather heavy, the actors not too bad, and the lions had not eaten the trainer. It would be discussed for a day or two more round the family table. And even when it was all forgotten—the band, the fireworks, the resplendent uniforms—there would still remain on the village green the holes of the tent pegs and a circle of sawdust. The rain and the shortness of man's memory would soon wipe out even those.[40]

Clostermann had generally been a perceptive observer of the war in the air. However, his prediction that the men of the wartime RAF would quickly be forgotten was to prove wide of the mark. The flyer was to be a central figure, not merely in British culture during the Second World War, but in the way the war was to be remembered and commemorated in the decades which followed. That, however, is a whole other story, which lies outside the remit of this study.

FLYERS AND POST-WAR POLITICS

In a radio interview soon after the publication of *The Last Enemy*, Richard Hillary claimed that most flyers were indifferent to politics, and felt they had little in common with the humdrum worlds of parliament or Whitehall.[41] When a newspaper covering the Beveridge Report, with its ambitious proposals for post-war welfare reform, appeared in Hillary's mess in 1942, he scorned the widespread public interest in social reconstruction: 'Beveridge Report? Oh, the fellow is thinking about after the war: we'll probably all be dead anyway.'[42] Hillary, of course, did not live to see 'after the war' and the implementation of Beveridge's recommendations in the programme of the Labour government elected soon after the end of hostilities in Europe in 1945. However, Hillary's disdain was not universally shared. Indeed, as the end of the war approached many flyers gave serious consideration to pursuing a post-war career in politics. One of the dominant motifs of Guy Gibson's *Enemy Coast Ahead*, which he composed in 1943–4, was the necessity for the young who had done the fighting to wrest power from the old men whose failures in the inter-war years had brought Britain to the brink of calamity in the first half of the war. While still a serving officer, Gibson shared a platform with the controversial political figure Lord Vansittart, and gave speeches to military audiences which made no attempt to conceal his partisan politics, one such address being dedicated to the subject of 'This Amazing Empire'. Gibson, as one of Churchill's 'young men', inevitably benefited from the patronage of the prime minister, and he was chosen as the Conservative Party candidate for the Macclesfield constituency. He later withdrew his candidacy, and was killed in action before he could realize his post-war political ambitions. Significantly, another name on the party's selection list for the Macclesfield seat was Air Vice-Marshal Donald Bennett, the 34-year-old leader of the elite Pathfinder bomber force. Bennett's brand of Conservative politics were much more sophisticated than those of his flyer rival. While Gibson simply assumed that the Tories were the natural party of government, Bennett was more reflective, believing that the war had revealed the need to embrace an agenda of—albeit managed—social change.[43]

Peter Townsend, despite being the cousin of leading Labour politician Hugh Gaitskell, also felt that his loyalties lay with the Conservatives. Like Bennett, he had little sympathy for Gibson's reactionary and imperialist brand of Toryism, characterizing himself as a pragmatic, 'modern' Conservative. Townsend allowed his name to be put forward as the candidate for a West Country seat, but he was clearly conflicted about the idea of entering parliament. His ambivalence was sufficiently evident for the local party chairman to advise him to drop the idea.[44] Townsend chose instead to make a contribution to public life as a member of the royal household. King George VI wanted his new equerries to be selected on the basis, not (as had been the case previously) of family or regional connections, but for their military records. In so doing, he failed to take into account the effect the arrival of a dashing former fighter ace was to have on the sensibilities of the young and impressionable Princess Margaret, thereby sowing the seeds of a doomed romance which culminated in a royal scandal.[45] Fighter pilots seem to have displayed a particular predilection for the Conservatives. 'Laddie' Lucas, a Spitfire pilot who had taken part in the Battle of Malta, was approached by Lord Beaverbrook at the end of the war and asked if he was interested in becoming a Tory MP. Lucas stood unsuccessfully against Edith Summerskill in West Fulham during the 1945 general election. Douglas Bader (himself courted by a number of Conservative constituency associations) and a glittering array of fighter-boy celebrities from RAF Tangmere came to speak on Lucas's behalf, but after a riotous meeting at which Bader was heckled, the government intervened to forbid serving officers from taking any further part in the election. In 1950 Lucas became MP for Brentford and Chiswick, and was later offered a junior ministerial position, which he declined in favour of leaving parliament to become the managing director of the Greyhound Racing Association.[46] Douglas Bader was not the only disabled fighter pilot to favour the Conservatives, Colin Hodgkinson declaring that his experience of losing his legs had led him to believe that an excess of security resulted in the death of initiative. With such unimpeachably Tory sentiments, he was adopted as the Conservative candidate for Islington in 1955.[47] A recent survey of former Battle of Britain fighter pilots reveals that the vast majority of 'the Few' voted Conservative in the 1945 general election.[48] John Collins, an RAF chaplain during the war, recalled the undisguised horror he encountered in many officers' messes following the news that Labour had won a landslide victory: 'Was it for this, they seemed to be saying to themselves, that the war had been fought and won?'[49]

Tory flyers insisted that their wartime experiences had made them suspicious of utopianism, and had fostered an individualism that would be incompatible with Labour's collectivist vision. However, some observers, including J. B. Priestley, believed that the relative informality and classlessness of the wartime RAF station might prove a worthy model for the communal and egalitarian society the Labour Party sought to establish after the war.[50] Indeed, the RAF's meritocratic and technocratic cultures suggested an obvious affinity with Attlee's Labour Party, with its emphasis on social opportunity, economic efficiency, and dispassionate expertise. One prominent member of the RAF hierarchy, Sholto Douglas, was a lifelong Fabian socialist, taking the Labour whip when he entered the House of Lords in 1948.[51] Nor should one forget the legacy of Mick Mannock, the First World War fighter ace who had also been a prominent Independent Labour Party activist.[52] Most bomber aircrew were possessed of a political outlook that has been characterized by one recent author as 'a mildly sceptical socialism and belief in social justice'.[53] Even those who were not partisan socialists would undoubtedly have subscribed to the sentiments of that celebrated fictional flyer Flight Lieutenant Peter Carter, hero of *A Matter of Life and Death*, who quips that he is 'Conservative by instinct, Labour by experience'. Left-leaning flyers who wanted to enter politics found Labour Party selection committees were sometimes ambivalent about the prospect of sending former servicemen to Westminster. John Pudney was shortlisted for the North Paddington seat, where he faced a rigorous interrogation at the hands of a selection committee 'of elderly doctrinaire people with strong pacifist leanings, who cross-examined me about my blameless, almost non-combatant, RAF career as if I were still dripping with the blood of innocent Germans'.[54] However, it is significant that Dick Windle, Labour's national agent, was eager to exploit the glamour and heroism associated with the men of the RAF. Among former flyers who became Labour MPs was Anthony Wedgwood-Benn, who had not merely served as aircrew himself, but had a flyer brother who was killed in action and a father who served as secretary of state for air in the 1945 Labour government.[55]

Some former flyers pursued their post-war political convictions in the context of the Empire-Commonwealth. In South Africa, public opinion had been deeply divided over the Dominion's support of Britain during the war, with many Afrikaners feeling they had more in common with Nazi Germany than with the supposed mother country. Many veterans returning from wartime service found themselves shunned by their fellow countrymen, a sense of alienation that deepened when the Nationalist Party swept to power in 1948, committed to a programme not merely of intensified racial segregation, but of hostility to the Anglophile sentiments of the Smuts era. Among those ex-servicemen was Group Captain Adolph Gysbert Malan, DSO and Bar, DFC and Bar, veteran of the Battle of Britain and generally regarded as one of the greatest fighter pilots of all time. While an Afrikaner, 'Sailor' Malan was disgusted at the Nationalist Party's malicious wrecking of the historic ties which had encouraged young men like himself to fight alongside Britain during the war. Initially, his response was to retreat into farming, but in 1951 he entered politics, provoked by the decision of the administration headed by his namesake, D. F. Malan, to disenfranchise the 'coloured' voters of the Cape, without observing the terms laid down in the 1909 South African constitution. Malan, sporting his wartime flying jacket and medals, mobilized thousands of his fellow veterans into what became known as the Torch Commando movement, its name derived from the torchlight processions which accompanied its meetings.[56] Malan had little interest in, let alone commitment to, racial equality. His movement was more concerned with the discontent of white veterans than it was with the political rights of 'coloured' voters. Unlike more radical veterans' associations, such as the Springbok Legion, Malan certainly had no desire to include either 'coloured' or black veterans in Torch, and his movement developed within the racial parameters of the colonial order. As he made clear to a rally in Johannesburg in May 1951: 'Who has the greatest claim to talk about saving white civilization? The moles who now pay lip service to it, or the men who fought for it?' For Malan, his wartime RAF service had provided a template for the post-war Commonwealth, in which equality and partnership between Britain and its Dominions would supersede the traditional hierarchy of imperial authority. However, he clearly understood such international interaction and solidarity in terms of an exclusive fellowship of white men, which meant that Torch was complicit in a racialized conception of South Africa, and the Empire-Commonwealth more generally.[57]

A former flyer with a much more explicit commitment to the preservation of racial difference was to become a central figure in the tragic history of Africa's other last redoubt of white supremacy, Rhodesia-Zimbabwe. During the war Ian Douglas Smith had been a fighter pilot with 237 (Rhodesia) Squadron, flying both Hurricanes and Spitfires in the Mediterranean theatre. On returning to Africa at the end of the war he initially pursued a career in farming, but in 1948 he became Southern Rhodesia's youngest MP. By the time he became the nation's premier in 1964, he had emerged as an uncompromising opponent of black majority rule, a stance which led to him declaring a unilateral declaration of independence from Britain in the following year. Smith's rhetoric of white resistance made constant reference to his wartime service. No white Rhodesian kitchen in the 1960s and 1970s was complete without an illustrated dishcloth featuring 'Good Old Smithy' and his trusty Spitfire.[58] Tributes to the Rhodesian security services published in these years always included prefatory chapters which reminded readers that between 1939 and 1945 a total of 2,409 Rhodesians joined the air force, of whom 498 were killed. During the war three RAF squadrons were awarded the designation 'Rhodesia'—237 and 266 Squadrons of Fighter Command and 44 Squadron, which flew Lancaster bombers and was famed for the raid on Augsburg and the precision bombing of the German warship

Tirpitz.[59] However, this emphasis on the flyer did more than register Rhodesia's not-insubstantial contribution to the war effort and permit reference to Smith's personal credentials as a war hero. It also allowed Rhodesia's white resistance campaign to identify itself with the particular esteem and public affection which had attached itself to the RAF's wartime flyboys. In so doing, it helped Smith attain considerable support in Britain, from backbench Conservative MPs, newspaper columnists, businessmen, and the general public. Some of Smith's more devoted admirers in Britain were responsible, in February 1966, for sending the beleaguered Rhodesian premier the gift of a painting, accompanied by a special dedication, boasting that it was 'presented to the Honourable I. D. Smith MP, Prime Minister of Rhodesia, at an epic period in her history, on behalf of many British people who remained true despite the misguidance of government'. Significantly, the painting itself depicted two Spitfires taking off on a wartime mission at dawn.[60]

Smith was able to reinforce the association of white Rhodesia's struggle with the cult of the wartime flyer through the support he received from former fighter ace Douglas Bader. While Bader's wartime career had been controversial, his undoubted bravery, his energetic post-war campaigning on behalf of the disabled, and the appearance of Paul Brickhill's hagiographic biography in 1954 ensured his heroic status among the post-war British public. From the late 1950s he became a regular newspaper columnist, airing his views first in the *News of the World* and later the *Daily Express*. Here he revealed himself to be an unapologetic reactionary, his hostility to black majority rule in Rhodesia part of a depressingly familiar litany of established diehard bugbears, including Commonwealth immigration, the creation of the Race Relations Board, the European Economic Community, the repeal of the death penalty, and the failure to take draconian measures against the terrorists of the IRA. In the case of Rhodesia, Bader was disgusted that Britain's leaders were destroying 'our gallant ally of two world wars'. As his biographer points out, this desperate cry from the heart to save a nation which, 'in his view was utterly British in thought and action', was also a 'sad lament for his own nation'. Bader had regular meetings with Smith throughout the long-drawn-out death-rattle of white resistance (and even claimed to have acted as an unofficial emissary between the Rhodesian premier and Harold Wilson in 1965), and also became a close friend of Rhodesian fighter ace Johnny Plagis.[61]

In fact, neither Smith nor Bader fitted comfortably into the dominant myths of the wartime RAF. Bader, the belligerent hearty, and Smith, the charmless puritan, in their radically different ways, could hardly be said to have corresponded to the image of the dashing and chivalric flyer. Moreover, political opponents were able to isolate a critical weakness in the deployment of the cult of the wartime flyer by the advocates of white resistance. The *Sunday Mirror* pointed out, in a profile of Bader: 'Here is a man who risked his life a hundred times in a war which was fought against tyranny, censorship and racism—the very stuff the Rhodesian rebels are made of. If Bader's views on such matters were the same in 1940 as they are today, what was he fighting for? It is a curious predicament to feel grateful to someone whose views one finds so repulsive.'[62] Bader's deployment of the myth of the anti-Nazi struggle was also jeopardized by his ill-advised attempts to extend the hand of friendship to former enemies in the Luftwaffe, which left him exposed to charges of colluding in the rehabilitation of the Nazi war effort. In 1955 he wrote the foreword to the memoirs of Germany's leading wartime fighter pilot, Adolf Galland, declaring: 'By any criterion, Galland is a brave man, and I personally shall look forward to meeting him again at any time, anywhere and in any company.'[63] Such sentiments might have been indulged as a case of adopting a chivalric outlook towards a vanquished, but valiant, enemy. However, three years previously he had offered similar praise to Hans Ulrich Rudel, a Stuka pilot whom Bader had met in 1945, and for whom he had secured an artificial leg. Rudel, Bader reassured the readers of a translation of the German flyer's memoir, 'is, by any standards, a gallant chap and I wish him luck'.[64] If Bader was trying here to create a post-war international fellowship of former (white) flyers, or indeed press the claims for Germany to be readmitted into the western fold as the Cold War deepened (Bader was, needless to say, a fanatical anti-communist), he had woefully miscalculated. A storm of controversy broke out when it became clear that Rudel was an unapologetic Nazi, and that the publisher of the English edition of his book was a former member of the British Union of Fascists who had been detained during the war. The association of the wartime flyer with the triumph over Nazi racism could serve as a credible alibi for the racial prejudices of Smith and Bader, but it could just as easily function as a highly convincing witness for the prosecution. Moreover the mono-racial fantasies of Britain's recent past history peddled by the two former flyers also required the erasure of the contribution of non-white aircrew from the dominant cultural memory of the Second World War. This shameful oversight may have still been possible in the 1960s and 1970s, but it became less sustainable by the end of the century, as Britain began to confront its too long neglected multicultural past.[65]

THE SLEEPING DEAD AND THE WAKING DEAD

Whether on the left or the right, flyers who pursued post-war political careers undoubtedly hoped that their participation in public life might offer some guarantee that their wartime comrades who had made the ultimate sacrifice had not done so in vain. Over 70,000 RAF personnel lost their lives during the Second World War, the overwhelming majority of them Bomber Command aircrew. In proportionate terms, the figures are even more stark. One in six of the Fighter Command pilots who fought in the Battle of Britain were killed that summer. Over 50 per cent of the aircrew who flew in Bomber Command throughout the war died.[66] For those who survived, the dead were never far away. Flyers were understandably protective of the memory of fallen comrades. Jules Roy, in a diary entry for December 1944, protested that non-combatants had no right to pay tribute to the dead. 'We'—by which he meant his fellow aircrew—'are the only ones who have the right to speak of them, and we must not tolerate the utterances of those who were not with us, who put false emotion into their voices when evoking their memory.'[67] Of course, in the years which followed the war former flyers were obliged to collaborate with the wider civilian world to facilitate formal public commemoration of their dead comrades, in the form of remembrance ceremonies or the dedication of memorials and monuments. However, the dead lived on, not so much in the rituals of public commemoration such as the Battle of Britain anniversary service in Westminster Abbey, as in the private memories of those who had been fortunate enough to live to see the end of the war. Fallen comrades were remembered with pride, but there were inevitably also highly personalized feelings of sadness, regret, guilt, and anger.

Some flyers sought, or at least accepted the possibility of, a psychic connection with their departed comrades that transcended death. The supernatural and the occult have always been significant in war, offering as they do a way for fighting men to establish a level of control over an environment which is terrifyingly unpredictable. Guardian angels and phantom warriors are therefore a perennial feature of military cultures. More specifically, the scale of loss in the First World War had eroded the boundary between the worlds of the living and the dead and, as a result, there was a widespread revival of spiritualist belief in early twentieth-century Britain.[68] Spiritualism remained popular in the inter-war years, benefiting from both the legacy of the mass bereavement of the Great War and a populist disposition that made it compatible with the democratic temper of the times. During the Second World War public and official responses to the occult were more ambiguous. As the apparent *sang froid* of the flyer reflected, the dominant wartime ethos was 'carrying on regardless', which required a public suppression of the emotional impact of death. Middle-class technocrats also saw (largely working-class) astrologers, clairvoyants, mediums, and faith-healers as relics of a superstitious past that must be replaced by rational expertise and enlightened progress. As a result, the last years of the war saw increased official intolerance of spiritualism, with a number of high-profile mediums being convicted of fraud and imprisoned.[69] However, it is estimated that there were a million spiritualist believers in Britain in 1944, and not just on the home front. In 1941 the Royal Navy recognized spiritualism as a religion. George Mackie, an RAF wing commander, was present at the January 1944 seance which saw the arrest of the notorious materialization medium Helen Duncan, the last woman to be jailed under the Witchcraft Act of 1735. Mackie actually testified in support of Duncan at her Old Bailey trial. For three years during the war the circle of medium Charles Glover Botham included Air Chief Marshal Sir Trafford Leigh-Mallory, commander of No. 12 Fighter Group during the Battle of Britain, who believed he had conversed at these seances with his brother George, lost on Everest in 1924. Leigh-Mallory's superior in 1940 had been Air Chief Marshal Sir Hugh Dowding. 'Stuffy' Dowding was a leading believer in spiritual survival after death, especially after his retirement from the RAF in 1942. In 1943 he created a storm by publishing in a Sunday newspaper letters from dead servicemen—including many of his own fighter boys—which he claimed to have received through automatic writing.[70] Undaunted by the controversy he created, he went on to author a number of impenetrably turgid spiritualist manifestos.[71] A guest at Tony Bartley's marriage to Deborah Kerr in 1947, Dowding unnerved the bridegroom's father by claiming that, during the ceremony, he could detect the astral presence of his son's dead comrades.[72]

Given that flyers were already associated with the ethereal, it is not surprising that several wartime authors found the RAF a prime candidate for exploring the connection between war and the weird. Arthur, the Spitfire pilot in Eileen Marsh's *We Lived in London*, has lost two comrades, Mike and Charlie, during the Battle of Britain. One day, patrolling on his own, he accidentally encounters a formation of German fighters and is shot down. As he hurtles through the air, he becomes aware that he is no longer alone. On each side of him a sister aircraft was diving, in perfect alignment with his own: 'There they were, two Spitfires, one to port and one to starboard, flying in close formation. Then he understood. It was Mike flying to port and Charlie to starboard. He knew what it meant! They had come to escort him in.'[73] What Marsh was doing here was placing an aeronautical twist on the classic 'wraith' or 'fetch' tale, in which a soldier killed in battle returns to visit a close friend at the moment of the latter's death. However, fictional stories featuring phantom airmen were also turned out by RAF authors, who drew on first-hand knowledge of the supernatural folklore of the flyer. A fondness for the esoteric and the occult was particularly evident in the wartime short stories of Roald Dahl. In 'Katina', the ghost of Peter, a downed fighter pilot, returns at night to the tent he had shared with a fellow flyer. 'They Shall Not Grow Old' recounts the story of Fin, a Hurricane pilot who disappears for two days while on a routine patrol over Syria. On his return, he relates to his fellow pilots how he had flown into a mysterious cloud, before emerging into a clear blue sky, 'a pure shining colour which I had never seen before and which I cannot describe'. Looking above him, Fin spies hundreds of aircraft moving in a single black line, all at the same speed and in the same direction. Flying higher and closer, he realizes that the long procession is made up of every type of aircraft, from all the belligerent nations: 'I do not know why or how I knew it, but I knew as I looked at them that these were the pilots and air crews who had been killed in battle, who now, in their own aircraft were making their last flight, their last journey.' Fin's Hurricane is dragged into this formation, but he found himself suddenly free of all worry or fear, feeling 'only pleasure at being where I was'. He notices that all the pilots are waving at one another, 'like children on a rollercoaster'. He then sees his final destination, a vast plain, 'green and smooth and beautiful', illuminated by an unnatural white light, 'shining bright and without any colour'. However, just at that moment Fin is torn away from this flyer's Valhalla, and, his time on earth clearly not yet up, he is returned to the skies above the Lebanon hills.[74]

Flyer diaries and memoirs often contain references to mystical visions or speculation about spiritual continuity after death. Navigator George Hull confessed to Joan Kirby that, while his scientific training has 'tended to make me believe in physical rather than spiritual things', and that he seriously doubted whether the dead could communicate with the living, nevertheless he was still undecided about the possibility of life after death.[75] Michael Scott's journal reveals that he had been reading, shortly before his death in action, John William Dunne's *The New Immortality*. 'If Dunne's theories are correct,' the young Blenheim pilot mused, 'we have an endless existence to enjoy after life . . . This thought makes war seem far less terrible.'[76] Leonard Cheshire had once imagined, on a mission in which he was close to sleep, seeing dead comrades 'flitting in and out of the clouds, laughing, hovering around, as if a barrier between danger and us'.[77] If such visions anticipated Cheshire's later reputation as a mystic, it should be noted that the much more worldly fighter pilot Jim Bailey was willing to grant credibility to claims by fellow flyers that, having got lost, they had landed on unfamiliar air bases and gone into the mess, only to see the ghostly figures of dead comrades sitting there.[78]

Fictional narratives suggested that a desire to retain some form of psychical or emotional fellowship with fallen brothers-in-arms remained an important element in the disposition of some flyers long after the end of the war. In Walter Clapham's *Night Be My Witness*, Johnny Somers, the former Wellington bomb-aimer, tells a friend that those, like himself, who had survived had more in common with his deceased comrades than they did with those who had never 'brushed the fringes of the mystery, in high places, and saw the earth dwindling to a star'. Indeed, while those who were killed were 'the sleeping dead', those who survived constituted 'the waking dead', different only by degree, not in substance. Between the former flyboys and their dead comrades was a bond 'which is imperishable and beyond your understanding'.[79] *The Last Reunion*, scripted by Kenneth Hyde, and one of the first 'weekend dramas' to appear on independent television in 1955, explored the agony of Simmie (Eric Portman), a former wing commander, who had accompanied a bomber crew on their last mission. While he had managed to survive, the crew had all been killed. Simmie, burdened with remorse, finds himself, even ten years later, unable to banish the ghosts of his deceased comrades and to escape the 'everlasting aeroplane' in which the dead and the living remain trapped together for eternity.[80] By contrast, in Powell and Pressburger's cinematic fantasy *A Matter of Life and Death*, the relationship of the flyer to the supernatural is used to deliver a rather different take on the issues of survival and guilt. Peter Carter (David Niven), having leapt from his stricken Lancaster without a parachute, insists that he was incorrectly chosen to die, and claims the right to plead for his life in a heavenly court. At the beginning of the movie Peter has flown sixty-seven missions, and has already come to terms with the fact that he cannot expect to outlive the war. When he realizes that he may, in fact, have escaped a fate he had believed to be virtually foreordained, Peter is initially subject to an overwhelming sense of remorse that he is still alive after six years of war, when so many of his comrades have died. Ultimately, however, Peter's passion for June (Kim Hunter), the control-tower operator with whom he has fallen in love, restores his desire to live on after the war. Guilt at survival is abrogated, while love, not to say life itself, are joyfully embraced.[81]

The necessity, now that the war had ended, of repudiating the self-reproach which regularly beset those who found they were still alive at the end of hostilities was a significant motif in a number of post-war fictional texts which referenced the wartime flyer, albeit in absentia. For these narratives tended to focus on the mindset, not of former flyers mourning comrades, but of civilians who had lost flyboy lovers, brothers, and sons. *Broken Journey*, a 1947 film about a passenger plane which crashes in the Alps, featured Mary (Phyllis Calvert), a stewardess who is forced to come to terms with the fact that her idealization of a wartime romance with a RAF boyfriend who had been killed in action was ultimately an act of monstrous self-deception. She eventually understands the need to move on, and allows herself to pursue a new, and much healthier, love affair with Bill, the co-pilot of the airliner on which she works.[82] A more agonized attempt to move out from under the shadow of the dead flyer is related in Mary Renault's novel *North Face*. Neil Langton, a schoolteacher, and Ellen Shortland meet while rock-climbing in Devon after the war. They are both emotionally damaged, Neil by his wife's infidelity and Ellen by the loss of her boyfriend, Jock, an RAF pilot killed over the Channel in 1940. Ellen is upset when they come upon the body of a dead airman, washed up on the shore, his skull smashed open and still wearing his parachute harness. Neil reassures her that this is a recent death, and cannot possibly be Jock's body. Ellen continues to wear a gold St Christopher medal with RAF wings on the other side, a gift from Jock, around her neck. As Neil falls in love with Ellen, he becomes obsessed with this token of her former lover's affection. When she wears a dress cut high at the throat he still imagines the medal underneath, and compares her to the mythical queen of Sparta imprisoned by Zeus: 'As clearly as if nothing had intervened, he could see the disc lying between her breasts . . . he could see the enamelled wings. She seemed to lie abandoned to it, like Leda to the swan.' Ellen cannot reciprocate Neil's increasingly obvious attachment, telling him that she feels responsible for Jock's death. She had refused to sleep with Jock and had, as a consequence, come to realize she did not really love him. However, she had then tortured herself over what she believed to be her selfishness when Jock had been facing possible death. Having decided that she will make herself love him, she writes a letter to Jock, agreeing to marry him. Unfortunately, she delays posting it, and in the meantime Jock is killed in action. On receiving the news of his death, she experiences a strange sense of exaltation: 'It seemed everything was resolved between us, that I'd always loved him, and that now it was perfect and spiritual and he must know it too.' However, almost at once 'a sort of shrivelling light burst in', and Ellen 'knew what all this ecstasy really was. It was relief.' This is why she has to reject Neil's love: 'I can't feel any pleasure now, without a sense of sin.' When Neil finally convinces Ellen that she has no need to feel guilty, they make love—'a casual epilogue, after an exhausting emotional crisis'—and Ellen agrees to marry him, but not before he symbolically removes her St Christopher medal and places it on her bedside table.[83]

Real-life narratives echoed such fictionalized renderings of the need to move on, although that did not necessarily imply that a fallen flyer would be completely forgotten. Her fighter pilot fiancé Denis Wissler having been shot down in November 1940, Edith Heap married someone else after the war. The marriage was short-lived and, in an interview fifty years later, she expressed the conviction that she had, over the years, often felt Denis's continued presence.[84] Joan Kirby, to whom George Hull addressed so many heartfelt letters, after the young navigator's death married in 1947, but preserved their wartime correspondence, before handing it over to the Imperial War Museum. There was nothing disrespectful or callous about putting the past behind one. Both flyers who had lost their comrades and women who had lost their flyboy lovers entered the post-war world in the knowledge that, despite all that they had already experienced, they still had most of their lives left to run. However, as the decades passed, the numbers of those flyers who had survived the war themselves began to dwindle. Now only a handful remain, the last survivors of a cohort of young men who had captured the imaginations of both their contemporaries and the generations which have come after. Ironically, as they reached their twilight years and became acutely conscious—for the second time in their lives—of their mortality, these veterans made more effort than they had done immediately after the war to record their experiences, to look up their former comrades, and to secure fitting memorials for those who had never returned home.[85]

The reintegration of the flyer into peacetime society was decidedly uneven. Some men found it difficult to renounce the excitement of flying or the fellowship of service life. Novels and films in the immediate post-war years featured a variety of maladjusted ex-flyers. Despite their successful careers in public life, many of those flyers who had entered politics appeared no less disenchanted, alienated by either the collectivist spirit of the post-war Labour government or the dramatic unravelling of Britain's imperial obligations. Flyers returning to a now communist-dominated eastern Europe found themselves resented and persecuted. Non-white flyers met with racial intolerance in both Britain and the colonies. Other flyers found it difficult to overcome the feelings of guilt and regret which were an understandable by-product of outliving the war, when so many of their comrades had died. This said, the overwhelming majority of flyers successfully managed the return to civilian life, and while it wasn't always easy, settled down into regular employment and family life. Unfortunately, such relatively mundane narratives were not necessarily attractive to novelists and screenwriters, which meant that this essentially congenial narrative is frequently absent from the domain of cultural representation in the immediate post-war years. Nevertheless, a successful readjustment to domesticity was the dominant experience of most flyers, and it is one which provides further evidence that their masculine identities tell us as much about mid-twentieth-century British society as a whole, as they do about the specific military culture of the wartime RAF.

Conclusion

If this author's recent visit to a provincial branch of a popular British bookstore chain is a reliable indicator, the men of the wartime RAF seem no less ubiquitous in 2007 than they did when Lord David Cecil went in search of them sixty-six years ago. A perusal of the military-history section produced a host of titles dedicated to the exploits and aircraft of the wartime flyboys. Shelved under biography was Geoffrey Wellum's best-selling memoir of his career as a Spitfire pilot in 1940, while the fiction section included not merely a reprint of H. E. Bates's Flying Officer X short stories, but three contemporary novels featuring wartime fighter pilots.[1] From the shelves dedicated to romance novels it was possible to retrieve two recently published potboilers, which portrayed on their covers a boyish flyer and a misty-eyed WAAF.[2] Among the bookstore's stock of DVDs one could find copies of *Dark Blue World*, a feature film about Czech flyers in the Battle of Britain, and *Piece of Cake*, a television drama serial about a fictional Spitfire squadron stationed in France in the first nine months of the war.[3] Judging from the range of genres represented in this single outlet, the allure of the fighter boys and bomber boys continues to capture the imagination of a broad swathe of the British public.

At times it is difficult not to feel a little wary towards this ongoing enchantment with the men in air-force blue. It might seem tainted by an unedifying national parochialism, a failure to recognize the more substantial military victories achieved, or the extent of sacrifices borne, by other peoples and nations whose lives were overshadowed by the terror of Nazism. The cult of the flyer may appear to be yet another example of the nation's neurotic, almost pathological, obsession with the Second World War, in which, unable to face (let alone mourn) its post-war decline, Britain, even at the opening of the twenty-first century, has taken refuge in comforting myths of a wartime 'finest hour'.[4] It is also possible that a celebration of the wartime flyboys betrays a desire to return to an ideal of masculinity defined in terms of the stoic and unreflective warrior, as opposed to more contemporary configurations of male identity, most notably the 'new man', enfeebled by his capitulation to the forces of second-wave feminism.

However, a sustained examination of the lives of the men of the RAF, and of the representations of them which existed in wartime, suggests that such reactionary fantasies are ultimately untenable. Those who have failed to come to terms with post-war multiculturalism will have to account for the contribution of non-white flying personnel to the war in the air. Acknowledging the presence of Irish or Indian flyers in the skies over Kent in the summer of 1940 should make it impossible for the Battle of Britain to any longer serve the mono-racial fantasies of little-Englanders. Likewise, those who look to the war years as a model of robust and undomesticated masculinity will need to disregard 'Sailor' Malan's heartfelt declarations of uxoriousness, or overlook the fact that Guy Gibson, on the eve of the legendary Dambusters raid, had been eager to snatch a few hours of comfort with a woman with whom he had fallen in love, but who, frustrated at his unavailability, had married someone else. The fact that the flyer may, on occasion in the post-war period, have been pressed into the service of those wedded to the politics of cultural intransigence and national consolation has been unfortunate, not least because it belies the airman's complicated relationship to the social, national, racial, and gender identities of his own age. Such complexity was inevitable, given that the flyer belonged to a military culture that was simultaneously distinct from, and yet an intrinsic part of, a wider society that recent historical research has revealed to be markedly heterogeneous.

A more congenial explanation for the continued esteem in which the flyer has been held is that his courage and sacrifice coincided with the last hurrah of the romance of flight. The arrival, at the close of the Second World War, of the jet engine, ballistic missile, and atomic bomb marked the closing of the heroic era of military aviation. The men who flew in the Second World War were the products of an inter-war culture that had passionately celebrated the aeroplane as the purest product of the machine age. In the early 1940s flying still possessed a magical and aesthetic quality which it was unable to sustain in a post-war era characterized by the depersonalization of military aviation and the demotion of civil aviation to a banal and routine means of mass transportation. The flyer was one of the last representatives of that passion for wings that had captivated the western imagination in the opening decades of the twentieth century. This, combined with his bravery in combat, ensured a star appeal which not merely made him a popular subject in the fictional narratives of novelists, playwrights, and filmmakers, but guaranteed a warm welcome for the real-life flyer in places as diverse as the Hollywood studio and the floor of the House of Commons.

However, while he had attained rarefied status through his ability to ride above the clouds, in a world still inaccessible and unfamiliar to his contemporaries, the flyer was also grounded in the sensibilities, values, and social fabric of the society from which he came, albeit one that was being violently refashioned by the requirements of wartime mobilization. The flyer reflected the conflict between increased egalitarianism and continued middle-class hegemony which characterized Britain throughout the 1940s. He disclosed the racial and national tensions which arose from Britain's tortured efforts to replace traditional imperial authority by a less hierarchical Commonwealth. The flyer who fell in love with the cookhouse WAAF exemplified a wartime culture which presented heterosexual romance as one of the rewards of citizenship available to men and women who had borne the obligations and sacrifices of national duty. For all his genuine attachment to the fraternity of flyers, the wartime airman also displayed that lionization of domesticity which had become the touchstone of masculinity in Britain by the mid-twentieth century. Their understandings of fear and courage were closely attuned to the emotional codes and standards of a wider society which was increasingly beholden to the authority of psychoanalytical expertise. Those flyers who were disfigured or dismembered in combat found that public responses were different only in degree from those faced by disabled civilians. More generally, the airman encapsulated Britain's fraught encounter with modernity, his ambivalent persona symbolizing a society that was capable of developing the extraordinarily advanced technology which made the air war possible, but which remained fixated on the values of a fantasized pre-industrial past.[5] For all his particular allure, uncommon courage, and singular achievements, the flyer's story is therefore also very much Britain's story, in the century of total war.

Notes

NOTES TO INTRODUCTION

1. David Cecil, 'The RAF: A Layman's Glimpse', in *Men of the RAF* (London: Oxford University Press, 1942), 65.

2. Ibid. 66.

3. e.g. Paul Addison and Jeremy A. Crang (eds.), *The Burning Blue: A New History of the Battle of Britain* (London: Pimlico, 2000); Stephen Bungay, *The Most Dangerous Enemy: A History of the Battle of Britain* (London: Aurum Press, 2001); Richard Overy, *The Battle of Britain* (London: Penguin, 2004).

4. Keith Lowe, *Inferno: The Devastation of Hamburg, 1943* (London: Viking, 2007); Frederick Taylor, *Dresden: Tuesday, 13 February 1945* (London: Bloomsbury, 2005); Richard Knott, *Black Night for Bomber Command: The Tragedy of 16 December 1943* (Barnsley: Pen and Sword, 2007).

5. e.g. Frank H. Ziegler, *The Story of 609 Squadron* (Manchester: Crecy Books, 1993); Larry Forrester, *Fly for Your Life: The Story of Bob Stanford Tuck* (Bristol: Cerberus Publishing, 2006); David Ross, *Stapme: The Biography of Squadron Leader Basil Gerald Stapleton, DFC* (London: Grub Street, 2002); Richard Morris, *Guy Gibson* (London: Viking, 1994); Tim Vigors, *Life's Too Short to Cry: The Compelling Memoirs of a Battle of Britain Ace* (London: Grub Street, 2006); Eric Brown, *Wings on My Sleeve* (London: Weidenfeld & Nicolson, 2006).

6. e.g. Harry Holmes, *Avro Lancaster: The Definitive Record* (Shrewsbury: Airlife, 2001). For a more imaginative variant of this genre, Jonathan Glancey, *Spitfire: The Biography* (London: Atlantic Books, 2006).

7. John Terraine, *The Right of the Line: The Royal Air Force in the European War, 1939–1945* (London: Hodder & Stoughton, 1985); Mark Connelly, *Reaching for the Stars: A New History of Bomber Command in World War Two* (London: I. B. Tauris, 2001).

8. e.g. James Taylor and Martin Davidson, *Bomber Crew: Survivors of Bomber Command Tell Their Own Story* (London: Hodder & Stoughton, 2004); Tony Rennell and John Nichol, *Tail End Charlies: The Last Battles of the Bomber War, 1944–45* (London: Viking, 2004); John Sweetman, *Bomber Crew: Taking on the Reich* (London: Little, Brown, 2004).

9. Patrick Bishop, *Fighter Boys: Saving Britain, 1940* (London: HarperCollins, 2004); id., *Bomber Boys: Fighting Back, 1940–1945* (London: HarperCollins, 2007).

10. Michael Roper and John Tosh (eds.), *Manful Assertions: Masculinities in Britain Since 1800* (London: Routledge, 1991).

11. Keith McClelland, 'Masculinity and the "Representative Artisan" in Britain, 1850–80', in Roper and Tosh (eds.), *Manful Assertions*; John Tosh, *A Man's Place: Masculinity and the Middle-Class Home in Victorian England* (New Haven: Yale

University Press, 1999); Nancy W. Ellenberger, 'Constructing George Wyndham: Narratives of Aristocratic Masculinity in Fin-de-siecle England', *Journal of British Studies*, 39 (2000), 487–517; Andrew Davies, 'Youth Gangs, Masculinity and Violence in Late Victorian Manchester and Salford', *Journal of Social History*, 32 (1998), 349–70; A. James Hammerton, 'The English Weakness? Gender, Satire and "Moral Manliness" in the Lower Middle Class, 1870–1920', in Alan Kidd and David Nicholls (eds.), *Gender, Civic Culture and Consumerism: Middle-Class Identity in Britain, 1800–1940* (Manchester: Manchester University Press, 1999); Angela V. John and Claire Eustance (eds.), *The Men's Share? Masculinities, Male Support and Women's Suffrage in Britain, 1890–1920* (London: Routledge, 1997); Kelly Boyd, *Manliness and the Boys Story Paper, 1855–1940* (Basingstoke: Palgrave, 2002); Paul Thompson, 'Playing at Being Skilled Men: Factory Culture and Pride in Work Skills among Coventry Car Workers', *Social History*, 13 (1988), 45–69; Graham Dawson, *Soldier Heroes: British Adventure, Empire and the Imagining of Masculinities* (London: Routledge, 1994); Mrinalini Sinha, *Colonial Masculinity: The 'Manly Englishman' and the 'Effeminate Bengali' in the Late Nineteenth Century* (Manchester: Manchester University Press, 1995); Heather Streets, *Martial Races: The Military, Race and Masculinity in British Imperial Culture, 1857–1914* (Manchester: Manchester University Press, 2004); Wendy Webster, *Englishness and Empire, 1939–1965* (Oxford: Oxford University Press, 2005), 182–217; Patrick F. McDevitt, 'Muscular Catholicism: Nationalism, Masculinity and Gaelic Team Sports, 1884–1916', *Gender and History*, 9 (1997), 262–84; Marcus Collins, 'Pride and Prejudice: West Indian Men in Mid-Twentieth-Century Britain', *Journal of British Studies*, 40 (2001), 391–418; Lesley Hall, *Hidden Anxieties: Male Sexuality, 1900–1950* (Cambridge: Polity, 1991); Christopher Breward, *The Hidden Consumer: Masculinities, Fashion and City Life, 1860–1914* (Manchester: Manchester University Press, 1999); Frank Mort, *Cultures of Consumption: Masculinities and Social Space in Late Twentieth-Century Britain* (London: Routledge, 1996); Michael Roper, *Masculinity and the British Organization Man Since 1945* (Oxford: Oxford University Press, 1994); Andrew Spicer, *Typical Men: the Representation of Masculinity in Popular British Cinema* (London: I. B. Tauris, 2001).

12. e.g. Chris Waters, 'Disorders of the Mind, Disorders of the Body Social: Peter Wildeblood and the Making of the Modern Homosexual', in Becky Conekin, Frank Mort, and Chris Waters (eds.), *Moments of Modernity: Reconstructing Britain, 1945–64* (London: Rivers Oram, 1994); Matt Houlbrook, *Queer London: Perils and Pleasures in the Sexual Metropolis, 1918–1957* (Chicago: University of Chicago Press, 2005).

13. Sandra Gilbert, 'Soldier's Heart: Literary Men, Literary Women and the Great War', and Elaine Showalter, 'Rivers and Sassoon: The Inscription of Male Gender Anxieties', in Margaret Higonnet *et al.* (eds.), *Behind the Lines: Gender and the Two World Wars* (New Haven: Yale University Press, 1987). Adrian Caesar, *Taking It Like a Man: Suffering, Sexuality and the War Poets* (Manchester: Manchester University Press, 1993); Alfredo Bonadeo, *Mark of the Beast: Death and Degradation in the Literature of the Great War* (Lexington, Ky.: University Press of Kentucky, 1989).

14. Joanna Bourke, *Dismembering the Male: Men's Bodies, Britain and the Great War* (Chicago: University of Chicago Press, 1996).

15. Nicoletta Gullace, *The Blood of Our Sons: Men, Women and the Renegotiation of British Citizenship During the Great War* (Basingstoke: Palgrave, 2002); Deborah Cohen, *The War Come Home: Disabled Veterans in Britain and Germany, 1914–1939* (Berkeley: University of California Press, 2001).

16. Sonya O. Rose, *Which People's War? National Identity and Citizenship in Wartime Britain, 1939–1945* (Oxford: Oxford University Press, 2003), 151–96.

17. Penny Summerfield, *Reconstructing Women's Wartime Lives: Discourse and Subjectivity in Oral Histories of the Second World War* (Manchester: Manchester University Press, 1998), 115–60.

18. Joanna Bourke, *An Intimate History of Killing: Face-to-Face Killing in Twentieth-Century Warfare* (London: Granta, 1998).

19. Christina S. Jarvis, *The Male Body at War: American Masculinity During World War Two* (De Kalb, Ill.: Northern Illinois University Press, 2004).

20. John Tosh, 'What Should Historians Do With Masculinity? Reflections on Nineteenth-Century Britain', *History Workshop Journal*, 38 (1994), 179–202.

21. Toby L. Ditz, 'The New Men's History and the Peculiar Absence of Gendered Power: Some Remedies from Early American Gender History', *Gender and History*, 16 (2004), 1–35.

22. Penny Summerfield, *Women Workers in the Second World War: Production and Patriarchy in Conflict* (London: Croom Helm, 1984); Christine Gledhill and Gillian Swanson (eds.), *Nationalising Femininity: Culture, Sexuality and British Cinema in the Second World War* (Manchester: Manchester University Press, 1996); Rose, *Which People's War?*; Antonia Lant, *Blackout: Reinventing Women for Wartime British Cinema* (Princeton: Princeton University Press, 1991); Lucy Noakes, *War and the British: Gender, Memory and National Identity* (London: I. B. Tauris, 1998).

23. Most of this literature is concerned with civil, rather than military, aviation. For example, Joseph Corn, *The Winged Gospel: America's Romance with Aviation, 1900–1950* (New York: Oxford University Press, 1983), 71–90; Susan Ware, *Still Missing: Amelia Earhart and the Search for Modern Feminism* (New York: Norton, 1993); Suzanne L. Kolm, 'Who Says It's a Man's World? Women's Work and Travel in the First Decades of Flight', in Dominick A. Pisano (ed.), *The Airplane in American Culture* (Ann Arbor, Mich.: University of Michigan Press, 2003), 147–64; Kathleen Barry, *Femininity in Flight: A History of Flight Attendants* (Durham, NC: Duke University Press, 2007); Elizabeth Millward, 'Scaling Airspace: Gender in the British Imperial Skies, 1922–1937', Ph.D dissertation, York, Ontario (2003).

24. Angus Calder, *The People's War: Britain, 1939–1945* (London: Cape, 1969).

25. Jeremy A. Crang, *The British Army and the People's War* (Manchester: Manchester University Press, 2000).

26. For middle-class resilience, Ross McKibbin, *Classes and Cultures: England, 1918–1951* (Oxford: Oxford University Press, 1998).

27. Richard Weight, *Patriots: National Identity in Britain, 1940–2000* (London: Macmillan, 2006); Marika Sherwood, *Many Struggles: West Indian Workers and*

Service Personnel in Britain, 1939–1945 (London: Karia, 1985); Ian Spencer, *British Immigration Policy Since 1939: The Making of Multicultural Britain* (London: Routledge, 1997).

28. Joanna Bourke, *Fear: A Cultural History* (London: Virago, 2005), 6.

29. Frank Costigliola, ' "I Had Come as a Friend": Emotion, Culture and Ambiguity in the Formation of the Cold War', *Cold War History*, 1 (2000), 103–28; Michael Roper, 'Maternal Relations: Moral Manliness and Emotional Survival in Letters Home During the First World War', in Stefan Dudink, Karen Hagemann, and John Tosh (eds.), *Masculinities in Politics and War: Rewritings of Modern History* (Manchester: Manchester University Press, 2004); Luisa Passerini, *Europe in Love, Love in Europe: Imagination and Politics in Britain Between the Wars* (London: I. B. Tauris, 1998).

30. For works focusing on public codes relating to emotional expression, William H. Reddy, *The Invisible Code: Honor and Sentiment in Postrevolutionary France, 1814–1848* (Berkeley: University of California Press, 1997); Peter N. Stearns and Jan Lewis (eds.), *An Emotional History of the United States* (New York: NYU Press, 1998).

31. For an assertion of the need to reach beyond representation to subjectivity, albeit one which insists on a psychoanalytical methodology, Michael Roper, 'Slipping Out of View: Subjectivity and Emotion in Gender History', *History Workshop Journal*, 59 (2005), 57–73.

32. Geoff Eley, 'Finding the People's War: Film, British Collective Memory and World War Two', *American Historical Review*, 105 (2001), 818–38; Mark Connelly, *We Can Take It! Britain and the Memory of the Second World War* (Harlow: Longman, 2004); Malcolm Smith, *Britain and 1940: History, Myth and Popular Memory* (London: Routledge, 2000); Martin Evans and Ken Lunn (eds.), *War and Memory in the Twentieth Century* (Oxford: Berg, 1997); Robert Murphy, *British Cinema and the Second World War* (London: Continuum, 2000); Neil Rattigan, 'The Last Gasp of the Middle Class: British War Films of the 1950s', in Wheeler Winston Dixon (ed.), *Re-Viewing British Cinema, 1900–1992* (New York: State University of New York Press, 1994), 143–54.

33. Noakes, *War and the British*, 3.

34. Figures from Terraine, *Right of the Line*, 3–6.

35. For examples of the experiences of flyers based in the Far East, Imperial War Museum Department of Documents [hereafter IWM] 91/35/1 HT Radford; Conshelf Flying Officer C. Crichton.

36. For a sophisticated interpretation of the complex relationship between experience and memory in the war-memoir genre, Leonard V. Smith, *The Embattled Self: French Soldiers' Testimony of the Great War* (Ithaca, NY: Cornell University Press, 2007).

37. For a recent example of such scepticism, Dan Todman, *The Great War: Myth and Memory* (London: Hambledon, 2005), 159–60.

38. Charles Bernheimer, *Figures of Ill Repute: Representing Prostitution in Nineteenth-Century France* (Cambridge, Mass.: Harvard University Press, 1989); Mary Poovey,

Uneven Developments: The Ideological Work of Gender in Mid-Victorian England (Chicago: University of Chicago Press, 1988); Alison Light, *Forever England: Femininity, Literature and Conservatism Between the Wars* (London: Routledge, 1991).

39. Janet S. K. Watson, *Fighting Different Wars: Experience, Memory, and the First World War in Britain* (Cambridge: Cambridge University Press, 2004), 10.

40. Rosa Maria Bracco, *Merchants of Hope: British Middlebrow Writers and the First World War, 1919–1939* (Oxford: Berg, 1993); Nicola Humble, *The Feminine Middlebrow Novel, 1920s to 1950s: Class, Domesticity and Bohemianism* (Oxford: Oxford University Press, 2001).

41. e.g. Geoffrey Wansell, *Terence Rattigan: A Biography* (London: Fourth Estate, 1995); Lynn Knight, 'Introduction' to *Dangerous Calm: Selected Stories of Elizabeth Taylor* (London: Virago, 1995).

42. Mark Rawlinson, *British Writing of the Second World War* (Oxford: Oxford University Press, 2000), 39–67; Samuel Hynes, *The Soldier's Tale: Bearing Witness to Modern War* (New York: Penguin, 1998), 125–9.

NOTES TO CHAPTER 1

1. Michael Paris, 'The Rise of the Airmen: The Origins of Air Force Elitism, c.1890–1918', *Journal of Contemporary History*, 28 (1993), 123–41.

2. Kay Carroll, *Compass Course: The Log of an Air Force Officer's Wife* (London: Hutchinson, n.d. [1941]), 25–6, 62–3.

3. Tony Mansell, 'Flying Start: Educational and Social Factors in the Recruitment of Pilots of the Royal Air Force in the Interwar Years', *History of Education*, 26 (1997), 71–90; John James, *The Paladins: A Social History of the RAF up to the Outbreak of World War Two* (London: Macdonald, 1990).

4. John Pudney, *A Pride of Unicorns: Richard and David Atcherley of the RAF* (London: Oldbourne, 1960), 198.

5. Sweetman, *Bomber Crew*, 10–11, Bishop, *Fighter Boys*, 91–3.

6. Anthony Bartley, *Smoke Trails in the Sky: From the Journals of a Fighter Pilot* (London: William Kimber, 1984), 16.

7. Peter Townsend, *Time and Chance: An Autobiography* (London: Collins, 1978), 65.

8. Richard Hillary, *The Last Enemy* (1942; London: Pimlico, 1997), 44.

9. David Omissi, 'The Hendon Air Pageant, 1920–37', in John M. Mackenzie (ed.), *Popular Imperialism and the Military, 1850–1950* (Manchester: Manchester University Press, 1992), 198–220.

10. Ira Jones, *King of Air Fighters: A Biography of Major Mick Mannock* (London: Nicholson & Watson, 1934); Walter Alwyn Briscoe, *The Boy Hero of the Air* (London: Oxford University Press, 1921); R. H. Kiernan, *Captain Albert Ball, VC* (London: John Hamilton, 1933).

11. W. E. Johns, *Biggles of the Camel Squadron* (London: John Hamilton, 1934); id., *Biggles Flies Again* (London: John Hamilton, 1934); Peter Ellis, *Biggles! The*

Life Story of Captain W. E. Johns (Godmanstone: Veloce, 1993); Susan Ottaway, *Dambuster: A Life of Guy Gibson, VC* (London: Leo Cooper, 1996), 22.

12. Linda A. Robertson, *The Dream of Civilized Warfare: World War One Flying Aces and the American Imagination* (Minneapolis: University of Minnesota Press, 2003).

13. Omissi, 'Hendon Air Pageant'; Robert Wohl, *The Spectacle of Flight: Aviation and the Western Imagination, 1920–1950* (New Haven: Yale University Press, 2005), 49–106, 305–8; Valentine Cunningham, *British Writers of the Thirties* (Oxford: Oxford University Press, 1988), 156–210; Ian Patterson, *Guernica and Total War* (London: Profile Books, 2007).

14. Hector Bolitho, *A Penguin in the Eyrie: An RAF Diary, 1939–1945* (London: Hutchinson, 1955), 84–5.

15. Jane Oliver, *In No Strange Land* (London: Collins, 1944), 221–2.

16. Carroll, *Compass Course*, 12, 16, 32.

17. Noel Monks, *Squadrons Up!* (London: Victor Gollancz, 1940), 74–5.

18. Bishop, *Fighter Boys*, 147–96.

19. Christopher Seton-Watson, *Dunkirk–Alamein–Bologna: Letters and Diaries of an Artilleryman, 1939–1945* (London: Buckland Publications, 1993), 38.

20. Norman Franks, *Air Battle Dunkirk* (London: Grub Street, 2000).

21. Alan C. Deere, *Nine Lives* (London: Hodder & Stoughton, 1959), 60–6.

22. Guy Gibson, *Enemy Coast Ahead* (1946; London: Pan Books, 1955), 80–2.

23. Bartley, *Smoke Trails*, 27, 29.

24. Philip Toynbee, *Friends Apart: A Memoir of Esmond Romilly and Jasper Ridley in the Thirties* (London: MacGibbon & Kee, 1954), 165.

25. IWM 03/34/1, Flight Lieutenant G. Shackleton, ms. notes on 'Friendly Fire'.

26. Nevil Shute, *Landfall* (1940; London: House of Stratus, 2000).

27. Bishop, *Bomber Boys*, p. xxxiii.

28. Mass-Observation Archive, University of Sussex [hereafter M-O] File Report 886–7, 'Civilian Attitudes to the Navy Compared with the RAF and Army' (1941), 2.

29. *We Speak from the Air: Broadcasts by the RAF, Issued for the Air Ministry by the Ministry of Information* (London: HMSO, 1942); *Over to You: New Broadcasts by the RAF* (London: HMSO, 1943).

30. *Target for Tonight*, dir. Harry Watt (1941). For Bomber Command's initial lack of success, Robin Neillands, *The Bomber War* (New York: Overlook Press, 2001), 56–7.

31. Helen Jones, *British Civilians in the Front Line: Air Raids, Productivity and Wartime Culture, 1939–45* (Manchester: Manchester University Press, 2006), 126–7.

32. Colin Curzon, *Flying Wild* (London: Hurst & Blackett, 1941); Denise Robins, *Winged Love* (London: Hutchinson, 1941); Carol Gaye, *Air Force Girl* (London: Collins, 1941); Oliver Sandys, *Wellington Wendy* (London: Hurst & Blackett, 1941).

33. M-O File Report 968, Tom Harrisson, 'War Books' (20 Nov. 1941), 2.

34. M-O File Report 895, 'Public Attitude to RAF News' (Oct. 1941), 1–2.

35. Bartley, *Smoke Trails*, 42.

36. Ibid. 50.

37. Ibid. 61–2. See also Johnny Kent, *One of the Few* (Stroud: Tempus, 2000), 88.

38. Cuthbert Orde, *Pilots of Fighter Command: Sixty-Four Portraits* (London: George Harrap, 1942), 25.

39. Bartley, *Smoke Trails*, 19.

40. C. H. Ward-Jackson, *No Bombs At All: Some Short Stories of the Royal Air Force* (London: Sylvan Press, 1944), 107–13.

41. Orde, *Pilots of Fighter Command*, 25.

42. IWM PP/MCR/C45 JMVC, J. M. V. Carpenter DFC, biographical notes filed among correspondence of Squadron Leader John Carpenter.

43. Jeffrey S. Reznick, *Healing the Nation: Soldiers and the Culture of Caregiving in Britain During the Great War* (Manchester: Manchester University Press, 2004), 99–111.

44. E. M. Delafield, *The Provincial Lady in Wartime* (New York: Harper & Bros., 1940), 268.

45. John Watson, *Johnny Kinsman: A Novel* (London: Cassell, 1955), 31–3.

46. Alexander Baron, *With Hope, Farewell* (London: Jonathan Cape, 1952), 135, 244.

47. Geoffrey Wellum, *First Light* (London: Viking, 2002), 84.

48. Pierre Clostermann, *The Big Show*, trans. Oliver Berthoud (Harmondsworth: Penguin Books, 1958), 250.

49. Colin Hodgkinson, *Best Foot Forward* (London: Odhams, 1957), 119.

50. William Simpson, *I Burned My Fingers* (London: Putnam, 1955), 115–16.

51. Joan Wyndham, *Love Is Blue: A Wartime Diary* (London: Heinemann, 1986), 179–84.

52. Ibid. 10.

53. Derek Gilpin Barnes, *Cloud Cover: Recollections of an Intelligence Officer* (London: Rich & Cowan, 1944), 61–2.

54. Cecil Beaton, *The Years Between: Diaries, 1939–44* (London: Weidenfeld & Nicolson, 1965), 69–100.

55. Cecil Beaton, *Winged Squadrons* (London, Hutchinson, 1942), 46–7.

56. Barnes, *Cloud Cover*, 49–50.

57. Arthur Gwynn-Browne, *Gone for a Burton* (London: Chatto & Windus, 1945), 336.

58. 'A Day in a Pilot's Life', in Ivor Halstead (ed.), *Wings of Victory: A Tribute to the RAF* (New York: E. P. Dutton, 1941), 91.

59. *Ships With Wings*, dir. Sergei Nolbandov (1942); diary entry, 24 Apr. 1942, quoted in Audrey Tucker, *Just an Echo* (Stratford: Eastside Community Heritage, n.d. [2001]).

60. David Niven, *The Moon's a Balloon* (London: Coronet, 1973), 209; Graham Lord, *Niv: The Authorized Biography of David Niven* (London: Orion, 2004); *The First of the Few*, dir. Leslie Howard (1942); *A Matter of Life and Death*, dir. Michael Powell and Emeric Pressburger (1946).

61. Bartley, *Smoke Trails*, 68, 75–6.

62. David Ross, *Richard Hillary* (London: Grub Street, 2000), 268–9.

63. Ibid. 218–20.

64. Geoffrey Page, *Shot Down in Flames: A World War Two Fighter Pilot's Remarkable Tale of Survival* (London: Grub Street, 1999), 7, 160–8.

65. Leonard Cheshire, *Bomber Pilot* (London: Hutchinson, 1943), 111–14; Richard Morris, *Cheshire: The Biography of Leonard Cheshire* (London: Penguin, 2001), 76–8.

66. Morris, *Guy Gibson*, 197–210.

67. Bartley, *Smoke Trails*, 167–71, 193–204.

68. Roald Dahl, *Going Solo* (London: Jonathan Cape, 1986), 114–18.

69. *Dangerous Moonlight*, dir. Brian Desmond Hurst (1941); British Film Institute, London [hereafter BFI], Pressbook: *Dangerous Moonlight* (1941).

70. Joyce Grenfell, *Joyce Grenfell Requests the Pleasure* (London: Macmillan, 1976), 167.

71. James Roos-Evans (ed.), *Joyce Grenfell, the Time of My Life: Her Wartime Journals* (London: Hodder & Stoughton, 1989), 169.

72. IWM 99/86/1 Miss J. Barclay, diary and minute book of Marion Jean Barclay, 23–4.

73. Ward-Jackson, *No Bombs At All*, 117–23.

74. Morris, *Gibson*, 234.

NOTES TO CHAPTER 2

1. Bourke, *Intimate History of Killing*, 112.

2. This phrase is from Hector Bolitho, *Combat Report: The Story of a Fighter Pilot* (London: Batsford, 1943), 18.

3. Jim Bailey, *The Sky Suspended: A Fighter Pilot's Story* (1964; London: Bloomsbury, 2005), 131.

4. John Pudney, *Who Only England Know: Log of a Wartime Journey of Unintentional Discovery* (London: Bodley Head, 1943), 85–6.

5. Beaton, *Winged Squadrons*, 43–5.

6. Oliver Walker, *Sailor Malan: A Biography* (London: Cassell, 1953), 57–8.

7. Athol Forbes and Hubert Allen, *Ten Fighter Boys* (London: Collins, 1942), 104.

8. Miles Tripp, *The Eighth Passenger: A Flight of Recollection and Discovery* (London: Heinemann, 1969), 75.

9. Ronald Sherbrooke-Walker, *Khaki and Blue* (London: St Catherine Press, 1952), 2–11.

10. Bishop, *Fighter Boys*, 66.

11. Pudney, *Who Only England Know*, 114.

12. Paul Brickhill, *Reach for the Sky: The Story of Douglas Bader* (1954; London: Companion Book Club, 1955), 178.

13. Townsend, *Time and Chance*, 80–1.

14. Ibid. 82.

15. This is not to say that the public house was an exclusively homosocial environment. For evidence that the pub became a venue more frequently used by women as well as men during the war, Claire Langhamer, ' "A Public House is for All Classes, Men and Women Alike": Women, Leisure and Drink in Second World War England', *Women's History Review*, 12 (2003), 423–43.

16. Sir Arthur Harris, 'Introduction' to Gibson, *Enemy Coast Ahead*, p. viii.

17. For Wooldridge, Gibson, *Enemy Coast Ahead*, 184–5; for Finucane, Doug Stokes, *Paddy Finucane: Fighter Ace* (London: William Kimber, 1983), 160.

18. IWM 91/41/1, Pilot Officer D. H. Wissler, ms. diary entries for 24 Apr. 1940, 8 June 1940, 9 June 1940, 17 July 1940.

19. [Paul Richey], *Fighter Pilot: A Personal Record of the Campaign in France* (London: Batsford, 1941), 31–2.

20. Bishop, *Fighter Boys*, 327–8; Bailey, *Sky Suspended*, 72–4.

21. IWM 03/34/1, Flight Lieutenant G. Shackleton, ms. memoir, 'Flying in the 40s: Memories of a Wartime Pilot', 61.

22. IWM 01/35/1, C. F. Smith, typescript, 'My Time in the Royal Air Force, by Cyril Smith', 9.

23. Forbes and Allen, *Ten Fighter Boys*, 174–6.

24. *Angels One Five*, dir. George More O'Ferrall (1952).

25. Eric H. Partridge, 'Slanguage', in R. Raymond and David Langdon (eds.), *Slipstream: A Royal Air Force Anthology* (London: Eyre & Spottiswoode, 1946), 60–5.

26. Townsend, *Time and Chance*, 111.

27. Richard Lumford, *My Father's Son* (London: Jonathan Cape, 1949), 195–6.

28. Tripp, *Eighth Passenger*, 19.

29. Noble Frankland, *History at War: The Campaigns of a Historian* (London: Giles de la Mere Publishers, 1998), 19–20.

30. Bishop, *Bomber Boys*, 183–4.

31. William Somerset Maugham, *Strictly Personal* (New York: Doubleday, 1941), 192–3.

32. Richard Vinen, *A History in Fragments: Europe in the Twentieth Century* (London: Little, Brown, 2000), 87.

33. IWM PP/MCR/C45 JMVC, J. M. V. Carpenter DFC, letters from John Carpenter to his parents, esp. 6 July 1940, 9 July 1940, 26 Dec. 1940.

34. IWM 04/24/1, Pilot Officer J. R. Byrne, ms. diary and scrapbook, entries for 26 May 1944, 4 July 1944, 30 July 1944, 16 Dec. 1944.

35. Lovat Dickson, 'Introduction' to Barry Sutton, *The Way of a Pilot: A Personal Record* (London: Macmillan, 1942), pp. xiii–xiv.

36. Bartley, *Smoke Trails*, 64.

37. IWM Conshelf, Flying Officer C. Crichton, letter from Charles Crichton to his mother, 17 May 1945.

38. Bailey, *Sky Suspended*, 76.

39. Helen Zenna Smith, *Not So Quiet . . .* (1930; London: Feminist Press, 1989), 166.

40. Gibson, *Enemy Coast Ahead*, 28.

41. Morris, *Guy Gibson*, p. xxii.

42. *The Dam Busters*, dir. Michael Anderson (1955); Murphy, *British Cinema and the Second World War*, 185–6.

43. Alexandra Shepard, *The Meanings of Manhood in Early Modern England* (Oxford: Oxford University Press, 2003), 93–126.

44. *One of Our Aircraft is Missing*, dir. Michael Powell and Emeric Pressburger (1942). Discussed in Murphy, *British Cinema and the Second World War*, 93–5.

45. Miles Tripp, *Faith is a Windsock* (London: Peter Davies, 1952), 126–7, 199–200.

46. Watson, *Johnny Kinsman*, 210.

47. Murphy, *British Cinema and the Second World War*, 189.

48. Tripp, *Faith is a Windsock*, 61–2.

49. R. C. Rivaz, *Tail Gunner* (London: Jarrolds, n.d. [1943]), 23.

50. IWM 94/37/1, Flight Lieutenant J. M. Catford, typescript memoir, 72.

51. 'The Squash Racquet', in Ward-Jackson, *No Bombs At All*, 17–26.

52. Rivaz, *Tail Gunner*, 16–17.

53. IWM 88/2/1, Mrs E. Kup, 'Memoirs of a Wartime WAAF, by Edith M Kup, née Heap', 60.

54. Bartley, *Smoke Trails*, 58

55. IWM PP/MCR/C45 JMVC, J. M. V. Carpenter DFC, letter from John Carpenter to his parents, 26 June 1940.

56. Monks, *Squadrons Up*, 163–4.

57. Brickhill, *Reach For the Sky*, 164–8.

58. Townsend, *Time and Chance*, 95.

59. Bailey, *Sky Suspended*, 32.

60. Bolitho, *Combat Report*, 70–1.

61. Simpson, *I Burned My Fingers*, 210.

62. Orde, *Pilots of Fighter Command*, 9.

63. Beaton, *Winged Squadrons*, 21, 29

64. Keith Ayling, *RAF: The Story of a British Fighter Pilot* (New York: Henry Holt, 1941), 183.

65. Cecil, 'The RAF', 81.

66. IWM 91/41/1, Pilot Officer D. H. Wissler, ms. diary entry, 20 Mar. 1940.

67. Gibson, *Enemy Coast Ahead*, 114–17, 120.

68. Beaton, *Winged Squadrons*, 10–11.

69. 'The Greatest People in the World', in Flying Officer X [H. E. Bates], *The Greatest People in the World* (London: Jonathan Cape, 1942), 69.

70. Gibson, *Enemy Coast Ahead*, 117–18.

71. Arthur Marwick, *Britain in the Century of Total War: War, Peace and Social Change, 1900–1967* (London: Bodley Head, 1970), 257–326.

72. e.g. Harold L. Smith (ed.), *War and Social Change: British Society in the Second World War* (Manchester: Manchester University Press, 1986); Rose, *Which People's War?*, 29–70.

73. James Hinton, *Women, Social Leadership and the Second World War: Continuities of Class* (Oxford: Oxford University Press, 2002).

74. For a useful reminder of Churchill's overwhelmingly aristocratic world-view, David Cannadine, 'Winston Churchill as Aristocratic Adventurer', in his *Aspects of Aristocracy: Grandeur and Decline in Modern Britain* (New Haven: Yale University Presss, 1994), 130–62.

75. Crang, *British Army and the People's War*.

76. Mark Harrison, *Medicine and Victory: British Military Medicine in the Second World War* (Oxford: Oxford University Press, 2004), esp. 126–7, 183–4, 231, 280–2.

77. David Cannadine, *The Decline and Fall of the British Aristocracy* (New Haven: Yale University Press, 1990), 606–36.

78. Beaton, *Winged Squadrons*, 43.

79. Ayling, *RAF*, 21–2.

80. *The Lion Has Wings*, dir. Michael Powell, Brian Desmond-Hurst, and Adrian Brunel (1939). Discussed in Anthony Aldgate and Jeffrey Richards, *Britain Can Take It: The British Cinema in the Second World War* (Edinburgh: Edinburgh University Press, 1994), 21–8.

81. *Journey Together*, dir. John Boulting (1945). Discussed in Toby Haggith, '*Journey Together*', in Alan Burton, Tim O' Sullivan, and Paul Wells (eds.), *The Family Way: The Boulting Brothers and British Film Culture* (Trowbridge: Flicks Books, 2000), 109–21.

82. Rattigan, 'Last Gasp of the Middle Class'.

83. Bishop, *Fighter Boys*, 75–80.

84. National Archive, Kew [hereafter NA] Air Ministry [hereafter AIR] 2/8061, 'Air Ministry Notice No.52: Aviation Candidates Selection Boards', 31 Aug. 1940.

85. Edward Smithies, *Aces, Erks and Backroom Boys: Aircrew, Ground Staff and Warplane Builders Remember the Second World War* (London: Cassell, 2002), 62–3.

86. NA AIR 2/8061, unsigned memorandum, discussed at Air Ministry meeting to review Bartlett Intelligence Test for aircrew candidates, 3 Oct. 1940.

87. Rivaz, *Tail Gunner*, 25.

88. IWM 86/18/1, F. C. Welding, ms. letters from Fred Welding to his mother, 8 July 1940 and 18 Sept. 1940.

89. IWM 03/34/1, Flight Lieutenant G. Shackleton, ms. memoir, 'Flying in the 40s', 1, 32–4, 46.

90. IWM Conshelf, G. J. Hull, ms. letter to Joan Kirby, 16 Feb. 1944.

91. Brickhill, *Reach for the Sky*, 172.

92. Morris, *Guy Gibson*, 113–14.

93. Sweetman, *Bomber Crew*, 92–3.

94. Bartley, *Smoke Trails*, 63.

95. Simpson, *I Burned My Fingers*, 63–5.

96. Smithies, *Aces, Erks and Backroom Boys*, 282–3; Bishop, *Bomber Boys*, 187–9.

97. John Braine, *Room at the Top* (1957; Harmondsworth: Penguin, 1963), 40–1, 66–7.

98. [Richey], *Fighter Pilot*, 36.

99. Robert Collins, *The Long and the Short and the Tall: An Ordinary Airman's War* (Saskatoon: Western Producer Prairie Books, 1986), 106.

100. Ward-Jackson, *No Bombs At All*, 39–48.

101. M-O File Report 569, 'Airmen: Morale and Attitudes' (1941), 5.

102. Bolitho, *Penguin in the Eyrie*, 77.

103. IWM 97/25/1, Miss J. M. Brotherton, typescript memoir, 'Press on Regardless' (Oct. 1945), 10.

104. Alex Kershaw, *The Few: The American 'Knights of the Air' Who Risked Everything to Fight in the Battle of Britain* (Cambridge, Mass.: Da Capo Press, 2006); Arthur Gerald Donahue, *Tally-Ho! Yankee in a Spitfire* (London: Macmillan, 1942).

105. R. Sidney Brown, *Dave Dawson with the RAF* (New York: Crown Publishers, 1941); *A Yank in the RAF*, dir. Henry King (1941).

106. Kershaw, *The Few*, 5–7, 64–5.

107. Bolitho, *Penguin in the Eyrie*, 191.

108. Claudio Meunier and Carlos Garcia, *Alas De Trueno* [*Wings of Thunder*] (Buenos Aires: C. G. Gustavo, 2004).

109. Diana Barnato Walker, *Spreading My Wings* (Sparkford: Patrick Stephens, 1994), 58.

110. George Armour Bell, *To Live Among Heroes: A Medical Officer's Dramatic Insight into the Life of 609 Squadron in Northwest Europe, 1944–45* (London: Grub Street, 2001), 71–2; Christopher Frayling, *Ken Adam: The Art of Production Design* (London: Faber, 2005), 23–40. For wartime anti-Semitism, Rose, *Which People's War?*, 92–106; Tony Kushner, *The Persistence of Prejudice: Antisemitism in*

British Society During the Second World War (Manchester: Manchester University Press, 1989).

111. Richard Doherty, *Irish Men and Women in the Second World War* (Dublin: Four Courts, 1999), 97–124, 225–40.

112. Adrian Smith, *Mick Mannock, Fighter Pilot: Myth, Life and Politics* (Houndmills: Palgrave, 2001), 144.

113. Stokes, *Paddy Finucane*, 137–9.

114. Preface to Jules Roy, *The Happy Valley: A War Novel* (London: Viking Press, 1952).

115. René Mouchotte, *The Mouchotte Diaries*, trans. Philip John Stead (London: Hamish Hamilton, 1957), 55, 71.

116. Ibid. 83–4, 86–7, 173–4.

117. Roy, *Happy Valley*; id., *The Navigator: A Novel*, trans. Mervyn Saville (New York: Knopf, 1955).

118. Jules Roy, *Return from Hell* (London: William Kimber, 1954), 15.

119. Roy, *Happy Valley*, 57–9, 145.

120. Roy, *Return from Hell*, 46, 53, 60, 71.

121. M. A. Liskutin, *Challenge in the Air: A Spitfire Pilot Remembers* (London: William Kimber, 1988), 176–8.

122. Ibid. 67, 91–2.

123. Nicholas Atkin, *The Forgotten French: Exiles in the British Isles, 1940–44* (Manchester: Manchester University Press, 2003).

124. Jules Roy, *Mémoires Barbares* (Paris: Albin Michel, 1989), 222–4.

125. Ashley Jackson, *The British Empire and the Second World War* (London: Hambledon, 2006), 38–40.

126. Paul Addison, 'National Identity and the Battle of Britain', in Barbara Korte and Ralf Schneider (eds.), *War and the Cultural Construction of Identities in Britain* (Amsterdam: Rodopi Books, 2002), 225–40.

127. 'Laddie' Lucas, *Five Up: A Chronicle of Five Lives* (London: Sidgwick & Jackson, 1978), 67–70, 72–3.

128. Peter Joyce, *Anatomy of a Rebel: Smith of Rhodesia* (Salisbury: Graham Publishing, 1974), 48–60.

129. John Darwin, 'A Third British Empire? The Dominion Idea in Imperial Politics', in Judith Brown and William Roger Louis (eds.), *The Oxford History of the British Empire*, vol. iv, *The Twentieth Century* (Oxford: Oxford University Press, 1999), 64–87.

130. Toynbee, *Friends Apart*, 161–2.

131. Jeff Keshen, *Saints, Sinners and Soldiers: Canada's Second World War* (Vancouver: University of British Columbia Press, 2004).

132. Walker, *Sailor Malan*.

133. Pip Beck, *A WAAF in Bomber Command* (London: Goodall, 1989), 35.

134. IWM 91/27/1, Miss V. E. E. Cossar, ms. letter from Flight Sergeant G. A. McGarvey, 6 May 1941.

135. IWM 04/24/1, Pilot Officer J. R. Byrne, ms. diary entry, 30 July 1944.

136. Rose, *Which People's War?*, 239–44, 267–77, 280–4.

137. Priya Satia, 'The Defense of Inhumanity: Air Control in Iraq and the British Idea of Arabia', *American Historical Review*, 111 (2006), 16–51; Omissi, 'Hendon Air Pageant'.

138. Tripp, *Eighth Passenger*, 11.

139. Norman Franks, *Sky Tiger: The Story of Group Captain Sailor Malan* (London: William Kimber, 1980), 163.

140. NA AIR 2/6876, 'Coloured RAF Personnel: Report on Progress and Suitability', n.d. [Feb. 1945]. See also AIR 2/6876, 'List of Colonial Aircrew', n.d.

141. *The League of Coloured Peoples Newsletter*, 33 (June 1942), 75; 37 (Oct. 1942), 9; 60 (Sept. 1944), 97; 63 (Dec. 1944), 59–60, 63.

142. Webster, *Englishness and Empire*, 31–2, 34, 41–2. Frances Thorpe and Nicholas Pronay, *British Official Films of the Second World War: A Descriptive Catalogue* (Oxford: Clio Press, 1980), 158, 163, 179.

143. NA AIR 2/665, 'Indians in the RAF: Press Publicity', n.d.

144. *Listener*, 24 (17 Oct. 1940), 559–60.

145. Rose, *Which People's War?*, 277–80

146. *Burma Rani*, dir. T. R. Sundaran (1944). Further details can be found in Ashish Rajadhyakalsha and Paul Willemen (eds.), *Encyclopedia of Indian Cinema* (New Delhi: Oxford University Press, 1999), 301.

147. Francis Yeats-Brown, *Martial India* (London: Eyre & Spottiswoode, 1945), 167.

148. Royal Air Force Museum, Hendon [hereafter RAF Museum], X003-6126/001, scrapbook of Mahindra Singh Pujji.

149. Streets, *Martial Races*.

150. Tripp, *Faith is a Windsock*, 16, 21, 48.

151. Raymond and Langdon (eds.), *Slipstream*, 162–5.

152. NA AIR 2/6876, 'Coloured RAF Personnel'.

153. For an example of a black Jamaican who enlisted as a flight engineer, but was remustered for clerical ground-staff duties, E. Martin Noble, *Jamaica Airman: A Black Airman in Britain, 1943 and After* (London: New Beacon Books, 1984), 43.

154. Robert N. Murray, *Lest We Forget: The Experiences of World War Two West Indian Ex-Service Personnel* (Nottingham: NWICEA Press, 1996), 74–6.

155. Ibid. 80–1, 89.

156. Ibid. 74–5, 80.

157. Smithies, *Aces, Erks and Backroom Boys*, p. xxii.

158. Bourke, *Dismembering the Male*, 124–70.

NOTES TO CHAPTER 3

1. Nevil Shute, *Pastoral* (New York: William Morrow, 1944), 89–90.

2. Beaton, *Winged Squadrons*, 17–18.

3. Reproduced in Robin Derrick and Robin Muir, *Unseen Vogue: The Secret History of Fashion Photography* (London: Little, Brown, 2002), 30–1.

4. Rom Landau, *The Fool's Progress: Aspects of British Civilization in Action* (London: Faber & Faber, 1942), 79.

5. Ross, *Richard Hillary*, 230–1.

6. IWM Conshelf, G. J. Hull, ms. letter to Joan Kirby, n.d. [Jan. 1944].

7. Townsend, *Time and Chance*, 96.

8. Shute, *Pastoral*, 98, 121–2.

9. Wellum, *First Light*, 295.

10. Watson, *Johnny Kinsman*, 165–7.

11. Walter Clapham, *Night Be My Witness* (London: Jonathan Cape, 1952), 281.

12. Ibid. 246–50.

13. Eric Taylor, *Force's Sweethearts: Service Romances in World War Two* (London: Robert Hale, 1990), 46.

14. Bailey, *Sky Suspended*, 64.

15. Watson, *Johnny Kinsman*, 215–20, 264.

16. Shute, *Landfall*. The novel was subsequently adapted for the screen: *Landfall*, dir. Ken Annakin (1949).

17. IWM Conshelf, G. J. Hull, ms. letter to Joan Kirby (21 Nov. 1943).

18. Sweetman, *Bomber Crew*, 123, 140–1.

19. Robert B. Westbrook, ' "I Want a Girl, Just Like the Girl that Married Harry James": American Women and the Problem of Political Obligation in World War Two', *American Quarterly*, 42 (1990), 587–614.

20. Lewis A. Erenberg, 'Swing Goes to War: Glenn Miller and the Popular Music of World War II', in Lewis A. Erenberg and Susan E. Hirsch (eds.), *The War in American Culture: Society and Consciousness During World War Two* (Chicago: University of Chicago Press, 1996), 144–65.

21. Stephen Kern, *The Culture of Love: Victorians to Moderns* (Cambridge, Mass.: Harvard University Press, 1992), 1.

22. e.g. Ann Swidler, *Talk of Love: How Culture Matters* (Chicago: Chicago University Press, 2001).

23. Karen Lystra, *Searching the Heart: Women, Men, and Romantic Love in Nineteenth-Century America* (New York: Oxford University Press, 1989); Beth L. Bailey, *From Front Porch to Back Seat: Courtship in Twentieth-Century America* (Baltimore: Johns Hopkins University Press, 1988); Kern, *Culture of Love*; Deborah A. Field, 'Romantic Love and the Emotional Basis of a Private Sphere', in *Private Life and Communist Morality in Khrushchev's Russia* (New York: Peter Lang, 2007), 39–50.

24. Marcus Collins, *Modern Love: An Intimate History of Men and Women in Twentieth-Century Britain* (London: Atlantic Books, 2003).

25. Claire Langhamer, 'Love and Courtship in Mid-Twentieth-Century England', *Historical Journal*, 50 (2007), 173–96.

26. Lystra, *Searching the Heart*, 6.

27. See Ch. 7, below.

28. Bishop, *Bomber Boys*, 288.

29. E. S. Turner, *A History of Courting* (London: Michael Joseph, 1954), 248–9.

30. For a discussion, and critique, of this notion, Sheila Sullivan, *Falling in Love: A History of Torment and Enchantment* (London: Macmillan, 1999), 117–30.

31. Forbes and Allen (eds.), *Ten Fighter Boys*, 157.

32. IWM 03/34/1, Flight Lieutenant G. Shackleton, 'Flying in the 40s', 60–1.

33. Wyndham, *Love Is Blue*; Patrick Marnham, *Wild Mary: A Life of Mary Wesley* (London: Chatto & Windus, 2006), 74–6, 86–7.

34. NA AIR 10/5571, 'Statistics on the Health of the Royal Air Force and Women's Auxiliary Air Force for the Year 1943', Table 3. For context see John Costello, *Love, Sex and War: Changing Values, 1939–45* (London: Guild Publishing, 1985), 17–33; Cate Haste, *Rules of Desire: Sex in Britain, World War One to the Present* (London: Vintage, 1992), 99–138.

35. John Sommerfield, 'Worm's Eye View', in *The Survivors* (Letchworth: John Lehmann, 1947), 15.

36. Gwynn-Browne, *Gone for a Burton*, 201.

37. *Millions Like Us*, dir. Frank Launder (1943).

38. IWM Conshelf, G. J. Hull, ms. letter to Joan Kirby (17 Nov. 1943).

39. Shute, *Pastoral*, 73.

40. Watson, *Johnny Kinsman*, 199–200.

41. Roald Dahl, 'Only This', in *Over to You: Ten Stories of Flyers and Flying* (1945; London: Penguin, 1973), 144–50.

42. *A Matter of Life and Death*, dir. Michael Powell and Emeric Pressburger (1946).

43. Cheshire, *Bomber Pilot*, 48–9.

44. IWM 91/41/1, Pilot Officer D. H. Wissler, ms. diary entry (6 Nov. 1940).

45. NA AIR 10/2144, *Not To Be Carried in Aircraft: Instructions and Guide to All Officers and Airmen of the Royal Air Force*, 3rd edn. (London: HMSO, 1936).

46. H. E. Bates, 'How Sleep the Brave', in *The Stories of Flying Officer X* (1952; London: Jonathan Cape, 1967), 85.

47. Gilbert, 'Soldier's Heart'.

48. Vera Brittain, *A Testament of Youth: An Autobiographical Study of the Years 1900–1925* (London: Gollancz, 1933).

49. Carol Acton, 'Writing and Waiting: The First World War Correspondence Between Vera Brittain and Ronald Leighton', *Gender and History*, 11 (1999), 54–83.

50. [Bates], *Greatest People in the World*, 18–19.

51. H. E. Bates, *Fair Stood the Wind for France* (London: Michael Joseph, 1944), 71–2.

52. Sweetman, *Bomber Crew*, 114–17, 246–7.

53. H. E. Bates, *The Day of Glory: A Play in Three Acts* (London: Michael Joseph, 1945), 22, 27, 30, 61–6.

54. Tessa Stone, 'Creating a (Gendered?) Military Identity: The Women's Auxiliary Air Force in Great Britain in the Second World War', *Women's History Review*, 8 (1999), 605–24.

55. IWM 98/9/1, Mrs J. Myler, typescript memoir, 'The War Under the City', 76.

56. Beck, *WAAF in Bomber Command*, 115.

57. IWM 88/2/1, Mrs E. Kup, 'Memoirs of a Wartime WAAF', 65.

58. Theodora Benson, *Sweethearts and Wives: Their Part in War* (London: Faber & Faber, 1942), 42–3.

59. Bartley, *Smoke Trails*, 77.

60. Taylor, *Forces Sweethearts*, 163–4.

61. NA AIR 2/8865, 'Air Council Letter A.30859/39/S.10c' (8 Nov. 1943).

62. NA AIR 2/8865, 'RAF Dances for All Ranks—Policy' (31 Jan. 1944).

63. IWM 93/22/1, Mrs M. Brookes, ms. memoir, 'A WAAF's Tale' (1993).

64. Taylor, *Forces Sweethearts*, 165–6.

65. IWM 98/9/1, Mrs N. J. Sandy, ms. letter (20 Aug. 1943).

66. IWM 88/2/1, Mrs E. Kup, 'Memoirs of a Wartime WAAF', 10.

67. IWM 88/2/1, Mrs N. C. Walton, typescript memoir, 'Memories of WAAF Service, 1942–46', n.d.

68. Pat Kirkham, 'Beauty and Duty: Keeping Up the (Home) Front', in Pat Kirkham and David Thoms (eds.), *War Culture: Social Change and Changing Experience in World War Two* (London: Lawrence & Wishart, 1995), 13–28.

69. IWM 88/2/1, Mrs E. Kup, 'Memoirs of a Wartime WAAF', 62.

70. Beck, *WAAF in Bomber Command*, 23.

71. Wyndham, *Love Is Blue*, 10.

72. M-O File Report 757, 'General Picture of WAAF Life' (25 June 1941), 4.

73. Beck, *WAAF in Bomber Command*, 73.

74. Liskutin, *Challenge in the Air*, 82.

75. Deere, *Nine Lives*, 164.

76. IWM 88/53/1, Mrs R. Sumner, ms. memoir, n.d.

77. Helena Schrader, *Sisters in Arms* (Barnsley: Pen and Sword, 2006), 5, 29, 199–209; Rosemary du Cros, *ATA Girl: Memoirs of a Wartime Ferry Pilot* (London: Frederick Muller, 1983), 77.

78. Benson, *Sweethearts and Wives*, 39.

79. IWM 95/20/1, E. Featherstone RAFVR, typescript memoir, 'A Worm's Eye View of RAF Millom, Cumberland, 1 November 1941–26 March 1943', n.d.

80. Schrader, *Sisters in Arms*, 90–1.

81. Bartley, *Smoke Trails*, 80.

82. Barnato Walker, *Spreading My Wings*, 58–62, 73–4, 142–3, 164–7.

83. e.g. Marilyn Lake, 'Female Desires: the Meaning of World War Two', in Joy Damousi and Marilyn Lake (eds.), *Gender and War: Australians at War in the Twentieth Century* (Cambridge: Cambridge University Press, 1995), 60–80.

84. Beck, *WAAF in Bomber Command*, 20.

85. Wyndham, *Love Is Blue*, 4, 10.

86. RAF Museum H/332/6204/00005 X002-5445, Mrs. Marjorie Hazell, typescript memoir, 'All the Same Buttons' (1970), 111–12, 196.

87. Tripp, *Eighth Passenger*, 145.

88. Beck, *WAAF in Bomber Command*, 71, 91–2.

89. Benson, *Sweethearts and Wives*, 28–9.

90. Richard Pape, *Boldness Be My Friend* (London: Elek, 1953), 9.

91. Shute, *Pastoral*, 147–50.

92. Beck, *WAAF in Bomber Command*, 94–5.

93. IWM 94/27/1, Miss R. Britten, typescript, 'Operation Varsity'.

94. This image can be viewed at http://www.ww2images.com.

95. Tripp, *Eighth Passenger*, 110–11.

96. IWM 91/36/1, Mrs J. Wallace, 'Recollections of a Servicewoman in the WAAF During the Second World War', n.d.

97. Raymond and Langdon (eds.), *Slipstream*, 224–6.

98. Beck, *WAAF in Bomber Command*, 24.

99. Wyndham, *Love Is Blue*, 5.

100. Peter Townsend, 'Foreword' to Bailey, *Sky Suspended*, 3.

101. Shute, *Pastoral*, 207–24.

102. IWM 88/2/1, Mrs E. Kup, 'Memoirs of a Wartime WAAF', 26.

103. Ibid. 61.

104. Beryl E. Escott, *Women in Air Force Blue: The Story of Women in the Royal Air Force from 1918 to the Present Day* (Wellingborough: Patrick Stephens, 1989), 143.

105. IWM 93/22/1, Mrs M. Brookes, 'A WAAF's Tale'.

106. IWM 91/36/1, Mrs J. Wallace, 'Recollections'.

107. IWM 83/46/1, Miss B. J. Wright, 'The Adventures of a Nobody in the WAAF', 61–2.

108. IWM 88/2/1, Mrs E. Kup, 'Memoirs of a Wartime WAAF', 62.

109. IWM 97/25/1, Miss J. M. Brotherton, typescript memoir, 'Press on Regardless' (Oct. 1945), 35–6, 45–6, 79.

110. IWM 88/2/1, Mrs E. Kup, 'Memoirs of a Wartime WAAF', 62.

111. IWM 91/36/1, Mrs J. Wallace, 'Recollections'.

112. Janet Finch and Penny Summerfield, 'Social Reconstruction and the Emergence of the Companionate Marriage, 1945–59', in David Clark (ed.), *Marriage, Domestic Life and Social Change: Writings for Jacqueline Burgoyne* (London: Routledge, 1991), 7–32.

113. Susan Kingsley Kent, *Making Peace: The Reconstruction of Gender in Interwar Britain* (Princeton: Princeton University Press, 1993).

NOTES TO CHAPTER 4

1. Air Ministry, *Psychological Disorders in Flying Personnel of the Royal Air Force, Investigated During the War, 1939–1945* (London: HMSO, 1947), 60–1.

2. Roland Winfield, *The Sky Belongs to Them* (London: William Kimber, 1976), 150.

3. *Psychological Disorders*, 61.

4. Gibson, *Enemy Coast Ahead*, 166–7.

5. 'Wives of the RAF', *Daily Sketch*, 2 Jan. 1941.

6. Hillary, *Last Enemy*, 69, 44–5.

7. M. C. 'Bush' Cotton, *Hurricanes Over Burma* (London: Grub Street, 1995), 108.

8. Ian Gleed, *Arise To Conquer* (London: Victor Gollancz, 1942), 24–5.

9. Beck, *WAAF in Bomber Command*, 41–2, 66–7.

10. Ibid. 24.

11. For attitudes towards premarital sex in the context of courtship, Claire Langhamer, *Women's Leisure in England, 1920–1960* (Manchester: Manchester University Press, 2000), 113–32.

12. RAF Museum, H/332/6203/00003 X002-5545, ms. letter from Pilot Officer Rohan Evans, Oct. 1939. Name changed in order to preserve anonymity of correspondent, at request of the archive.

13. Clapham, *Night be My Witness*, 240.

14. Campbell, *Maximum Effort*, 191.

15. John Pudney and Henry Treece (eds.), *Air Force Poetry* (London: The Bodley Head, 1944), 61.

16. Campbell, *Maximum Effort*, 90–1.

17. Bates, 'How Sleep the Brave', 89–90, 126–8.

18. Eileen Tremayne, *Four Who Came Back* (London: Hutchinson, 1941), 113.

19. Bishop, *Fighter Boys*, 101–2.

20. Carroll, *Compass Course*, 214.

21. *RAF Welfare Bulletin*, 8 (Dec. 1943), 4.

22. Escott, *Women in Air Force Blue*, 143.

23. Ayling, *RAF*, 233.

24. British Library [hereafter BL], Terence Rattigan Manuscripts [hereafter Rattigan Ms.], ADD. 74302, typescript of 'Signed With Their Honour', 202–3.

25. Tripp, *Faith is a Windsock*, 13, 54–5, 67, 156–7.

26. Barnes, *Cloud Cover*, 29.

27. Orde, *Pilots of Fighter Command*, 19, 18.

28. Bartley, *Smoke Trails*, 84–5.

29. Bader, *Reach for the Sky*, 112, 139, 329, and 251.

30. IWM 94/40/1, G. T. Lang, typescript memoir (written in 1991–3), 21, 24, 32, 47.

31. Carroll, *Compass Course*, 11–12.

32. Clapham, *Night Be My Witness*, 239.

33. IWM 88/26/1, Mrs J. F. P. Hambly, typescript memoir, 41–2, 45.

34. Carroll, *Compass Course*, 17–24, 126, 159–66, 267–8.

35. RAF Museum, X002-9360/004, ms. diary of Sam Miara, Jan.–Feb. 1941; X002-9360/005, ms. letters from Sam Miara to Doris Miara, 5 Feb. 1941, 20 Feb. 1941, 3 Apr. 1941.

36. [Bates], *Greatest People in the World*, 77; Bates, 'How Sleep the Brave', 91, 93–4, 127–8.

37. Ward-Jackson, *No Bombs At All*, 7–14.

38. Raymond and Langdon (eds.), *Slipstream*, 38–40.

39. Townsend, *Time and Chance*, 116–17.

40. Alfred A. Denney, *The Fairy Who Lost Her Wings* (Sevenoaks: Chadwell, 2002).

41. Ottaway, *Dambuster*, p. xi; Hillary, *Last Enemy*, 78–9.

42. Dahl, *Over to You*, 83–107.

43. Tosh, *Man's Place*, 1, 170–94. See also Martin Francis, 'The Domestication of the Male? Recent Research on Nineteenth- and Twentieth-Century British Masculinity', *Historical Journal*, 45 (2002), 637–52.

44. Paul Fussell, *The Great War and Modern Memory* (Oxford: Oxford University Press, 1975), 86–90; Eric J. Leed, *No Man's Land: Combat and Identity in World War One* (Cambridge: Cambridge University Press, 1979), 189.

45. Bourke, *Dismembering the Male*, 167. See also Ilana R. Bet-El, *Conscripts: Forgotten Men of the Great War* (Stroud: Sutton, 2003), 131, 143.

46. Roper, 'Maternal Relations', 295–315.

47. Gullace, *'Blood of Our Sons'*, 49.

48. Rose, *Which People's War?*, 153–4, 195–6.

49. Stephane Audoin-Rouzeau, *Men at War, 1914–1918: National Sentiment and Trench Journalism in France During the First World War* (Oxford: Berg, 1992), 128.

50. Marcus Funck, 'Ready for War? Conceptions of Military Manliness in the Prusso-German Officer Corps Before the First World War', in Karen Hagemann and Stefanie Schüler-Springorum (eds.), *War/Front: The Military, War and Gender in Twentieth-Century Germany* (Oxford: Berg, 2002), 43–67.

51. Birthe Kundrus, 'Gender Wars: The First World War and the Construction of Gender Relations in the Weimar Republic', and Thomas Kuhne, 'Comradeship:

Gender Confusion and Gender Order in the German Military, 1918–1945', both in Hagemann and Schüler-Springorum (eds.), *War/Front*, 159–79, 233–54.

52. Christa Hämmerle, 'You Let A Weeping Woman Call You Home? Private Correspondence During the First World War in Germany and Austria', in Rebecca Earle (ed.), *Epistolary Selves: Letters and Letter Writers, 1600–1945* (Aldershot: Ashgate, 1999), 154–7.

53. Bourke, *Dismembering the Male*, 133–5; Roper, 'Maternal Relations', 295–315.

54. Tosh, *Man's Place*, 4.

55. Barnes, *Cloud Cover*, 29.

56. Townsend, *Time and Chance*, 103.

57. J. B. Priestley, 'Postscript', in Halstead (ed.), *Wings of Victory*, 205.

58. Beaton, *Winged Squadrons*, 46.

59. IWM 88/2/1, Mrs E. Kup, 'Memoirs of a Wartime WAAF', 70–1.

60. Carroll, *Compass Course*, 258.

61. Acton, 'Writing and Waiting', 54–83.

62. Sweetman, *Bomber Crew*, 47–50, 59.

63. Michael Darlow and Gillian Hodson, *Terence Rattigan: The Man and His Work* (London: Quartet Books, 1979), 101–2.

64. BL Rattigan Ms. ADD. 74300, ms. letter from Rattigan, while stationed at Freetown, to his parents, n.d. [1941].

65. Darlow and Hodson, *Terence Rattigan*, 110.

66. BL Rattigan Ms. ADD. 74300, ms. letter from Rattigan, on RAF Lough Erne stationery, to his parents, n.d. [1941].

67. Theatre Museum Archive, Blythe House, Olympia, Playbill: *Flare Path*, Apollo Theatre, 13 Aug. 1942.

68. IWM 04/24/1, Pilot Officer J. R. Byrne, scrapbook, Dec. 1944.

69. Darlow and Hodson, *Terence Rattigan*, 109, 114–15, 119–20.

70. Terence Rattigan, 'Flare Path', in *The Collected Plays, Volume One* (1953; London: Hamish Hamilton, 1968), 83–169.

71. BL Rattigan Ms. ADD. 74310, typescript (with ms. additions) of 'Rendezvous', n.d.

72. Ibid., ADD. 74311, typescript screenplay 'For Johnny', n.d.

73. *The Way to the Stars*, dir. Anthony Asquith (1945). BFI Pressbook: *The Way to the Stars* (1945). Discussed in Aldgate and Richards, *Britain Can Take It*, 277–98.

74. *Monthly Bulletin of the British Film Institute*, 12 (June 1945), 70. See also Tom Ryall, *Anthony Asquith* (Manchester: Manchester University Press, 2005), 90.

75. Jane Oliver, 'Preface', to John Llewelyn Rhys, *England Is My Village* (London: Faber & Faber, 1941), 9, 12–14.

76. Oliver, *In No Strange Land*, 219.

77. Rhys, *England Is My Village*, 32–4.

78. Jane Oliver, *The Hour of the Angel* (London: Collins, 1942), 35, 64–8, 71, 81–2, 112, 252–6.

79. Finch and Summerfield, 'Social Reconstruction'; Collins, *Modern Love*, 90–133.

80. Dawson, *Soldier Heroes*, 63–76.

NOTES TO CHAPTER 5

1. Bourke, *Fear*, 199.

2. Roy, *Happy Valley*, 21.

3. NA AIR 2/6668, Papers relating to insurance companies and RAF men killed in action, 1943.

4. Terraine, *Right of the Line*, 682.

5. Hillary, *Last Enemy*, 36.

6. Townsend, *Time and Chance*, 75.

7. Wellum, *First Light*, 44–5.

8. Liskutin, *Challenge in the Air*, 75.

9. Bolitho, *Combat Report*, 71.

10. Forbes and Allen (eds.), *Ten Fighter Boys*, 9.

11. Tripp, *Eighth Passenger*, 101.

12. Quoted in S. J. Rachman, *Fear and Courage*, 2nd edn. (New York: W. H. Freeman, 1990), 36–7.

13. NA AIR 10/5571 'Statistics on the Health of the Royal Air Force and Women's Auxiliary Air Force for the Year 1943', Table 8: 'Deaths'.

14. S. P. Mackenzie, *The Colditz Myth: British and Commonwealth Prisoners of War in Nazi Germany* (Oxford: Oxford University Press, 2004), 38–9, 40, 241–2.

15. IWM 94/37/1, Flight Lieutenant J. M. Catford, typescript memoir, 66.

16. IWM 97/25/1, Miss J. M. Brotherton, 'Press on Regardless', 25.

17. Watson, *Johnny Kinsman*, 84.

18. Harry Levy, *The Dark Side of the Sky: The Story of a Young Jewish Airman in Nazi Germany* (London: Leo Cooper, 1996), 12, 49.

19. Marnham, *Wild Mary*, 90–101.

20. Beaton, *Winged Squadrons*, 38.

21. Tripp, *Eighth Passenger*, 179–80.

22. Cecil, 'The RAF', 79.

23. Gleed, *Arise to Conquer*, 93.

24. Wellum, *First Light*, 142.

25. [Richey], *Fighter Pilot*, 61–2.

26. *Psychological Disorders*, 33–4.

27. Bourke, *Fear*, 7.

28. Bailey, *Sky Suspended*, 84.

29. Morris, *Guy Gibson*, pp. 132, xxvi.

30. Townsend, *Time and Chance*, 94.

31. Beaton, *Winged Squadrons*, 39.

32. Clostermann, *Big Show*, 41–2.

33. Dahl, *Over to You*, 12–13.

34. David Stafford-Clark, *Psychiatry Today* (Harmondsworth: Penguin, 1952), 248.

35. Morris, *Guy Gibson*, 132.

36. [Richey], *Fighter Pilot*, 121–2.

37. Gibson, *Enemy Coast Ahead*, 179.

38. Mouchotte, *Mouchotte Diaries*, 101.

39. IWM 03/34/1, Flight Lieutenant G. Shackleton, 'Flying in the 40s', 63–4.

40. Smithies, *Aces, Erks and Backroom Boys*, 52, 60, 182.

41. Rachman, *Fear and Courage*, 73.

42. Bourke, *Fear*, 208–10.

43. Joanna Bourke, 'Psychology at War, 1914–1945', in G. C. Bunn, A. D. Lovie, and G. D. Richards (eds.), *Psychology in Britain: Historical Essays and Personal Reflections* (London: BPS Books, 2001), 133–49; id., 'Disciplining the Emotions: Fear, Psychiatry and the Second World War', in Roger Cooter, Mark Harrison, and Steve Sturdy (eds.), *War, Medicine and Modernity* (London: Sutton, 1998), 234, 228–9; Michael Roper, 'Between Manliness and Masculinity: The "War Generation" and the Psychology of Fear in Britain, 1914–1950', *Journal of British Studies*, 44 (2005), 344, 356.

44. Harrison, *Medicine and Victory*, 279.

45. Stafford-Clark, *Psychiatry Today*, 244–9.

46. Bourke, 'Disciplining the Emotions', 233–4. See also Allan D. English, 'A Predisposition to Cowardice? Aviation Psychology and the Genesis of "Lack of Moral Fibre" ', *War and Society*, 13 (1995), 20–7.

47. Tripp, *Eighth Passenger*, 174–5.

48. H. L. Roxburgh, 'Introduction', to Winfield, *Sky Belongs to Them*, 1.

49. *Psychological Disorders*, passim.

50. Roy R. Grinker and John P. Spiegel, *Men Under Stress* (Philadelphia: Blakiston, 1945), 4–6.

51. *Psychological Disorders*, 33–5.

52. Ibid. 35–6.

53. Ibid. 51–3.

54. Ibid. 54–7, 60.

55. Ibid. 63–8.

56. NA AIR 2/8039, N. H. Bottomley to Arthur Harris, 20 Jan. 1943.

57. NA AIR 2/8039, Arthur Harris to N. H. Bottomley, 2 Feb. 1943.

58. Bishop, *Fighter Boys*, 226–7.

59. Hillary, *Last Enemy*, 96.

60. Tripp, *Eighth Passenger*, 181.

61. Cheshire, *Bomber Pilot*, 24–5.

62. Bell, *To Live Among Heroes*, 73.

63. Watson, *Johnny Kinsman*, 106, 135–6.

64. Roy, *Return from Hell*, 121–2.

65. Forbes and Allen (eds.), *Ten Fighter Boys*, 171–2.

66. *The Secret Life of Walter Mitty*, dir. Norman Z. McLeod (1947).

67. Walker, *Sailor Malan*, 104.

68. Bailey, *Sky Suspended*, 121.

69. John Pudney, *Dispersal Point and Other Air Poems* (London: Bodley Head, 1942), 30.

70. Beaton, *Winged Squadrons*, 18–19.

71. S. I. Ballard and H. G. Miller, 'Psychiatric Casualties in a Woman's Service', *British Medical Journal*, 3 Mar. 1945, pp. 193–4.

72. Erich Maria Remarque, *All Quiet on the Western Front* (1928; New York: Ballantine Books, 1987), 165.

73. Morris, *Guy Gibson*, p. xxiv.

74. Marnham, *Wild Mary*, 89.

75. Bolitho, *Combat Report*, 71.

76. *Psychological Disorders*, 35, 67–8.

77. Wyndham, *Love Is Blue*, 103, 145–6, 188.

78. Mary Renault, *The Charioteer* (1953; London: Longmans, 1968), 156.

79. Bartley, *Smoke Trails*, 24.

80. *RAF Welfare Bulletin*, 2 (June 1943), 3–6; 3 (July 1943), 3–7; 5 (Sept. 1943), 8.

81. *Psychological Disorders*, 59–60.

82. IWM Conshelf, G. J. Hull, ms. letters to Joan Kirby, 24 Sept. 1943, 29 Sept. 1943, 8 Oct. 1943, 4 Nov. 1943, 17 Nov. 1943.

83. Reprinted in Halstead (ed.), *Wings of Victory*, 13–16. A short film was made in 1941, in which the letter was recited by John Gielgud, accompanied by images of a downed flyer's childhood home: *An Airman's Letter to His Mother*, dir. Michael Powell (1941).

84. IWM 93/5/1, E. F. Rawlings, ms. letter addressed to his 'dearest folks', n.d.

85. John Sommerfield, *The Survivors* (Letchworth: John Lehman, 1947), 83.

86. Winfield, *Sky Belongs to Them*, 141–8.

87. Adrian Hastings, *A History of English Christianity, 1920–2000* (London: SCM Press, 2001), 355–402. Recent attempts to argue for the resilience of Christianity

in Britain during the two world wars have risked overstatement. For a misconceived effort to establish that soldiers' fatalistic sentiments and an emergency recourse to prayer indicate an 'enduring bond' between the mainstream churches and the British public in the first half of the twentieth century, Michael Snape, *God and the British Soldier: Religion and the British Army in the First and Second World Wars* (London: Routledge, 2005), 19–58.

88. Morris, *Cheshire*, 194–5.

89. Calder, *People's War*, 481.

90. John Collins, *Faith Under Fire* (London: Leslie Frewin, 1966), 67–8.

91. Frayling, *Ken Adam*.

92. Beaton, *Winged Squadrons*, 19.

93. Tripp, *Eighth Passenger*, 30.

94. Tripp, *Faith is a Windsock*, 150–1.

95. Clapham, *Night Be My Witness*, 152–3.

96. IWM 67/334/1, Mrs P. Brimson, typescript, 'A Day on a Lancaster Bomber Station, Winter 1943, by Les Bartlett, DFM', n.d.

97. Gleed, *Arise to Conquer*, 34.

98. Deere, *Nine Lives*, 163.

99. IWM 04/24/1, Pilot Officer J. R. Byrne, ms. diary entries, 4 July 1944, 6 Dec. 1944.

100. M-O File Report 975, 'Report on Superstition' (1941).

101. Quoted in Tripp, *Eighth Passenger*, 179–80.

102. Cheshire, *Bomber Pilot*, 102.

103. John McCarthy, 'Air Crew and "Lack of Moral Fibre" in the Second World War', *War and Society*, 2 (1984), 87–101; English, 'A Predisposition to Cowardice', Bishop, *Bomber Boys*, 239–40, 248–9.

104. Tripp, *Eighth Passenger*, 39.

105. Monks, *Squadrons Up*, 23–4.

106. Gleed, *Arise to Conquer*, 29–31.

107. Deere, *Nine Lives*, 101–3.

108. Roper, 'Between Manliness and Masculinity', 347–8, 350–3, 359–60; Ben Shephard, *A War of Nerves: Soldiers and Psychiatrists, 1914–1994* (London: Pimlico, 2002), 1–168; Peter Leese, *Shell Shock: Traumatic Neurosis and the British Soldiers of the First World War* (Houndmills: Palgrave, 2002).

109. Charles Moran, *The Anatomy of Courage* (London: Constable, 1945).

110. Bourke, *Fear*, 206.

111. John Strachey, 'Foreword' to Gleed, *Arise to Conquer*, 6.

112. Quoted in Connolly, *Reaching for the Stars*, 42.

113. Winfield, *Sky Belongs to Them*, 119.

114. Cheshire, *Bomber Pilot*, 26.

115. Morris, *Cheshire*, 180–1.

116. Sutton, *Way of a Pilot*, 46–7.

117. Hillary, *Last Enemy*, 14–15.

118. [Richey], *Fighter Pilot*, 79–80, 97.

119. Walker, *Sailor Malan*, 101–2.

120. Ibid. 101.

121. Brickhill, *Reach for the Sky*, 32; William Rothenstein, 'Some Account of Life in the RAF', in *Men of the RAF* (London: Oxford University Press, 1942), 42.

122. Orde, *Pilots of Fighter Command*, 19, 30–2.

123. Monks, *Squadrons Up*, 120.

124. Bailey, *Sky Suspended*, 59–60.

125. Somerset Maugham, *Strictly Personal*, 193.

126. Beaton, *Winged Squadrons*, 29–30.

127. Barnes, *Cloud Cover*, 93–5.

128. Philip Hoare, *Noel Coward: A Life* (New York: Sinclair-Stevenson, 1995), 340. For a narrative of a gay flyer in Bomber Command, Bishop, *Bomber Boys*, 274–5.

129. English, 'A Predisposition to Cowardice', 27–8.

130. Sommerfield, *The Survivors*, 76.

131. Bartley, *Smoke Trails*, 64.

NOTES TO CHAPTER 6

1. Elaine Scarry, 'Injury and the Structure of War', *Representations*, 10 (1985), 1.

2. Harrison, *Medicine and Victory*, 275.

3. David A. Gerber, 'Introduction', in David A. Gerber (ed.), *Disabled Veterans in History* (Ann Arbor, Mich.: University of Michigan Press, 2000), 5–7.

4. Seth Koven, 'Remembering and Dismemberment: Crippled Children, Wounded Soldiers and the Great War in Great Britain', *American Historical Review*, 99 (1994), 1167–1202.

5. Cohen, *The War Come Home*, 129–30.

6. Stephen Crane, *The Red Badge of Courage* (1895; New York: Modern Library, 2000).

7. Orde, *Pilots of Fighter Command*, 18.

8. Bishop, *Fighter Boys*, 323.

9. *Reach For the Sky*, dir. Lewis Gilbert (1956); Kenneth More, *Happy Go Lucky: My Life* (London: Robert Hale, 1959), 152–61.

10. 'Laddie' Lucas, *Flying Colours: The Epic Story of Douglas Bader* (London: Sidgwick & Jackson, 1990); Robert Jackson, *Douglas Bader: A Biography* (London: Arthur Barker, 1983).

11. Brickhill, *Reach for the Sky*, 106–7.

12. Brickhill, *Reach for the Sky*, 91–102.

13. Ibid. 137, 144–6.

14. Ibid. 181, 341–2.

15. Colin Hodgkinson, *Best Foot Forward* (London: Odhams, 1957), 12–14, 18, 21, 31–45.

16. Ibid. 81–2.

17. Ibid. 84, 95–6, 110–11, 139–40.

18. Ibid. 71, 104–5, 125, 169–71.

19. Arthur Koestler, *The Yogi and the Commissar* (New York: Macmillan, 1946); Sebastian Faulks, *The Fatal Englishman: Three Short Lives* (London: Vintage, 1997), 109–208.

20. E. R. Mayhew, *The Reconstruction of Warriors: Archibald McIndoe, the Royal Air Force and the Guinea Pig Club* (London: Greenhill Books, 2004), 23, 44, 70, 88.

21. Ibid. 58–64, 70–1, 76–81, 156–9, 166–70; Leonard Mosley, *Faces from the Fire: The Biography of Sir Archibald McIndoe* (London: Weidenfeld & Nicolson, 1962).

22. Mayhew, *Reconstruction of Warriors*, 202.

23. Quoted in Ross, *Richard Hillary*, 166.

24. Lovat Dickson, *Richard Hillary* (London: Macmillan, 1950), 98.

25. Simpson, *I Burned My Fingers*, 126, 71.

26. For the contrast between responses in East Grinstead and London, William Simpson, *The Way of Recovery* (London: Hamish Hamilton, 1944), 132–3.

27. Faulks, *Fatal Englishman*, 143.

28. Hillary, *Last Enemy*, 119, 172–4.

29. Dickson, *Richard Hillary*.

30. Page, *Shot Down in Flames*, 116–17.

31. Faulks, *Fatal Englishman*, 161.

32. Hillary, *Last Enemy*, 149–50, 125.

33. Dickson, *Richard Hillary*, 100, 145; Ross, *Richard Hillary*, 225–31; Michael Burn, *Mary and Richard: The Story of Richard Hillary and Mary Booker* (London: Deutsch, 1988).

34. Simpson, *I Burned My Fingers*, 34–7.

35. Ibid. 42, 46–7, 50–7. The memoirs Simpson published during the war itself made no reference to Hope's horror and rejection, and implied that he had already reconciled himself to the break-up of his marriage before his return to England: William Simpson, *One Of Our Pilots Is Safe* (London: Hamish Hamilton, 1942), 227; Simpson, *Way of Recovery*, 12.

36. Simpson, *I Burned My Fingers*, 182–4, 192, 267–70.

37. Page, *Shot Down in Flames*, 82–3, 86.

38. Ibid. 93–4, 100, 113, 160–8, 133.

39. This is also the case in films and novels concerned with disabled veterans in the United States: Jarvis, *Male Body at War*, 102–3.

40. Bates, *Fair Stood the Wind*, 104–5.

41. Ibid. 117–18, 163.

42. Moie Charles, *Eve at the Driving Wheel* (London: Chatto & Windus, 1957). Discussed in Deborah Phillips and Ian Haywood, *Brave New Causes: Women in Postwar British Fictions* (London: Leicester University Press, 1998), 69.

43. Warren Chetham Strode, *Young Mrs Barrington: A New Play in Three Acts* (London: Samuel French, 1947), 51, 53–4, 67–9, 81.

44. Bates, *Day of Glory*, 22, 30, 61, 66, 21.

45. Campbell, *Maximum Effort*, 59–60, 196, 179, 251.

46. *Cage of Gold*, dir. Basil Dearden (1950). BFI, Pressbook: *Cage of Gold* (1950). Discussed in Murphy, *British Cinema and the Second World War*, 189.

47. Elizabeth Taylor, *At Mrs Lippincote's* (1945; London: Virago, 2000), 5, 105, 179, 190–3, 206, 214.

48. Terence Rattigan, *The Deep Blue Sea* (1952; London: Nick Hearn Books, 1999), 32–5, 55–6, 61–2, 72.

49. *Squadron Leader X*, dir. Lance Comfort (1942).

50. *Monthly Bulletin of the British Film Institute*, 9 (Nov. 1942), 142.

51. Stephen Bourne, *Brief Encounters: Lesbians and Gays in British Cinema, 1930–1971* (London: Cassell, 1996), 55–6, 63–4.

52. Gleed, *Arise to Conquer*, 107.

53. Geoffrey Kerr, *Cottage to Let: A Play in Three Acts* (London: Samuel French, 1941), 12–13, 58–63, 99–100.

54. *Cottage to Let*, dir. Anthony Asquith (1941). Reviewed in *Monthly Bulletin of the British Film Institute*, 8 (Aug. 1941), 97, and *Kinematograph Weekly*, 1791 (14 Aug. 1941). The film is discussed in Gill Plain, *John Mills and British Cinema: Masculinity, Identity and Nation* (Edinburgh: Edinburgh University Press, 2006), 62–5.

55. *Holiday Camp*, dir. Ken Annakin (1948). See also Kit Porlock, *Holiday Camp: The Book of the Film* (London: World Film Publications, 1947), 6–7, 12, 17, 32–3, 52–3, 75–7.

56. Conrad Phillips, *Murderer's Moon: Being Studies of Heath, Haigh, Christie and Chesney* (London: Arthur Barker, 1956), 13, 20–1; Gerald Byrne, *Borstal Boy: The Uncensored Story of Neville Heath* (London: Headline, 1946); Macdonald Critchley (ed.), *The Trial of Neville George Clevely Heath* (London: William Hodge, 1951).

57. Phillips, *Murderer's Moon*, 37–45.

58. Francis Selwyn, *Rotten to the Core? The Life and Death of Neville Heath* (London: Routledge, 1988), 187.

59. Donald Thomas, *An Underworld at War* (London: John Murray, 2004), 39.

60. *Love Story*, dir. Leslie Arliss (1944). Discussed in Murphy, *British Cinema and the Second World War*, 173–4.

61. Hamilton Bertie 'Tony' Gibson, obituary, *Guardian*, 30 Apr. 2001.

62. More, *Happy Go Lucky*, 123–5, 152–61.

NOTES TO CHAPTER 7

1. Karl Marx, 'The German Ideology', in *Selected Writings*, 2nd edn. (Oxford: Oxford University Press, 2000), 175–208.

2. Barnes, *Cloud Cover*, 49–50.

3. Hillary, *Last Enemy*, 43.

4. Rothenstein, 'Some Account of Life in the RAF', 20, 55.

5. Ibid. 61.

6. James Lees-Milne, *Diaries, 1942–1945* (London: John Murray, 1995), 53.

7. M-O File Report 734, 'Morale in the Ranks of the RAF' (June 1941), 6.

8. *RAF Welfare Bulletin*, 15 (July 1944), 3–4.

9. Bishop, *Bomber Boys*, 264–5.

10. Walker, *Sailor Malan*, 104–5.

11. Robert Wohl, *A Passion for Wings: Aviation and the Western Imagination, 1908–1918* (New Haven: Yale University Press, 1994), 260–72.

12. IWM 74/93/1, Pilot Officer M. A. Scott, ms. diary entries, 21 Jan. 1941, 10 Jan. 1941.

13. IWM 88/2/1, Mrs E. Kup, 'Memoirs of a Wartime WAAF', 70.

14. IWM Conshelf, G. J. Hull, ms. letter to Joan Kirby, 11 Jan. 1944.

15. Morris, *Guy Gibson*, 111.

16. Tucker, *Just an Echo*, diary entries for 10 June 1942, 14 June 1942.

17. Fussell, *Great War and Modern Memory*, 157. For working-class authors and the autodidact tradition, Jonathan Rose, *The Intellectual Life of the British Working Classes* (London: Yale University Press, 2001); Christopher Hilliard, *To Exercise Our Talents: The Democratization of Writing in Britain* (Cambridge, Mass.: Harvard University Press, 2006).

18. Bates, *Day of Glory*, 43.

19. M-O File Report 968, Harrisson, 'War Books', 9.

20. Hynes, *Soldier's Tale*, 125–6.

21. Somerset Maugham, *Strictly Personal*, 193–5; Bolitho, *Penguin in the Eyrie*, 107–11.

22. M-O File Report 968, Harrisson, 'War Books', 12–13; see also File Report 1253–4, 'Air Superiority' (May 1952), 1.

23. Sanford Sternlicht, *R. F. Delderfield* (Boston: Twayne Publishers, 1988), 12–14, 24–6; R. F. Delderfield, *The Avenue Goes to War* (London: Hodder & Stoughton, 1958); id., *The Green Gauntlet* (London: Hodder & Stoughton, 1968).

24. Bolitho, *Penguin in the Eyrie*, 16–17, 119.

25. Raymond and Langdon (eds.), *Slipstream*.

26. Gwynn-Browne, *Gone For a Burton*.

27. H. E. Bates, *The Blossoming World: An Autobiography* (London: Michael Joseph, 1971), 180–2.

28. [Bates], *Greatest People in the World*; Flying Officer X [H. E. Bates], *How Sleep the Brave* (London: Jonathan Cape, 1943).

29. H. E. Bates, *The World in Ripeness: An Autobiography* (London: Michael Joseph, 1972), 16, 18–19, 31, 32–3.

30. Bates, *Fair Stood the Wind for France*.

31. H. E. Bates, *The Cruise of the Breadwinner* (London: Michael Joseph, 1946); id., *Day of Glory*; id., *The Purple Plain* (London: Michael Joseph, 1947).

32. For Bates's literary reputation, Dennis Vannatta, *H. E. Bates* (Boston: Twayne Publishers, 1983), 51–69.

33. IWM 74/93/1, Pilot Officer M. A. Scott, ms. diary entry, 8 Jan. 1941.

34. Jane Oliver, 'Preface', to Rhys, *England Is My Village*, 12.

35. Dahl, *Going Solo*, 101, 122–3.

36. Dahl, *Over to You*, 52–82, 39–51, 113–30, 24–38. For Dahl's literary reputation, Mark I. West, *Roald Dahl* (New York: Twayne Publishers, 1992).

37. Rawlinson, *British Writing of the Second World War*, 39–67.

38. Ross, *Richard Hillary*, 231.

39. Faulks, *Fatal Englishman*, 165–6, 200.

40. Ibid. 203–4.

41. *Listener*, 26 (23 Nov. 1941), 567.

42. Miranda Seymour, *Robert Graves: Life on the Edge* (New York: Doubleday, 1995).

43. Calder, *The People's War*, 518–23.

44. Toynbee, *Friends Apart*, 12–13.

45. Calder, *The People's War*, 517.

46. *Listener*, 26 (30 Nov. 1941), 603.

47. The collection Jones had in mind was most likely R. De la Bère (ed.), *Icarus: An Anthology of the Poetry of Flight* (London: Macmillan, 1938).

48. M-O File Report 968, Harrisson, 'War Books', 28.

49. John Pudney and Henry Treece (eds.), *Air Force Poetry* (London: The Bodley Head, 1944), 5.

50. Margery Fisher, *Henry Treece* (London: The Bodley Head, 1969), 9–11.

51. John Pudney, *Home and Away: An Autobiographical Gambit* (London: Michael Joseph, 1960), 93–100, 120–6; id., *Dispersal Point*, 24.

52. BL, Rattigan Ms. ADD. 74302, 'Signed With Their Honour', 37–8.

53. Eric Warman, *A Matter of Life and Death: The Book of the Film* (London: World Film Publications, 1946), 8–10; Ian Christie, *A Matter of Life and Death* (London:

British Film Institute, 2000), 10, 50, 72–4; Robert Shail, 'Officers and Gentlemen: Masculinity in Powell and Pressburger's Wartime Films', in Ian Christie and Andrew Moor (eds.), *The Cinema of Michael Powell* (London: BFI, 2005), 248.

54. Lumford, *My Father's Son*, 199–201.

55. Bailey, *Sky Suspended*, 55–6.

56. Wellum, *First Light*, 127, 191–2.

57. *Over to You*, 16.

58. Forbes and Allen (eds.), *Ten Fighter Boys*, 124.

59. Roy, *Return from Hell*, 176, 219.

60. Winfield, *Sky Belongs to Them*, 139.

61. Ernst Jünger, *Storm of Steel*, trans. Michael Hoffman (1920; London: Penguin, 2004), pp. xix–xx; Edmund Blunden, *Undertones of War* (London: Cobden-Sanderson, 1928). See also Fussell, *Great War and Modern Memory*, 231–69.

62. Pudney, *Dispersal Point*, 7.

63. Wohl, *Spectacle of Flight*, 266.

64. Gwynn-Browne, *Gone for a Burton*, 21.

65. Townsend, *Time and Chance*, 79–80.

66. Bishop, *Bomber Boys*, 57–9, 91–2.

67. Shute, *Landfall*, 190.

68. Gibson, *Enemy Coast Ahead*, 237, 252–6, 222.

69. Forbes and Allen (eds.), *Ten Fighter Boys*, 98, 100.

70. Walker, *Sailor Malan*, 65–6.

71. Smithies, *Aces, Erks and Backroom Boys*, 34–5; Bishop, *Fighter Boys*, 86–7.

72. Liskutin, *Challenge in the Air*, 74–5.

73. Wellum, *First Light*, 105, 101.

74. Clostermann, *Big Show*, 19.

75. Hillary, *Last Enemy*, 58, 46.

76. Bates, *Blossoming World*, 166–7; Renault, *Charioteer*, 70.

77. Collins, *Long and the Short and the Tall*, 102.

78. Bailey, *Sky Suspended*, 33, 124–5.

79. J. C. M. Gibb, 'The Bomber', in Pudney and Treece (eds.), *Air Force Poetry*, 36.

80. IWM Conshelf, G. J. Hull, ms. letter to Joan Kirby, 6 Jan. 1944.

81. Antoine de Saint-Exupéry, *Flight to Arras*, trans. Lewis Galantière (1942; Harmondsworth: Penguin, 1969), 30.

82. Wellum, *First Light*, 104; Clostermann, *Big Show*, 42.

83. Sommerfield, *The Survivors*, 77.

84. 'Death of an Old Man', in Dahl, *Over to You*, 18.

85. Paul Nash, 'The Personality of Planes' (1942), quoted in Wohl, *Spectacle of Flight*, 270.

86. Clostermann, *Big Show*, 42.

87. Cecil, 'The RAF', 70, 83–4.

88. Wellum, *First Light*, 146.

89. Dahl, *Going Solo*, 149–55; 'Katina' in Dahl, *Over to You*, 98–9.

90. Quoted in James Chapman, *Past and Present: National Identity and the British Historical Film* (London: I. B. Tauris, 2005), 122.

91. Elizabeth Bowen, *The Heat of the Day* (1949; New York: Anchor Books, 2002), 310.

92. Mark Girouard, *The Return to Camelot: Chivalry and the English Gentleman* (New Haven: Yale University Press, 1981), 275–93.

93. Bourke, *Intimate History of Killing*, 359.

94. Allen J. Frantzen, *Bloody Good: Chivalry, Sacrifice and the Great War* (Chicago: University of Chicago Press, 2004), esp. 1–3, 265. A more nuanced account of how the Crusades, chivalry, and medieval mythology all figured centrally in the remembrance of the First World War is provided by Stefan Goebel, *The Great War and Medieval Memory: War, Remembrance and Medievalism in Britain and Germany, 1914–1940* (Cambridge: Cambridge University Press, 2007).

95. Dawson, *Soldier Heroes*, 167–230.

96. Wohl, *Passion for Wings*, 239–41; Goebel, *Great War and Medieval Memory*, 223–9.

97. Cecil Lewis, *Sagittarius Rising* (1936; London: Warner Books, 1998), 45.

98. Robertson, *Dream of Civilized Warfare*.

99. 'The Necessity of Chivalry' [1940], in C. S. Lewis, *Essay Collection and Other Short Pieces* (London: HarperCollins, 2000), 717–20.

100. Rothenstein, 'Some Account of Life in the RAF', 39.

101. Eric Kennington, *Drawing the RAF: A Book of Portraits* (Oxford: Oxford University Press, 1942), 22.

102. Ross, *Richard Hillary*, 280–3.

103. Monks, *Squadrons Up*, 27–8. Although note that Paul Richey's squadron entertained a downed German flyer in their mess during the winter of 1939–40, [Richey], *Fighter Pilot*, 12.

104. Brickhill, *Reach for the Sky*, 273.

105. Cecil, 'The RAF', 83.

106. Bolitho, *Combat Report*, 103.

107. Townsend, *Time and Chance*, 97, 106.

108. [Richey], *Fighter Pilot*, 102–3.

109. Hynes, *Soldier's Tale*, 134.

110. Bishop, *Fighter Boys*, 208.

111. Gleed, *Arise to Conquer*, 103.

112. Forbes and Allen (eds.), *Ten Fighter Boys*, 7.

113. IWM 90/32/1, Flying Officer G. A. Stillingfleet, ms. letter to his parents, 26 June 1941.

114. Page, *Shot Down in Flames*, 133.

115. For various contributions to this debate, Stephen A. Garrett, *Ethics and Airpower in World War Two: The British Bombing of German Cities* (New York: St Martin's Press, 1993); Donald Bloxham, 'Dresden as a War Crime', in Paul Addison and Jeremy A. Crang (eds.), *Firestorm: The Bombing of Dresden, 1945* (London: Pimlico, 2006), 180–208; Jörg Friedrich, *The Fire: The Bombing of Germany, 1940–1945*, trans. Allison Brown (New York: Columbia University Press, 2006).

116. Connelly, *Reaching for the Stars*, 162; Garrett, *Ethics and Airpower*, 84.

117. Friedrich, *The Fire*, 44–6,

118. Garrett, *Ethics and Airpower*, 118.

119. Andrew Chandler, 'The Church of England and the Obliteration Bombing of Germany in the Second World War', *English Historical Review*, 108 (1993), 920–46.

120. Gordon C. Zahn, *Chaplains in the RAF: A Study in Role Tension* (Manchester: Manchester University Press, 1969), 166–75, 262.

121. Vera Brittain, *Seed of Chaos: What Mass Bombing Really Means* (London: New Vision, 1944).

122. Garrett, *Ethics and Airpower*, 77–8.

123. M-O File Report 569, 'Airmen: Morale and Attitudes', 9–10.

124. Beaton, *Winged Squadrons*, 31–2.

125. Roy, *Return from Hell*, 110–11.

126. Jo Capka, *Red Sky at Night* (London: Anthony Blond, 1958), 102.

127. Bishop, *Bomber Boys*, 136–7.

128. Peter Johnson, *The Withered Garland: Reflections and Doubts of a Bomber* (London: New European Publications, 1995), 189–92, 230–2, 246–8, 342.

129. IWM 67/334/1, Mrs P. Brimson, typescript 'A Day on a Lancaster Bomber Station, Winter 1943, by Les Bartlett, DFM', n.d.

130. Morris, *Cheshire*, 266–7.

131. Rivaz, *Tail Gunner*, 39.

132. Winfield, *The Sky Belongs to Them*, 149–50.

133. Hillary, *Last Enemy*, 97.

134. Friedrich, *The Fire*, 84.

135. Dahl, *Over to You*, 152–3, 157–8.

136. Campbell, *Maximum Effort*, 63.

137. *Tawny Pipit*, dir. Bernard Miles and Charles Saunders (1944), reviewed in *Monthly Bulletin of the British Film Institute*, 11 (May 1944), 53; Shute, *Pastoral*, 32–3, 39.

138. Tripp, *Faith is a Windsock*, 30–1.

139. Connelly, *Reaching for the Stars*, 143–7.

140. e.g. D. M. Crook, *Spitfire Pilot* (London: Faber & Faber, 1942), 54, 84.

141. Bolitho, *Combat Report*, 103.

142. Smithies, *Aces, Erks and Backroom Boys*, 38

143. 'The Dog Who Spoke Polish', in Ward-Jackson, *No Bombs At All*, 71–7.

144. Barbara Stanton, *WAAF into Wife* (London: Mills & Boon, 1943).

145. Landau, *Fool's Progress*, 74–5.

146. Lynne Olson and Stanley Cloud, *For Your Freedom and Ours: The Kosciuszko Squadron, Forgotten Heroes of World War Two* (London: Arrow Books, 2004), 177–81.

147. Bates, *Day of Glory*, 20, 23.

148. Wyndham, *Love Is Blue*, 170–1, 183.

149. Watson, *Johnny Kinsman*, 67–8, 71.

150. Costello, *Love, Sex and War*, 80.

151. Wohl, *Spectacle of Flight*, 49–106, 305–8.

152. Rex Warner, *The Aerodrome: A Love Story* (1941; Chicago: Elephant Paperbacks, 1993), esp. 20–1, 187, 222–4.

153. Ibid. 6.

154. Gwynn-Browne, *Gone for a Burton*, 24, 246–7, 300–11.

155. Pudney, *Who Only England Know*, 19, 82.

156. John Lehmann, *I Am My Brother* (London: Longmans, 1960), 204.

157. Ottaway, *Dambuster*, 126–7; Morris, *Guy Gibson*, 176.

158. Morris, *Guy Gibson*, 65.

159. Ibid. 114.

160. Ibid. 197, 200; Ottaway, *Dambuster*, pp. xi, 177.

NOTES TO CHAPTER 8

1. Tripp, *Faith is a Windsock*, 222.

2. Ibid. 216.

3. Ross, *Richard Hillary*, 262.

4. Stokes, *Paddy Finucane*, 161.

5. Bartley, *Smoke Trails*, 28–9.

6. Ibid. 202.

7. Mary Abbott, *Family Affairs: A History of the Family in Twentieth-Century England* (London: Routledge, 2003), 84–5.

8. Martin Francis, 'A Flight from Commitment? Domesticity, Adventure and the Masculine Imaginary in Britain after the Second World War', *Gender and History*, 19 (2007), 163–85.

9. Clostermann, *Big Show*, 247–50.

10. Bailey, *Sky Suspended*, 137–8.

11. Bishop, *Bomber Boys*, 367.

12. IWM 94/37/1, Flight Lieutenant J. M. Catford, typescript memoir, 169.

13. IWM 88/2/1, Mrs E. Kup, 'Memoirs of a Wartime WAAF', 95–6.

14. Brian Nolan, *Hero: George Beurling* (Toronto: Lester and Orpen Denys, 1981).

15. Maurice Edelman, *The Happy Ones* (London: Allan Wingate, 1957), 166.

16. *They Made Me a Fugitive*, dir. Cavalcanti (1947). Discussed in Robert Murphy, *Realism and Tinsel: Cinema and Society in Britain, 1939–1949* (London: Routledge, 1992), 146–90.

17. *Escape*, dir. Joseph Mankiewicz (1948); BFI Pressbook: *Escape* (1948).

18. David A. Gerber, 'Heroes and Misfits: The Troubled Social Reintegration of Disabled Veterans in *The Best Years of Our Lives*', *American Quarterly*, 46 (1994), 551–2.

19. Lumford, *My Father's Son*, 215.

20. Waters, 'Disorders of the Mind', 134–51; Patrick Higgins, *Heterosexual Dictatorship: Male Homosexuality in Post-War Britain* (London: Fourth Estate, 1996).

21. John Bierman and Colin Smith, *Fire in the Night: Wingate of Burma, Ethiopia, and Zion* (London: Macmillan, 1999), 392–3.

22. Lumford, *My Father's Son*, 216–18.

23. Morris, *Cheshire*, 232–46.

24. Hodgkinson, *Best Foot Forward*, 220–2.

25. IWM 01/35/1, C. F. Smith, typescript, 'My Time in the Royal Air Force, by Cyril Smith', 21.

26. Thomas, *Underworld at War*, 364.

27. Smithies, *Aces, Erks and Backroom Boys*, 138.

28. Philip Gibbs, *The New Elizabethans* (London: Hutchinson, 1953), 100.

29. John Pudney, *Six Great Aviators* (London: Hamish Hamilton, 1955), 215–17.

30. *The Sound Barrier*, dir. David Lean (1952).

31. Quoted in Darlow and Hodson, *Terence Rattigan*, 195.

32. Roberta Cowell, *Roberta Cowell's Story, by Herself* (London: Heinemann, 1954), 114.

33. Ibid. 58, 64–5, 72–6, 119.

34. Liskutin, *Challenge in the Air*, 187, 199–217, 225–6.

35. Capka, *Red Sky at Night*, 176–80.

36. Olson and Cloud, *For Your Freedom and Ours*, 301, 401–2.

37. Ibid. 420.

38. IWM 90/11/1, B. J. Solak, typescript memoir, 'Yoga of the Sun', n.d.

39. Murray, *Lest We Forget*, 132–3.

40. Clostermann, *Big Show*, 250–1.

41. Ross, *Richard Hillary*, 262.

42. Ibid. 309.

43. Morris, *Guy Gibson*, 228–31, 241–2, 245.

44. Townsend, *Time and Chance*, 128–9, 120.

45. Sarah Bradford, *George VI* (London: Weidenfeld & Nicolson, 1991), 549–51.

46. Lucas, *Five Up*, 114–15, 119–25, 130, 156.

47. Hodgkinson, *Best Foot Forward*, 246–8.

48. Addison, 'National Identity and the Battle of Britain', 238.

49. Collins, *Faith Under Fire*, 89–90.

50. J. B. Priestley, 'Postscript', in Halstead (ed.), *Wings of Victory*, 206.

51. Sholto Douglas, *Years of Command* (London: Collins, 1966), 363.

52. Smith, *Mick Mannock*, 9.

53. Bishop, *Bomber Boys*, p. xxxv.

54. Pudney, *Home and Away*, 163–74.

55. Tony Benn, *Years of Hope: Diaries, Letters and Papers, 1940–1962* (London: Hutchinson, 1994), 24, 66–7.

56. Walker, *Sailor Malan*, 159–75.

57. Neil Roos, *Ordinary Springboks: White Servicemen and Social Justice in South Africa* (Aldershot: Ashgate, 2005), 129–57.

58. Joyce, *Anatomy of a Rebel*, 48–60, 61–9; Peter Godwin and Ian Hancock, *'Rhodesians Never Die': The Impact of War and Political Change in White Rhodesia, c.1970–1980* (Oxford: Oxford University Press, 1993), 61.

59. John Lovett, *Contact: A Tribute to Those Who Serve Rhodesia* (Salisbury: Galaxie Press, 1977), 20.

60. Reproduced in Ian Douglas Smith, *The Great Betrayal* (London: Blake, 1997), opp. 274.

61. Jackson, *Douglas Bader*, 147–62.

62. Ibid. 153.

63. Douglas Bader, 'Foreword', to Adolf Galland, *The First and the Last*, trans. Mervyn Saville (1955; London: Fontana, 1970), p. xii.

64. Douglas Bader, 'Foreword', to Hans Ulrich Rudel, *Stuka Pilot*, trans. Lynton Hudson (Dublin: Euphorion Books, 1952), p. xiii.

65. For further discussion of this topic, Martin Francis, 'Men of the Royal Air Force, the Cultural Memory of the Second World War and the Twilight of the British Empire', in Susan Grayzel and Philippa Levine (eds.), *Gender, Labour, War and Empire: Essays on Modern Britain in Honour of Sonya Rose* (Houndmills: Palgrave, 2009).

66. Figures from Bishop, *Fighter Boys*, 378; Bishop, *Bomber Boys*, 389.

67. Roy, *Return from Hell*, 157.

68. David Clarke, *The Angel of Mons: Phantom Soldiers and Ghostly Guardians* (Chichester: Wiley, 2004), 5–10.

69. Jenny Hazelgrove, *Spiritualism and British Society Between the Wars* (Manchester: Manchester University Press, 2000), 2, 271–6.

70. Malcolm Gaskill, *Hellish Nell: Last of Britain's Witches* (London: Fourth Estate, 2001), 175, 207–8, 282–4.

71. Hugh Dowding, *Many Mansions* (London: Rider and Co., 1943); id., *Lychgate: On Spiritualism* (London: Rider and Co., 1945).

72. Bartley, *Smoke Trails*, 204.

73. Eileen Marsh, *We Lived in London* (London: Lutterworth Press, 1942), 160–5.

74. Dahl, *Over to You*, 97–8, 118–24.

75. IWM Conshelf, G. J. Hull, ms. letter to Joan Kirby, 11 Jan. 1944.

76. IWM 74/93/1, Pilot Officer M. A. Scott, ms. diary entries, 16 Jan. 1941; John William Dunne, *The New Immortality* (London: Faber, 1938).

77. Cheshire, *Bomber Pilot*, 126–8.

78. Bailey, *Sky Suspended*, 77–8.

79. Clapham, *Night Be My Witness*, 280.

80. *The Last Reunion*, dir. Leonard Brett (1955), made for ABC Television.

81. Philip Horne, 'Life and Death in *A Matter of Life and Death*', in Christie and Moor (eds.), *Cinema of Michael Powell*, 123–8.

82. *Broken Journey*, dir. Ken Annakin (1947). Discussed in Tony Williams, *Structures of Desire: British Cinema, 1939–1955* (Albany: State University of New York, 2000), 97–8.

83. Mary Renault, *North Face* (London: Longman, 1949), 133–5, 264–73, 293–307.

84. Edith Kup, interview with Patrick Bishop, in Bishop, *Fighter Boys*, 404.

85. Bishop, *Bomber Boys*, 394–5.

NOTES TO CONCLUSION

1. Wellum, *First Light*; H. E. Bates, *How Sleep the Brave: The Complete Stories of Flying Officer X* (London: Vintage, 2002); Andrew Greig, *That Summer* (London: Faber, 2000); James Holland, *The Burning Blue* (London: Arrow Books, 2004); Frank Barnard, *Blue Man Falling* (London: Headline, 2006).

2. Margaret Dickson, *Wish Me Luck* (London: Pan Books, 2007); Lilian Harry, *A Song at Twilight* (London: Orion Books, 2006).

3. *Dark Blue World*, dir. Jan Sverák (2001); *Piece of Cake*, dir. Ian Toynton (1988), made for London Weekend Television.

4. For a powerful polemic on this theme, see Paul Gilroy, *Postcolonial Melancholia* (New York: Columbia University Press, 2005), 87–95, 116.

5. David Edgerton, *England and the Aeroplane: An Essay on a Militant and Technological Nation* (Basingstoke: Macmillan, 1991).

Bibliography

A. UNPUBLISHED PRIMARY SOURCES

British Film Institute, London

Pressbooks

British Library, London

Terence Rattigan Manuscripts

Imperial War Museum, London (Department of Documents)

Papers of Miss J. Barclay
Papers of Mrs P. Brimson
Papers of Miss R. Britten
Papers of Mrs M. Brookes
Papers of Miss J. M. Brotherton
Papers of Pilot Officer J. R. Byrne
Papers of J. M. V. Carpenter
Papers of J. M. Catford
Papers of Miss V. E. E. Cossar
Papers of Flying Officer C. Crichton
Papers of E. Featherstone, RAFVR
Papers of Mrs J. F. P. Hambly
Papers of G. J. Hull
Papers of Mrs E. Kup
Papers of G. T. Lang
Papers of Mrs J. Myler
Papers of Mrs D. Plant
Papers of H. T. Radford
Papers of E. F. Rawlings
Papers of Mrs N. J. Sandy
Papers of Pilot Officer M. A. Scott
Papers of Flight Lieutenant G. Shackleton
Papers of C. F. Smith
Papers of B. J. Solak
Papers of Flying Officer G. A. Stillingfleet
Papers of Mrs R. Sumner
Papers of Mrs J. Wallace
Papers of Mrs N. C. Walton
Papers of F. C. Welding
Papers of Pilot Officer D. H. Wissler
Papers of Miss B. J. Wright

Mass-Observation Archive, University of Sussex
File Reports (Microfilm)

National Archive, Kew
Air Ministry Files (AIR)

Royal Air Force Museum, Hendon
Papers of Mrs Marjorie Hazell
Papers of Sam Miara and Doris Miara
Scrapbook of Mahindra Singh Pujji

Theatre Museum Archive, Blythe House, Olympia
Playbills

B. PUBLISHED SOURCES

Journals

Kinematograph Weekly
The League of Coloured Peoples Newsletter
The Listener
Monthly Bulletin of the British Film Institute
RAF Welfare Bulletin

Autobiographies, Biographies, and Published Diaries

Bailey, Jim, *The Sky Suspended: A Fighter Pilot's Story* (1964; London: Bloomsbury, 2005).
Barnes, Derek Gilpin, *Cloud Cover: Recollections of an Intelligence Officer* (London: Rich & Cowan, 1944).
Barnato Walker, Diana, *Spreading My Wings* (Sparkford: Patrick Stephens, 1994).
Bartley, Anthony, *Smoke Trails in the Sky: From the Journals of a Fighter Pilot* (London: William Kimber, 1984).
Bates, H. E., *The Blossoming World: An Autobiography* (London: Michael Joseph, 1971).
—— *The World in Ripeness: An Autobiography* (London: Michael Joseph, 1972).
Beaton, Cecil, *The Years Between: Diaries, 1939–44* (London: Weidenfeld & Nicolson, 1965).
Beck, Pip, *A WAAF in Bomber Command* (London: Goodall, 1989).
Bell, George Armour, *To Live Among Heroes: A Medical Officer's Dramatic Insight into the Life of 609 Squadron in Northwest Europe, 1944–45* (London: Grub Street, 2001).
Benn, Tony, *Years of Hope: Diaries, Letters and Papers, 1940–1962* (London: Hutchinson, 1994).
Bierman, John, and Smith, Colin, *Fire in the Night: Wingate of Burma, Ethiopia, and Zion* (London: Macmillan, 1999).
Bolitho, Hector, *Combat Report: The Story of a Fighter Pilot* (London: Batsford, 1943).
—— *A Penguin in the Eyrie: An RAF Diary, 1939–1945* (London: Hutchinson, 1955).
Bradford, Sarah, *George VI* (London: Weidenfeld & Nicolson, 1991).

Brickhill, Paul, *Reach for the Sky: The Story of Douglas Bader* (1954; London: Companion Book Club, 1955).

Briscoe, Walter Alwyn, *The Boy Hero of the Air* (London: Oxford University Press, 1921).

Brittain, Vera, *A Testament of Youth: An Autobiographical Study of the Years 1900–1925* (London: Gollancz, 1933).

Brown, Eric, *Wings on My Sleeve* (London: Weidenfeld & Nicolson, 2006).

Burn, Michael, *Mary and Richard: The Story of Richard Hillary and Mary Booker* (London: Deutsch, 1988).

Byrne, Gerald, *Borstal Boy: The Uncensored Story of Neville Heath* (London: Headline, 1946).

Capka, Jo, *Red Sky at Night* (London: Anthony Blond, 1958).

Carroll, Kay, *Compass Course: The Log of an Air Force Officer's Wife* (London: Hutchinson, n.d. [1941]).

Cheshire, Leonard, *Bomber Pilot* (London: Hutchinson, 1943).

Clostermann, Pierre, *The Big Show*, trans. Oliver Berthoud (Harmondsworth: Penguin Books, 1958).

Collins, John, *Faith Under Fire* (London: Leslie Frewin, 1966).

Collins, Robert, *The Long and the Short and the Tall: An Ordinary Airman's War* (Saskatoon: Western Producer Prairie Books, 1986).

Cotton, M. C. 'Bush', *Hurricanes Over Burma* (London: Grub Street, 1995).

Cowell, Roberta, *Roberta Cowell's Story, by Herself* (London: Heinemann, 1954).

Critchley, Macdonald (ed.), *The Trial of Neville George Clevely Heath* (London: William Hodge, 1951).

Crook, D. M., *Spitfire Pilot* (London: Faber & Faber, 1942).

Dahl, Roald, *Going Solo* (London: Jonathan Cape, 1986).

Darlow, Michael, and Hodson, Gillian, *Terence Rattigan: The Man and His Work* (London: Quartet Books, 1979).

Deere, Alan C., *Nine Lives* (London: Hodder & Stoughton, 1959).

Dickson, Lovat, *Richard Hillary* (London: Macmillan, 1950).

Donahue, Arthur Gerald, *Tally-Ho! Yankee in a Spitfire* (London: Macmillan, 1942).

Douglas, Sholto, *Years of Command* (London: Collins, 1966).

Du Cros, Rosemary, *ATA Girl: Memoirs of a Wartime Ferry Pilot* (London: Frederick Muller, 1983).

Ellis, Peter, *Biggles! The Life Story of Captain W. E. Johns* (Godmanstone: Veloce, 1993).

Fisher, Margery, *Henry Treece* (London: The Bodley Head, 1969).

Forbes, Athol, and Allen, Hubert Allen, *Ten Fighter Boys* (London: Collins, 1942).

Forrester, Larry, *Fly for Your Life: The Story of Bob Stanford Tuck* (Bristol: Cerberus Publishing, 2006).

Frankland, Noble, *History at War: The Campaigns of a Historian* (London: Giles de la Mere Publishers, 1998).

Franks, Norman, *Sky Tiger: The Story of Group Captain Sailor Malan* (London: William Kimber, 1980).

Frayling, Christopher, *Ken Adam: The Art of Production Design* (London: Faber, 2005).

Galland, Adolf, *The First and the Last*, trans. Mervyn Saville (1955; London: Fontana, 1970).

Gaskill, Malcolm, *Hellish Nell: Last of Britain's Witches* (London: Fourth Estate, 2001).

Gibson, Guy, *Enemy Coast Ahead* (1946; London: Pan Books, 1955).

Gleed, Ian, *Arise To Conquer* (London: Victor Gollancz, 1942).

Grenfell, Joyce, *Joyce Grenfell Requests the Pleasure* (London: Macmillan, 1976).

Hoare, Philip, *Noel Coward: A Life* (New York: Sinclair-Stevenson, 1995).

Hodgkinson, Colin, *Best Foot Forward* (London: Odhams, 1957).

Hillary, Richard, *The Last Enemy* (1942; London: Pimlico, 1997).

Jackson, Robert, *Douglas Bader: A Biography* (London: Arthur Barker, 1983).

Johnson, Peter, *The Withered Garland: Reflections and Doubts of a Bomber* (London: New European Publications, 1995).

Jones, Ira, *King of Air Fighters: A Biography of Major Mick Mannock* (London: Nicholson & Watson, 1934).

Joyce, Peter, *Anatomy of a Rebel: Smith of Rhodesia* (Salisbury: Graham Publishing, 1974).

Kent, Johnny, *One of the Few* (Stroud: Tempus, 2000).

Kiernan, R. H., *Captain Albert Ball, VC* (London: John Hamilton, 1933).

Lees-Milne, James, *Diaries, 1942–1945* (London: John Murray, 1995).

Lehmann, John, *I Am My Brother* (London: Longmans, 1960).

Levy, Harry, *The Dark Side of the Sky: The Story of a Young Jewish Airman in Nazi Germany* (London: Leo Cooper, 1996).

Lewis, Cecil, *Sagittarius Rising* (1936; London: Warner Books, 1998).

Liskutin, M. A., *Challenge in the Air: A Spitfire Pilot Remembers* (London: William Kimber, 1988).

Lord, Graham, *Niv: The Authorized Biography of David Niven* (London: Orion, 2004).

Lucas, 'Laddie', *Five Up: A Chronicle of Five Lives* (London: Sidgwick & Jackson, 1978).

—— *Flying Colours: The Epic Story of Douglas Bader* (London: Sidgwick & Jackson, 1990).

Lumford, Richard, *My Father's Son* (London: Jonathan Cape, 1949).

Marnham, Patrick, *Wild Mary: A Life of Mary Wesley* (London: Chatto & Windus, 2006).

Maugham, William Somerset, *Strictly Personal* (New York: Doubleday, 1941).

More, Kenneth, *Happy Go Lucky: My Life* (London: Robert Hale, 1959).

Morris, Richard, *Cheshire: The Biography of Leonard Cheshire* (London: Penguin, 2001).

—— *Guy Gibson* (London: Viking, 1994).

Mosley, Leonard, *Faces from the Fire: The Biography of Sir Archibald McIndoe* (London: Weidenfeld & Nicolson, 1962).

Mouchotte, René, *The Mouchotte Diaries*, trans. Philip John Stead (London: Hamish Hamilton, 1957).

Niven, David, *The Moon's a Balloon* (London: Coronet, 1973).

Noble, E. Martin, *Jamaica Airman: A Black Airman in Britain, 1943 and After* (London: New Beacon Books, 1984).

Nolan, Brian, *Hero: George Beurling* (Toronto: Lester & Orpen Denys, 1981).

Ottaway, Susan, *Dambuster: A Life of Guy Gibson, VC* (London: Leo Cooper, 1996).

Page, Geoffrey, *Shot Down in Flames: A World War Two Fighter Pilot's Remarkable Tale of Survival* (London: Grub Street, 1999).

Pape, Richard, *Boldness Be My Friend* (London: Elek, 1953).

Phillips, Conrad, *Murderer's Moon: Being Studies of Heath, Haigh, Christie and Chesney* (London: Arthur Barker, 1956).

Pudney, John, *Home and Away: An Autobiographical Gambit* (London: Michael Joseph, 1960).

——*A Pride of Unicorns: Richard and David Atcherley of the RAF* (London: Old-bourne, 1960).

—— *Six Great Aviators* (London: Hamish Hamilton, 1955).

—— *Who Only England Know: Log of a Wartime Journey of Unintentional Discovery* (London: Bodley Head, 1943).

[Richey, Paul], *Fighter Pilot: A Personal Record of the Campaign in France* (London: Batsford, 1941).

Rivaz, R. C., *Tail Gunner* (London: Jarrolds, n.d. [1943]).

Roos-Evans, James (ed.), *Joyce Grenfell, The Time of My Life: Her Wartime Journals* (London: Hodder & Stoughton, 1989).

Ross, David, *Richard Hillary* (London: Grub Street, 2000).

—— *Stapme: The Biography of Squadron Leader Basil Gerald Stapleton, DFC* (London: Grub Street, 2002).

Roy, Jules, *Mémoires Barbares* (Paris: Albin Michel, 1989).

—— *Return from Hell* (London: William Kimber, 1954).

Rudel, Hans Ulrich, *Stuka Pilot*, trans. Lynton Hudson (Dublin: Euphorion Books, 1952).

Ryall, Tom, *Anthony Asquith* (Manchester: Manchester University Press, 2005).

Selwyn, Francis, *Rotten to the Core? The Life and Death of Neville Heath* (London: Routledge, 1988).

Seton-Watson, Christopher, *Dunkirk–Alamein–Bologna: Letters and Diaries of an Artil-leryman, 1939–1945* (London: Buckland Publications, 1993).

Seymour, Miranda, *Robert Graves: Life on the Edge* (New York: Doubleday, 1995).

Sherbrooke-Walker, Ronald, *Khaki and Blue* (London: St Catherine Press, 1952).

Simpson, William, *I Burned My Fingers* (London: Putnam, 1955).

—— *One Of Our Pilots Is Safe* (London: Hamish Hamilton, 1942).

—— *The Way of Recovery* (London: Hamish Hamilton, 1944).

Smith, Adrian, *Mick Mannock, Fighter Pilot: Myth, Life and Politics* (Houndmills: Palgrave, 2001).

Smith, Ian Douglas, *The Great Betrayal* (London: Blake, 1997).

Sternlicht, Sanford, *R. F. Delderfield* (Boston: Twayne Publishers, 1988).

Stokes, Doug, *Paddy Finucane: Fighter Ace* (London: William Kimber, 1983).

Sutton, Barry, *The Way of a Pilot: A Personal Record* (London: Macmillan, 1942).

Townsend, Peter, *Time and Chance: An Autobiography* (London: Collins, 1978).

Toynbee, Philip, *Friends Apart: A Memoir of Esmond Romilly and Jasper Ridley in the Thirties* (London: MacGibbon & Kee, 1954).

Tripp, Miles, *The Eighth Passenger: A Flight of Recollection and Discovery* (London: Heinemann, 1969).

Tucker, Audrey, *Just an Echo* (Stratford: Eastside Community Heritage, n.d. [2001]).

Vannatta, Dennis, *H. E. Bates* (Boston: Twayne Publishers, 1983).

Vigors, Tim, *Life's too Short to Cry: The Compelling Memoirs of a Battle of Britain Ace* (London: Grub Street, 2006).

Walker, Oliver, *Sailor Malan: A Biography* (London: Cassell, 1953).

Wansell, Geoffrey, *Terence Rattigan: A Biography* (London: Fourth Estate, 1995).

Wellum, Geoffrey, *First Light* (London: Viking, 2002).

West, Mark I., *Roald Dahl* (New York: Twayne Publishers, 1992).

Winfield, Roland, *The Sky Belongs to Them* (London: William Kimber, 1976).
Wyndham, Joan, *Love Is Blue: A Wartime Diary* (London: Heinemann, 1986).

Novels, Short Stories, Plays, and Poetry Collections

Ayling, Keith, *RAF: The Story of a British Fighter Pilot* (New York: Henry Holt, 1941).
Barnard, Frank, *Blue Man Falling* (London: Headline, 2006).
Baron, Alexander, *With Hope, Farewell* (London: Jonathan Cape, 1952).
Bates, H. E., *The Cruise of the Breadwinner* (London: Michael Joseph, 1946).
—— *The Day of Glory: A Play in Three Acts* (London: Michael Joseph, 1945).
—— *Fair Stood the Wind for France* (London: Michael Joseph, 1944).
—— *How Sleep the Brave: The Complete Stories of Flying Officer X* (London: Vintage, 2002).
—— *The Purple Plain* (London: Michael Joseph, 1947).
—— *The Stories of Flying Officer X* (1952; London: Jonathan Cape, 1967).
Blunden, Edmund, *Undertones of War* (London: Cobden-Sanderson, 1928).
Bowen, Elizabeth, *The Heat of the Day* (1949; New York: Anchor Books, 2002).
Braine, John, *Room at the Top* (1957; Harmondsworth: Penguin, 1963).
Brown, R. Sidney, *Dave Dawson with the RAF* (New York: Crown Publishers, 1941).
Charles, Moie, *Eve at the Driving Wheel* (London: Chatto & Windus, 1957).
Clapham, Walter, *Night Be My Witness* (London: Jonathan Cape, 1952).
Crane, Stephen, *The Red Badge of Courage* (1895; New York: Modern Library, 2000).
Curzon, Colin, *Flying Wild* (London: Hurst & Blackett, 1941).
Dahl, Roald, *Over to You: Ten Stories of Flyers and Flying* (1945; London: Penguin, 1973).
De la Bère, R. (ed.), *Icarus: An Anthology of the Poetry of Flight* (London: Macmillan, 1938).
Delafield, E. M., *The Provincial Lady in Wartime* (New York: Harper & Bros., 1940).
Delderfield, R. F., *The Avenue Goes to War* (London: Hodder & Stoughton, 1958).
—— *The Green Gauntlet* (London: Hodder & Stoughton, 1968).
Denney, Alfred A., *The Fairy Who Lost Her Wings* (Sevenoaks: Chadwell, 2002).
Dickson, Margaret, *Wish Me Luck* (London: Pan Books, 2007).
Edelman, Maurice, *The Happy Ones* (London: Allan Wingate, 1957).
Flying Officer X [H. E. Bates], *The Greatest People in the World* (London: Jonathan Cape, 1942).
—— *How Sleep the Brave* (London: Jonathan Cape, 1943).
Gaye, Carol, *Air Force Girl* (London: Collins, 1941).
Greig, Andrew, *That Summer* (London: Faber, 2000).
Gwynn-Browne, Arthur, *Gone for a Burton* (London: Chatto & Windus, 1945).
Harry, Lilian, *A Song At Twilight* (London: Orion Books, 2006).
Holland, James, *The Burning Blue* (London: Arrow Books, 2004).
Johns, W. E., *Biggles Flies Again* (London: John Hamilton, 1934).
—— *Biggles of the Camel Squadron* (London: John Hamilton, 1934).
Jünger, Ernst, *Storm of Steel*, trans. Michael Hoffman (1920; London: Penguin, 2004).
Kerr, Geoffrey, *Cottage to Let: A Play in Three Acts* (London: Samuel French, 1941).
Marsh, Eileen, *We Lived in London* (London: Lutterworth Press, 1942).
Oliver, Jane, *The Hour of the Angel* (London: Collins, 1942).
—— *In No Strange Land* (London: Collins, 1944).
Porlock, Kit, *Holiday Camp: The Book of the Film* (London: World Film Publications, 1947).

Pudney, John, *Dispersal Point and Other Air Poems* (London: Bodley Head, 1942).

——and Treece, Henry (eds.), *Air Force Poetry* (London: Bodley Head, 1944).

Rattigan, Terence, *The Deep Blue Sea* (1952; London: Nick Hearn Books, 1999).

——'Flare Path', in *The Collected Plays, Volume I* (1953; London: Hamish Hamilton, 1968), 83–169.

Remarque, Erich Maria, *All Quiet on the Western Front* (1928; New York: Ballantine Books, 1987).

Renault, Mary, *The Charioteer* (1953; London: Longmans, 1968).

——*North Face* (London: Longman, 1949).

Rhys, John Llewelyn, *England Is My Village* (London: Faber & Faber, 1941).

Robins, Denise, *Winged Love* (London: Hutchinson, 1941).

Roy, Jules, *The Happy Valley: A War Novel* (London: Viking Press, 1952).

——*The Navigator: A Novel*, trans. Mervyn Saville (New York: Knopf, 1955).

Saint-Exupéry, Antoine de, *Flight to Arras*, trans. Lewis Galantière (1942; Harmondsworth: Penguin, 1969).

Sandys, Oliver, *Wellington Wendy* (London: Hurst & Blackett, 1941).

Shute, Nevil, *Landfall* (1940; London: House of Stratus, 2000).

——*Pastoral* (New York: William Morrow, 1944).

Smith, Helen Zenna, *Not So Quiet . . .* (1930; London: Feminist Press, 1989).

Sommerfield, John, *The Survivors* (Letchworth: John Lehmann, 1947).

Stanton, Barbara, *WAAF into Wife* (London: Mills & Boon, 1943).

Strode, Warren Chetham, *Young Mrs Barrington: A New Play in Three Acts* (London: Samuel French, 1947).

Taylor, Elizabeth, *At Mrs Lippincote's* (1945; London: Virago, 2000).

Tremayne, Eileen, *Four Who Came Back* (London: Hutchinson, 1941).

Tripp, Miles, *Faith is a Windsock* (London: Peter Davies, 1952).

Ward-Jackson, C. H., *No Bombs At All: Some Short Stories of the Royal Air Force* (London: Sylvan Press, 1944).

Warman, Eric, *A Matter of Life and Death: The Book of the Film* (London: World Film Publications, 1946).

Warner, Rex, *The Aerodrome: A Love Story* (1941; Chicago: Elephant Paperbacks, 1993).

Watson, John, *Johnny Kinsman: A Novel* (London: Cassell, 1955),

Films and Television Programmes

An Airman's Letter to His Mother, dir. Michael Powell (1941).

Angels One Five, dir. George More O'Ferrall (1952).

Broken Journey, dir. Ken Annakin (1947).

Burma Rani, dir. T. R. Sundaran (1944).

Cage of Gold, dir. Basil Dearden (1950).

Cottage to Let, dir. Anthony Asquith (1941).

The Dam Busters, dir. Michael Anderson (1955).

Dangerous Moonlight, dir. Brian Desmond Hurst (1941).

Dark Blue World, dir. Jan Sverák (2001).

Escape, dir. Joseph Mankiewicz (1948).

The First of the Few, dir. Leslie Howard (1942).

Holiday Camp, dir. Ken Annakin (1948).

Journey Together, dir. John Boulting (1945).
Landfall, dir. Ken Annakin (1949).
The Last Reunion, dir. Leonard Brett (1955), made for ABC Television.
The Lion Has Wings, dir. Michael Powell, Brian Desmond-Hurst, and Adrian Brunel (1939).
Love Story, dir. Leslie Arliss (1944).
A Matter of Life and Death, dir. Michael Powell and Emeric Pressburger (1946).
Millions Like Us, dir. Frank Launder (1943).
One of Our Aircraft is Missing, dir. Michael Powell and Emeric Pressburger (1942).
Piece of Cake, dir. Ian Toynton (1988), made for London Weekend Television.
The Secret Life of Walter Mitty, dir. Norman Z. McLeod (1947).
Ships with Wings, dir. Sergei Nolbandov (1942).
The Sound Barrier, dir. David Lean (1952).
Squadron Leader X, dir. Lance Comfort (1942).
Target for Tonight, dir. Harry Watt (1941).
Tawny Pipit, dir. Bernard Miles and Charles Saunders (1944).
They Made Me a Fugitive, dir. Cavalcanti (1947).
The Way to the Stars, dir. Anthony Asquith (1945).
A Yank in the RAF, dir. Henry King (1941).

Books and Articles

Abbott, Mary, *Family Affairs: A History of the Family in Twentieth-Century England* (London: Routledge, 2003).
Acton, Carol, 'Writing and Waiting: The First World War Correspondence Between Vera Brittain and Ronald Leighton', *Gender and History*, 11 (1999), 54–83.
Addison, Paul, 'National Identity and the Battle of Britain', in Barbara Korte and Ralf Schneider (eds.), *War and the Cultural Construction of Identities in Britain* (Amsterdam: Rodopi Books, 2002), 225–40.
—— and Crang, Jeremy A. (eds.), *The Burning Blue: A New History of the Battle of Britain* (London: Pimlico, 2000).
Air Ministry, *Psychological Disorders in Flying Personnel of the Royal Air Force, Investigated During the War, 1939–1945* (London: HMSO, 1947).
—— *We Speak from the Air: Broadcasts by the RAF, Issued for the Air Ministry by the Ministry of Information* (London: HMSO, 1942).
—— *Over to You: New Broadcasts by the RAF* (London: HMSO, 1943).
Aldgate, Anthony, and Richards, Jeffrey, *Britain Can Take It: The British Cinema in the Second World War* (Edinburgh: Edinburgh University Press, 1994).
Atkin, Nicholas, *The Forgotten French: Exiles in the British Isles, 1940–44* (Manchester: Manchester University Press, 2003).
Audoin-Rouzeau, Stephane, *Men at War, 1914–1918: National Sentiment and Trench Journalism in France during the First World War* (Oxford: Berg, 1992).
Bailey, Beth L., *From Front Porch to Back Seat: Courtship in Twentieth-Century America* (Baltimore: Johns Hopkins University Press, 1988).
Ballard, S. I., and Miller, H. G., 'Psychiatric Casualties in a Woman's Service', *British Medical Journal* (3 Mar. 1945), 193–4.
Barry, Kathleen, *Femininity in Flight: A History of Flight Attendants* (Durham, NC: Duke University Press, 2007).

Beaton, Cecil, *Winged Squadrons* (London, Hutchinson, 1942).

Benson, Theodora, *Sweethearts and Wives: Their Part in War* (London: Faber & Faber, 1942).

Bernheimer, Charles, *Figures of Ill Repute: Representing Prostitution in Nineteenth-Century France* (Cambridge, Mass.: Harvard University Press, 1989).

Bet-El, Ilana R., *Conscripts: Forgotten Men of the Great War* (Stroud: Sutton, 2003).

Bishop, Patrick, *Bomber Boys: Fighting Back, 1940–1945* (London: HarperCollins, 2007).

—— *Fighter Boys: Saving Britain, 1940* (London: HarperCollins, 2004).

Bloxham, Donald, 'Dresden as a War Crime', in Paul Addison and Jeremy A. Crang (eds.), *Firestorm: The Bombing of Dresden, 1945* (London: Pimlico, 2006), 180–208.

Bonadeo, Alfredo, *Mark of the Beast: Death and Degradation in the Literature of the Great War* (Lexington, Ky.: University Press of Kentucky, 1989).

Bourke, Joanna, 'Disciplining the Emotions: Fear, Psychiatry and the Second World War', in Roger Cooter, Mark Harrison, and Steve Sturdy (eds.), *War, Medicine and Modernity* (London: Sutton, 1998).

—— *Dismembering the Male: Men's Bodies, Britain and the Great War* (Chicago: University of Chicago Press, 1996).

—— *Fear: A Cultural History* (London: Virago, 2005).

—— *An Intimate History of Killing: Face-to-Face Killing in Twentieth-Century Warfare* (London: Granta, 1998).

—— 'Psychology at War, 1914–1945', in G. C. Bunn, A. D. Lovie, and G. D. Richards (eds.), *Psychology in Britain: Historical Essays and Personal Reflections* (London: BPS Books, 2001), 133–49.

Bourne, Stephen, *Brief Encounters: Lesbians and Gays in British Cinema, 1930–1971* (London: Cassell, 1996).

Boyd, Kelly, *Manliness and the Boys Story Paper, 1855–1940* (Basingstoke: Palgrave, 2002).

Bracco, Rosa Maria, *Merchants of Hope: British Middlebrow Writers and the First World War, 1919–1939* (Oxford: Berg, 1993).

Breward, Christopher, *The Hidden Consumer: Masculinities, Fashion and City Life, 1860–1914* (Manchester: Manchester University Press, 1999).

Brittain, Vera, *Seed of Chaos: What Mass Bombing Really Means* (London: New Vision, 1944).

Bungay, Stephen, *The Most Dangerous Enemy: A History of the Battle of Britain* (London: Aurum Press, 2001).

Caesar, Adrian, *Taking it Like a Man: Suffering, Sexuality and the War Poets* (Manchester: Manchester University Press, 1993).

Calder, Angus, *The People's War: Britain, 1939–1945* (London: Cape, 1969).

Cannadine, David, *The Decline and Fall of the British Aristocracy* (New Haven: Yale University Press, 1990).

Cannadine, David, 'Winston Churchill as Aristocratic Adventurer', in *Aspects of Aristocracy: Grandeur and Decline in Modern Britain* (New Haven: Yale University Presss, 1994), 130–62.

Cecil, David, 'The RAF: A Layman's Glimpse', in *Men of the RAF* (London: Oxford University Press, 1942), 65–84.

Chandler, Andrew, 'The Church of England and the Obliteration Bombing of Germany in the Second World War', *English Historical Review*, 108 (1993), 920–46.

Chapman, James, *Past and Present: National Identity and the British Historical Film* (London: I. B. Tauris, 2005).

Christie, Ian, *A Matter of Life and Death* (London: British Film Institute, 2000).

Clarke, David, *The Angel of Mons: Phantom Soldiers and Ghostly Guardians* (Chichester: Wiley, 2004).

Cohen, Deborah, *The War Come Home: Disabled Veterans in Britain and Germany, 1914–1939* (Berkeley: University of California Press, 2001).

Collins, Marcus, *Modern Love: An Intimate History of Men and Women in Twentieth-Century Britain* (London: Atlantic Books, 2003).

—— 'Pride and Prejudice: West Indian Men in Mid-Twentieth-Century Britain', *Journal of British Studies*, 40 (2001), 391–418.

Connelly, Mark, *Reaching for the Stars: A New History of Bomber Command in World War Two* (London: I. B. Tauris, 2001).

Connelly, Mark, *We Can Take It! Britain and the Memory of the Second World War* (Harlow: Longman, 2004).

Corn, Joseph, *The Winged Gospel: America's Romance with Aviation, 1900–1950* (New York: Oxford University Press, 1983).

Costello, John, *Love, Sex and War: Changing Values, 1939–45* (London: Guild Publishing, 1985).

Costigliola, Frank, ' "I Had Come as a Friend": Emotion, Culture and Ambiguity in the Formation of the Cold War', *Cold War History*, 1 (2000), 103–28.

Crang, Jeremy A., *The British Army and the People's War* (Manchester: Manchester University Press, 2000).

Cunningham, Valentine, *British Writers of the Thirties* (Oxford: Oxford University Press, 1988).

Darwin, John, 'A Third British Empire? The Dominion Idea in Imperial Politics', in Judith Brown and William Roger Louis (eds.), *The Oxford History of the British Empire*, vol. iv, *The Twentieth Century* (Oxford: Oxford University Press, 1999), 64–87.

Davies, Andrew, 'Youth Gangs, Masculinity and Violence in Late Victorian Manchester and Salford', *Journal of Social History*, 32 (1998), 349–70.

Dawson, Graham, *Soldier Heroes: British Adventure, Empire and the Imagining of Masculinities* (London: Routledge, 1994).

Derrick, Robin, and Muir, Robin, *Unseen Vogue: The Secret History of Fashion Photography* (London: Little, Brown, 2002).

Ditz, Toby L., 'The New Men's History and the Peculiar Absence of Gendered Power: Some Remedies from Early American Gender History', *Gender and History*, 16 (2004), 1–35.

Doherty, Richard, *Irish Men and Women in the Second World War* (Dublin: Four Courts, 1999).

Dowding, Hugh, *Lychgate: On Spiritualism* (London: Rider & Co., 1945).

—— *Many Mansions* (London: Rider & Co., 1943).

Dunne, John William, *The New Immortality* (London: Faber, 1938).

Edgerton, David, *England and the Aeroplane: An Essay on a Militant and Technological Nation* (Basingstoke: Macmillan, 1991).

Erenberg, Lewis A., 'Swing Goes to War: Glenn Miller and the Popular Music of World War II', in Lewis A. Erenberg and Susan E. Hirsch (eds.), *The War in American*

Culture: Society and Consciousness During World War Two (Chicago: University of Chicago Press, 1996), 144–65.

Escott, Beryl E., *Women in Air Force Blue: The Story of Women in the Royal Air Force from 1918 to the Present Day* (Wellingborough: Patrick Stephens, 1989).

Evans, Martin, and Lunn, Ken (eds.), *War and Memory in the Twentieth Century* (Oxford: Berg, 1997).

Eley, Geoff, 'Finding the People's War: Film, British Collective Memory and World War Two', *American Historical Review*, 105 (2001), 818–38.

Ellenberger, Nancy W., 'Constructing George Wyndham: Narratives of Aristocratic Masculinity in Fin-de-siecle England', *Journal of British Studies*, 39 (2000), 487–517.

English, Allan D., 'A Predisposition to Cowardice? Aviation Psychology and the Genesis of "Lack of Moral Fibre" ', *War and Society*, 13 (1995), 20–7.

Faulks, Sebastian, *The Fatal Englishman: Three Short Lives* (London: Vintage, 1997).

Field, Deborah H., *Private Life and Communist Morality in Khrushchev's Russia* (New York: Peter Lang, 2007).

Finch, Janet, and Summerfield, Penny, 'Social Reconstruction and the Emergence of the Companionate Marriage, 1945–59', in David Clark (ed.), *Marriage, Domestic Life and Social Change: Writings for Jacqueline Burgoyne* (London: Routledge, 1991), 7–32.

Francis, Martin, 'The Domestication of the Male? Recent Research on Nineteenth- and Twentieth-Century British Masculinity', *Historical Journal*, 45 (2002), 637–52.

——— 'A Flight from Commitment? Domesticity, Adventure and the Masculine Imaginary in Britain after the Second World War', *Gender and History*, 19 (2007), 163–85.

——— 'Men of the Royal Air Force, the Cultural Memory of the Second World War and the Twilight of the British Empire', in Susan Grayzel and Philippa Levine (eds.), *Gender, Labour, War and Empire: Essays on Modern Britain in Honour of Sonya Rose* (Houndmills: Palgrave, 2009).

Franks, Norman, *Air Battle Dunkirk* (London: Grub Street, 2000).

Frantzen, Allen J., *Bloody Good: Chivalry, Sacrifice and the Great War* (Chicago: University of Chicago Press, 2004).

Friedrich, Jörg, *The Fire: The Bombing of Germany, 1940–1945*, trans. Allison Brown (New York: Columbia University Press, 2006).

Funck, Marcus, 'Ready for War? Conceptions of Military Manliness in the Prusso-German Officer Corps before the First World War', in Karen Hagemann and Stefanie Schüler-Springorum (eds.), *War/Front: The Military, War and Gender in Twentieth-Century Germany* (Oxford: Berg, 2002), 43–67.

Fussell, Paul, *The Great War and Modern Memory* (Oxford: Oxford University Press, 1975).

Garrett, Stephen A., *Ethics and Airpower in World War Two: The British Bombing of German Cities* (New York: St Martin's Press, 1993).

Gerber, David A. (ed.), *Disabled Veterans in History* (Ann Arbor, Mich.: University of Michigan Press, 2000).

——— 'Heroes and Misfits: The Troubled Social Reintegration of Disabled Veterans in *The Best Years of Our Lives*', *American Quarterly*, 46 (1994), 545–74.

Gibbs, Philip, *The New Elizabethans* (London: Hutchinson, 1953).

Gilbert, Sandra, 'Soldier's Heart: Literary Men, Literary Women and the Great War', in Margaret Higonnet *et al.* (eds.), *Behind the Lines: Gender and the Two World Wars* (New Haven: Yale University Press, 1987).

Gilroy, Paul, *Postcolonial Melancholia* (New York: Columbia University Press, 2005).

Girouard, Mark, *The Return to Camelot: Chivalry and the English Gentleman* (New Haven: Yale University Press, 1981).

Glancey, Jonathan, *Spitfire: The Biography* (London: Atlantic Books, 2006).

Gledhill, Christine, and Swanson, Gillian (eds.), *Nationalising Femininity: Culture, Sexuality and British Cinema in the Second World War* (Manchester: Manchester University Press, 1996).

Godwin, Peter, and Hancock, Ian, *'Rhodesians Never Die': The Impact of War and Political Change in White Rhodesia, c.1970–1980* (Oxford: Oxford University Press, 1993).

Goebel, Stefan, *The Great War and Medieval Memory: War, Remembrance and Medievalism in Britain and Germany, 1914–1940* (Cambridge: Cambridge University Press, 2007).

Grinker, Roy R., and Spiegel, John P., *Men Under Stress* (Philadelphia: Blakiston, 1945).

Gullace, Nicoletta, *The Blood of Our Sons: Men, Women and the Renegotiation of British Citizenship During the Great War* (Basingstoke: Palgrave, 2002).

Haggith, Toby, *'Journey Together'*, in Alan Burton, Tim O' Sullivan, and Paul Wells (eds.), *The Family Way: The Boulting Brothers and British Film Culture* (Trowbridge: Flicks Books, 2000), 109–21.

Hall, Lesley, *Hidden Anxieties: Male Sexuality, 1900–1950* (Cambridge: Polity, 1991).

Halstead, Ivor (ed.), *Wings of Victory: A Tribute to the RAF* (New York: E. P. Dutton, 1941).

Hämmerle, Christa, 'You Let A Weeping Woman Call You Home? Private Correspondence During the First World War in Germany and Austria', in Rebecca Earle (ed.), *Epistolary Selves: Letters and Letter Writers, 1600–1945* (Aldershot: Ashgate, 1999).

Hammerton, A. James, 'The English Weakness? Gender, Satire and "Moral Manliness" in the Lower Middle Class, 1870–1920', in Alan Kidd and David Nicholls (eds.), *Gender, Civic Culture and Consumerism: Middle-Class Identity in Britain, 1800–1940* (Manchester: Manchester University Press, 1999).

Harrison, Mark, *Medicine and Victory: British Military Medicine in the Second World War* (Oxford: Oxford University Press, 2004).

Haste, Cate, *Rules of Desire: Sex in Britain, World War One to the Present* (London: Vintage, 1992).

Hastings, Adrian, *A History of English Christianity, 1920–2000* (London: SCM Press, 2001).

Hazelgrove, Jenny, *Spiritualism and British Society Between the Wars* (Manchester: Manchester University Press, 2000).

Higgins, Patrick, *Heterosexual Dictatorship: Male Homosexuality in Post-War Britain* (London: Fourth Estate, 1996).

Hilliard, Christopher, *To Exercise Our Talents: The Democratization of Writing in Britain* (Cambridge, Mass.: Harvard University Press, 2006).

Hinton, James, *Women, Social Leadership and the Second World War: Continuities of Class* (Oxford: Oxford University Press, 2002).

Holmes, Harry, *Avro Lancaster: The Definitive Record* (Shrewsbury: Airlife, 2001).

Horne, Philip, 'Life and Death in *A Matter of Life and Death*', in Ian Christie and Andrew Moor (eds.), *The Cinema of Michael Powell* (London: BFI, 2005), 117–42.

Houlbrook, Matt, *Queer London: Perils and Pleasures in the Sexual Metropolis, 1918–1957* (Chicago: University of Chicago Press, 2005).

Humble, Nicola, *The Feminine Middlebrow Novel, 1920s to 1950s: Class, Domesticity and Bohemianism* (Oxford: Oxford University Press, 2001).

Hynes, Samuel, *The Soldier's Tale: Bearing Witness to Modern War* (New York: Penguin, 1998).

Jackson, Ashley, *The British Empire and the Second World War* (London: Hambledon, 2006).

James, John, *The Paladins: A Social History of the RAF up to the Outbreak of World War Two* (London: Macdonald, 1990).

Jarvis, Christina S., *The Male Body at War: American Masculinity During World War Two* (De Kalb, Ill.: Northern Illinois University Press, 2004).

John, Angela V., and Eustance, Claire (eds.), *The Men's Share? Masculinities, Male Support and Women's Suffrage in Britain, 1890–1920* (London: Routledge, 1997).

Jones, Helen, *British Civilians in the Front Line: Air Raids, Productivity and Wartime Culture, 1939–45* (Manchester: Manchester University Press, 2006).

Kennington, Eric, *Drawing the RAF: A Book of Portraits* (Oxford: Oxford University Press, 1942).

Kent, Susan Kingsley, *Making Peace: The Reconstruction of Gender in Interwar Britain* (Princeton: Princeton University Press, 1993).

Kern, Stephen, *The Culture of Love: Victorians to Moderns* (Cambridge, Mass.: Harvard University Press, 1992).

Kershaw, Alex, *The Few: The American 'Knights of the Air' Who Risked Everything to Fight in the Battle of Britain* (Cambridge, Mass.: Da Capo Press, 2006).

Keshen, Jeff, *Saints, Sinners and Soldiers: Canada's Second World War* (Vancouver: University of British Columbia Press, 2004).

Kirkham, Pat, 'Beauty and Duty: Keeping Up the (Home) Front', in Pat Kirkham and David Thoms (eds.), *War Culture: Social Change and Changing Experience in World War Two* (London: Lawrence & Wishart, 1995), 13–28.

Knight, Lynn, 'Introduction' to *Dangerous Calm: Selected Stories of Elizabeth Taylor* (London: Virago, 1995).

Knott, Richard, *Black Night for Bomber Command: The Tragedy of 16 December 1943* (Barnsley: Pen and Sword, 2007).

Koestler, Arthur, *The Yogi and the Commissar* (New York: Macmillan, 1946).

Kolm, Suzanne L., 'Who Says It's a Man's World? Women's Work and Travel in the First Decades of Flight', in Dominick A. Pisano (ed.), *The Airplane in American Culture* (Ann Arbor, Mich.: University of Michigan Press, 2003), 147–64.

Koven, Seth, 'Remembering and Dismemberment: Crippled Children, Wounded Soldiers and the Great War in Great Britain', *American Historical Review*, 99 (1994), 1167–1202.

Kuhne, Thomas, 'Comradeship: Gender Confusion and Gender Order in the German Military, 1918–1945', in Karen Hagemann and Stefanie Schüler-Springorum (eds.), *War/Front: The Military, War and Gender in Twentieth-Century Germany* (Oxford: Berg, 2002), 23–54.

Kundrus, Birthe, 'Gender Wars: The First World War and the Construction of Gender Relations in the Weimar Republic', in Karen Hagemann and Stefanie Schüler-Springorum (eds.), *War/Front: The Military, War and Gender in Twentieth-Century Germany* (Oxford: Berg, 2002), 159–79.

Kushner, Tony, *The Persistence of Prejudice: Antisemitism in British Society During the Second World War* (Manchester: Manchester University Press, 1989).

Lake, Marilyn, 'Female Desires: The Meaning of World War Two', in Joy Damousi and Marilyn Lake (eds.), *Gender and War: Australians at War in the Twentieth Century* (Cambridge: Cambridge University Press, 1995), 60–80.

Landau, Rom, *The Fool's Progress: Aspects of British Civilization in Action* (London: Faber & Faber, 1942).

Langhamer, Claire, 'Love and Courtship in Mid-Twentieth-Century England', *Historical Journal*, 50 (2007), 173–96.

—— ' "A Public House is for All Classes, Men and Women Alike": Women, Leisure and Drink in Second World War England', *Women's History Review*, 12 (2003), 423–43.

—— *Women's Leisure in England, 1920–1960* (Manchester: Manchester University Press, 2000).

Lant, Antonia, *Blackout: Reinventing Women for Wartime British Cinema* (Princeton: Princeton University Press, 1991).

Leed, Eric J., *No Man's Land: Combat and Identity in World War One* (Cambridge: Cambridge University Press, 1979).

Leese, Peter, *Shell Shock: Traumatic Neurosis and the British Soldiers of the First World War* (Houndmills: Palgrave, 2002).

Lewis, C. S., 'The Necessity of Chivalry' [1940], in *Essay Collection and Other Short Pieces* (London: HarperCollins, 2000), 717–20.

Light, Alison, *Forever England: Femininity, Literature and Conservatism Between the Wars* (London: Routledge, 1991).

Lovett, John, *Contact: A Tribute to Those Who Serve Rhodesia* (Salisbury: Galaxie Press, 1977).

Lowe, Keith, *Inferno: The Devastation of Hamburg, 1943* (London: Viking, 2007).

Lystra, Karen, *Searching the Heart: Women, Men, and Romantic Love in Nineteenth-Century America* (New York: Oxford University Press, 1989).

McCarthy, John, 'Air Crew and "Lack of Moral Fibre" in the Second World War', *War and Society*, 2 (1984), 87–101.

McClelland, Keith, 'Masculinity and the "Representative Artisan" in Britain, 1850–80', in Michael Roper and John Tosh (eds.), *Manful Assertions: Masculinities in Britain Since 1800* (London: Routledge, 1991).

McDevitt, Patrick F., 'Muscular Catholicism: Nationalism, Masculinity and Gaelic Team Sports, 1884–1916', *Gender and History*, 9 (1997), 262–84.

Mackenzie, S. P., *The Colditz Myth: British and Commonwealth Prisoners of War in Nazi Germany* (Oxford: Oxford University Press, 2004).

McKibbin, Ross, *Classes and Cultures: England, 1918–1951* (Oxford: Oxford University Press, 1998).

Mansell, Tony, 'Flying Start: Educational and Social Factors in the Recruitment of Pilots of the Royal Air Force in the Interwar Years', *History of Education*, 26 (1997), 71–90.

Marwick, Arthur, *Britain in the Century of Total War: War, Peace and Social Change, 1900–1967* (London: Bodley Head, 1970).

Marx, Karl, 'The German Ideology', in *Selected Writings*, 2nd edn. (Oxford: Oxford University Press, 2000), 175–208.

Mayhew, E. R., *The Reconstruction of Warriors: Archibald McIndoe, the Royal Air Force and the Guinea Pig Club* (London: Greenhill Books, 2004).

Meunier, Claudio, and Garcia, Carlos, *Alas De Trueno* [*Wings of Thunder*] (Buenos Aires: C. G. Gustavo, 2004).

Monks, Noel, *Squadrons Up!* (London: Victor Gollancz, 1940).

Moran, Charles, *The Anatomy of Courage* (London: Constable, 1945).

Mort, Frank, *Cultures of Consumption: Masculinities and Social Space in Late Twentieth-Century Britain* (London: Routledge, 1996).

Murphy, Robert, *British Cinema and the Second World War* (London: Continuum, 2000).

—— *Realism and Tinsel: Cinema and Society in Britain, 1939–1949* (London: Routledge, 1992).

Murray, Robert N., *Lest We Forget: The Experiences of World War Two West Indian Ex-Service Personnel* (Nottingham: NWICEA Press, 1996).

Neillands, Robin, *The Bomber War* (New York: Overlook Press, 2001).

Noakes, Lucy, *War and the British: Gender, Memory and National Identity* (London: I. B. Tauris, 1998).

Olson, Lynne, and Cloud, Stanley, *For Your Freedom and Ours: The Kosciuszko Squadron, Forgotten Heroes of World War Two* (London: Arrow Books, 2004).

Omissi, David, 'The Hendon Air Pageant, 1920–37', in John M. Mackenzie (ed.), *Popular Imperialism and the Military, 1850–1950* (Manchester: Manchester University Press, 1992), 198–220.

Orde, Cuthbert, *Pilots of Fighter Command: Sixty-Four Portraits* (London: George Harrap, 1942).

Overy, Richard, *The Battle of Britain* (London: Penguin, 2004).

Paris, Michael, 'The Rise of the Airmen: The Origins of Air Force Elitism, c.1890–1918', *Journal of Contemporary History*, 28 (1993), 123–41.

Partridge, Eric H., 'Slanguage', in R. Raymond and David Langdon (eds.), *Slipstream: A Royal Air Force Anthology* (London: Eyre & Spottiswoode, 1946), 60–5.

Passerini, Luisa, *Europe in Love, Love in Europe: Imagination and Politics in Britain Between the Wars* (London: I. B. Tauris, 1998).

Patterson, Ian, *Guernica and Total War* (London: Profile Books, 2007).

Phillips, Deborah, and Haywood, Ian, *Brave New Causes: Women in Postwar British Fictions* (London: Leicester University Press, 1998).

Plain, Gill, *John Mills and British Cinema: Masculinity, Identity and Nation* (Edinburgh: Edinburgh University Press, 2006).

Poovey, Mary, *Uneven Developments: The Ideological Work of Gender in Mid-Victorian England* (Chicago: University of Chicago Press, 1988).

Rachman, S. J., *Fear and Courage*, 2nd edn. (New York: W. H. Freeman, 1990).

Rajadhyakalsha, Ashish, and Willemen, Paul (eds.), *Encyclopedia of Indian Cinema* (New Delhi: Oxford University Press, 1999).

Rattigan, Neil, 'The Last Gasp of the Middle Class: British War Films of the 1950s', in Wheeler Winston Dixon (ed.), *Re-Viewing British Cinema, 1900–1992* (New York: State University of New York Press, 1994), 143–54.

Rawlinson, Mark, *British Writing of the Second World War* (Oxford: Oxford University Press, 2000).

Raymond, R., and Langdon, David (eds.), *Slipstream: A Royal Air Force Anthology* (London: Eyre & Spottiswoode, 1946).

Reddy, William H., *The Invisible Code: Honor and Sentiment in Postrevolutionary France, 1814–1848* (Berkeley: University of California Press, 1997).

Rennell, Tony, and Nichol, John, *Tail End Charlies: The Last Battles of the Bomber War, 1944–45* (London: Viking, 2004).

Reznick, Jeffrey S., *Healing the Nation: Soldiers and the Culture of Caregiving in Britain During the Great War* (Manchester: Manchester University Press, 2004).

Robertson, Linda A., *The Dream of Civilized Warfare: World War One Flying Aces and the American Imagination* (Minneapolis: University of Minnesota Press, 2003).

Roos, Neil, *Ordinary Springboks: White Servicemen and Social Justice in South Africa* (Aldershot: Ashgate, 2005).

Roper, Michael, 'Between Manliness and Masculinity: The "War Generation" and the Psychology of Fear in Britain, 1914–1950', *Journal of British Studies*, 44 (2005), 344–63.

Roper, Michael, *Masculinity and the British Organization Man Since 1945* (Oxford: Oxford University Press, 1994).

Roper, Michael, 'Maternal Relations: Moral Manliness and Emotional Survival in Letters Home During the First World War', in Stefan Dudink, Karen Hagemann, and John Tosh (eds.), *Masculinities in Politics and War: Rewritings of Modern History* (Manchester: Manchester University Press, 2004).

——'Slipping Out of View: Subjectivity and Emotion in Gender History', *History Workshop Journal*, 59 (2005), 57–73.

——and Tosh, John (eds.), *Manful Assertions: Masculinities in Britain Since 1800* (London: Routledge, 1991).

Rose, Jonathan, *The Intellectual Life of the British Working Classes* (London: Yale University Press, 2001).

Rose, Sonya O., *Which People's War? National Identity and Citizenship in Wartime Britain, 1939–1945* (Oxford: Oxford University Press, 2003).

Rothenstein, William, 'Some Account of Life in the RAF', in *Men of the RAF* (London: Oxford University Press, 1942), 11–64.

Satia, Priya, 'The Defense of Inhumanity: Air Control in Iraq and the British Idea of Arabia', *American Historical Review*, 111 (2006), 16–51.

Scarry, Elaine, 'Injury and the Structure of War', *Representations*, 10 (1985), 1–51.

Schrader, Helena, *Sisters in Arms* (Barnsley: Pen and Sword, 2006).

Shail, Robert, 'Officers and Gentlemen: Masculinity in Powell and Pressburger's Wartime Films', in Ian Christie and Andrew Moor (eds.), *The Cinema of Michael Powell* (London: BFI, 2005), 239–52.

Shepard, Alexandra, *The Meanings of Manhood in Early Modern England* (Oxford: Oxford University Press, 2003).

Shephard, Ben, *A War of Nerves: Soldiers and Psychiatrists, 1914–1994* (London: Pimlico, 2002).

Sherwood, Marika, *Many Struggles: West Indian Workers and Service Personnel in Britain, 1939–1945* (London: Karia, 1985).

Showalter, Elaine, 'Rivers and Sassoon: The Inscription of Male Gender Anxieties', in Margaret Higonnet *et al.* (eds.), *Behind the Lines: Gender and the Two World Wars* (New Haven: Yale University Press, 1987).

Sinha, Mrinalini, *Colonial Masculinity: The 'Manly Englishman' and the 'Effeminate Bengali' in the Late Nineteenth Century* (Manchester: Manchester University Press, 1995).

Smith, Leonard V., *The Embattled Self: French Soldiers' Testimony of the Great War* (Ithaca, NY: Cornell University Press, 2007).

Smith, Harold L. (ed.), *War and Social Change: British Society in the Second World War* (Manchester: Manchester University Press, 1986).

Smith, Malcolm, *Britain and 1940: History, Myth and Popular Memory* (London: Routledge, 2000).

Smithies, Edward, *Aces, Erks and Backroom Boys: Aircrew, Ground Staff and Warplane Builders Remember the Second World War* (London: Cassell, 2002).

Snape, Michael, *God and the British Soldier: Religion and the British Army in the First and Second World Wars* (London: Routledge, 2005).

Spencer, Ian, *British Immigration Policy Since 1939: The Making of Multicultural Britain* (London: Routledge, 1997).

Spicer, Andrew, *Typical Men: The Representation of Masculinity in Popular British Cinema* (London: I. B. Tauris, 2001).

Stafford-Clark, David, *Psychiatry Today* (Harmondsworth: Penguin, 1952).

Stearns, Peter N., and Lewis, Jan (eds.), *An Emotional History of the United States* (New York: NYU Press, 1998).

Stone, Tessa, 'Creating a (Gendered?) Military Identity: The Women's Auxiliary Air Force in Great Britain in the Second World War', *Women's History Review*, 8 (1999), 605–24.

Streets, Heather, *Martial Races: The Military, Race and Masculinity in British Imperial Culture, 1857–1914* (Manchester: Manchester University Press, 2004).

Sullivan, Sheila, *Falling in Love: A History of Torment and Enchantment* (London: Macmillan, 1999).

Summerfield, Penny, *Reconstructing Women's Wartime Lives: Discourse and Subjectivity in Oral Histories of the Second World War* (Manchester: Manchester University Press, 1998).

—— *Women Workers in the Second World War: Production and Patriarchy in Conflict* (London: Croom Helm, 1984).

Sweetman, John, *Bomber Crew: Taking on the Reich* (London: Little, Brown, 2004).

Swidler, Ann, *Talk of Love: How Culture Matters* (Chicago: Chicago University Press, 2001).

Taylor, Eric, *Force's Sweethearts: Service Romances in World War Two* (London: Robert Hale, 1990).

Taylor, Frederick, *Dresden: Tuesday, 13 February 1945* (London: Bloomsbury, 2005).

Taylor, James, and Davidson, Martin, *Bomber Crew: Survivors of Bomber Command Tell Their Own Story* (London: Hodder & Stoughton, 2004).

Terraine, John, *The Right of the Line: The Royal Air Force in the European War, 1939–1945* (London: Hodder & Stoughton, 1985).

Thomas, Donald, *An Underworld at War* (London: John Murray, 2004).

Thompson, Paul, 'Playing at Being Skilled Men: Factory Culture and Pride in Work Skills Among Coventry Car Workers', *Social History*, 13 (1988), 45–69.

Thorpe, Frances, and Pronay, Nicholas, *British Official Films of the Second World War: A Descriptive Catalogue* (Oxford: Clio Press, 1980).

Todman, Dan, *The Great War: Myth and Memory* (London: Hambledon, 2005).

Tosh, John, *A Man's Place: Masculinity and the Middle-Class Home in Victorian England* (New Haven: Yale University Press, 1999).

—— 'What Should Historians Do with Masculinity? Reflections on Nineteenth-Century Britain', *History Workshop Journal*, 38 (1994), 179–202.

Turner, E. S., *A History of Courting* (London: Michael Joseph, 1954).

Vinen, Richard, *A History in Fragments: Europe in the Twentieth Century* (London: Little, Brown, 2000).

Ware, Susan, *Still Missing: Amelia Earhart and the Search for Modern Feminism* (New York: Norton, 1993).

Waters, Chris, 'Disorders of the Mind, Disorders of the Body Social: Peter Wildeblood and the Making of the Modern Homosexual', in Becky Conekin, Frank Mort, and Chris Waters (eds.), *Moments of Modernity: Reconstructing Britain, 1945–64* (London: Rivers Oram, 1994).

Watson, Janet S. K., *Fighting Different Wars: Experience, Memory, and the First World War in Britain* (Cambridge: Cambridge University Press, 2004).

Webster, Wendy, *Englishness and Empire, 1939–1965* (Oxford: Oxford University Press, 2005).

Weight, Richard, *Patriots: National Identity in Britain, 1940–2000* (London: Macmillan, 2006).

Westbrook, Robert B., ' "I Want a Girl, Just Like the Girl that Married Harry James": American Women and the Problem of Political Obligation in World War Two', *American Quarterly*, 42 (1990), 587–614.

Williams, Tony, *Structures of Desire: British Cinema, 1939–1955* (Albany, NY: State University of New York, 2000).

Wohl, Robert, *A Passion for Wings: Aviation and the Western Imagination, 1908–1918* (New Haven: Yale University Press, 1994).

—— *The Spectacle of Flight: Aviation and the Western Imagination, 1920–1950* (New Haven: Yale University Press, 2005).

Yeats-Brown, F., *Martial India* (London: Eyre & Spottiswoode, 1945).

Zahn, Gordon C., *Chaplains in the RAF: A Study in Role Tension* (Manchester: Manchester University Press, 1969).

Ziegler, Frank H., *The Story of 609 Squadron* (Manchester: Crecy Books, 1993).

Index